In The Studio

In The Studio

Jake Brown

First published in Great Britain in 2011 by Cherry Red Books
(a division of Cherry Red Records Ltd.), Power Road Studios
114 Power Road, Chiswick, London W4 5PY

Copyright Jake Brown © 2011

ISBN: 9781901447620

All rights reserved. No part of this book may be reproduced
or transmitted in any form or by any means, electronic
or mechanical, including photocopying, recording or any
information storage and retrieval system, without permission
in writing from the publisher.

This book is sold subject to the condition that it shall not, by
way of trade or otherwise, be lent, resold, hired out or otherwise
circulated without the publisher's prior consent in any form of
binding or cover other than that in which it is published and
without a similar condition being imposed on the subsequent
purchaser.

Design: Nathan Eighty

CONTENTS

9	INTRODUCTION:	Tom Waits In The Studio...An Overview
21	PART I:	Tom Waits: The Roots Of A Songwriter
29	PART II:	Closing Time (1973)
37	PART III:	Bones Howe... He's Got The Jazz!
45	PART IV:	The Heart Of Saturday Night (1974)
55	PART V:	Nighthawks At The Diner (1975)
63	PART VI:	Small Change (1976)
75	PART VII:	Foreign Affairs (1977)
81	PART VIII:	Blue Valentine (1978)
87	PART IX:	Heartattack And Vine (1980)
95	PART X:	One From The Heart (1982)
105	PART XI:	Swordfishtrombones (1983)
119	PART XII:	Rain Dogs (1985)
135	PART XIII:	Frank's Wild Years (1987)
147	PART XIV:	Big Time (1988)
153	PART XV:	Bone Machine (1992)
173	PART XVI:	Night On Earth (1992)
177	PART XVII:	Black Rider (1993)
185	PART XVIII:	Mule Variations (1999)
205	PART XIX:	Alice (2002)
213	PART XX:	Blood Money (2002)
221	PART XXI:	Real Gone (2004)
233	PART XXII:	Orphans: Brawlers, Ballers & Bastards (2006)
247	CONCLUSION:	Looking Past The Confines Of Legacy...
253	AUTHOR BIO	

ACKNOWLEDGEMENTS

This book is dedicated to my Wooster college roommate crew – Adam 'The Skipper' Perri, Matt Pietz and Christie 'Wyatt' Beilharz for making Waits part of our Juke Box and by extension once-in-life nights and times!!

Author Note of thanks: To Tom Waits, without sounding indulgent, thank you for creating this epic catalogue of records that belongs to a sub-genre all your own. It has inspired so many generations of artists to take bold chances, big or small, over the past four decades, and no doubt will continue to with future generations.

Project Thank You(s): I would first and foremost like to thank Richard Anderson and everyone at Cherry Red Books for taking the chance on such an ambitious catalogue of music; Bones Howe, Jerry Yester, and Bob Musso for your interviews (both for my 'Behind the Boards' Anthology and by extension for this book); and last but definitely not least, the indispensable and definitive Tom Waits fan site www.TomWaitsLibrary.com for the amazing interview archive, going all the way from 1970 up through the present – this book would not have been possible without your amazing collection of interview archives.

Personal Thank You(s): First and foremost, as always, I would like to thank my parents, James and Christina-Thieme Brown, for continuing to tirelessly support my various artistic goings-on (both literary and musically); my brother Joshua T. Brown (K-9 Catalyst, proud of you bud); the extended Brown and Thieme Families; Alex Schuchard and Jackson Schuchard for being the coolest Godson in the world!; my beautiful girl Dena; Andrew and Sarah McDermott; 'The' Sean and Amy Fillinich; Adam Perri; Chris 'SEE' Ellauri; Matt, Eileen and Kamelya Ellen Peitz; Richard (thanks for the past 10 years re Versailles), Lisa and Regan Kendrick; Paul and Helen WATTS!; Bob O'Brien and Cayenne Engel; Lexi 'Clown' Federov; Rose Reiter and Gerry Plant; MVD Distribution/Big Daddy Music; Aaron 'Whippit' Harmon for continuing to have my back musically week in and out; Joe Viers/Sonic Lounge Studios for 10 years of great ears; Andrew Neice @ Melodic Rock; Keavin Wiggins @ Antimusic.com; Cheryl Hoahing at Metal Edge; Tim @ Brave Words/Bloody Knuckles; Rock and Roll Report; John Lavallo and Take Out Marketing; Larry, Joel, James, and everyone at Arbor Books; Aaron, Gabriel, Victor, John and everyone at SCB Distribution/Rock N Roll Books; Bookmasters; To Jasmin St Claire, thanks for hanging in there, we finally made it!; Lemmy Kilmister; Curt and Cris Kirkwood/Dennis; Ben Ohmart/BearManor Media; Jack, Crissy, David, Simon et all at ECW Press; Tony (congrats on beating the big C!) & Yvonne Rose at Amber Books; Richard Anderson at Cherry Red Books; Jason Rothberg and Tracii Guns, thanks for the opportunity to be involved with telling this amazing story; Stephan Jenkins and Third Eye Blind for the opportunity to work on an 'In the Studio' book with you!; and finally and without arrogance of any sort implied, thank you to the music fans who buy/read my books, and specifically this series, as you keep them coming!

INTRODUCTION: Tom Waits In The Studio... An Overview

As great American songwriters go, it is impossible and irresponsible not to recognise Tom Waits' singular genius in speaking for the underdog. Music historians and critics have studied him for decades like religious scholars do the Scriptures. He has always communicated in his own, singularly unique musical language and lyrical dialect to millions of fans for decades, astounding and confounding outsiders. Without any outside interpretation required to justify his record sales or loyal following, Waits' listeners were fluent from the moment they first heard him mirror their story in a way they could relate to.

Waits' words wind through the fringes and frays of life's most authentic moments, in terms both of errant adventure and consequence after the 'thrill' is gone. Told through a sympathetic lens and narrative much in the way a rapper speaks defensively of a pimp or drug dealer, Tom Waits was an advocate for the urban dwellers who were arguably the white counterpart to the black working-class artists like Sly Stone and Stevie Wonder represented in the early Seventies.

Waits was one of the all-night diner patrons; the broken-down waitress who served them; the 3am newsstand regular who knew all the prostitutes by name; the hooker who couldn't shake her lifestyle; the small-time bookie who placed bets for gamblers he knew could never pay – but did so anyway out of habit; the bum in the alley or the hobo riding by railcar aimlessly from town to town; the junkie stripper dancing to support a child or an alcoholic boyfriend who beats her with routine; the down and out loser living in a hotel that rented by the week; or perhaps the deadbeat laying low in a seedy strip club to avoid the realities and responsibilities of family life.

At the same time, Waits was the lonely truck driver on the open road, free of the commitment or consequence of settling down; the small-town gas station attendant living in his own head; the recently paroled convict trying to go straight, leading a 'regular' life devoid of all excitement; the average family Joe who hates his job but sucks it up because he loves and takes pride in providing for his kids; or the young forbidden lovers who go for it anyway in spite of the consequences. Waits' melodic commonwealth covered every facet of the human experience – the sunny days and romantic nights; the glory of dreams and the sadness of their failure to blossom into truth; and the lies we tell ourselves and others to get by; the ways we live with those lies inside ourselves. Waits' songs were like modernised passages from SE Hinton novels like Rumblefish and The Outsiders, which gave an identity and sympathetic light to the underdog.

Tom Waits sung in almost constant metaphor in the context of cause and effect, playing a chord harmonious with everyone's inner demons and desires, and the helpless and often simultaneous indulgence of both of those opposing entities. He also spoke of the consequences – whether impending or already cast – as the characters in his songs made their way through the wreckage of human mistakes in a societal framework. He spoke broadly for and to the drifters, the castaways, the conned, the broken-hearted and the corrupted – anyone who once had promise they either betrayed by some misfortune of their own doing or who were victims of the lies those promises turned out to be. Waits' lyrics were graphic passages from the diary of society's underbelly – naked, gripping confessions that came at our most random and vulnerable moments, secrets sloppily spilled which soaked into our conscience like bloodstains that could not be cleaned up from innocence's murder.

Delving into the creative cocoon he'd created for himself amid that world, Tom began by recalling years later to Mojo that "when I was writing, I kind of made up my own little Tin Pan Alley so I could sit at the piano, like a songwriter, with a bottle and an ashtray and come out of the room with a handful of songs, as they did," adding to the BBC that "in the old days, I would go into a room with a piano and an ashtray and a bottle and come back with all the songs." Setting up shop at the appropriately seedy Tropicana Hotel in Hollywood, Tom explained of his decision to stay in the heart of Hollywood rather than drift into its more luxurious hills like many of his peers had been an effort to "have a genuine, authentic artistic experience," adding in the same comments to GQ that, to that end, "I had a piano in the kitchen, and in those days I'd stay up all night, sleep half the day."

Soaking up the scene that so inspired him, Tom recalled years later to the Star Tribune that in doing so "I was living out my dream... I stayed in hotels where I thought stories grew. I'd get a chance to inhale all those things that happened in rooms before I was born. My idea of going on the road was not the Holiday Inn or Hyatt House. It was some kind of older dream, like a vaudeville dream." The singer-songwriter shared his memory with Rock's Backpages that "when I moved into the Tropicana in LA, that place it was nine dollars a night. But it became a stage, because I became associated with it, and people came looking for me and calling me in the middle of the night. I think I really wanted to kind of get lost in it all, so I did. When they painted the pool black, that's when I said this has gone too far. It was a pretty heavy place at times. I had a good seat at the bar, and I could see everyone in the room."

Waits confirmed the authenticity of the media's depiction of him during that period as very much a character out of one of his songs to the LA Times. "There's not much difference between what I appear to be on stage and what I am. I think people like that, that I'm not trying to pull a caper. It's easy for me, 'cause it's not such a large jump. I don't have to get into a costume. I'm in contact and I'm in context... But all of a sudden it becomes your image, and it's hard to tell where the image stops and you begin or where you stop and the image begins. Any image I have, it's just what I do, but it comes off as being very pretentious. When you're a bit in the public astigmatism, anything you do seems like you did it so somebody would see you do it, like showing up at the right parties." Melody Maker would later conclude that "albums like 'The Heart Of Saturday Night', 'Small Change' and 'Blue Valentine'…confirmed him as America's leading street poet."

Tom Waits' lyrical landscape was a crime scene for every conceivable sin of man, but also a dancefloor for the celebration of our most immoral yet satisfying indulgences – those that can't be helped. Risk was inbred in every line he spoke or sang, yet the characters Waits played in his lyrics often had nothing to lose. Often he seemed to write from the vantage point of what they had left. In the same time, he sang of the beauty of redemption like no other because there was nothing shallow about the back story of his characters' triumphs in context of their adversities.

Waits' musical novella was a reality television show for every human emotion, offering characters so vividly described and embodied that you felt you knew them, or were perhaps like them in some significant vice, mannerism or experience. More importantly, Tom Waits was a classic blues vocalist, delivering his confessionals with a voice authentically worn from the worlds of his characters, one that gravelled the way man naturally does within himself over the right and wrong of things he does in and with his life.

Songwriting society ASCAP commented in their bio on the performer that the period between 1974 and 1980 "was an incredibly prolific period for Waits and one that solidified his reputation as one of America's new leading songwriters. As a singer, his trademark gravelly voice became one of the most unique voices ever heard in pop music." Summarising the stylistic diversity of that catalogue of eight LPs, Time Out magazine noted that "his music took strands from folk, jazz, country and blues then pulled them together behind narratives which explored an America populated by transients, drunks and whores. It was the America of Kerouac, Bukowski and Chandler brought up to date. The style of many of the songs was lush and heart-rending. Waits shaped the stuff of everyday life into beautiful myth."

Waits had established a safe, successful signature sound by the early Eighties, but found himself unfulfilled, confessing to Mojo magazine years later that "I had been so frustrated at that point." The catalyst for one of the most radical stylistic and sonic shifts by an established artist in the history of the record business came in 1981 when Tom met the woman who would change the direction of both his career and life. While working from Francis Ford Coppola's studios on the soundtrack for One From The Heart he met screenwriter Kathleen Brennan. Within two months, they married at the Always Forever Yours Wedding Chapel on Manchester Boulevard in Watts, Tom quipping to GQ that "it was planned at midnight for a 1am wedding. We made things happen around here!"

The pair then went about radically re-working Waits' plans for the future, which he confessed at the time were in some disarray due to the reckless state of his personal life. He confessed years later to journalist Sean O'Hagan that meeting Brennan had inspired him to believe "I would not go down the drain, I would not light my hair on fire, I would not put a gun in my mouth. I had something abiding in me that was moving me forward. I was probably drawn to her because I saw that there was a lot of hope there… It was tough. I went to AA. I'm in the programme. I'm clean and sober. Hooray. But, it was a struggle… I'm happy to be sober. Happy to be alive. I found myself in some places I can't believe I made it out of alive."

Waits added to GQ that the process felt like "I hatched out of the egg I was living in. I had nailed one foot to the floor and kept going in circles, making the same record. Kathleen was the first person who convinced me that you can take James White and the Blacks, Elmer Bernstein and Leadbelly – folks that could never be on the bill together – and that they could be on the bill together in you." Once he began to pay attention to how his life had come to destructively imitate art, he added to the San Diego Union Tribune that "I really went through a lot of changes when I got married, and my music changed."

The catalyst for that change first came when Waits and Brennan began discussing Tom's desire to re-invent both his musical direction and his image, which by that point, according to the LA Weekly, had cast him as "kind of hero to the pop discontent". In reasoning why he needed to move beyond that stage of his career – both professionally and personally – Tom offered to the Orange County Register that "I kind of grew up in public; I was 22 when I made my first record, I was falling down the stairs. I didn't know what I was doing, but I knew I was gonna be in music. Some people come out fully formed, like an egg. Not me. I was gathering things as I moved forward. A stage persona is very different from who you are. In fact, a persona is basically someone you don't believe you are that you're trying desperately to convince other people that you are."

Waits would credit new wife Kathleen as the first to recognise that inner desire on the singer's part, recalling to Newsweek that "she was the one that encouraged me to start producing my own records. At that point I had done all my records with a producer. I kind of got stuck. I needed something to kick me. I needed some kind of car wreck or something. She was the one that started playing bizarre music.

"She said, 'You can take this and this and put all this together. There's a place where all these things overlap. Field recordings and Caruso and tribal music and Lithuanian language records and Leadbelly. You can put that in a pot. No one's going to tell you you can't. You like James Brown and you also like Mabel Mercer. There's nothing wrong with that.' We're all that way. We all have disparate influences. And we all know people that don't know each other! Right? I mean, some people are afraid to have parties and invite them all."

Rather than becoming a Yoko Ono, Brennan would push Waits to move past the first sonic stage of his career and help him rethink himself. "Because my music up to that point was still in the box – I was still in the box; hadn't unwrapped myself yet. She let me take my shoes off and loosen up – back then I was still wearing suits to the park. I think from that point on I really tried to grow.

"Growth is scary," he continued in an interview with Mojo years later "because you're a seed and you're in the dark and you don't know which way is up, and down might take you down further into a darker place, you know? I felt like that: I don't know which way to grow. I don't know what to incorporate into myself. What do you take from your parents? What did you come in with? What did you find out when you got here? I was sorting all that out."

He began writing with Brennan for what would become his next studio LP and felt "liberated...I felt like I had found my voice." Unfortunately, not everyone in Waits' camp was a fan of that new voice, beginning with longtime label Asylum who said "You'll get no new fans and you'll lose all the ones you used to have." His wife encouraged him to dig in his heels. "Kathleen said: 'Look, we can find musicians. We'll find the engineer. We can get money from the record company. We have 12 songs here. Let's go, we'll do it ourselves. You don't have to give six points to a producer.'"

Indeed, to achieve the vision they had for Waits' new sound they would have to self-produce the album – as much a first for the singer-songwriter as anything else he was trying. "It was really Kathleen that said, 'Look, you can do this. You know, I'd broken off with Herbie (Cohen, former manager), we were managing my career at that point and there were a lot of decisions to make. I thought I was a millionaire, and it turned out that I had, like 20 bucks. And what followed was a lot of court battles, and it was a difficult ride for both of us, particularly being newlyweds.

"At the same time, it was exciting, because I had never been in a studio without a producer. I came from that whole school where an artist needs a producer. You know, they know more than I do, I don't know anything about the board. I was really old-fashioned that way. Kathleen listened to my records and she knew I was interested in a lot of diverse musical styles that I'd never explored myself on my own record. So she started talking to me about that – you know, 'You can do that.' She's a great DJ, and she started playing a lot of records for me. I'd never thought of myself being able to go in and have the full responsibility for the end result of each song. She really co-produced that record with me, though she didn't get credit. She was the spark and the feed."

Once they had made the decision to take the gamble of producing the album themselves, Waits admitted readily to NPR that, at the time, "the idea of going into the studio and doing your own record is a little scary: pick the engineer, pick all the musicians, write some kind of mission-statement for yourself where you want it to be and sound like and feel like and take responsibility for everything that goes on tape. That's a lot to do, especially it's a lot for a record company to let you do when you behave like I did. And I think they thought I was a drunk. I was really non-communicative. I scratched the back of my neck a lot and I looked down at my shoes a lot. You know, and I wore old suits.

"They were nervous about me. But it's understandable. And in those days they didn't really let artists produce themselves. 'Cause that was also the day of the producer. You know, the big shining producer who would be, I guess, like the director of a film. They give you the money and they say: 'Go make a record with this guy over here.'"

As the pair began plotting the record's sonic direction, Waits found Brennan's input invaluable, quipping to journalist Sean O'Hagan that "I didn't just marry a beautiful woman, I married a record collection. I had something in me, too."

In a business where careers have lived and died on taking chances, Waits was putting it all on the line with his new LP. "I was trying to find some new channel or breakthrough for myself," he told Mojo, adding that personally, the process felt "like growing up and hitting the roof because you have this image that other people have of you, based on what you've put out there so far and how they define you and what they want from you. It's difficult when you try to make some kind of a turn or a change in the weather for yourself."

Tom told journalist Mike Jollett that his breakthrough came during their demoing process. "Someone was fixing a mic and dragging a chair across the floor and it made the most beautiful sound like, 'eeeeeehhh'. And I was thinking, jeez, that's as musical as anything I heard all day, and I'm here to make music. So maybe I should be paying more attention to the things that are outside what we think we're here to do."

A series of demos laid out the sonic blueprint for where Waits was heading with his musical reinvention. He recalled to Mojo that we "did four songs, went and played them to Joe Smith at Elektra-Asylum, and he didn't know what to make of it, and at that point I was kind of dropped from the label." Speaking more candidly to Harp years later, Tom added more specifically in terms of how the label head felt that, in fact, "He hated it! I mean, this is a guy who looked like a sports announcer, so I didn't really have much of a rapport with him. I felt like I was talking to an insurance agent... I think he even called me 'kid'. He fancied himself as something of a mob boss but he also had a little bit of a fraternity feel to him. It was discouraging, but we were able to get off the label on a loophole." That loophole allowed Waits and Brennan – now officially his manager – to take the demos to Island Records owner Chris Blackwell, who Waits recalled thankfully "loved the record. He came out to LA, we had coffee and he said, 'Yeah, I'll put it out.' And that was it."

The move to Island gave him the artistic freedom and financial backing to add on to the new sound he was constructing, sharing years later with Irish radio host Dave Fanning that "it was a big turning point for me in 1980 when I started hearing things differently and doing things differently."

Waits explained to the Chicago Tribune that, in the course of producing the 'Swordfishtrombones' album, "I tried to open my eyes and ears to things that I had been listening to for a long time. I just had never before found a way to incorporate those things into my own music and my own ideas. I've always liked the idea of musical cross-fertilization, any kind of mutant cannibalisation of music that's imposed over another culturally."

The results would dazzle critics like the LA Times who noted in their glowing review that Waits' new sound "explored his scrapyard symphonies and customised cabaret with a bracing sense of risk and freedom," while GQ would quip accurately in later years that the sound Waits and Brennan had succeeded in producing was "an album like none before it. A boldly drawn line, running right through the centre of Tom Waits' work, dividing his life into two neat categories:

before Kathleen Brennan and after Kathleen Brennan."

He had succeeded in shedding his first generation of musical skin, and NPR would note that, in the process, "the barroom piano of 'Closing Time' gave way a decade later to the bizarre, horn-based experimentation of 1983's 'Swordfishtrombones'. His style...(became) more distinctive...(weaving) new elements into his music, in the process sealing his reputation as one of the rock era's most important artists."

Examining the transition from a broader vantage point, the New York Times would note that, heading into the mid Eighties, "since...his own ground-breaking album 'Swordfishtrombones', he has been resolutely broadening his musical palette...has been creating a music that is beyond category – and beyond the scope of the character he portrayed in his early performances, the hard-drinking, gruff-voiced chronicler of bleak rooming house days and road-weary nights... Gravitating toward odd instruments (including a wheezing old proto-synthesiser called the Chamberlin and a percussive sound sculpture known as the conundrum) and sonic textures."

His next studio LP, 1985's 'Rain Dogs', built on the creative and commercial momentum achieved with 'Swordfishtrombones'. By that point, he told Mojo, he'd developed "a lot more self-esteem. We'd done something on our own. It just felt more honest. I was trying to find music that felt more like the people that were in the songs, rather than everybody being kind of dressed up in the same outfit. The people in my earlier songs might have had unique things to say and have come from diverse backgrounds, but they all looked the same."

Stylistically, Waits would add in the same conversation that "I got to a point where I became more eccentric – my songs and my world view. And I started using experimental instruments and ethnic instruments and trying to create some new forms for myself. Using found sounds and so forth."

Tom experienced another sonic epiphany that would become and remain a central tenet of his production philosophy throughout the balance of his career, describing the moment for fans years later in a Epitaph label blog by recalling that "my most thrilling musical experience was in Times Square, over 30 years ago. There was a rehearsal hall around the Brill Building where all the rooms were divided into tiny spaces with just enough room to open the door. Inside was a spinet piano – cigarette burns, missing keys, old paint and no pedals.

"You go in and close the door and it's so loud from other rehearsals you can't really work – so you stop and listen and the goulash of music was thrilling. Scales on a clarinet, tango, light opera, sour string quartet, voice lessons, someone belting out 'Everything's Coming Up Roses', garage bands, and piano lessons. The floor was pulsing, the walls were thin. As if ten radios were on at the same time, in the same room. It was a train station of music with all the sounds milling around... for me it was heavenly."

He branched out further into the realm of experimentation, using the natural soundscape of New York City to help him craft 'Rain Dogs'. Tom explained to the Austin Chronicle that "since 'Swordfishtrombones' I've tried to explore diverse musical styles and that type of thing. I touched on a few of them here, on this record. You know, some blues and a lot of...different kinds of things. I think there's a lot of variety."

The city's endless energy affected his creative incorporation process. "I couldn't sleep on 23rd Street in New York – it was a musical traffic jam session. You can hear a melody, a horn section, haaa heee haaa, broken glass jig-jag clack whack shuffle shuffle. And a radiator with all those little Doc Severinsens playing. There's food for thought at our fingertips and it begs to be dealt with."

As he and Brennan wove those sounds into the broader fabric of the record itself in the studio, he recalled to Mojo that he "was exposed to a kind of mélange of sounds out there," the results of which he later explained to Film Threat magazine sounded like "a whole pageant. It's very rich, there's a lot of noises that you either become compatible with or they drive you away. It's just very surreal living with so much impact and so much input."

The decade would produce 'Swordfishtrombones' 'One From The Heart', 'Rain Dogs', 'Frank's Wild Years' and 'Big Time', a quintet described by the San Francisco Chronicle as "a masterful series of experimental yet deeply traditional albums. He took swatches of immigrant music – secondhand tangos, pub ballads, Weimar-era cabaret songs – and made them uniquely American, uniquely his own."

Waits kicked off the Nineties by pushing his musical boundaries even further, seeming to find both artistic comfort and commercial success in the freedom he gave himself to experiment with anything that itched at his muse. He told Interview magazine that "after a while you realise that music – the writing and enjoying of it – is not off the coast of anything. It's not sovereign, it's well woven, a fabric of everything else." He confirmed to GQ years later that "I wanted to take it all in – and then kind of, y'know, set it all on fire and see what remained. I didn't really want to be part of a clique or a niche. But I also was looking for my own voice as a writer, y'know? And a world I could call my own."

The next landmark in that ever-evolving search would come with 1992's 'Bone Machine', where Waits felt he'd completed his first new wave of experimentation. In the first two decades of his career as a songwriter, he told Harp magazine, "I was just studying the whole thing, trying to find out what I could bring to it that hadn't been brought to it before. Which is really hard to do. Most American culture – we just bury things so we can dig them up again. There's nothing new under the sun, certainly not in popular music. By its very nature, popular music is repetitive and it's constantly masquerading and then exposing itself again. If you just keep stirring it, different things come to the surface. So it's sort of interesting to watch what's bubbling up. What you recognised from before that you thought had gotten hidden at the bottom is now up at the top again."

Certain characteristics of his classic sound remained intact, the BBC noting that Waits in the Nineties would remain "famous for his gravelly voice and a penchant for unusual and exotic instruments, not to mention a bizarre and exaggerated public persona." The Houston Chronicle would further argue that Waits had remained successful in retaining and even expanding that fan base by maintaining an "enduring allure...(of) mystique...throughout his career, a foreignness and an ability to surprise." 'Bone Machine' would accomplish all of the above, garnering Waits in the process a new generation of fans and a Grammy Nomination for Best Alternative Album in 1994.

As the Nineties unfolded and alternative rock went mainstream, Tom had succeeded in cornering his own musical market, a self-invented sub-genre that thrived on what American Songwriter highlighted as a "brilliance...(that) has been found in his ability to create albums that are perfectly sequenced to showcase his eclecticism and range as an artist." His next project 'The Black Rider', was no exception as an illustration of that brilliance in action. Having built up enough creative capital to approach one of his lifelong literary heroes about collaborating on new music together, Waits reached out to the legendary beat writer William S Burroughs, who, Tom explained to the Chicago Tribune, he viewed artistically as "the crooked sheriff in a bad town. Kind of like the real Mark Twain, the one standing in the shadows that nobody wants to look at, particularly the literary side."

Meeting the reclusive Burroughs meant "going to Lawrence, Kansas" where, Waits shared with the Daily News, "there was a little summit meeting out there, and it was really exciting getting this whole thing off the ground. Nobody knew what it would be or the form it would take. I remember Burroughs started singing, 'Ain't no sin to take off your skin and dance around in your bones.' For some reason, with him looking all skeletal himself, holding a drink in his hand and kind of doing a little jig in the middle of the floor, it was inspiring."

Tom seemed to have found a sense of inner peace, taking a few years off in the mid Nineties to raise his children. An interview with journalist Michael Fuchs-Gambock revealed that "I had no choice but to grow up fast. You can't bring kids up if you're still one yourself. On top of that, being a father has a lot of advantages. You get healthier. Life is quieter and you can concentrate on work better. I am my work, and only when I work can I really express myself and what's inside me. I learn more about myself through it. To get to that stage I have to have peace and quiet and the family is a vital part of that."

Tom and Brennan returned in 1999 with their next studio opus, 'Mule Variations', opting to leave Island Records, his home for much of the past two decades, in favour of indie label Epitaph who, Waits recalled to Mojo, "convinced me that I belonged there and that what I was doing was perfectly valid, and that gave me confidence."

Back in the studio, Waits and Brennan were as strong a production team as ever, engineer Steve Hodges recalling to author Barney Hoskyns that "they sang stuff together and she commented on his phrasing, helped with the enunciations. They definitely worked together at sculpting this thing, and they were really honest about how much they needed each other. It's a fucking beautiful thing they have. Who wouldn't think it's pretty cool that these guys can relate on stuff and work together? Tom is a renaissance man of a sort. To be so powerful without being macho is...very cool."

A Mojo magazine cover story framed him as "a master songwriter who likes to pretend he's a bin raider, not so much composing his demented nerve-jangles and sentimental broken beauties as welding together a bunch of found sounds with some new ideas, cobbled-together instruments with traditional ones, speaking with singing and mouth-rhythms that sound like both field recordings and computer loops. His creations have become even more experimental with age."

His Epitaph debut 'Mule Variations' went gold and reaffirmed the currency of Waits' influence through a Grammy Award for Best Contemporary Folk Album and a nomination for Best Male Rock Performance. The singer-songwriter entered the Millennium and his 30-year mark in the business as viable as ever.

An Epitaph label press release cited a range of influences including "Kerouac, Dylan, Bukowski, Rod Serling, Don Van Vliet, Cantinflas, James Brown, Harry Belafonte, Ma Rainey, Big Mama Thornton, Howlin' Wolf, Leadbelly, Lord Buckley, Mabel Mercer, Lee Marvin, Thelonious Monk, John Ford, Fellini, Weegee, Jagger, Richards, Willie Dixon, John McCormick, Johnny Cash, Hank Williams, Frank Sinatra, Louis Armstrong, Robert Johnson, Hoagy Carmichael, Enrico Caruso."

Tom had succeeded through his own sub-genre in becoming what Mojo concluded by that point was "a totemic figure for a generation of alternative acts who want their music to sound dirty, visceral, and human. From the gothic swamp-rock of Nick Cave and PJ Harvey to the muddy grooves of the Beta Band and the stomping blues-punk of Jon Spencer, Waits is the hidden presence behind so much music that rages against mechanical blandness."

Waits was as busy as ever as the decade unfolded, remaining popular not only with his multi-generational base of fans from the Seventies, Eighties and Nineties, but equally as relevant to a new generation of college-aged fans. Chart Attack's report on the success of his 2008 live album stated that "there's a new Number 1 album courtesy Tom Waits, a veteran of the college radio wars. His latest album, 'Glitter And Doom Live', rises two places to capture the Number 1 spot on this week's charts.

"Holding this spot on the campus charts is nothing new for this wily old veteran. Since engaging in his musical comeback a decade ago, all but one of his six most recent releases have topped the campus charts, beginning with his Grammy Award-winning 'Mule Variations' which held the Number 1 position for seven straight weeks in 1999. Waits' other Number 1 albums include 2002's 'Blood Money', 2004's 'Real Gone' and the triple-album release 'Orphans: Brawlers, Bawlers & Bastards' which remained at Number 1 for three weeks exactly three years ago. The only album in that period to not hit Number 1 was 'Alice', which Waits released concurrently with 'Blood Money'. 'Alice' reached Number 4 when 'Blood Money' was also in the Top 10."

Putting the depth and breadth of that ever-influential and growing catalogue under a complete and comprehensive examination for the first time in the pages of Tom Waits: In The Studio, we now begin an exploration of the behind-the-scenes process by which the alt-jazz/folk-pop sub-genre he still chairs today was first invented, beginning with an examination of the Seventies Asylum years.

Via beloved early LPs like the latter-mentioned 'The Heart Of Saturday Night', 'Small Change' and 'Heartattack And Vine', the singer-songwriter succeeded in singularly standing out among what Harp magazine concluded was "a musical era overpopulated with coke fiends and jaded hippies, Waits was the personification of a new kind of vintage cool – a technologically advanced hipster. Raymond Chandler for the counterculture. Hoagy Carmichael for folkies. Lord Buckley for the Cheech and Chong generation."

For fans of Waits' later decades of multiple musical evolutions, stylistically and sonically, that produced equally-and-in-some-cases more broadly celebrated LPs like 'Swordfishtrombones', 'Rain Dogs', 'Bone Machine', 'Mule Variations', 'Real Gone' and beyond, an equally as thrilling period of production is explored. In light of the Miami Herald's recent conclusion that "you could say Waits is the king…of turning idiosyncrasies and eccentricities into artistic statements and masterpieces," this journey promises to be as unique as Tom Waits' artistic self.

"I was born on 7 December 1949 in the back seat of a yellow cab in Murphy Hospital parking lot in Pomona, California." – TOM WAITS

"I remember when I was a kid I heard a songwriter in a club and it gave me some purpose and an idea that I also wanted to be a performer. I didn't know anything about it, but I knew what I didn't want to do and just narrowed it down to that." – TOM WAITS

PART I: Tom Waits:
The Roots Af A Songwriter

Tom Waits would become an overnight poet and musical advocate for the 'real people' of the world with his very first album. His lyrics, twisting along the boulevards and back roads of society's underbelly, expressed what Rolling Stone concluded was "passionate love for the seamier side of Los Angeles and its environs. Booze, cigarettes and gasoline fuel his world of neon signs, gas stations, diners, bus depots, barmaids and sailors."

In looking back on his own childhood, the singer/songwriter admits that, on the surface, "my own background was very middle class... I was a kid...(and) had a pretty normal childhood. I learned to handle silverware and all of that stuff."

Still, the suburban subterfuge faded fast with Waits' next revelation – one that could have been pulled right out of one of his songs – that "my parents divorced when I was 10 years old. My father's been married about three times, so I moved around quite a lot." Initially staying in his father's custody, Waits' vagabond roots were planted in the years that followed, the singer recalling in a conversation with ZigZag magazine that "my father was a Spanish teacher, so we lived in Whittier, Pomona, LaVerne, North Hollywood, Silver Lake, metropolitan areas surrounding Los Angeles."

This domestic transience would go on to inform Waits' real-world experience speaking on and for those who, like him, hadn't lived a life of traditional white-picket life, reflective in Waits' childhood memory with Smash Hits magazine that "when I was ten, we lived on a chicken ranch in Baja California for about five months. I spent a lot of time in Mexico."

When he wasn't moving around with his father's family, Waits shared with Melody Maker that "sometimes I lived with my mother and two sisters... I kinda took care of my (sisters). I was at home with these three women, my mother and an older sister and a younger sister...and although they were there, I was on my own a lot."

During these formative years, Tom's escape from the realities of growing up bouncing back and forth between his parents came, not surprisingly, via music, beginning with his parents' respective vinyl collections, which he recalled to Contemporary Keyboard magazine "wasn't anything real eclectic...mostly the hit parade, that kind of stuff: Frank Sinatra, Bing Crosby, Gene Krupa, Benny Goodman, Harry Belafonte, Glenn Miller – nothing real 'inside.' But as an alternative to Blue Cheer, it was a welcome relief... There was always music in the house."

As he began to dig deeper than his folks' record collections' in search of a sound that spoke more really to him, Waits shared that "the first album I bought was James Brown's 'Papa's Got A Brand New Bag.'"

From there, a pallet of wildly colourful influences as eclectic as Waits' own style would eventually emerge that, he explained to Crawdaddy Radio, included "Clarence 'Frogman' Henry, Huey 'Piano' Smith, Harry 'The Hipster' Edison. I listened to Lord Buckley for a long time. I was always fond of George and Ira Gershwin and Jerome Kern and Johnny Mercer and Cole Porter and Irving Berlin. As far as contemporary artists at the time, I wasn't listening to them. I was never a real trendsetter... I was never particularly excited about the Beach Boys, a lot of their albums were good for keeping the dust off your turntable."

He would add years later in a walk down memory lane with NPR that "the early songs I remember was 'Abilene'. When I heard 'Abilene' on the radio it really moved me. And then I heard you know: 'Abilene, Abilene, prettiest town I have ever seen. Women there don't treat you mean. And Abilene...' I just thought that was the greatest lyric you know 'Women there don't treat you mean.' And then, you know, 'Detroit City'. 'Last night I went to sleep in Detroit City.' 'And I dream about the cotton fields back home.'

"I liked songs with the names of towns in them and I liked songs with weather in them and something to eat. So I feel like there's a certain anatomical aspect to a song that I respond to. I think: 'Oh yeah, I can go into that world. There's something to eat, there's the name of a street, there's a saloon, okay.' So probably that's why I put things like that in my songs."

Waits' own musical development began, the singer recalled to Folkscene, when "I went to O'Farrell Junior High School, an all-black junior high. I was under certain social pressures, so I listened to what was around me. I listened to a lot of black artists, quite a few black artists – James Brown, the Supremes, Wilson Pickett – but by then I'd had a lot of incongruous musical influences: jazz, Gershwin, Porter, Kern, Arlen, Carmichael, Mercer, Louis Armstrong, Stravinsky, Reverend Gary Davis, Mississippi John Hurt. I had a real interest in that. James Brown was my idol at the time...and the Flames were real big... I saw James Brown live – he knocked me out, man, when I was in 7th grade."

Tom's experience with the Godfather of Soul sparked the same ambition and inspiration that had gripped John Lennon on seeing Elvis Presley perform for the first time on Ed Sullivan Live and less than a decade later, resulted in his own band's appearance on the same stage, inspiring an entire new generation of music fans. Waits explained to SOMA magazine that he'd already begun to discover a talent of his own at a younger age, beginning with "the ukulele when I was a kid and I played a guitar my dad gave me...(and) played trumpet in elementary school."

Waits recalled to Contemporary Keyboard that he joined his first band at age 12. "I played rhythm guitar and sang in a band called the Systems...(We played) rhythm and blues – a lot of black hit parade stuff, white kids trying to get that

Motown sound... I don't know if it was a soul band. It was surf and soul." Eager to begin honing his own live musical instincts, Tom explained to journalist Mikel Jollett that, initially, being stunted in that ambition by the fact that "in those days, you didn't play a lot of gigs. You'd play a dance every now and then. I knew I wanted to do something with music, but navigating that seems almost impossible. It's like digging through a wall with a spoon and your only hope is that what's on the other side is digging with the same intensity towards you."

At age 14, Tom, living again with his father after he opened a translation business in San Diego, enrolled in Hill Top High School in the Chula Vista neighborhood of San Diego. From the outset, he confessed to Rambler magazine, "I was kind of an amateur juvenile delinquent... When I was a kid, I was pretty normal. Used to go to Dodger Stadium, was a real avid Dodger fan. I did all the usual things like hang around parking lots, had paper routes, vandalised cars, stole things from dime stores and all that stuff."

Crediting his rebellion in part to the fact that "I felt really peculiar when I was going through puberty. That was a very peculiar period for me," Waits soon found refuge – and arguably his foot in the door to a world that would eventually come to define him as a songwriter – working the graveyard shift at Napoleon's Pizza Parlour in the National City neighborhood of San Diego, a job he comically recalled to Smash Hits magazine that he landed "when I was 14.

"My brother-in-law, who weighed about 300 pounds, was working in a small Italian restaurant and they decided that there was no room for him in the kitchen, so they sacked him and I got the job... I stayed in school, but worked every night until four in the morning." The nocturnal nature of his new job allowed Waits "the freedom to take off at five in the afternoon and come back at five in the morning, no questions asked... I would stay out all night, I loved it."

Tom also found himself instantly attracted to the gritty narrative of the 'real world' vibe National City offered him in contrast to his family's middle-class suburban existence, describing his workplace to WAMU Radio as "a tiny community – this Naugahyde town in Southern California – a sailor town, lots of vinyl white-booted go-go dancers...The main drag was a transvestite (row) and the average age was deceased... Hookers would come in, brag and play with me. The point was to wash enough dishes as you could so you could go outside and smoke a cigarette... I encountered a whole different element – people a lot older than me, pool hustlers and Mafioso types." Taking the young, eagerly impressionable Waits under their wing, the singer-songwriter volunteered that "I grew up real fast."

He recalled in a conversation with the New Yorker a feeling in his gut that "I knew when I was working there I was going to do something with it. I didn't know how, but I felt it every night... I worked until four in the morning in a pizza house as a cook, started off as a dishwasher, worked for Sal Crivello and Joe Sardo, worked there for five years as a matter of fact... I was dishwasher, waiter, cook, janitor, plumber – everything. They called me Speed O Flash. Sundays, I'd come in at 6 am and wash, buff and wax the floors. There was a good jukebox – played 'Cryin' Time' and 'I Can't Stop Loving You.'"

The musical influences that captured his ear in his later teens included "James Brown and Bobby Blue Bland, Jimmy Witherspoon, Bob Dylan and Ray Charles. I think most singers, when they start out, are doing really bad impersonations of other singers that they admire. You kind of evolve into your voice. Or maybe your voice is out there waiting for you to grow up and then it meets you."

Waits' nocturnal lifestyle left no real energy or passion for days as a student to the point where, by the age of 17, Tom recalled to journalist Peter O'Brien that high school had become "a big pain... When I was in school, I was in trouble a lot. Conflict with teachers. I got no sympathy from my folks, being teachers themselves. I was wasted all day, because I worked in a restaurant until four in the morning... I became a day sleeper... I'd worked all the way through high school – bus boy, cook, janitor, plumber, maintenance man. I was never voted 'Most Likely to Succeed' in school, but, what the hell. I'm glad I wasn't!... I didn't find much in school. I was just getting in a lot of trouble so I hung it up."

He now had more time on his hands to continue soaking up as much real-life experience as he could. While continuing to hold down his night-job at Napoleon's Pizza Parlor, Tom took on any part-time job he could get, recalling to WAMU Radio that these included "all the odd jobs... I drove taxis, sold vacuum cleaners and encyclopedias, worked in gas stations and liquor stores, at a jewellery store, as a janitor, a delivery boy, a labour organiser at a maternity ward, in a commissary on a Navy base, as a street sweeper, a bouncer at a coffee house and even had a paper route. I sold night crawlers to fishermen – you can buy live worms in the mail, you know... I worked a lot of different jobs."

Waits admits in hindsight he was "desperately keen to get away (from)" in part because he felt socially alienated from the Sixties hippie/flower-power social movement. Tom's decision to follow his own path would later be depicted by Newsweek as an age where "a middle-class southern California kid...dropped out of the hippie generation."

He addressed his alienation from both a social and artistic perspective in a conversation with New Times magazine. "I was kinda lost in the Sixties... I didn't have black lights or incense or Jimi Hendrix posters, so I was really going through an identity crisis...knowing I wanted to do something creative and not knowing how or where to do it... I felt a little misplaced."

All of that changed, as the Los Angeles Free Press would report, "in his mid teens...(at) a time when some of us discovered Dylan; some of us discovered swing; and when some of us are discovering Springsteen. The mod teens are an important, impressionable age. Waits discovered Jack Kerouac."

Tom candidly told Now magazine that discovering Kerouac and Ginsberg at such a crucial and pivotal time in his teens "saved me. Growing up without a dad, I was always looking for a father figure and those guys sorta became my father figures. Reading On The Road added some interesting mythology to the ordinary and sent me off on the road myself with an investigative curiosity about the minutiae of life."

Waits added to Rolling Stone that "Kerouac liked to consider himself a jazz poet, using words the same way Miles (Davis) uses his horn. And it's a beautiful instrument. He had melody, a good sense of rhythm, structure, colour, mood and intensity. I couldn't put the book down. And I got a subscription to Downbeat afterwards."

The writer would serve in time as a tour guide as Waits made his way through an era where, he admits, "I was kinda groping for something to hang on to, stylistically." He added in the same conversation with NME that "even though I was growing up in Southern California, he made a tremendous impression on me... I guess everybody reads him at some point in their life...and I loved (him) since I first discovered him... (At the time), I was obsessed with Kerouac (and) he remained my hero. I think it's good to have heroes."

Waits own rejection of the mainstream "during the height of rock and roll, (when) I kept a low profile," fitted perfectly with Kerouac's On The Road philosophy of exploring life at a time when Waits' ambitions 'didn't go much beyond just working in a restaurant, maybe buying into a place. Music was just such a vicarious thing, I was a patron. No more, no less."

Crediting his favourite Beat writer with giving him the focus to think freely of those sorts of conventional boundaries, Tom admitted years later to Melody Maker that "I discovered him at the time I could have ended up at Lockheed Aircraft, a jewellery store or a gas station, married with three children, lying on the beach...a lot of Americans went off on the road, just get into a car and drive, for 3,000 miles, East or West."

Waits would soon follow suit, fully embracing the concept of life imitating art when he "hitchhiked to Arizona with Sam Jones while I was still a high school student," beginning his own journal of experiences that he recalled became a regular feature to his post-high school life in the late Sixties. In an Asylum Records promo interview Waits revealed that he and buddy Sam Jones would "hitchhike all the time from California to Arizona. We would just see how far we could go in three days, on a weekend and see if we could get back by Monday... I rode the rails and slept in a graveyard."

Waits' days as a regional vagabond exploring the highways and byways of the Southwest included adventures such as one he recalled to Magnet magazine where "one night in a fog...we got lost on the side road and didn't know where we were exactly. And the fog came in and we were really lost then and it was very cold. We dug a big ditch in a dry river bed and we both laid in there and pulled all this dirt and leaves over us like a blanket. We're shivering in this ditch all night and we woke up in the morning and the fog had cleared and right across from us was a diner; we couldn't see it through the fog. We went in and had a great breakfast, still my high-water mark for a great breakfast. The phantom diner."

Waits added in Island promo interview that "another time we wound up) on a New Year's Eve in front of a Pentecostal church and an old woman named Mrs Anderson came out. We were stuck in a town, with like seven people in this town and trying to get out you know? And my buddy and I were out there for hours and hours and hours getting colder and colder and it was getting darker and darker. Finally she came over and she says: 'Come on in the church here. It's warm and there's music and you can sit in the back row.' And then we did and they were singing and had a tambourine, an electric guitar and a drummer.

"They were talking in tongues and then they kept gesturing to me and my friend Sam: 'These are our wayfaring strangers here.' So we felt kinda important. And they took up a collection, they gave us some money, bought us a hotel room and a meal. We got up the next morning, then we hit the first ride at seven in the morning and then we were gone. It was really nice, I still remember all that and it gave me a good feeling about travelling."

Followng the same path toward artistic discovery that heroes like Kerouac had through their fascinations with American literature, Tom recalled to the New Yorker that "I became curious about style more than anything else...(so) I read a lot. I used to read Hubert Selby, Larry McMurtry, John Rechy, Nelson Algren. I liked comedians and storytellers: Wally Cox, Harry the Hipster, Rodney Dangerfield, Redd Foxx, Lord Buckley... I discovered Gregory Corso, Lawrence Ferlinghetti...

"Ginsberg still comes up with something every now and again... Charles Bukowski is probably one of the most colourful and most important writers of modern fiction, poetry and prose, in contemporary literature... I'd say he's at the vanguard in my book, he just levels me." To accompany his beatnik image, Waits happily dressed the part, recalling that, in 1968, "I started wearing dark glasses and got myself a subscription to (jazz magazine) Downbeat."

By that age, he was finally able to begin putting the proverbial puzzle pieces of what to do with his life. He revealed to Rambler that "since I was a kid I had an image of me in a dark sport coat and clean tie getting up and entertaining people." In his late teens, he told Sounds magazine, "I heard a songwriter in a club and it gave me some purpose and an idea that I also wanted to be a performer. I didn't know anything about it, but I knew what I didn't want to do and just narrowed it down to that."

Tom had put the guitar aside to explore life over the preceding few years. He next found himself sitting in his parents' garage before a piano that he admitted up to that point, he'd avoided because "it scared me to death... I wouldn't go near it because...I didn't know how to approach it." Summoning the same fearless spirit that had first sent him exploring the open roads, Waits recalled to the New Yorker becoming "an investigator at the keyboard... I finally broke down (and) started sitting down, fooling around with it... No academic study at all. I just listened to records."

His technique came from a collection of influences that, he recalled to Downbeat magazine, included legendary pianists like "Red Tyler, Huey Piano Smith, Art Tatum, Professor Longhair and Thelonious Monk... Another composer I like is Bob Dorough. He wrote 'Baltimore Oriole' back in the Fifties... The first time I got hip to him was on an album called 'Poetry And Jazz'. John Carradine was on it reading some Dylan Thomas stuff."

Tom recalled to Folkscene that a favourite was a spoken-word LP by Steve Allen and Jack Kerouac, explaining that "Steve Allen played some stuff and he just talked over the top of it and it was real, real effective... It was essentially Steve Allen playing jazz behind Kerouac and Kerouac was just telling stories...

(From there), I listened to Rudy Ray Moore, Oscar Brown Jr, Ken Nordine, Lord Buckley... I had never heard anything like it – so I wrote a few little things... It frees you as a songwriter to be able to just throw down some colour and not worry about any sort of meter at all, so I enjoyed (that)."

As Waits laid it down on the piano day after day, the singer/songwriter soon found himself becoming more and more "curious about melody. If I wanted to learn a key, I'd write a melody in that key... I soon taught myself to play everything in F sharp and little by little I got to be all right... I taught myself primarily so that I could understand what I was trying to do technically on the piano. Usually you write within a framework, however limited you are, then that's as far as you'll go. Instead of learning theory and then learning how to play the piano, I learned theory through writing."

This was an early and important underpinning to any composer who would later – with that knowledge of song structure – be free to explore many uncharted musical territories. His discovery of the piano would be the catalyst to launching Tom's career as a songwriter.

Waits' songwriting craft continued to evolve in a free-form style that reflected what he explained to the San Diego Weekly was an ongoing desire to avoid "any real academic stuff, which I think becomes sort of obvious when you notice my pedestrian style... I'm real ragged. To use the word ragtime would be about right. I'm just real pedestrian in how I approach it. It's mainly from a writing standpoint... It provides a lot more freedom for me."

San Diego's live music scene was as much his classroom as the recorded and written influences described above, Waits used his love of life as inspiration as he continued to refine his songwriting instincts, recalling to Folkscene that "my musical education began at a folk club – the Heritage, a small club in San Diego which had a lot of traditional music, a lot of country artists, bluegrass, that sort of thing. I soaked it in like a sponge. I sat on the door and I listened to as much as I possibly could."

Landing his first regular gig was no easy task, with Waits explaining to the San Diego Weekly that "I was the doorman and that was one of the important steps for me because I got to listen every weekend. It was one place you could run into someone you haven't seen in three of four years and that was usually the place you went when you got back in town to see who was in town. All those people that used to hang out there. When the Heritage closed it was hard for a long time...

"Bob Webb gave me a weekend there. I'd been hootin' for quite a while and I had a girlfriend who got a job waiting tables too. So she was kind of putting a good word in for me with Bob and finally he came around and said, 'We'll risk it.'"

As he became further immersed into the live folk scene, Tom explained that the club offered his first face-to-face exposure to "the first real songwriters I came into first-hand contact with were around San Diego. All local people at the Heritage and the Candy Company and the Back Door and, eventually, Jack Tempchin, Ray Bierl and Ted Staak. There weren't that many, but the ones that were playing here were all worth listening to."

The fledgling songwriter explained to Rambler that "I was working the door, taking tickets at the time and listening to all kinds of acts from the door... I heard bluegrass, comics, folk singers, string bands... I knew one day I would perform myself, but I was trying to soak up as much before I did so I wouldn't make an ass of myself."

In a short time, Waits' plan paid off. "I first got on stage, slowly I worked up to where I was doing a weekend now and then and I was playing a little guitar, a little piano, doing Mississippi John Hurt songs and Reverend Gary Davis and it was basically a traditional club with emphasis on string, bands, banjo, fiddle, bluegrass folk music, traditional blues, very few songwriters.

"I was just one of many and it was kind of a beach community musical school where people come and hang out, just local talent... It was just something I wanted to try my hand at, so I tried my hand at it... I guess you get better as you go along, the more music you listen to and the more perceptive you become towards melody and lyric and all."

As an ever-evolving songwriter, Waits soon found his core creative comfort zone intermingling a love for improvisation, both in his life and musical stylings, that was reminiscent of his hero Jack Kerouac. He reasoned that while "some people choose to write about cosmic garbage, what sign are you and how many limousines there are, I just write about things that I see around me." Drawing on his years working and walking among the proverbial 'real people' of the world, Waits further explained that in the course of acquiring his street smarts he was also developing his creative intelligence as a songwriter.

"I was picking up people's conversations in all-night coffee shops – ambulance drivers, cabdrivers, street sweepers. I did research there as an evening curator and I started writing gingerly. I thought at some point I'd like to forge it all into something meaningful and give it dignity."

Waits began to invent what would become his signature art-imitating-life style of songwriting. Years later, he would explain that the aforementioned wouldn't have been possible without his having personally walked enough in those characters' shoes to give them a real voice, reasoning to WAMU Radio that "I'm concerned about imagery in a song and not going for the easiest possible description.

"It helps when I sit down to write something to be able to use my imagination and it certainly is a craft after a while, it's a whole combination of craft and your own past experience and your own crazy ideas about things. I come from a good family and everything but I've over the years developed some ways about me that just aren't right – you just have to look for the kinks in your personality and it helps sometimes."

PART II: 'Closing Time' (1973)

Having decided on his career path by the age of 19, Waits recalled to Folkscene feeling at the time that "I couldn't think of anything else I really wanted to be. Seems to be today nobody wants to be...a baseball player anymore or anything – everybody wants to be a rock'n'roll star. I was always real interested in music (which) beat the hell out of putting aluminum siding on recreational vehicles, or fixing radios... Even though I've had to do a lot of other things to make a buck, this is what I've always wanted to do."

Seeking more promising professional horizons than San Diego's folk clubs, Waits turned his ambition north toward Los Angeles, sharing his memory with New Times magazine of feeling "like a lion ready to pounce on the music scene... I was as ambitious as hell. I wasn't any good, but I was ambitious and I thought I was better than anybody and I sucked raw eggs. But you have to think that way. To let an audience intimidate you is musical suicide."

He commuted back and forth on a weekly basis between Los Angeles and San Diego, as Melody Maker magazine later recalled. "Waits took his bluesy, boozy act to amateur night at Los Angeles' Troubadour Club...on Monday evenings, when the club opened its stage to all-comers... Tom would take the 150-mile bus ride up from San Diego; after standing in line for several hours, he would be called onstage in time to do only a few numbers before catching a bus that would deliver him back home as the sun was coming up... Within a year he had gathered an impressive following including Elton John, Bette Midler and Joni Mitchell."

Waits' live gigs at the Troubadour attracted attention in the same vein of Jimi Hendrix's residence at the Bag O'Nails club in London, where like Waits, while still an unknown, Hendrix boasted a loyal audience including Eric Clapton, Pete Townshend, John Lennon, Mick Jagger, Brian Jones, Jeff Beck, Rod Stewart, Jimmy Page, Ronnie Wood and Paul McCartney. One member of that audience would soon step forward and help in launching Tom's career as a recording artist.

The night that would change Waits' life, as Melody Maker recounted, came one night in the summer of 1971 when "Frank Zappa/Tim Buckley manager Herb Cohen heard Tom perform at the Troubadour. Impressed, Cohen added the singer to his client roster." Years later, Cohen would share his memory of that first encounter with journalist Stan Soocher. "I was on my way to the toilet when

I heard Tom sing. When I came out of the toilet, I asked him what he was doing and he said, 'Nothing'. So I signed him up." Signing Waits to a development deal with Bizarre/Straight Records, the label Cohen co-owned with star client Frank Zappa, "Herb got me a songwriting contract and I wrote for a (year) before I got a recording contract with Asylum Records."

Jerry Yester, who had produced 'Goodbye And Hello' and 'Happy Sad' for Tim Buckley, as well as hit albums for the Turtles and the Association, was chosen to oversee Waits' debut album. Recounting his first face-to-face meeting with Waits, Yester recalled that "I'd got a call from Tom's manager about the project, who was also my manager at the time and rather than send me any demos, he sent Tom my address and phone number and he showed up at my house in Burbank.

"My house was located across the street from a church and Hungarian deli, and so I got this call, 'Is this Jerry?' And I said 'Yes', and he said 'This is Tom, I'm standing in front of this place called Olive Imports.' So I directed him to my house and he walked right in, sat down at my living room baby grand piano and played me all the songs from the album." The set, Waits explained to WAMU Radio, was culled from "a collection of a lot of old songs of mine...that I'd been keeping around until I got a record contract. A lot of the songs were already three years old!"

Yester was as impressed with Waits as the characters in his songs. "He came off as a character right away, very eccentric. (Drummer) Shelly Manne put it best years later during the 'Small Change' LP sessions, which was the first time he'd met Tom, when he came into the control room after the first take of a song called 'Step Right Up' and asked us 'Who is this guy? He's the oldest guy I've ever met.' And we were all laughing because Tom really was in good possession of his character. He was self-invented and had a lot going for him at such a young age, because he was only 25 at that time and even younger – 21 at the time we first started working together.

"When he started playing in my living room my wife, who had been washing the tub in the bathroom, heard Tom and came in with this 'What the hell' look on her face, sat down alongside me and listened to him the rest of the time he was playing. I recorded Tom at my house that afternoon on a Sony two-inch machine to make my own demos. After listening through again and reaching the same conclusion that pre-production on the songs was done, my next thought was: okay, what's next? Which was the band."

Though he hadn't played with a band backing him since Junior High, Yester remembered Waits knowing right off the bat what instrumentation he wanted behind his songs. It began, as the producer recalled, with "Tom saying 'I like an upright bass', so I said 'Okay, I'll find a good player' and came up with Bill Plummer. Then I said, 'I think an electric guitar would sound good on this stuff'. He said 'Yeah?' And I said 'I know this young guy who I've known since he was six, who is one of the best guitar players I've ever heard, Peter Klimes', and next I said 'I think on drums, I don't think you can do better than John Seiter (who had been the drummers for the Turtles). He had a lot of soul and was a great natural player.'

"So we tried the band out in a rehearsal, and it just clicked, Tom loved them all. They really gelled from the start, fell right into the tunes and the arrangements evolved naturally. There was no real talk about it, I don't remember anything except that they evolved naturally and very quickly, maybe over one afternoon as I recall, and then we went right into the studio." Tom, for his own part, recalled to the San Diego Weekly that "I had a good group and we got along fine. We had a week and a half, two weeks, of rehearsal and then went right into the studio."

Though he'd clocked up recording time already between August and December, 1971 demoing songs for manager Herb Cohen, 'Closing Time' would mark Waits' first time formally entering a studio to record, the prospect of which the singer-songwriter would admit years later to The Scene "was kind of frightening... You know when ya go into the studio for the first time you get a little nervous and you don't know as much." Jerry Yester felt far more confident because "I felt the songs were really there already, I was stunned, because it was amazing material. Tom seemed to be coming from a totally artistic point of view and there was no chaff at all; he was done with pre-production and that kind of gave me a sonic blueprint for the record as a producer in that I knew right away I wanted to keep it very simple and non-technical and let the songs speak for themselves. There were no snags and it was one of the easiest things I've ever recorded in my life."

Though the album would ultimately be titled 'Closing Time' – in line with the dive-bar subject matter of its songs – Jerry Yester joked about finding a small amount of irony in the fact that sessions for the record began early in the morning, explaining that "the only time we could get in the studio was from 10 in the morning to six in the evening. Tom and I were both night owls, everybody was, but because we both wanted to get right to work in a studio, rather than waiting for a couple months, so we settled for a day-time booking at Sunset Sound. We went in within a couple of weeks to Sunset Sound to begin work. I remember we had both grumbled a lot about the daytime schedule at first, but after the first day we were really into the music we were making so it didn't take long to adjust to the hours. It was a really productive time and there was something nice about working in the daytime."

"I was fortunate enough to have pretty much my own rein in the studio," Waits recalled to the San Diego Weekly, describing his greatest challenge as the realisation "that because any fine, competent studio musician in LA can play any number of different styles, you have to know exactly what you want... It was the matter of being explicit enough in the studio to tell a musician exactly what you want." The sound Waits invented in the course of 'Closing Time' was one Melody Maker would later compare to something "like the Beat poets whose readings were accompanied by unobtrusive jazz. Tom utilises a simple, jazz-flavoured instrumentation. On his album...he plays a soft piano and is backed by a small, bass-dominated ensemble."

Detailing the studio's layout, famed producer Bruce Botnick (at the time an engineer at the studio) shared with Music Angle that "the main room was a compression room...the back wall was all brick, the floor was asphalt tile, the right wall looking out to the studio was shelving with sliding doors. That's where we put the tapes, because we didn't have a tape vault. Then there was the glass window and there were three Altec Lansing 604e loudspeakers hanging above that. The left was a block wall covered with acoustical tile, and then there was a big door, which held the famous Sunset Sound echo chamber, and then there was the entrance into the control room. The console was a custom tube console with 14 inputs that Alan Emig designed."

Yester added of the studio's design that "the whole control room was all brick and it had individual panels of acoustical tile to deaden it down. Basically, it was a very live room. The console sat on a platform, which was about six or eight inches off the floor. The tape machine sat behind us; we had an old Ampex 200 three-track, which had separate record and playback electronics so that you could select separate record or playback curves. They had a thing back then called AME, which was Ampex Master Equalisation, and then they had NAB, so if you recorded AME and played it back NAB it would come out brighter. It's like recording with Dolby and not decoding. We also had an Ampex 300, I believe, three-track, which I converted over to a four-track with sel-sync (the ability to perform overdubs)."

Jerry Yester explained that "as far as the micing, I remember our engineer Ritchie loved U87s, U67s and U47s, but he would also use ribbon mics in different places in front of the drums and on Tom's piano we used a pair of Neumann KM-87s. Tom played on a Steinway grand piano and everything just sounded great together. We spent three to four days on tracking and the band was done; it didn't really take long to get the basic recording finished. Then Tom and I booked time over at this little studio on Cahuenga Boulevard, down toward Sunset, to record his overdubs."

Waits would later express amazement at the freedom Sunset Sound gave him in the course of building the album's instrumentation, explaining to the San Diego Weekly that "you just realise how much you have at your disposal...you have all this equipment, you're open for 24 tracks, you can just shoot your rocks. The hardest thing is to be discrete. Definitely a learning experience. I was pleased with it."

'Closing Time' opened with 'Ol' 55', a song the Eagles would go on to cover and Rolling Stone hailed as "one of the album's finest cuts". It is the rapturous evocation of driving the freeway in the early morning in a state of post-coital euphoria." Waits, in a conversation with New Times magazine, pinpointed the song's originality. "Ol' 55' is not just nostalgic, I drive a '55 Cadillac. That's the car I've always driven. It has nothing to do with nostalgia. That's why I never do any oldies. You can't improve on 'Minnie The Moocher'. Cab Calloway did it best. I'm not going to do anything old until I think I can do it better. I'm not at all into the musical retread tire scene, like say the Manhattan Transfer or the Pointer Sisters. They're just ripping off the past."

Turning to the album's title cut, Jerry Yester recalled its serendipitous creation as "probably the most magical moment of the album, which occurred three weeks into recording on a Sunday afternoon. Tom and I wanted to record something, and the only studio I could find that was open was Western, which is now Ocean Way Studios, and it was a big studio where Sinatra and the Association used to record.

"I remember at first it was like the total opposite of the way the album had moved so far because nothing was coming together, so we were sitting in the studio with nothing to do and this time booked, and I asked Tom 'What do you want to do?' And he said 'Well, how about 'Closing Time'?' This was an instrumental, so I asked him 'Okay, how do you want to do it?' And he replied 'I hear a horn doing the melody, and the bass', and then one of us – I don't remember who – said 'How about a cello?'"

Sensing he needed to seize the moment, Yester "started calling people... It was a Sunday, so I thought it might be slim pickings, but luckily I found three or four players who weren't doing anything, and they were all these at the studio within 45 minutes – Arni Egilsson, Tony Terran, who was an incredible trumpet player, and Jesse Ehrlich, who played cello. So Tom just started talking to him, running over parts, and the engineer Ritchie was so excited because it was such a nice grouping of instruments." Agreeing, Waits added that the collection of players was "real effective...an instrumental done with standup bass, trumpet and piano."

Continuing with the specifics of the song's charmed recording session, Yester recalled that engineer Ritchie Moore "didn't want any baffles, he wanted to use the big room and record it Quad (which meant two mics in front, and two in back). Ritchie wanted to just placing players in the right places with the right mics, and record it live two-track, backing the session up on the 16-track. So that afternoon, when these guys started playing, they just clicked so well together that it was just magical, one of those incredible storybook moments. It was like they'd known each other all their lives, even in this short time. Directionally, Tom didn't need to say much of anything, other than little things like, 'The trumpet should play melody here, and then I'll play, then you'll come back in...'"

Offering the recording as a perfect example of studio serendipity, the producer recalled that "the whole thing was improvised. I made a chord chart for whoever needed it, but we only did two takes, and the second take was the one. Tony played the sweetest trumpet, the cello and bass players were both incredible and Tom – who played piano live with them – was just blown away. Everyone was, it was just one of those moments where, when it was over, no-one really wanted to leave. No-one wanted to even move from the spot they were in, even like an hour and a half after the session was over. I've had maybe three recording moments like that in my life, where it was so wonderful no-one wanted it to end."

'I Hope That I Don't Fall in Love with You' was highlighted by Rolling Stone as "melodically the album's most beautiful song. In this story about meeting eyes with a girl in a bar... Waits doesn't just sing the song, he phrases it like the interior monologue of a method actor." Jerry Yester found it impossible to pick favourites. It was like 'Which is your favourite kid?' It's hard to say, because they all had different things going for them. I love 'Ice Cream Man', 'Virginia Avenue', 'Little Trip', 'Love' – they were all so different from anything that was going on."

As production approached its close after about four weeks of tracking, producer Yester, who was wrapping up instrumental overdubs, shared some of his favourite collaborative moments between Tom and his band as including when "drummer John Seiter said 'Hey, what about a harmony on this?' So he sang the harmony vocal on 'Rosie' and Tom loved his singing, so he ended up singing on a couple of other things. I also sang the high falsetto harmony on…just light stuff. Tom was very clear that he didn't want a big, fancy production, and I was right with him on that and didn't want one either. I remember talking him into strings on 'Martha', and he said 'I don't know man, I don't know about that.' So I said 'I'm just talking about a string quartet, let's bring them in and if you don't like it, we'll take it right off.' So he was agreeable to that, and when we did it he loved it, and from then on he loved strings."

Upon release, although still an unknown, Waits' sound embodied a sonic signature so instantly familiar that Billboard magazine argued it "announces the arrival of a talented songwriter whose…(debut LP is) a minor-key masterpiece." Fellow critics were equally keen to acclaim the first great singer-songwriter of the decade. It was a depiction producer Jerry Yester would agree with in his recollection that "when that album was completed, listening back through the tracks, I knew instinctively and instantly that Tom was going to something very special and unique, it was very obvious. He stood out for his songwriting ability with both melody and lyrics, and for the fact that he didn't try to change himself for any reason.

"He didn't think about it, he just did what he did, and wouldn't compromise. There was a lot of good stuff around, but nobody was doing anything like Tom. Still, having said that, his songs were still very accessible to other people, from the Eagles, who covered 'Ol' 55', to any number of other artists who have covered his songs over the years. But back then, he was very much in a class of his own, and wasn't influenced by anything going on at the time around him. I was proud to have produced 'Closing Time' in its entirety."

Billboard would continue by observing that "within the apparently narrow range of the cocktail-bar pianistics and muttered vocals, Waits and producer Jerry Yester manage a surprisingly broad collection of styles, from the jazzy 'Virginia Avenue' to the uptempo funk of 'Ice Cream Man'", while the magazine would equally hail Waits' "gift for gently rolling pop melodies…He can come up with striking, original scenarios, as on…'Martha.'"

Rolling Stone paid him the compliment of noting that "Waits sings with such conviction that the…language of cliché is transmuted into the super-articulate vehicle for expression of gut feeling. It's no wonder then that Waits' personal narratives are ultimately not all that different in spirit from his parodies, for they too are stamped with the same emotional realism… In both his songs and in his lazy, strolling piano playing, he parodies the lounge music sub-genre so perfectly that we wonder if he's putting us on or if he's for real, and it is his especial triumph that in the end he has it both ways: he is able to deliver whole both the truth and the sham of the music… In particular, Waits is master of the pictorial vignette that crystallises the emotions of a specific common experience in a uniquely moving way."

Waits' hometown newspaper, the San Diego Daily, led the praise parade with their conclusion that "Waits evokes a nostalgic feeling for the good old days without sacrificing originality… Tom is a collector and researcher of stories and songs… He has a keen interest in the music, events, and Beat culture of the late Fifties yet his songs and performance stand up in today's music market."

New Times magazine hailed music that "calls forth a vision found in movies of the Forties and Fifties. It's a vision of all-night talks among would-be novelists and poets in New York cafeterias, of lonely World War II sailors standing out on Front Street hoping for love but settling for a pint of rot-gut rye and a flophouse floozy – the stuff mined by novelists like Nelson Algren, directors like Elia Kazan. And yet, that's not all there is to Waits' music. He takes the American loser/hero – the cocktail piano player, the wise-assed smacked-around rogue who plays the nags and loses the winning ticket – and infuses the figure with new life, in a style that is at once nostalgic and completely contemporary."

As much a gypsy by nature as many of the characters in the stories told on 'Closing Time', Tom was eager to hit the road in support of the album following its release in March 1973. He shared with the Colorado Daily his feeling that "a first album is like a diploma… Having a record out gets your foot in the door. You can't play these fucking clubs like…no matter how good you are…if you don't have an album out."

Waits was granted both visibility and an open-minded audience by the opening slot he landed supporting Frank Zappa's Mothers of Invention, recalling to Crawdaddy Radio that "Herb Cohen was working closely with Frank Zappa and (hooked that up)… A little recognition goes a long way, I started to get a little reinforcement and that helped. I ended up doing three tours with the Mothers… (I also) opened up shows for Billy Preston and Charlie Rich and Jerry Jeff Walker and Buffalo Bob and Martha and the Vandellas and the Temptations." Life on the road suited Tom, who added later to NME that "singing and writing and travelling attracted me at that age – like running away to the circus, I guess."

Off the road, Tom and Jerry Yester became "very close. Tom liked my writing, I had kind of introduced him to strings, so he brought me along on his other projects after that with Bones Howe, even though I wasn't producing any more. The upside of recording in the daytime had been, when we were through, we had the entire evening in front of us, so we'd all go out to dinner, and he and my wife and I hung out quite a bit." Though the pair would not work together in a production context again, Waits would explain that "as far as I'm concerned, Jerry Yester's a great man and a great producer."

Waits seemed pleased that his family were supportive of his talent, explaining to Relix magazine that, at the time, "my parents support what I do. My mother was real pleased that I got a page in Time. My father thinks I'm a chip off the ol' block." Looking toward the future, Tom quipped that "I'd like to do my second album because the first one's old already." And indeed he would, heading into 'The Heart Of Saturday Night'…

PART III: BONES HOWE...
HE'S GOT THE JAZZ!

Waits' lyrical carnival of vagabond city-dwellers and their downtown adventures was framed a jazz-based musical foundation as improvisational as the characters' fluid lives. For producer Bones Howe, drawing upon his 15-year background as one of the hottest jazz engineers on the West Coast, the pairing was a natural fit.

Howe began by explaining that "most of the people who have lasted as producers will tell you, I started out as a bass player, or whatever, they all have different histories. I came to California to be a recording engineer because I had been influenced by guys like Shelly Manne. Max Bennett and Bill Louis, people who played in road bands that came through Atlanta where I was going to school, and playing around town six nights a week. They said to me, 'Well, with your experience as a musician, and training as an engineer, you should come to California and be a recording engineer. Because most guys are old radio engineers, and don't know what a rhythm section is supposed to sound like.'

"The light went on, and I said 'That is something I'd like to do, or at least would like to try', so that's what I did. In the spring of 1956 I drove out here to California with $200 in my pocket to make jazz records, and took a job for $72 a week working at a recording studio, just to find out if it was something I could do. The rest, as they say, is history."

Howe went to work at Radio Recorders, at the time the biggest independent recording studio in Los Angeles. "They had two large recording studios and a smaller studio in their complex. I started as an apprentice, where I swept floors and took out the trash just to be in the room with that kind of activity. Just to be around that, I would have started anywhere. I never started out to be a producer, I was in hog heaven by the time I was engineering jazz records with Bud Shank, Bill Holman and Shorty Rodgers, the guys who were the big names in those days, I was done as far as I was concerned. If I could just keep on doing this, I was great. I never intended to be a producer in the first place, and again, that's where I get my philosophy that if you're in the business for 10 years you just don't know what's going to happen to you."

As he began to find his niche within the studio, Howe decided he wanted to be a mixer. "I did want to be an actual recording engineer, I wanted to be in charge of recording sessions. I did a lot of session for in those days for Verve, and Atlantic, and Pacific Jazz, and Jean Norman's company, I went through all these guys making jazz records as an engineer, and the guys at Atlantic used to always send me copies of the albums when they came out that I'd worked on.

"I'd done Harold Land and a Red Mitchell record, and on the back of the album, be had me listed as a co-producer. So I was actually producing records before I knew I was producing them. These are just things that happen to you in the process of going to work every day and trying to be better at what you do. I was working for the guys at the studio, so my head was always on the other side of the glass, I was always trying to make better-sounding records."

Elaborating on his early collaborations with many of the biggest names in jazz in the Fifties and how those sessions informed his philosophy and approach to capturing live sound on two-inch tape, Howe recalls that "I did the first two Ornette Coleman albums for Atlantic, and the thing with those guys was they used to rehearse in Ornette's apartment, they would all sit up in a little circle together and practice. And from playing in a rhythm section, I knew that you couldn't really get a good feeling as a rhythm-section player if you weren't sitting close, like the bass player next to the drummer or piano player, so I always set the guys up really close together.

"They were astounded when they came into the studio that I put them all facing each other in a circle, but that's the way they played so that's the way we made the record. Now the sound may not have been perfectly separated but they played great that way, and I always felt that the engineering was there to capture the music – not that the music was there to satisfy engineering egos. So I always made my records on that basis, and musicians loved to work with me because of that. Obviously the sound was up to par because the record companies kept coming back to me."

As to the secret of his success as a producer, Bones reasoned that "I kept a simple philosophy that I was there for the music, and to make it sound great. And when I started engineering, I was the youngest kid in the studio mixing, which caused a little resentment, because the guys there were mostly in their forties and I was 24, 25. So when I came to the studio to start a session in the morning, and opened the door to the mic closet, I always got what was left over. Everybody else had taken the good stuff – so, to compensate, what I learned to do was make the acoustic properties of the room and the microphones work for me."

Focusing on the technical side of the Fifties-era studio tracking process, Howe explained that "in those days, you were recording to two-track stereo, you weren't multi-tracking things, so it wasn't like today with Pro Tools where everything goes on a separate track. In those days, everything went onto the same track, so what you wanted to do was create the most satisfying sound for the listener and make the environment the best for the band to give you the most exciting performance. That's what I was always trying to do, and I was not concerned with trying to make a perfect-sounding record at the expense of the performance.

"One way I tried to achieve that was to always use the room, and every room had different properties, but they were all those Celotex panels with the holes with them, and peg-board to soak up the low-end – all the tried and true acoustic things of the day. So what you tried to do was set up a rhythm section in a place where the guys could all hear each other, but the sound wouldn't bounce around a lot. It was always trial and error till you found a great place to work, and then you would just build on that. I always tried different set-ups. I always believed a big band had to be set up the way a big band is when it plays in concert, because that's the way everybody's used to hearing each other. You can't separate the trumpet from the trombone."

Reasoning that harmony is best achieved in this context when "a brass section plays together," Howe added that "they're used to sitting together when they play – saxophones are used to being grouped together, so you have to be respectful of those kind of thing. You want them to play well, and hear themselves the way they're used to hearing themselves when they play live, that's how always how you get the best take. I don't believe you can make a great jazz record without everybody breathing the same air at the same time. No glass houses, no earphones.

"I've made records the other way, and sometimes you have to because you're restricted by a record company who wants to do it a different way for audio file purposes. It's separation for separation's sake, and not for the sake of the music. And guys feel alienated when they're in a different room than the guys their playing with. It's the responsibility of the producer to make sure the performances sound like they were recorded with everybody sitting together in the same room."

Throughout the late Fifties and the first half of the Sixties, Howe's studio credits piled up as high as the stacks of hit jazz LPs and singles he was recording for artists including Ornette Coleman, Bud Shank, Bobby Troup, Bill Holman, Bing Crosby and the Big Band All Stars. Transitioning into the world of pop in the mid Sixties, Howe logged time as an engineer alongside Phil Spector for the Righteous Brothers' 'Ebb Tide' hit, as well as with the Mamas and the Papas and the Crickets before stepping out into his own as a pop producer in 1966. With the Turtles, he created a greatest-hits collection worth of jukebox smashes, including 'You Baby', 'Can I Get To Know You Better', 'She'd Rather Be With Me,' 'Happy Together,' and 'Making My Mind Up' among others.

In describing his approach to producing pop records, Howe explains that "I always used to joke that I was the first rock'n'roll producer to put major sevenths in vocal groups. Where that translated to making pop records, I'll make one comment about it working with different people in different tracks at different times, and that's that I had the best success working with just chord sheets. All the records that I made, the rhythm section parts were never written down, nothing was ever written down except the number of bars, where there were just empty bars with chord symbols written over top of them. Then what I would do is go in and stand in the studio with the guys, with the rhythm section – because I always started with the full rhythm section. Even if it was just guitar, a couple of keyboards, bass and drums, I would stand in the room with them, and say 'Okay, here's the feel.'

"I would sing kind of the idea of the parts to the guys, and they would just start playing, and because there was nothing there except the chord symbols, things would begin to happen. So then I would say 'That's great, keep that, don't change that.' And by the time we'd been through it five or six times, they had what amounted to a really good rhythm section part. And I've got the vocal going in my head, so I know whether it's going to work or not against the vocal. So that's how I always began these sessions."

As a specific example, Howe offers the Turtles. "When you work with a group that's an organised group like that, you work up the tune in rehearsal, then they play it on stage, then you come to the studio, and for the most part they're locked into that because those kind of players are not ready to make major changes to their parts – they've already cemented it all down in their minds, and that's how they play it. So when you make a record like 'It Ain't Me Babe', you're basically working with the arrangement that was worked up on stage."

The Turtles gave Howe his first taste of commercial success as a Top 40 pop producer, but it was his next collaborations, with Sixties folk-psychedelia groups the Association – via hits like 'Windy' and 'Never My Love' – and the Fifth Dimension – via hits like "Go Where You Want To Go' and the Grammy-winning 'Let The Sunshine In' – that took him into the big league.

Recalling his rise up the charts as a pop producer, Howe explained that his main duties behind the boards included that of "always being the song picker. Every hit I've had, I picked the song. So the point of pre-production was to pick the song, find the key that's right for the group or the lead singer; those things have to be done in pre-production. Then we worked with an arranger – say it was a vocal arranger for the Association or the Fifth Dimension – you have to know who's going to sing what parts, and the way the song's going to develop.

"So that part all gets developed very, very early on, even before you cut the track, because you want to make sure that the key that its put in is going to work for everybody that's singing, and for all the parts. So most times, there was a kind of sketch of the vocal arrangement worked out with the vocal arranger before I ever cut the track. And gradually, what happened was I gravitated to having the guy who was the vocal arranger write out the rhythm parts, and we would just build a track on the session. I was always making less and less people involved if I possibly could, depending on where it all went. So most times there were horns and strings later, and I did those usually with Bill Holman, who was a jazz arranger and one of my favourites of all time.

"As it turned out," he continued, "most of the biggest hits I had were with vocal groups…so I suppose, in terms of my pop music career as a producer, that would be where my signature is. I enjoyed making those records, I think they were a step ahead each time in the evolution of pop vocal group sound, so I'm very happy with that. What happens is you look back after a long time and realise that opportunities are created by being there every day. I went to work every day, and I often joke about the fact that it only took me 11 years to become an overnight success. So people who go into this business trying to define the kind of success they're going to have is a really chancy business."

By the end of the Sixties, Howe had arrived at the peak of pop production and, based on his reputation as one of the specialists in capturing live bands in a studio context, the producer was drafted for one of the biggest gigs in the business –

Elvis Presley's comeback television special in 1968. Ironically, it was not Howe's first collaboration with Presley, the producer recalling that "I grew up in Sarasota, Florida, so I remember when Elvis used to come through town on those country tours and they would play in the theatres. To me, he was a country artist. I was interested in jazz, not in country music.

"I remember being in Atlanta, and seeing his name on the marquee at the Fox Theatre, and thinking 'Woah, this guy is really taking off.' By then he had sort of morphed into a rockabilly artist. So when I was out in LA and first worked with him, I wasn't really thrilled. Although when I did work with him, I liked him. He was a good guy, had a great sense of humour, and was fun to be around, and had a great feel for music, as basic as the music was. You never know. There again, I was working as a second engineer, starting and stopping tape machines and making edits."

Howe was responsible for making "the first edit that Elvis ever saw: just because he made a great take and the ending got spoiled. Scotty hit a wrong chord or something happened, so I said to the first engineer, 'Go ahead and have them play the ending again, and I'll cut it off.' So he said to Elvis, 'Just have the guys play the ending again.' They played it, I cut it off, and Elvis's eyes got real big, he said 'You're gonna put those scissors into my tape?' And I did, put it together, played it for him and he said 'I don't hear it', referring to the edit.

"So that was the way it kind of began for me in the early days. I was a really good tape editor because I could pause without counting and I learned the technique very quickly because it was music and rhythm-related. I helped having the music background in combination with the engineering skills I was developing toward my eventual career as a producer. I know guys who are wonderful arrangers, and have written songs, but can't work in the studio with an artist. It depends on the personality."

Howe recalled that "by the time I got around to producing Elvis's television special in 1968, I had won Grammys for my work with groups like Fifth Dimension and the Turtles. Also, I hadn't seen Elvis since the mid Fifties, and this TV showcase was designed to be a comeback of sorts. The thing about working with him was, first of all, he was a wonderful singer; he could imitate anybody and would do it at the drop of a hat. He had a great sense of humour and fooled around a lot, but was very professional about what he did. So when you gave him a song to learn, he learned it. So those performances are his performances on that special are his, not someone else's off a demo. He took those songs and learned them."

Seeking to maintain the integrity of that vibe, Howe – turning to the television special – offered that when it came time to map out the live performances "it was even less so, because we didn't do a demo with someone who sounded like Elvis singing it. The people who wrote the songs sat with him at the piano and taught him the songs, so those are really his performances, and there was a kind of freshness that came from that. It kind of goes back to the early days in the Fifties when he first started coming to California to record.

"He made those songs his own, and as he got to be more famous, and there was more and more money involved in an Elvis Presley record, more and more of the demos for his singles were made with sound-alikes like Jeff Powers, who used to do a perfect Elvis imitation on a microphone and later became an Elvis imitator they would hire to sing on all his demos. So when you got the demos, they already sounded like finished Elvis Presley songs. But the special was done from the ground up, and Elvis was involved in developing the script, choosing the material. Even though that special re-launched his career, you never know when you're developing it."

Elaborating on the show from a recording perspective, Howe explains that "we were all just having a good time, and it shows. The performances were all shot live and I did the mixes live. For live recording, first of all, you're setting up for the stage, not like you do in the studio. So whatever the accompaniment is musically, they're set up onstage with the singer. The audience is there too, so you have additional audio considerations you have to be mindful of. It's meant to be part of the recording, so nobody's expecting it to sound like it was done in a recording studio, but these recordings still became singles.

"There's just every consideration – you're setting up for the stage, micing for the stage, generally working with portable equipment. Also, there's a lot of noise an audience gives off even if they're not making a lot of noise; a room makes a certain kind of noise when its full of people, even if they're not cheering and yelling. There's just a sound that people make when they fill up a room, and people listening to a live recording expect to hear that."

The key, Howe explains, is to make all those elements work well together in a sonic context. "What you're trying to do is get the excitement of a live recording in terms of the spontaneous thing that happens with a live performance. When micing a live performance, you need really good directional mics, and sometimes stage mics are better that studio mics for that – like the ElectroVoice stage mics, in a lot of cases those mics are better to use in live situations because they're very directional and you don't have the sound of the room coming back in quite so much.

"It also depends on how big the room is – if it's a small room, it's a different consideration than if its an auditorium or concert hall. Every one of them is different. For the Elvis special, in the live segments, he had a hand mic, I think an ElectroVoice. In the informal segments, we just had mics on little short booms, and I think we probably had some overhead mics to give it the sound of an open room so it wouldn't sound so much like they were in a closet."

The success of the television special and its LP release relaunched Presley as a recording artist, re-establishing the singer's credibility among both fans and critics, with Rolling Stone writer (and future Bruce Springsteen producer) Jon Landau commenting for one that "it was the finest music of his life. If ever there was music that bleeds, this was it."

As the Sixties came to a close, and the rock-rock heavy Top 40 era of the Seventies began, Bones Howe was in the market for a new sound which, as the producer recalled, came via "a very close friend of mine, David Geffen, whom I had known since he was a junior agent at William Morris.

"I had put together with the Association because David wanted to handle the Association as a live act. And David and I remained friends through the years as we moved up the latter of success, and eventually, he started Asylum Records. I'd produced Warren Zevon's first record and had him signed for a time to my company as a writer; David signed Warren for his second record, on the recommendation of Jackson Browne."

Not long afterwards, Geffen called Howe, "possibly returning the favour, and said 'I have an artist I think you should hear, I think its different than what you have done, but I think you and he will really hit it off.' David always had a great gut about putting people together, and he was a big fan. He always promoted me. He'd wanted me to do Crosby, Stills, Nash and Young, and we had a couple meetings and I told David 'We'll kill each other.' I loved Buffalo Springfield, but by the time they had started a band together they were all doing drugs. I told David 'I don't do drugs, and we're all going to end up hacking each other to death, cause they're going to get high in the studio…'

"I always believed the studio is business, and so for them, I guess all of that lifestyle was part of the business. So working with a group during that period was really, really difficult, but I always had really great working relationships with individual artists. So it just wasn't meant to be, and I didn't take things – no matter how successful I thought it would be – that I felt I couldn't be a part of."

"The material on 'Heart' ranges from spoken jazz-poetry to doleful melodic lyricism." – ROLLING STONE MAGAZINE

"I'm a professional nighthawk." – TOM WAITS, 1973

"He wrote this album on skid row." – PRODUCER BONES HOWE

PART IV: 'THE HEART OF SATURDAY NIGHT' (1974)

With the release of 1974's 'The Heart Of Saturday Night', Tom Waits began introducing the world at large to his own musical sub-genre which, along with its creator, was still a work in progress. Rolling Stone noted that, with his sophomore studio LP, "Waits had begun to play with his language and to inject some swing into his arrangements; images were striking and original; he had matured as a singer." From a songwriting perspective, Waits had immersed himself creatively into fully capturing a culture he felt very much a part of.

Doing so provided him an authenticity that, he explained in an Asylum Records press release, stemmed from his having "tasted Saturday nights in Detroit, St Louis, Tuscaloosa, New Orleans, Atlanta, NYC, Boston, Memphis. I've done more travelling in the past year than I ever did in my life so far, in terms of my level of popularity, on the night-spot circuit, I remain in relative obscurity and now, upon the release of a second album, which I believe a comprehensive study of a number of aspects of this search for the centre of Saturday night, which Jack Kerouac relentlessly chased from one end of this country to the other, and I've attempted to scoop up a few diamonds of this magic that I see."

Elaborating on the kind of Saturday night he wished to spend with his listeners, Tom told Folkscene that "conceptually, I had in mind an album storyline with some sort of collection of songs like chapters – that weren't just a random handful of ballads but something that tied together – so I guess I did. Once I wrote 'Saturday Night' I started thinking in terms of other ways of approaching Saturday night and things like that." The result, as celebrated by Rolling Stone, would become an adventure far and away from those Waits' contemporaries sought to take their fans on. "While so many singer-songwriters concern themselves with escape from the city, Waits' songs express passionate love for the seamier side of Los Angeles and its environs.

"Booze, cigarettes and gasoline fuel his world of neon signs, gas stations, diners, bus depots, barmaids and sailors, all of which merge into an evocation of ecstatic nighttime restlessness…Waits' excellent first album, 'Closing Time', conjured this vision less directly than 'The Heart Of Saturday Night', which obsessively searches it out."

Feeling as fresh as a Saturday night would after anyone's long working week, the album was Waits' escape from a debut album that, he confessed to journalist

Jim Gerard, was "a collection of a lot of old songs of mine... Ever since 'Closing Time' came out, I've been on the road ever since. Continually, I write all the stuff out here now and my schedule has changed a great deal. That is bound to have an effect on what I do and what I say."

Along that 'road', Waits found himself in a constant and inevitable state of research, playing dive bars and lounges along America's every highway and byway, witnessing what the New Yorker observed as "a landscape that is bleak, lonely, contemporary: all-night diners; cheap hotels; truck stops; pool halls; strip joints; Continental Trailways buses; double knits; full table rail shots; jumper cables; Naugahyde luncheonette booths; Foster Grant wraparounds; hash browns over easy; glasspacks and overhead cams; dawn skies 'the colour of Pepto Bismol.'"

Comparisons to his hero Jack Kerouac were frequent and unavoidable. Melody Maker would effectively argue that "the very title of Waits' second album, 'The Heart Of Saturday Night', is in direct reference to a passage from Kerouac's book Visions Of Cody, and the theme of the whole album is essentially little more than an elaboration, albeit articulate, on this self-same passage." Its review further noted that Waits' lyrics "evidences a continuing fascination with the ephemeral ecstasies previously explored by such writers as Jack Kerouac, Lawrence Ferlinghetti, Allen Ginsberg, Ray Charles and Mose Allison."

Acknowledging readily in an interview with WAMU Radio that "I'm fascinated with American literature. I read a lot," Waits would elaborate on his own style of communicating with his listeners in context. "I'm concerned about imagery in a song and not going for the easiest possible description. It helps when I sit down to write something to be able to use my imagination and it certainly is a craft after a while; it's a whole combination of craft and your own past experience and your own crazy ideas about things. I come from a good family and everything but, over the years, I've developed some ways about me that just aren't right so you just have to look for the kinks in your personality and it helps sometimes."

The singer-songwriter seemed content to acknowledge the influence of his beatnik heroes on his own writing for the LP. At the same time, he revealed to the LA Times that "I hate that reference because of the stigma that's attached to it – Maynard G Krebs with some bongos. I'm not having a vicarious Fifties thrill or trying to come off like Manhattan Transfer. Stylistically, most writers and performers draw from wherever they can. There's all kinds of resource out there. You suck it up if you can. You should be thirsty for it, whatever it is, and then integrate it into what you're doing."

Offering fans some insight into this specific aspect of his writing process, he began from a technical angle by explaining to WAMU Radio that "I bring a tape recorder with me and when I get back to the hotel I talk to myself and I'm working on some spoken-word pieces that I want to do with accompaniment." The result, Tom explained to Folkscene, wasn't one he was sure was "really poetry but it's just like – instead of writing a song I just wrote a mouthful of words and just talked 'em instead of singin' 'em. I guess you could call them poems, yeah. There are a lot more; they can be palatable for an audience I think, in a lot of cases more so than a song when you get hung up on the melody and the mood and what kind of voice this guy's got and the sound of his instrument."

Waits added in a conversation with Melody Maker that, though "I'm doing spoken word now, I'm considered a songwriter so it's something I gotta watch. But I'm getting tired of hearing myself sing and I like talking bits. I don't call them poetry, 'cause there's too many poets I admire; but they're in an oral tradition. I call 'em 'metropolitan doubletalk.'"

Waits shared with Melody Maker a steadfast rule of his for maintaining consistent access to the 'real people' of the world he captured so brilliantly in words. It was the importance of "keeping your anonymity...as a writer, so that you can go anywhere, any part of town, sit in a corner," adding in a self-penned Asylum Records press release that, among his favourite corners of the world to compose from were "coffee shops, bars, and parking lots".

Like many of the characters in his songs, Tom offered in a conversation with the Onion his feeling that "most songs have meagre beginnings. You wake up in the morning, you throw on your suspenders and you sub-vocalise and just think. They seem to form like calcium. I can't think of a story right off the bat that was that interesting. I write things on the back of my hand, usually, and sing into a tape recorder." When it came down to the physical composition of his tunes, Tom shared with Melody Maker that "songwriting is a very solo effort. You just come to grips with your own creative imagination and work at it and it's yours. You know what you're proud of in what you do. You know where you are; you know how far you've come."

The result of that process, as Waits viewed it, was not the product of "some kind of divine inspiration or anything," but rather the hardest work he did as a recording artist, offering in the same dialogue with Folkscene that, while "there are times when you're moved to write something...I don't think you quake and talk in tongues or anything, I think that's a lot of poppycock and balderdash myself. You work on a concept, work on an idea, and you read and you listen to other writers and you listen to the radio and you listen to the hit parade and you listen to KPFK – and then you get better, hopefully.

"Of course it's all a matter of opinion, there are songwriters that I like that aren't so well liked – it's still a matter of what your own taste is but I do think there's a strong difference between someone like Randy Newman who is certainly a craftsman when it comes to putting a song together, someone who can evoke such a feeling from his listeners and it comes from him really sweating over a song and then you take somebody like – I don't want to slander anybody, we're on the air – but take somebody who really writes ridiculously childish songs that don't have meat to them or real vision. I think it's certainly craft. It's a craft by all means."

Waits now wrote primarily on piano rather than his other primary instrument, the acoustic guitar, claiming that "It provides a lot more freedom for me." He told Folkscene that "writing on the piano is different than writing on guitar," remarking that "you get different feels – in fact a lot of times you write a tune with some other artist in mind."

When Tom opened up to journalist Howard Larman about the artists currently influencing his compositional process, he began by citing "Ray Charles. I got a lot of old Ray Charles records, let's see – Diana Ross – I like her a lot, got some old Billie Holliday records, I listen to her, and Mose Allison, I'm real fond of Mose Allison, Dale Evans, Miles Davis, a little bit of everything. I try to integrate different styles in my writing, it's important to do that. With a piano it's easier for me to write, I can find a lot more things that I could never find on guitar so it helps with writing on the piano.

"I played guitar before I played piano, I'm no technician, no big fancy fingers. Writing on an instrument is different than being a real master of an instrument. It's more of a process of investigation than anything else so you may be lacking in technique but high on the investigation scale."

Humbly referring to himself in a self-penned Asylum Records press release as "a pedestrian piano player with poor technique but a good sense of melody," the singer-songwriter added "Thelonious Monk, George Gershwin, Irving Berlin, Stephen Foster, and Frank Sinatra" to the pool of players he drew inspiration from. Music World magazine at the time would observe that "Tom's music is characterised by a moody, almost sullen but not self-pitying, atmosphere; a tinkling piano and muted trumpet underscoring his emotional output and a drawling delivery that draws the listener into his grasp."

Amazingly, for all his endless nights and miles on the road researching the album, Tom revealed to journalist Jim Gerard that "all of the material was written in a couple of weeks." The album's title track was allegedly "spat out in 5 minutes. It's a problem with writing songs, for me it's just conceiving the idea for a song, visualising it in your head and then putting it down is nothing, it comes out real easy. Trying to come up with something that's challenging for me, I guess, to deal with as the raw material for a song, something to take and develop rather than just, say, well, a love song, well, 'I love you and…'

"It's usually the idea, like that 'Semi Suite' song came out real quick too. I don't know – the ones that come out hard are usually the ones that aren't any good, I guess. You can usually tell if a tune was hard to write or you were having trouble deciding whether to use love or dove or above, you know."

Recalling the song's inspiration, Waits explained that "it's kind of about driving down Hollywood Boulevard on Saturday night. Bob Webb and I were kicking this around one afternoon, Saturday afternoon it was, the idea of looking for the heart of Saturday night, hadn't really worked on any tune about it yet. We're both real Jack Kerouac fans and this is kind of a tribute to Kerouacians I guess."

Acknowledging Waits' achievement, Rolling Stone would deem the tribute "one of the most haunting, exquisite songs ever written about the cruel myth of eternal youth. The yearning was still there but it was partially mitigated by the carefree exuberance of 'Depot, Depot' and the compelling 'Diamonds On My Windshield'. 'Diamonds…' the one entirely spoken cut, celebrates being on the road. A first-person monolog delivered Oscar Brown-style, 'Diamonds' reads like poetry."

Turning to the writing of the last-mentioned piece, Waits confessed to WAMU that initially "I didn't really know what to do with that piece 'cause it was written out just as some spontaneous verse that I had written on the back of an itinerary and I didn't know what the hell to do with it. So we went in the studio and I tried singing it, tried doing it acappella – nothing worked. Jim Hughart was playing the upright bass with me for that session just started playing a modal bass line and I just started talking and Jim Gordon started playing a cool 12-bar shuffle on brushes and we just winged it in one take and we had it and I like the way it came out."

As for its deeper lyrical meaning, Tom revealed to Folkscene that "this is about driving in the rain. I used to make that track from San Diego to Los Angeles a lot, usually with several pit stops on the way with engine trouble. So this is about driving in the rain, circa 1973."

In the same conversation, the singer-songwriter would describe 'Depot, Depot' as "a bit of local colour... This is about 6th & Los Angeles in downtown Los Angeles, about the Greyhound Bus Depot, about going down to the depot on a Saturday night with plenty of quarters for the TV chairs and it's just a great place to take a date."

Expanding on some of his personal observations that composed the song's lyrical landscape, he recalled to journalist Howard Larman that "not many people go to downtown LA. Free Press did a big article called 'Downtown LA, Who Needs It?' I've been going there since I moved here, I've been here a year, I go to hang out down there, I live in Silver Lake so I'm about 10 minutes from downtown. I go down there just to hang out – not too many people live down there, really, people work down there and hang out, that's all."

Using the muse of another city's seedy, downtown to create 'Drunk On The Moon', Waits took KPFK-FM on a journey cross-country to "Denver, Colorado. I always stayed at a place called the Oxford Hotel which is down on 17th & Wazee about a block away from Larimer Street. Larimer being just full of a lot of ghosts down there...shopping for images in the trash cans – boy, that's old Kerouac and Cassady stomping grounds. It's really changed quite a bit. They put up what's called Larimer Square now, which is kind of like a contemporary little boutique sort of shopping centre. It looks awful ridiculous cause right across the street is some real bona fide serious winos – right out in front of a place called the Gin Mill, another place called the Terminal Bar.

"Terminal Bar is a block away from the Santa Fe train depot so they called it the Terminal Bar but they had no idea that like 20 years later the place'd be filling up with terminal cases. This is called 'Drunk On The Moon', there's all different kinds of moons – silver slipper moons and there's cue-ball moons and there's buttery cue ball moons and moons that are all melted off to one side and this is about a muscatel moon."

Compositionally, the singer-songwriter revealed to Folkscene that fitting lyrics to the song's tune was a challenge. "It was a matter of taking a whole bunch of words and trying to hang them in the right place on a melody. Sometimes you get so many words you don't know what to do and you – sometimes you don't need 'em all, sometimes you do, so I think that's a crafty song."

Waits was equally happy to call on his home town of San Diego for inspiration in the journey that was writing 'Saturday Night'. The roots of 'The Ghosts Of Saturday Night', he explained in a conversation with KPFK-FM, came from "National City, which is primarily a sailor town, a suburb of San Diego, where the infamous Mile Of Cars is on National Avenue and at the north end of National Ave is the Berge-Roberts Mortuary and the Golden Barrel, Escalante's Liquor Store, sandwiched in between a Triumph motorcycle shop and Berge-Roberts' is Napoleon's Pizza House, it's been there for a good 25 years and I worked there when I was real young. I've worked since I was 15 there and I guess not 'til I was away from it for a long time I could really sit down and write something constructive about it."

Turning to 'San Diego Serenade', which Rolling Stone would later single out as the album's "most beautiful moment," Tom explained to Folkscene that, musically, "I kind of had Ray Charles in mind," while adding in a discussion with the Dallas Morning News that the "song was about a girl I knew once, I was crazy about her."

Once he'd completed writing the album, attention turned to the question of who was best suited to capture its magic on tape. Waits recalled his label laboured over the choice, given how important the album was to developing him as an artist who was inventing his very own sound and sub-genre. Pulling the curtain back a bit on that challenge at the time, Tom began a conversation with journalist Kenny Weissberg by sharing his opinion that "as far as I'm concerned, Jerry Yester's a great man and a great producer. I was expecting to record my second album with him, but Asylum wants to find someone that can take my songs and make hits out of them. I've been ready for about four months but they haven't found anyone yet."

He explained to WAMU Radio that the process took the time it did quite simply because "there's so much pressure in the studio, it's $100 an hour or whatever and time is money. It's a collective effort; there's six cats you're playing with and a producer and an engineer…a very highly concentrated sort of effort. I enjoy it when something happens in the studio, when you come up with something. It's exciting, it's work producing an album."

Waits shared years later with Mojo magazine his recollection that "in those days, nobody would even think of sending you into the studio without a producer. In their mind, they gave you 30 grand, you might disappear to the Philippines and they never see you again. They're not giving you 30 grand, they're giving this guy who plays tennis and wears sweaters and lives in a big house, they're giving him the money and he's paying for everything. Just show up on time and stay out of jail."

David Geffen eventually paired Tom with producer Bones Howe in what would become a truly kindred studio partnership over the course of the next six albums the pair would produce together. Recounting the genesis of that partnership, Howe recalled that "Out of the blue, one day David called me about working with Tom Waits, and I said 'Send me a tape.' And he said, 'No, no, I want you to come to my office.' So I went to his office, and he played me a few tracks off 'Closing Time', Tom's first album, which Jerry Yester had produced, and who I knew because his brother had been in the Association.

"I asked David if Tom was a folk artist, and he replied 'Well, I'm not really sure what he is. He's not really folk, but he's different. I saw him at the Troubadour and he's great live, so I signed him and made this record. But its not exactly what I think he is.' So after listening to a few tracks from 'Closing Time', I decided...there was kind of a jazz-tinged quality to it that I thought was really quite interesting.

"I asked if they were going to do another record like this. David told me he was working on some demos, and that when Tom was done with those he would send them to me; if I liked them, then Geffen would set up a meeting. That's the way David always worked, one step at a time."

As for his first impressions of Waits' vaudevillian, jazz/folk style of Beat-poet blues piano rock, Howe explained that "they sent the tape over to me the following week, and I thought 'God, this guy's like Jack Kerouac.' And as fate would have it, I had done a record with Norman Granz that Jack had done in a hotel room in Miami where he'd read his works and poetry into a microphone and tape recorder. They in turn sent them to Norman, who bought them, and sent them over to me and said 'Make an album out of this. I can't make head or tail out of it, you want to take a shot at it?' So I said 'Sure'.

"I sat with those tapes for two or three days, sorted through them and made an album out of them. In those days, if you were lucky, you could get an hour of spoken word if you used both sides of an LP."

Describing the impression Waits made on him in the context of Howe's past spoken-word artist collaborators, the producer recalled that "he had that kind of Beat generation sound in his writing, but there was a folk quality because he was playing an acoustic guitar along with a lot of the material. But there was also beauty in some of the songs where he played piano and accompanied himself, like 'San Diego Serenade' and 'Blue Skies', which was almost like a Ray Charles song to me. So I thought, 'God, this guy's got all kinds of things.' So I called David, and said 'I love what he does, I'd like to meet him, and if we like each other we can make a record together.'

Tom shared his reaction to the prospect of entrusting Howe with the responsibility of arguably the most important LP of his career with Mojo. He was intrigued by the producer because "Bones had a background in jazz, and he'd done a lot of records like that anyway." Detailing that first, fateful meeting, Howe recalled that "I sat down with Waits, and we ended up talking about Jack Kerouac and Steve Allen, and I told him I'd made a record with Kerouac. So he next asks me, 'Did you know Steve Allen made a record with Jack Kerouac?' And when I said no, he said 'I'll send you a tape of it if you'll send me a tape of yours.' So we started off exchanging Jack Kerouac tapes, and then he talked about a lot of stuff from the Beat generation, and I talked about the jazz musicians I had worked with; we immediately liked each other."

Once the pair had clicked on a personal level, Howe shared that, immediately thereafter, "we began talking about his demos, and a lot of the record thematically was about being on the road. He was fascinated with bus stations and people on the road, truck drivers and that sort of transient part of society that's out of the mainstream, and almost has its own world and language. He was fascinated by a lot of the language that goes along with that. On 'Shiver Me Timbers', like 'Truck Driving Man', that song arose out of Tom's fascination with people who worked on the hourly wage, the working class. Any of those kind of people he was fascinated with, and these ideas just bubbled out of him."

Once Waits had put muse to paper, the producer recalled that "he'd come into the studio with lyrics scribbled on a piece of paper. He was a great poet. The couplings and ideas that go together. There are people who I speak to who are songwriters who say 'All the really great lyrics have been used.' And I say 'Uh-uh, just go back and listen to some Tom Waits records and you'll find lyrics you haven't heard before and haven't heard since.' He wrote this album on skid row. I'd ask him, 'Tom, what did you do today?' And he'd say, 'I went down to skid row, there's some interesting people down there. I bought a pint of rye, went down to skid row, I talked to those guys. Every one of them – a woman put him there. I drank that pint of rye, went home, threw up and wrote 'Tom Traubert's Blues.'"

When talk turned to the pre-production task of "how we'd record the songs," Howe recalls that "Tom said 'I don't want to do a record like I did before. I want to make a record with some musicians in the studio.'" Waits would reason years later in an interview with Mojo that he wanted a group to bring his songs to life in the studio because "I think they complemented the songs rather than put a Band Aid on them like a lot of groups do to people's songs... On a record you're faced with a real collective effort with so many people that have to be happy with it, so it's not one man's decision at all. I enjoy working with a group."

In assembling that backing group, Howe next recalled that "I got a rhythm section together, and the pianist, Mike Melvoin, a jazz pianist, had also been an arranger. So we had a jazz rhythm section, with a couple of horns, and went in the studio and made 'The Heart Of Saturday Night.'" The end product, according to Melody Maker's ear, would be something akin to "the Beat poet whose readings were accompanied by unobtrusive jazz, Tom utilises a simple, jazz-flavoured instrumentation...(playing) a soft piano and is backed by a small, bass-dominated ensemble."

Once the pair had entered Wally Heider Studios in Hollywood and tracking was underway, Waits and Howe established a routine that would remain largely intact for all of their collaborations. The producer explains that "it was always the same with Tom and I when we were shaping the production of the songs. First of all, he wrote all the songs, and in some cases, the kind of quality of the song was in the way it was written and that he presented it to me – if it was a folk song he played on the piano, then it was a ballad by definition.

"For instance, 'San Diego Serenade' was a ballad, and the joke about that song always was it could go on for a year because there were a lot more verses than ended up on the record. He would come up with a verse talking about it, there were dozens. So the first thing we had to do was choose the verses he was going to do, and figure out from there how long the song was going to be. This was the beginning of our working relationship, so we were kind of feeling around a little bit."

Delving into some of the album's other standout tracks, the producer added that "there were some songs that were just gonna be kind of down and funky like 'Depot, Depot'; those kind of things were gonna be what they were, and there was no way you could change them. But 'San Diego Serenade' was a song that could almost have a pop flavour to it, so we let it go that way a little. Waits could always get his arms around these things, it was never meant to be a big production, it was meant to be a Tom Waits record."

Indeed, Waits explained his preference for "two-track records" in a conversation with Mojo years later, recalling that at the time, "even though there were more than four tracks available, I was paranoid about it... I was like, 'I don't like that. Let's just do it so it's done.'" Indeed, 'The Heart Of Saturday Night' "was recorded with just a bass and guitar – came off real nice, I like it."

Waits' improvisational approach to both living life and creating his songs and sound, was something to be cherished, Howe explained. "Tom, to me, was like a jazz artist, so as his producer my job was not to force him into a mould like I did with pop artists. He was not going to get played on the radio, so my job with Waits was to deliver the baby. He was the talent, and I was the one who was there to help him find the direction, cement it down and then go onto the next thing. So there's a lot of arrows pointing in different musical directions on that first record we made together, and he could have gone in a lot of different directions if he'd wanted to.

"After we were done tracking, we would just get together, usually in the evening, sit down, open a beer, talk about the sequence of the album, because all the pressure's off at that point. You're just gonna decide how to put the record together, and quite often Tom would say to me, 'You know, I think if I go to the studio and sing this by myself it will be better.' So you'll find on those album tracks it's all him, by himself, just sitting at the piano playing."

Describing the simple-by-design technical approach to capturing Waits' on tape, Howe recalled that "I'd go hang a microphone, usually a 77, and two mics on the piano, a U-47 on the low strings, and something with a real wide pattern on the high strings because I had no separation or leakage problems. It was just Tom at the piano singing live with a mic hanging in front of him, just like he would be if he was sitting on stage singing." Seeming appreciative of the producer's ability to translate his songs onto record, as recording on 'The Heart Of Saturday Night' wrapped, Tom shared with Folkscene that "I enjoyed very much working with Bones Howe and I had a good group behind me. The songs were strong, I thought."

Upon its release in October 1974, 'The Heart Of Saturday Night' marked a special moment of discovery – of the birth a new star for the listeners, and a new sound altogether in the process for critics to admire – like Rolling Stone magazine, whose highly complimentary review praised the singer-songwriter as "an urban romantic poet whose lyrics echo the oral Beat poetry pioneered by Kerouac, Ginsberg, Ferlinghetti and Corso in the Fifties. Like the Beats, Waits has an ear for the underlying rhythms of American speech and an impressive ability to catalogue and juxtapose provocative snatches of cityscape while creating a grandly sentimental vision. Waits has the special ability to redeem clichés — to make such phrases as 'lonesome ol' town' and 'ol' bloodshot moon' at once sincere and sardonic... Beneath the sophisticated brilliance of his lyrics, Waits reveals a haunting innocence – the sense of a loner circling and re-circling the same turf, musing out loud."

Along that ride, the San Diego Weekly would note that "Tom Waits evokes a nostalgic feeling for the good old days without sacrificing originality," while the LA Times felt for its part that Waits was "a specialist," producing a sound that Downbeat magazine concluded "can amaze with the sheer power of its imagery." Commenting on his artistic growth in the time that had passed between the release of 'Closing Time' and 'The Heart Of Saturday Night', the BBC would declare that "this is an altogether more confident album," while Waits for his own part clearly appeared to feel he was on the start of a journey that he confessed to journalist Peter Silverton was "something that I didn't completely understand" at the time. He added that "I thought: I'm going to ride this somewhere, it's going to take me somewhere. I couldn't go any other way. You're in the world of adventure. It literally takes you places. It's like you went to sleep in a small house on a quiet street and you woke up in New York. The idea that you can dream yourself someplace can change your world."

One element of that trajectory Waits was clear about was his desire to utilise the album's buzz as a "diploma" by which to graduate to better live venues, adding in the same comments to Melody Maker that "having a record out gets your foot in the door. You can't play these clubs without an album or two." Still, even with that advantage, the singer-songwriter seemed measured in terms of his expectations where commercial crossover was concerned, reasoning to Rolling Stone that while "I wouldn't be playing the Troubadour without a couple of records – when you get a record you're just thrown into another arena with the thousands of other cats who have records just like you. I'm not hooting anymore, but I'm still pimping. I'm just on a different corner."

Having successfully established the foundations of what many argued would become a signature sound throughout the balance of the decade, producer Bones Howe agreed with the almost-universal critical assessment that "its a lovely album," adding that more importantly, he felt the pair were headed down the right musical path, regarding the album as "the beginning" of something "very special." Looking to the future, Tom – in a reflective conversation with WAMU – appeared equally at home with the sonic seeds he and Howe had planted in the pop cosmos with 'The Heart Of Saturday Night', feeling his greatest growth had come with the fact that "the second album was a move in a new direction, as far as myself as a writer goes. I was developing and growing and I felt good about that..."

PART V: 'Nighthawks At The Diner' (1975)

By 1975, Tom Waits' one-of-a-kind niche of beatnik-jazz/blues singer-songwriting was catching everyone's ear who mattered. The word was spreading on what Newsweek advertised as his "syncopated, stream-of-consciousness tour of the seamy side streets of America, backed by a soulful jazz quartet. All this has already won him a cult following in the music industry."
Admiring the talent that had helped assemble that fanbase, the LA Times hailed Tom that year as "one of the most critically admired writers and performers around and the object of (a fan base that was)…intense and growing."
Exploring the sound and style Waits had invented to attract that cult following, Downbeat magazine – in a cover story – explained that "rhythm is his forte, the manic finger-snapping serving as the backdrop to an incessant collage of fantastic characters and bizarre events. It's not an easy brand of music to peg; it owes more to the era of beatnik jazz than it does to rock, with a healthy dose of Tin Pan Alley more than occasionally making its presence felt. The songs never come across the same way twice, as Tom's rambling palaver mutates the arrangements as well as the general aura surrounding them."

Illustrating precisely why "each vinyl work-of-art acts as a Polaroid snapshot" of an American underbelly, the University of Washington Newspaper concluded that Waits' uniquely-authentic observatory talent "captured the pulse of contemporary American life in the tradition of early Beat poets." A common comparison as most critics regarded the singer-songwriter lyrically as a revivalist of the aforementioned linguistic fad, Waits – for his own part – was quick to distinguish himself from the latter class of greats he so admired and had admitted to being inspired by.

"I don't like the word poetry," he told the LA Times, "I don't like poetry readings and I usually don't like poets. I would much prefer describing myself and what I do as: I'm kind of a curator, and I'm kind of a night-owl reporter. Maybe a little bit of Damon Runyon in me or something… I always had a great appreciation for jazz, but I'm a very pedestrian musician. I get by. I like to think that my main instrument is vocabulary… If I'm tied down and have to call myself something, I prefer 'storyteller'. Everybody has their own definition of what poetry is, and of who's a poet. I think that Charles Bukowski is a poet – and I think that most will agree to that… So I call what I'm doing an improvisational adventure or an inebriation travelogue, and all of a sudden it takes on a whole new form and meaning."

Still, against the backdrop of the latter-mentioned derivative influences, New Times magazine made the important observation regarding the original ground the Waits had covered since with his own sound that the comparison was in fact an advantage in the context of "his Beat predecessors, because he is first a songwriter. He makes the words and music fit. The Beats, in spite of their claims to spontaneity, had very little feel for words put to music. For the music of language, yes, but one or two listens to any of the old Beat-jazz combos tell you that Tom Waits is not merely cashing in on nostalgia. He is improving on the form."

Elaborating on how his own process worked as far as writing, Tom added to the latter analysis in his conversation with the LA Times that "I know what works and what doesn't, strictly by trial and error. People who like what I do have come to expect this narrative; this I-don't-give-a-shit shuffle that I've been doing for a few years. I'm aware that I cut a certain sort of figure on stage. It's the difference between lighting up a cigarette in your living room, and lighting one up on stage – a whole different attitude takes over. Everything is blown up beyond proportion. I want to be able to go up and be a caricature of myself on stage."

Delving more intimately into his compositional process for 'Nighthawks At The Diner', Waits began by explaining that he used the road as his muse, in fact shaping the record as a tribute to that aforementioned cult that he'd bonded with in the course of the preceding four years, reasoning to Melody Maker in terms of that backdrop that "everybody has their own climate. I mean, it's where you find it. Some people choose to write about cosmic garbage, what sign are you, and how many limousines there are. I just write about things that I see around me."

Broadening his explanation of that process, Tom shared with Downbeat magazine that "what you essentially do is just look around you, take the raw material and forge it into something meaningful. It's as much the way you deal with what you're dealing with as what you choose to write about. 'Nighthawks' was a result of spending eight months on the road; it's just a lot of travelogues strung together. When you're on the road doing clubs, it's hard to stay out of the bars in the afternoons. You got time to kill before the show.

Then you hang around the club all night and you're up till dawn, so you hang around coffee shops. It stops being somethin' you do – it becomes somethin' you are. I'm constantly jottin' things down. I keep the notebook in my pocket. That's why I'm so anxious to get home after a few months on the road, I just dump out all my suitcase full of things I've written. I take down people's conversations in cafes, then I make music over the notes."

Turning specifically to what the LA Times – continuing in their championing of all things Waits – hailed as "his flair for pungent detail and his sensuous imagery bringing vibrancy and dimension to his neon maze and its asphalt escape chutes," the singer-songwriter explained to Melody Maker that he regarded himself as "a kind of curator, a collector of improvisational adventures from the bowls of the night. I'm a kind of an imagist… I don't have enough of a thoroughbred pedigree to consider myself a poet. It may make me a storyteller. It don't necessarily make me a poet just because I talk instead of sing sometimes."

Those conversations, according to Downbeat magazine, produced "new images and occurrences...(that) are constantly popping up in the songs, phrases Waits hews from the conversations he is eavesdroppingly addicted to – the cliché-ridden, daily-burdened, colour-frocked jargon of the working class, a language that runs the gamut of human emotion, lauding the mundane at the expense of the maudlin." Discussing the tools of that trade, Tom shared with journalist Marv Hohman that "I don't just sit down at a typewriter and write. I pick up stuff from conversations in bars and cafes and cabs and clubs. The monologue generally comes out of stuff I experiment with onstage."

In matching those conversational dialogues – whether spoken or sung – with their appropriate musical soundscape, Waits offered to Crawdaddy Radio of his composing process that "I just write it down like a story and then when I get an opportunity to sit down at a keyboard, which is very rare, I usually jump at the chance and write a melody and then stick it all together into some kind of homogenised, pasteurised, copasetic sort of little piece of work." Using one aspect of his writing process to aid the other whenever he hit a creative roadblock, Waits began by explaining to Downbeat that "usually you write within a framework, however limited you are, then that's as far as you'll go. Instead of learning theory and then learning how to play the piano, I learned theory through writing."

Admitting there were times when he found himself "so musically constipated you don't know what the hell to do," Tom – in the same conversation with Melody Maker – seemed to take comfort in the fact that "the whole creative process. I can't boil that down. It's a lot easier to talk about than it is to do." One source for inspiration Waits continually visited throughout each of his records, with 'Nighthawks' as no exception, came with routinely hanging "around in bars and cafes taking down people's conversations, trying to keep the meter, picking up expressions. This stuff is my meat and potatoes... It concerns the art of storytelling."

Waits began in an interview with WMMS-FM discussing 'Better Off Without A Wife', of which he explained "here's one about matrimony...it's kind of an old song I kept working around. I used to do it like a blues and it ended up like a little ballad, like a little anthem. But I don't have any personal vendetta against the constipation (sic) of holy matrimony."

Turning to 'Big Joe And Phantom 309', the singer-songwriter recalled to journalist Jim Gerard of the song that "I liked the story – kind of like a 'Legend Of Sleepy Hollow' or 'Ichabod Crane' and that. It was one narrative I've always enjoyed." Of 'Eggs And Sausage', the singer-songwriter explained that the song was at heart an ode to the many diners he used as his office on the road, reasoning to WAMU Radio that "after you hang around enough diners, it seems a place you always go when you're feeling like a refugee from a disconcerted love affair – you end up at a 24-hour place, in LA we got a place called Norm's – all the losers are there and the waitresses are all good looking."

Waits told Folk Scene that the song 'On a Foggy Night' was inspired in part by a "soundtrack written quite a bit later than the film – the film came out about 1947 and I wrote it just a couple of weeks ago. It's about a foggy night on one of those 'triangle' films that you see on The Late Show and this is just about the eternal triangle – like George Raft and Fred MacMurray and Rosalind Russell – and somebody has to go and it's going to be George Raft in this case. And Fred MacMurray's got this old Plymouth and he's on this foggy road with MacMurray in the trunk, a little bit of his lapel sticking out the back of the trunk and this song comes on the radio."

Tom added to KPFK-FM 90.7 of the song's inspiration that "there's a stretch of highway from Blythe to San Diego – I drove all night from Nogalis and I got to Blythe and I hadn't washed my windshield. Driving through Blythe at about three o'clock in the morning I sort of imagined all these Eucalyptus trees hanging over the highway and these big radio towers which weren't really there. I was just driving a long time.

"I've talked to truck drivers that say that same stretch of highway they imagined being in a forest – if you've been driving for a long time but there's something about coming into town on Highway 8 that's exciting. But when we were going out there was a fog bank up around Hecumba and – God, a mysterious wet fog was hanging over the highway and so we're coming down and this is about driving on a foggy night on an abandoned road late at night."

Once attention turned to the production stage, Waits and producer Bones Howe decided the natural backdrop was a live crowd in celebration of the album's muse. While live albums were common to that era of the Seventies, 'Nighthawks' was, not surprisingly, unique in how the duo chose to track the record, with producer Bones Howe recalling that "out of our conversations post-tracking for 'Heart Of Saturday Night', out of that recording, came the band that played on 'Nighthawks At The Diner'.

"That album was an outgrowth of 'The Heart Of Saturday Night' because it came so quickly after that, and had come out of the ideas we'd generated from those sessions. So Tom wrote the songs, we then went over them and talked about how we wanted them to go, rehearsed with the group, and then went in and did it live at the back of the Record Plant. David said, 'Tom's great on stage, we should do a live album.'"

Confessing to Melody Maker at the time that "I've always found it awkward to adjust to the studio – that knowledge that you've got the same facilities as any other artist at your disposal – you can go in and make a great album or you can go in and suck raw eggs," Waits added in a conversation with ZigZag magazine that the whole process felt "really like pulling teeth, everything is real fastidious. I dunno, I'm afraid of it. I'm afraid of it, and I'm just a nervous wreck the whole time, because you spend a lot of time working on this material, which is really the crux of it, where the real sweat is. Then you can have major surgery done to something you just busted your chops over. So it's real sensitive, and a lot of heated arguments, a lot of fist fights. I don't look forward to it."

Producer Bones Howe wanted to keep the atmosphere light during recording, and shared his recollection of asking Waits, "Where are we going to do this? I don't want to do it at the Troubadour.' And I remembered one day that they had made a live Barbra Streisand album at the back of Record Plant, with a live concert audience and everything. So I called David back and asked him, 'Why in the world couldn't we take that place and turn it into a club?'

"So we turned this big, empty scoring stage in the back of the Record Plant into a club, put tables and chairs in it, got some waiters and people from Elektra Records to come over, poured some wine and beer, got some chips on the table, and next said 'Well, we need an opening act.' And Tom said 'I worked with this great stripper named Dewana at some joint I played. I'll call her up, her husband's a cab driver, he'll bring her over.' And I got his rhythm section to come on early and play for the stripper, and we had two nights running, did two shows a night."

Detailing his 'pre-production' process for the record, Waits recalled in a conversation with journalist Marv Hohman, "I spent two weeks rehearsing for it. It was done like a club date, nonstop. We invited 200 people and had booze, tables, chairs. A stripper named Dewana opened the show. The band played 'The Pink Panther' and 'Night Train'," adding to music writer Jim Gerard that the album had "no overdubbing".

The results Waits and his band produced – as reviewed by the LA Times – was indeed a "record, cut with an audience in the studio...(where) Waits breaks the mould of the conventional singer-songwriter and presents himself as a bebop raconteur, a scatting storyteller and spontaneous, rapid-fire imagist reciting to the fourth-gear highway rhythms of a smoky jazz trio. The inescapable first impression is that of the Fifties jazz-and-poetry format, but Waits is leery of the term poetry and thinks that too much is made of his beatnik connection."

Waits began by explaining to journalist Robert Ward that, in selecting the live band that accompanied him on the album, he was seeking something along the lines of "George and Ira Gershwin, Jerome Kern, Cab Calloway, and the old Nat King Cole Trio – I always liked that sort of trio sound," adding to the BBC of the specific line-up of players that "I have a copasetic Creole Sicilian tenor player, Frank Vicari. And uh, on parole on drugs and drums is Chip White. On upright bass uh is Dr. Fitzgerald Huntington Jenkins III junior. All from New York City. Three previously unemployed bebop musicians."

Once the group was assembled, Tom expressed his feeling to Downbeat magazine that he was "proud of (the line-up). Pete Christlieb played tenor sax on it, he's with the NBC Doc Severinsen orchestra. He also drives the Ontario Motor Speedway: he just plays with Severinsen as more or less as a sideline. Jim Hughart, the bassist, he's got a pedigree all his own. He does studio work in Los Angeles, he's done a lot of road work with Ella Fitzgerald. Bill Goodwin is on drums. He lives in Pocono, Pennsylvania, so he flew out for the date. I'd seen him before with Mose Allison in New York. Hughart lives in LA so does Mike Melvoin (the keyboardist on the album) and Christlieb. I was just trying to find a band that could naturally play what I wanted and not have to teach or tell 'em what to do. I wanted them to stretch out on their own."

In terms of how the band melded musically with Waits' ambitions for the live album, the New Times magazine reported that "the jazzmen obviously love the kid. They play in perfect sync with him, and as he sweats and shakes and lets the words fly, there is a moment when the stage is magical, spinning not out of control but pleasantly and beautifully like a great patched-up lyrical balloon...

Great wordplay and great energy combined perfectly with the sax and bass create a hypnotic, joyous floating sensation".

Waits – in a conversation with WMMS FM – explained that in adapting from a solo act to those performances "when I'm performing with the group, what I tend to do is do a lot of monologues, do a lot of nocturnal emissions and eh improvisational adventures," adding to NME that in the course of playing alongside the aforementioned musicians, "I just accompany, that's what I do. I'm glad to have my band with me, they're a real high-voltage bebop trio." For his spoken word moments on the record, Tom told Melody Maker that "if I can't find a melody to hang the words on to, I just don't worry about it. I do it anyway, without music."

Once the band's live performances had been tracked, producer Bones Howe recalled that "we wound up with four taped shows, then Tom and I went in the studio and put the album together. The idea for reading the weather report came about from, we're sitting around the studio with the rhythm section during the making of 'The Heart Of Saturday Night', and Waits starts reading the want ads. And the guys started playing, but it didn't have anything directly to do with the record we were making. It was an idea that got set aside for the next project, which happened to be the live album. So then Tom said, 'Well, I can read the weather report, which really has more emotion to it because it can have a second meaning.' So those kind of serendipitous moments happened all the time with us."

In highlighting some of his favourite musical moments from the sessions that comprised the final track listing for 'Nighthawks At The Diner', Tom told Melody Maker that "there's a new thing I've done called 'Eggs And Sausage' which I'm really pleased with, and another one called 'Warm Beer And Cold Women'… oh and there's one called 'Putnam County' which is a little vignette about a Naugahyde town in Kentucky."

Released in October, 1975, the critical response to Waits' newest LP was significant from past reviews in the way the media strove to explore and define the essence of the singer-songwriter's evolving sub-genre. The LA Times concluded that "'Nighthawks At The Diner' (was) the experiment that crystallised various elements of Waits' act: the sophisticated funk, the Skid Row baritone, the arranged disarray, the rocks upon which he built its musical church," adding that lyrically, "his discovery of the Beat writers came as a breath of fresh air and furnished a strong stylistic impulse which surfaced" on the LP.

Elaborating on the praise for Waits' channeling of the beatnik style in his sound, the University of Washington Newspaper declared that "Ferlinghetti would be proud," while Contemporary Keyboard magazine elaborated that "'Nighthawks At The Diner' clearly demonstrated Waits' debt to such late-Fifties 'jazz orators' as Ken Nordine and Oscar Brown Jr, coming prophets of the Beat era like Lord Buckley and Harry The Hipster Gibson, smut comics such as Redd Foxx and Rudy Ray Moore, poets and authors out of the mould of Jack Kerouac, Gregory Corso and Lawrence Ferlinghetti, and even Americana storytellers like Mark Twain and Will Rogers."

The BBC got more analytical in its review of the double LP, noting years later that the record marked the beginning of a time – in the legendary broadcast network's estimation – "where Tom Waits starts to sound like Tom Waits... his voice is much more gravelly than it was on his first two albums, though it's far from the ferocious growl present in his later works. 'Nighthawks' is a defiant fan favourite...(and) the final product...is a masterpiece. Accompanied by a drummer, saxophonist and a pianist, Waits weaves between hilarious anecdotes and terrific songs with unrivalled charm and charisma."

Newsweek, for its part, felt the record reflected "Waits' talent as an original writer with a unique mixture of blues and jazz in his music," while Time Out magazine highlighted the "excellent" LP as a "testament to Waits' power as a live act." Commenting for his own part on why he felt he was such a hit with the live audiences he played to night after night on the road three seasons out of the year, Tom offered to Newsweek that "I've got a personality that an audience likes. I'm like the guy they knew – someone raggedy and irresponsible – who never really amounted to much but was always good for a few laughs. A victim, just a victim. But I don't mind the image."

Billboard magazine offered perhaps the most rounded review of the LP by suggesting that the "major part of Tom Waits' mystique has always been his complex, intriguing persona; part Bukowski-esque barfly poet, part Kerouac-inspired hipster, part Hoagy Carmichael troubadour. Nowhere has that persona been more fully utilised than on 'Nighthawks At The Diner.' Throughout the album waits unfurls his colourful, charismatic, artfully amplified personality.

"It's like spending the evening with a lounge lizard/raconteur/beatnik standup comic who also happens to compose strikingly beautiful tunes that could have come from the Great American Songbook if not for their lyrical quirkiness... The character who stomps through your brain on 'Nighthawks' with both guns blazing is as original and impressive a character as you could want." The New York Times agreed, adding their opinion that "Waits' ability to rework the sleazy nightclub setting" was "proven by the double live album 'Nighthawks At The Diner.'"

Offering his reaction to the chorus of praise for what he'd accomplished, Tom began by quipping to NME that "they have a lot of faith in me over there, with the idea that sooner or later I'll do something significant," confessing to the University of Washington Newspaper that that expectation and what it implied in terms of "pressure is very hard to cope with sometimes. But the way I look at it, is that I quit my day-job and what I'm doing beats the shit out of wages. There was a time when I said to myself, 'I'd give my left nut to be doin' something other than working behind a goddamn register in a hobby shop. And now I'm doin' it. All I'm concerned about is continuing to write."

In that respect, Waits – through both his writing for 'Nighthawks' as well as the new songs he was already working on for his fifth studio album – revealed to ZigZag magazine that "I really have changed. I've become a little more ambitious about it. For me it's also a craft. It's not something that drops out of the sky. It's not something where you sit at your picture window and watch the sun glistening off the trees and a deer walks by and whispers in your ear. It's really a craft, and it's hard work. It's just a lot of discipline, and hopefully, you get better with each project. I've just about worked out the stuff for my next album, so what I'm going to do when I get back to Los Angeles is get drunk as a skunk and stay that way for about three days. Then I'm going right into the studio."

Offering the LA Times a glimpse into what would compose the subject matter of his next album, Waits explained that – as with past records – "I deal with the things that I know most about. You almost have to create situations in order to write about them, so I live in a constant state of self-imposed poverty. I don't want to live any other way... I have to be completely aware of the figure that I cut on stage. I'm a caricature of myself up there. It's just an exaggeration of my own personality... I'm just trying to be bona fide, and not have to compromise my integrity too much. It's a lot easier to deal with being an underdog than it is being a household word. I'm a legend in my own mind, a kind of tumour in my own mind. I'm not on the verge of national prominence or anything." Waits couldn't have been further from the truth on that score as his next album, the magical 'Small Change', would prove.

"Tom Waits is a twenty-six-year-old composer and performer who looks like an urban scarecrow...He is a private sort of person, older than his years; skinny, angular, and long faced; reflective eyes in the shadow of his cap brim."
– THE NEW YORKER

"I'm not a drunk, I'm not a lush. I work real hard all year. If I was a drunk I don't think I'd have five albums out." – TOM WAITS, 1976

PART VI: 'Small Change' (1976)

Tom Waits' fourth studio LP, 'Small Change', turned him into a critical favourite at a time when his career desperately needed the spotlight. Melody Maker declared in 1976 that "albums like 'The Heart Of Saturday Night' and 'Small Change'…have confirmed him as America's leading street poet, with a staunch cult following," one that media as stylistically diverse as Country Rambler noted was steadily expanding, declaring Waits "the fast-rising street rambling songwriter" that CBC Stereo, Canada's biggest radio network, concluded had "established himself as rock's paramount beat-poet."

Downbeat magazine hailed the singer-songwriter as "the most gifted and genuine folk musician-poet around today," in part because of a talent – as The Guardian observed in Britain – for turning "American music into the speech-song of ordinary men and women caught in that murky bad-smelling alleyway between the juvenile rhetoric of the American dream and the unforgiving adult reality of contemporary life."

Waits quipped to television host Barth Gimble at the time that "I live at Bedlam and Squalor," before confirming more accurately for the Dallas Morning News that "on stage, I'm not trying to be anyone else but me. I try not to be compromising and condescending. I talk about things I know about. deep down inside there isn't a man wearing a leisure suit. I live in a run-down hotel – the Tropicana. All room rents paid in advance. The other people who live there are four-speed automatic transvestites, unemployed firemen, dykes, hoods, hookers, sadists, masochists, Avon ladies on the skids, reprieved murderers, ex-bebop singers and one-armed piano players. The whole gambit – lock, stock and bagels."

Rolling Stone magazine, in a 1976 feature, reported at the time that "his tenuous home base was the Tropicana Motel in Los Angeles. The piano was in his kitchen. With gut-wrenching sincerity, his gravel-edged voice sang of those on the shadow line – prostitutes, derelicts and misfits – with equal measures of melancholy and desperation. He gained a strong following both here and abroad, but unlike most of the Seventies singer-songwriters, whose allegiance was to lyrical country-rock, Waits leaned towards Jack Kerouac's American wordscape and Stephen Foster's homesick melodies."

Leading a life that imitated the art of his music, the poetic portraits Waits painted on wax, according to the LA Times, via "such landmark albums as

1974's 'The Heart Of Saturday Night' and 1976's 'Small Change', " produced "wonderfully evocative songs about losers with big dreams and dreamers with unlikely victories," anthems that the New York Times noted were a result of his obsession "with America's low-life – the bars, the broads, the booze, the touts, the sleaze. His voice is variations on a gargle, half-conversational mutterings about life's disappointments and dreams."

Rolling Stone fleshed out this low-life demographic their observation "the people who populate Tom Waits' songs...(are) deeply rooted in 20th-century American mythology. They come from tough-guy novels, pulp magazines, radio serials and film noir. Waits isn't interested in the heroes of this fiction, but with the people who exist on its fringes: cabbies, newsstand dealers, shoeshine boys and all-night waitresses. In the perverted language of American politics, they are known as 'the little people', but Waits would agree with writer Joseph Mitchell that 'they are as big as you are, whoever you are'... With his cigarette dangling from his mouth, his cap slapped over his forehead, Waits slouches through these streets presenting himself not as a detached observer but as a full-fledged native."

Even as a major-label recording artist, Waits could speak so accurately to this 'off the grid' demographic's truths because, he explained to the New Yorker, "my creative climate is relatively the same as it used to be," adding that "I still love living in hotels. Transient hotels. I live in a nine dollar a night hotel in LA, I know every flop in every town. Cheap hotels remind me of home a lot more than some sanitary protection place. They're a little more humane." He could have left his roots with his star on the rise, but Waits revealed to journalist Rich Trenbeth that "I don't do a lot of hob-nobbing with household words. It's hard to keep one foot in the street because of how this business can be and this whole American Dream. There are different criteria for success – like the American credit card. But for me life in the streets is much more fascinating."

Having hit the road in the spirit of his hero Jack Kerouac and as a singer-songwriter building an audience with a tireless touring schedule, Tom's songwriting routine was one that, from a conventional standpoint, he explained to KPFK-FM 90.7, was "difficult to do because it's hard to be able to get the opportunity to sit down at the keyboard except to perform. I was mostly doing two, sometimes three shows a night, six nights and then leaving on the seventh night to open like on Monday. Some were Monday through Saturday, some were Monday through Sunday so it's hard to get a chance to sit down and concentrate and think in notes. So I wrote a lot of verse but it is a problem, the road, I don't know, everybody has to have a different climate in order to create so I managed okay...but it's hard to write out there."

Whether home in LA or out on the road, where he spent "eight months out of the year", Waits found the same muse at play, pointing out in an interview with Newsweek that he'd found throughout his travels "there's a common loneliness that just sprawls from coast to coast. It's like a common disjointed identity crisis. It's the dark, warm narcotic American night I just hope I'm able to touch that feeling before I find myself one of these days parked on Easy Street."

Waits' acute eye for imagery began with lyrics, which he revealed to journalist

Dan Forte "I usually have...written (first)... I just have to find something to hang them on... I start with a couple of changes, maybe a single-note melody sometimes." Discussing the rhythmic pace of his lyrical compositional style, Waits – in a conversation with WNEW FM – termed it as akin to a "road rhythm... I guess you can handle that any one of a numbers of different ways. But I just thought that there's something that's inherently rhythmic about a barker or a used car salesman or a, you know, a pitch man carney cat. You know there's always a rhythm there to hold your attention."

Turning to the musical side of his songwriting method, Tom told Dan Forte that his "approach to the keyboard is so much different as a writer – it's one of investigation, rather than learning technique. My technique is: I compose everything on the piano even if I'm going to play it on guitar. I used to have a little trumpet around here for when I was writing, like, a single-note melody line. I can construct melody; that's where I'm most comfortable."

He told journalist Bret Kofford that as he composed, "I play fake piano. I'm a composer, basically. When I sit down at the piano I don't sit down to play something or learn something. I sit down to discover." In discussing some of the derivative influences at work during the writing of 'Small Change', the singer-songwriter offered to music writer Rich Trenbeth that "my musical influence of songwriters were guys who are either old or dead and just not around anymore. They're a real incongruous group that somehow I had to fuse together."

Elaborating more specifically on some of those influences, Tom shared with Contemporary Keyboard that the "players that I was listening to, and continue to listen to...are Bill Evans, Mose Allison, (Thelonious) Monk, Art Tatum, Huey 'Piano' Smith, Professor Longhair, Doctor John... I like Jerome Kern, Irving Berlin, George and Ira Gershwin, Hoagy Carmichael, Cole Porter, Rodgers and Hammerstein, Johnny Mercer... But of the cats I admire, there's no trace of my admiration for them in my own style, you know what I mean? If I said I listen to Thelonious Monk, you wouldn't be able to go and find out where that comes into my playing."

The songs that came out of that playing, Telegraph magazine would conclude, were "songs that had a way of sidling up on you like a stranger in a bar with a story to tell, romantic celebrations of the bare and enduring fact of existence under even the most straitened of circumstances. The characters in his songs may have lost their shirts and their temper, but never their human dignity."

Amazingly, the "20 songs" he wrote for 'Small Change' were produced in an astonishingly-short "two weeks while I was in London," Waits told the Houston Post, adding that on the road, he used his performances themselves as opportunities to glean compositional ideas from. He told The New Yorker that he'd created this approach as a solution to "the problem with performing is it's repetitive, and unless I can come up with something new each night, I find it grueling. Like I'm just a monkey on a stick. So I try to stretch out nightly, make something of it. And that's very valuable to me, and a lot of songs come out of that."

Discussing some of the specific songs those months on the road had produced, beginning with 'Step Right Up', Waits explained to Rolling Stone that "through the songs I'm writing now I'm changing my attitude towards things. I'm becoming a little more shrewd, a little more (where)...I don't take things at face value like I used to. So I dispelled some things in these songs that I had substantiated before. I'm trying to show something to myself, plus get some things off my chest.

"'Step Right Up' – all that jargon we hear in the music business is just like what you hear in the restaurant or casket business. So instead of spouting my views in "'Scientific American' on the vulnerability of the American public to our product-oriented society, I wrote 'Step Right Up'." The Guardian would fall instantly in love with the song, celebrating the fact that "only Tom Waits could make an entire song out of a running string of infomercials ('Step Right Up') and somehow turn the list into an exhaustive, funny documentary on American credulousness and American cunning."

The more controversial title track was inspired by his witnessing a murder, sharing that "it was the first time I ever covered a homicide, and the incident is a true one. I was in New York City, stayin' at the Chelsea Hotel, and a young cat was shot and killed across the street from the restaurant where I was goin' to eat – just as I walked in the door. It happened two years before I wrote anything about it. I just didn't know how to deal with it. I was just trying to deal with the whole murder thing in New York, the whole ambience... It's all just like, 'So what? Somebody got shot and killed, I don't care.'"

Continuing on the subject of disassociation he was addressing with the song, Tom added that "by the time you read it in the newspapers, it's gone. I mean, a newspaper doesn't weep, it's not wet, it doesn't bleed, doesn't croak. It's just facts, no ideas, no mess, no funeral, no phone calls in the middle of the night explaining it to somebody, no tears, no nothing. The night I saw this cat blown away, the cops were sittin' around sayin', 'Hey, Charley, where you goin' on your vacation?' And there's this little cat oozin' life, lyin' in his own blood."

Perhaps viewing the song as a broader commentary on the fact that murder "happens all the time," Waits added in his discussion with journalist Jim Gerard that "its all over. I was there and some little kid got murdered. Stuff like that usually gets buried in the back pages of the papers. All I did was cover the homicide, so to speak."

Moving on, the singer-songwriter confessed to Rolling Stone that "I put a lot into 'Bad Liver And A Broken Heart'. I tried to resolve a few things as far as this cocktail – lounge, maudlin, crying-in-your-beer image that I have. There ain't nothin' funny about a drunk. You know, I was really starting to believe that there was something amusing and wonderfully American about a drunk. I ended up telling myself to cut that shit out. On top of everything else, talking about boozing substantiates the rumours that people hear about you, and people hear that I'm a drunk. So I directed that song as much to the people that listen to me and think they know me as much as I directed it to myself."

Waits attempted to correct the record where his image as a boozer was concerned, telling the Dallas Morning News that "I don't drink when I'm working. John, my road manager, does. He buys bargain stuff, like Frank's Scotch, or Benson & Hedges brewed in Rochester. He was my inspiration for my line, 'I'll meet you at the bottom of a bottle of bargain Scotch.' When I was on Fernwood 2Night, Martin Mull was the host and he apologised for having only a diet Pepsi to offer me. I started drinking from a flask I had in my coat and he said something about me sitting there with a bottle in front of me. So I said, 'I'd rather have a bottle in front of me than a frontal lobotomy.' Later I said, 'People who can't face drugs turn to reality.'"

Of 'Jitterbug Boy', Waits recalled to WNEW FM that "this is a song about… a cat I met at Pennsylvania station real late one night and his name's Rocky. It seems there's always a guy named Rocky at Pennsylvania station…or any station for that matter. If there isn't, you know, they usually have and rent one. And the guy'd been everywhere, done everything. I was going to Philadelphia. He said: 'Man, I'm going to Philadelphia.' He said: 'I'm gonna take a train.' I said: 'Well you know eh, don't take a train, let the train take you.'"

Musically, he added in a conversation with journalist Dan Forte that "on 'Jitterbug Boy', I was thinking about George Gershwin's 'I Got Plenty O' Nuthin', Nuthin's Plenty For Me.'" Turning to 'Tom Traubert's Blues', which blended a famous Australian bush ballad 'Waltzing Matilda' with his own composition, Tom offered in the same discussion with WNEW FM that his translation "just means, really just to take off, you know? Like blow town, that's what the song means, maybe…"

Producer Bones Howe shared of the deeper meaning behind fan favourite 'The Piano Has Been Drinking' that "the reason he wrote that song was because he would do it live at the clubs, we never did it on a record. There was a club owner that he really hated, and the guy used to get on Tom because he ran up a bar bill, so Tom wrote an ode to him. We recorded that just as if he was playing it live. 'Invitation To The Blues' was another example of the people in Tom's life who were cab drivers, bus drivers, strippers, waitresses – who he'd had relationships with, a lot of these people, where he'd either known them as friends, and also, a lot of failed romances, including Rickie Lee Jones and Bette Midler, they all informed his song writing. You hear these songs and they tear your heart out."

As Waits and mainstay producer Howe prepared to enter the studio to record his fourth studio LP, the producer recalled that their pre-production routine, "from the time of the 'Nighthawks' album on, began to change because Tom and I would see each other quite often in between albums, and would have long talks at Duke's over coffee about what the next record would be like, the atmosphere and what was going to happen.

"On average, we made a record a year, and the way we would work was, he would write the songs, then he would go into a demo studio, and just put down a demo on tape of all the songs he wanted to do, in whatever shape they were in. Some they were incomplete, sometimes it was just an intro and a verse, sometimes just a chorus with his voice saying 'Okay, there's a verse here, and then it goes dadada.'

"And then he would send me the tape, he'd never play those demos for me live. He'd always lay them down on tape. And then I'd get a copy of the tape, and I'd go through it, and then we'd have one of our 'production meetings' at Duke's or one of those coffee shops on the Sunset Strip. And we'd sit there for three hours and talk about it: I'd talk about the flavour, the feeling of the album was. Then we'd talk about what the album was gonna be like, and then the atmosphere of it. That all developed out of these conversations."

Turning specifically to Waits' thoughts for 'Small Change', Howe recalled that "these 'production meetings' usually began with Tom saying 'Well, tell me about those records you made in the Fifties with those jazz musicians.' And I would explain that it was live to two-track and mono, and so he said to me, 'You know, I want to do a record that's live to two-track and mono, because I like performing that way, being out there.' We had done some multi-track recording obviously for safety's sake on the live album, and we'd done some on 'The Heart Of Saturday Night', and Tom then said 'I think there's an immediate feel to doing recording that way.' So we began recording that way for the 'Small Change' sessions."

Indeed, Tom confirmed to journalist Jim Gerard that "the whole album was done live with no overdubbing. It was done on a direct two-track machine; everything was done on the spot while it was being recorded." Waits added in a discussion with journalist Peter Orr that the "live two-track came out of not wanting anybody else to mess with it. You know, it's done! None of thing going to 24-track. I didn't like having that many choices. didn't want that many options. I was very old-fashioned.

"I thought that it should be done, like, you come in and sing your song – you know your song, first of all, you know it really well. That's what Bob Dylan said: I will know my song before I sing it. And that became part of what I thought the song should be. You take it on the road and drive it so you really know it and it means something to you, and then when you sing it on record it's like taaa! You got it."

In selecting the band he would enter the studio with, rather than recruiting known heavy-hitters, the singer-songwriter explained to journalist Rich Trenbeth that "I found myself three previously unemployed bebop musicians. Except my tenor used to play with Maynard Ferguson and Woody Herman – he's been around the block several times. My upright player is Dr Fitzgerald Huntington Jenkins III. It's nice to have something to fall back on. He was a doctor and went to a concert, saw an upright player and went out. He quit his internship, split for Europe and studied bass with a guy. And my drummer grew up in Harlem in a drumming family. He was weaned on brushes. I got a black bass player, a Sicilian tenor and a Cherokee and Afro-American drummer. We can go into any neighbourhood in the world and hang out."

Arranger Jerry Yester offered his observation on the good vibes within the band that "Tom always saw himself as part of the group, even though obviously he had the last word. He knew that, but he never pushed it because he didn't have to. They would ask him what he wanted and he would tell them. He was very friendly with everyone, and loved the camaraderie of other musicians in the studio." In choosing his band's members, Waits added of the process in a conversation with Jim Gerard that economics played a role as well, reasoning that "when you decide to cut an album you sit down and decide what cast would be best to get a hold of. It has to do with availability and you see who is in town and who is not and who might be back and who is double scale and triple scale. Who is available has as much to do with it as who you would like."

Producer Bones Howe explained that "the records we made were so inexpensive. It wasn't like million dollar-recording budgets. Our records never cost more than $50,000, so we recouped with the first shipment. We always knew what we were gonna do, we went in, did it live, there was no overdubbing, and then we went in and put the album together. And even though sometimes there was a lot of production on those albums, we always went in and did them very quickly."

Indeed, Jerry Yester recalled that "for 'Small Change', at least the songs I worked on, it went pretty quickly because they didn't take a lot of takes on everything. One thing about Bones was he did his mixing as he went along recording, so the stuff was mixed when the song's tracking was done. That was the old style of engineering, so he could run the 16-track and you had a mix, and he also recorded everything live two-track at the same time."

Elaborating on Tom and his band's studio set-up, Howe explained that "I organised Waits' rhythm section like I was scoring for a movie – I did my share of movie scoring, so it was set up like a scoring orchestra, which means not every instrument has its own microphone. Sections have their own microphone, and you mic the sections because you mic them from farther away. You don't mic each instrument right down in the middle of the horn for instance, so sections have their microphones. Or in some cases, you may have two, like with the woodwind section you may have flutes and clarinets, and you can't mic them on the same mic because they're different animals. So you mic the flutes separately and the clarinets separately, but for the most part, they're treated as sections and not as individual instruments. And then, in general, the quality of the sound is not one of the horn or the instrument right in the microphone, its back a space. All of this has to do with perspective."

Elaborating on the mystery of this process, the producer offered that "when you're making a record, one thing you can't define – except aurally – is depth, and one of the big problems with making records on a computer is that there is only one depth. Everything is right in your face, like a flat piece of paper. There's nothing even artificial reverb does not give you the absence of presence is the absence of room sound. Well, if you don't have a room, you can't have room sound. And no matter how you record something – even if you add room sound to it – you still have the presence of the instrument being right there at the front level. With a scoring orchestra, everything is in the background, not just in terms of volume but also in terms of distance.

"Distance is what makes it possible for the music to be really loud and you can still understand the dialogue. Every one of the songs that went on 'Small Change' is a gem, and they were fun to record. On small change, a lot of the songs were recorded with almost an orchestra, those were recording live with Tom singing live while the band was playing. Some of the songs on that record were recorded in one take, others were three or four times through, and then we'd maybe put it off to the next day. Everything I did in terms of engineering when making those

Waits records was based on things other than engineering."

Waits, for his part, recalled in a conversation with 90 Minutes Live of the album's recording that "I stood in the studio – with the last album – in the middle of the studio were like 52 musicians. It was very exciting," while arranger and strings master Jerry Yester added of the sheer size of the band required to meet the singer-songwriter's orchestral vision for certain tracks from the record that "from the songs I'd heard, I figured the size of the strings section would be around 22 people, which is small actually compared with the size of a complete symphonic string group, which is usually around 60 people. Again, I called Edgar Lustgarten, who became my contractor for strings, in that he got the players together with me in the studio. We had eight first violins, six second violins, four violas, two cellos and one stand-up bassist."

Describing his interaction with Howe throughout the album's recording process, Yester recalled that "Bones was almost always out in the main room, setting up the mics himself or supervising the setting up of the mics, and then just usually tweak after that. When we were recording, I would be there conducting, but I'd told the players 'I'm not a conductor, so don't be looking to me except for indications, look at Tom's foot, because really that's the conductor, and they did, and were right there with him.' Tom played along live on piano during all the string section tracking, and they all worked so well together that it was easy."

Tom shared with journalist Dan Forte that, atmospherically, "I wanted to do all the piano myself, so that what I lay down on the record I could recreate on the road." He preferred to record on the same type of acoustic he used in the studio, explaining to Contemporary Keyboard that he avoided using a "Rhodes piano or any of that shit. I don't like the action, I don't like the sound, the flavour – and I don't like lugging them around. I just don't like them."

Discussing how he viewed himself as a player, Waits added in the same discussion that "I don't put myself off as any pioneer of the piano or anything. I feel a little funny even talking about it. I taught myself; I'm not anything to write home about. I don't spend evenings around the piano with friends and hot toddies, you know, singing old Gershwin songs. Nobody comes over here much. Look around and figure it out."

Howe elaborated on the specifics of the ambitious title track's development in the studio, explaining that "for 'Small Change', that song was done with the whole rhythm section and Jack Sheldon playing trumpet in the spaces between the verses, kind of an improvised little jazzy thing that we did. Often, what would happen with Waits and I is we would do something with the saxophone and bass, or trumpet and trombone, whatever the ensemble would be. We would do it all live to two-track, so there was no mixing, as Waits would say, 'There's no kitchen drudgery.'"

Detailing the recording of many fans' favourite from the album, its title track, Bones shared his memory that "on the reading of 'Small Change', he's talking about gangsters and gambling. He kind of made this circle through this underbelly, and it was always an adventure. On 'Small Change', when he said he wanted to do this reading, I said 'Well, we should score it like a movie.' And he said 'Oh

God, what a great idea.' So I got Bob to write some underscoring. What Tom did was just lay the reading down on tape, then we gave it to Bob, and Waits played some things in between to show Bob how he wanted it to go, and in turn Bob turned it into a film score. That was kind of the beginning of what we did on 'One From The Heart.'

"So I said, here's what we're gonna do, we're gonna just put the orchestra in the studio, and they're gonna play, and Bob's gonna conduct, and you're gonna recite it. Bob's gonna listen to you through earphones in the same room, and conduct this orchestra at the same time, and underscore it like it's a movie.' And that's what we did."

Continuing, the producer added that "we actually had to do it two nights running, because it turned out the first night that the transitions were too long between the verses, and also, Tom read some of it faster when the orchestra was live, so the pacing was different. So we went out and did it again the next night. Even the reading of 'Small Change (Got Rained On With His Own .38)', is the live reading over a live orchestra to two-track. We did make multi-track safeties, but we never used them, and all those recordings are first-generation two-track CD. I mean, when you hear those albums on compact disc, they were transferred right from the original two-track tape, so you're hearing it the way I did come through the monitors when I first recorded it. It's amazing and, looking back on the original recordings for 'Small Change', they were something that was a lot of fun to do."

Waits' lead vocals, Howe recalled, were recorded "on the microphone up close like he was reciting or singing, and with the orchestra in the background, which meant the orchestra could be up pretty good. It didn't have to be way down, because you had the depth of the room and the feeling that the orchestra is in the background. The trick is there is no trick, you just make sure to keep them from being as close to the mic as he is. And then you get a little room sound, which changes the wave form, and it kind of runs the music all together, and ease up close next to the mic and it's very clear, so you can hear Waits' voice and still have the music pretty loud.

"My one big regret with Tom was that he wrote such great melodies, but you didn't often get the melody because of the gruffness of his voice." That gruffness – which Rolling Stone noted found Waits "singing in a strangled cigarette-and-whiskey voice" – the singer himself conceded to Audio Media magazine required Howe to put "strings behind everything because of my cracked voice. It's kind of like a painting that's made out of mud, and putting a real expensive frame around it."

Once Waits was finished hanging his latest gallery of what the New Yorker would hail as "extraordinarily moving" music and attention turned to mixing, the singer-songwriter wasn't shy about confessing to Musician magazine that "the process of 'mixing' makes me insane. I feel like I'm underwater without scuba gear." To keep all parties accommodated on that accord, Bones Howe shared that "I generally mixed without the artist in the control room, and gave them finished mixes to listen to. Its one thing to be in the studio and singing, doing something you're really comfortable doing in the studio. But when it comes to mixing, its not something that you do, and you were also mixing – particularly in the Sixties and Seventies – because you knew it was going to come out of a radio first. And you also had to think about how your audience is going to hear it, so its not as pure."

Howe, pointing to the irony that "with Waits, it was purer because we never expected to get played on the radio, and then always did," added that "Tom and I mixed the first two records together, and after that, there was no mixing. Tom would listen to a take of a song back after tracking in the studio, and approve or not. Occasionally, he would say something like 'I want to hear the saxophone louder on the call and response parts.' So we'd do it and make another take, but basically we never had those kinds of discussion. You're taping live to two-track, so when we listened, if it was a record, it was a record.

"I think having an opinion about things is much more important than being able to do anything. I always had opinions about every song on the Hot 100, I either loved it or hated it, and I knew why. I think that you need to have opinions about other people's mixes, and know why, and that defines your style in a way – in terms of how you hear things. I don't know anyone who's a successful producer in this business who doesn't listen to everybody else's records, and either love them or hate them."

A highlight project for all involved, upon completion, Waits shared with journalist Pete Oppel his excited feeling that "I'm proud of that record," while Bones Howe – offering a deeper analysis – recalled that "with every record I made with Tom, I tried to keep up with him. He was evolving, and it was my job to capture his evolution. I always said a record is a snapshot, it's where you are today, tomorrow you may be a completely different artist. It's just where you are today, so lets try to make this the best photograph we can right now, because next year it will be completely different.

"And you see the evolution of an artist when you go back through all of Waits' albums from 'The Heart Of Saturday Night' through 'Foreign Affairs'. You see how he developed, and he used to say my job was 'to hold the stick higher for him to jump over every time.' But that was all that I did in terms of 'go running in front', if you know what I mean? Everything else was working with, we were a team, collaborative. So his job was to create it, my job was to realise it. That's the way we worked, and I had loads of fun working with him. I do agree with him that those sessions were over too quickly, but they were loads of fun."

On a more serious note, arranger Jerry Yester offered his opinion that "this record was a little more grown-up than his last record, which certainly was the case with 'Invitation To The Blues', which really showcased Tom's ability to evoke period or a feeling of place and time, so it was fun to write for because it wasn't a case of 'What do I do here?' I did five string arrangements for that record, and one I remember being a particular challenge was 'Tom Traubert's Blues', because it was so long and so much the same. I'm really not happy with that song. I love it, but that is one I'd love to do again."

Upon the album's release in October, 1976, Waits continued to impress both fans and critics alike, beginning with Rolling Stone, who hailed Waits as "a brilliant chronicler of our past," adding that he had "returned to the melodic style which highlighted his first two LPs... His songs focus on...mood: the late-night blues where fatigue and romance mingle. The piano and occasional strings and saxophone relentlessly reinforce this atmosphere. His language still sparkles, the one-liners still dazzle...(He) continues to write superb songs (particularly 'Tom Traubert's Blues' and 'Invitation To The Blues')... Waits...(remains) an appealing...artist." His hometown paper, the LA Times, agreed, concluding that the singer-songwriter "delivered his fourth album, 'Small Change', the rich, expressive tour de force that established his reputation as an outright original." Reflecting Waits' growing fan base overseas, the BBC's reviewer concluded "this is one of the best albums I've ever heard... Primarily Tom sings his songs over a luscious mix of piano, strings and saxophones and the effect is just sublime."

For Waits, looking to the future, his aim seemed squarely on keeping momentum moving, sharing with journalist Jim Gerard that "I got the writing covered as far as new musical fabric is concerned. I'm working on stuff for a new album now. Before 'Small Change' was released I was out on the road, though. As soon as I get home in February I'm going to start another album." Regardless of outside critical labels – and they were plentiful as every big critic was racing to contribute their own spin to Waits' relevance – Tom viewed himself as "just a performer, a songwriter (and) an entertainer, I guess," adding in the same discussion with Contemporary Keyboard that "I think of myself more as a curator, an imagist... (that's) my main forte."

Joking to journalist Pete Oppel that "as a merchandisable property with a residual future, ('Small Change') didn't have a Chinaman's chance," Waits still seemed focused ambitiously on the future, reasoning to Rolling Stone that while "I'm not money-oriented except to the point that I have bills to pay and I have to support a trio. I want to be respected by my peers and I want my old man to think that what I'm doing is good. For me, it's more of an internal thing. I'm just trying to do something that I think is viable, that I can be proud of, trying to create something that wasn't there before... I've got to cinch something before we get out of the Seventies. I've got a lot invested in this whole thing – just in confidence – in my development as a writer and all that. I don't want to be a has-been before I've even arrived."

Tom explained that he was fulfilling a dream he'd held since childhood. "Since I was a kid I had an image of me in a dark sport coat and clean tie getting up and entertaining people. Even though I've had to do a lot of other things to make a buck, this is what I've always wanted to do." Having come full circle with the first stage of that vision, Tom told the LA Times that he remained going forward by another dream that had come to him more recently, wherein "there was a time back then when I could see that we were all going to wind up in the Salvation Army bargain bins unless we did something unique. It came to me in a dream. There was my album sitting in this big stack of old records underneath a bunch of old clothes and old platform shoes and shovels. So, in some way I realised I wanted to try to make something unique, something that you'd want to keep."

"The tunes I've written, they're not just about drunks. They're about murder and car wrecks and love...a lotta different things." – TOM WAITS

"My voice is changing... I'm just going through puberty. I'm a late bloomer." – TOM WAITS

PART VII: 'Foreign Affairs' (1977)

By the time of his fifth album, 'Foreign Affairs', Waits had built what Billboard acknowledged as "a steady cult audience that enjoyed his verbal flights and boozy philosopher persona," one that inspired Sounds music paper in Britain to add at the time that "since 1973's 'Closing Time', Tom Waits has been seen as the archetypal chronicler of American subterranean lowlife blues." Still, in spite of speaking for that underbelly, Creem noted that, by 1977, "now that he's made Time magazine and has five albums out on Asylum ('Foreign Affairs' is the newest), Tom Waits is the cat's meow."

Time magazine had observed in a spotlight feature with the singer-songwriter that, indeed, six years into his career, "Waits is playing fewer of the seedy nightclubs that have long been his backdrop as a performer and his inspiration as an artist. At 27, he is a street-smart scuffler who writes knowingly of dingy bars, all-night diners and down-and-outers on the make."

In spite of his rising star, Tom was quick to clarify in an interview with the Colorado Daily that "I don't write for the radio. I'm more concerned with what I can do with it on stage," adding in a conversation with Mojo that, at that point in his career – having spent an average of eight months out of every year on the road – "I was still in the rhythm of making a record, going out on the road for eight months, coming home and making another record, living in hotels. That's kind of what my life was in those days. I was trying to find some new channel or breakthrough for myself."

Part of that breakthrough did not have to do with his albums' subject matter, even though he'd been painted on occasion by select critics as a case of life-imitating-art in the context of his lifestyle mirroring his image. In answer to such depictions, Waits defended himself to Spin magazine, arguing at the time that "I've written a lot of songs... The tunes I've written, they're not just about drunks. They're about murder and car wrecks and love and...I write about a lotta different things."

Tom stated in a discussion with Relix magazine that, at the time, his topical fascinations in song were moving "away from unrequited love and more into auto accidents and homicides. My road manager thinks I'm becoming the Sam Peckinpah of music. I've had a lot of experience on the road. I've eaten in truck stops and shopped at trucker's supermarkets. I've hitch-hiked but I hate it and I won't pick 'em up. People look just like Charlie Manson and they're on narcotics and probably have firearms and concealed weapons. I don't trust 'em. I'm not going to pick up a guy with devil eyebrows and 'cunt' tattooed on his bicep. In LA in particular on the corner of Santa Monica and Western, it's Charlie Starkweather and Charlie Whitman or some four-speed transvestite."

Recounting the conceptual approach that Waits sought to take toward the latter end of 'Foreign Affairs' production, producer Bones Howe recalled that "I thought it was like a black and white movie, and that's why they did that album cover. There's a kind of feeling you get from the material when you listen to it." Expanding on the jazz-blues rock fusion of their last studio effort, Howe felt by this album that "in a way it was kind of a full-circle thing for me because I was able to bring all these guys in I'd worked with on jazz records into the studio with Tom, and he just loved what they did. And then he would bring stuff he liked, so it was the kind of relationship where we were always moving ahead."

Indeed, Billboard magazine would later note that, via production of his latest LP, "Waits gives one side of his fifth album, 'Foreign Affairs', to his more structured, bluesy ballads and the other to his jazz raps." Discussing the writing of some of the albums' specific tracks, Tom began with 'Potter's Field', sharing with Circus that the song was biographically named, and "just a stone's throw from Riker's Island, you know, the prison. When someone is found cold on a street, with no identification, they freeze 'em until they're identified, and if nobody claims 'em, and they aren't identified, they just throw 'em in a pine box with all their personal belongings and effects...

"They put 'em on a barge and send 'em out to Potter's Field. Bela Lugosi (the original Hollywood Dracula), was buried in Potter's Field – he made eleven million dollars and died penniless on the Lower East Side... So 'Potter's Field' is my story about a stoolpigeon in a bar selling information to a hitman who's lookin' for a guy named 'Nightsticks' who's hidin' out in Potter's Field. It's mostly a mystery like 'Odd Man Out.'" The song became so involved for Waits during its writing that he confessed to journalist Larry Goldstein that "it took a long time. Just the writing of it took a long time... Believe me!"

'Burma Shave' was a song Rolling Stone concluded "cannot be ignored". Tom told Time Out magazine that "Burma Shave is an American shaving-cream company, like Colgate. They advertise on the side of the road and they have these limericks which are broken up into different signs like pieces of a fortune cookie. You drive for miles before you get the full message. 'PLEASE DON'T'...five miles...'STICK YOUR ARM OUT SO FAR'...another five miles...'IT MIGHT GO HOME'...five more miles...'IN ANOTHER MAN'S CAR – BURMA SHAVE.' They reel you in. So when I was a kid I'd see these signs on the side of the road – BURMA SHAVE, BURMA SHAVE – and I'm young and I think it's the name of a town and I ask my dad, 'When we getting to Burma Shave?' So in the song I used Burma Shave as a dream, a mythical community, a place two people are trying to get to. They don't make it."

Of his collaboration with Bette Midler, which NME called "a divine duet". the singer-songwriter shared of the roots of their personal relationship to journalist

Larry Goldstein that "I met her, now let me see, a couple of years ago at the Bottom Line (a nightclub) in New York, and we got along famously. I admire her a great deal. And you know… I'll kick anybody's ass who knocks her."

Waits next explained to Relix that the friendship evolved quickly to where she became "a friend of mine. She asked me to write her a song so I wrote 'I Never Talk To Strangers.' She likes those old songs like, 'Baby It's Cold Outside', so I decided to write something that sounds like a standard." Expanding on the song's musical vibe, Tom added in a discussion with 90 Minutes Live that "I wrote that tune…with a kind of a 'Baby It's Cold Outside' sort of flavour that I really like." Rolling Stone would conclude that the results the pair created together sounded "ragged but right".

Tom detailed his band's player line-up to Circus magazine, recalling that "I've got Frank Vicari on tenor sax. Frank's an old veteran of the Woody Herman Band and Maynard Ferguson. He spends a good deal of time with me, he's my right hand man. I look up to Frank a lot. Musically he's brilliant. I've learned a great deal from Frank. I've also got Chip White on vibes and percussion, and Andy Trifan on upright bass." Of Waits' musical role, Rolling Stone would report that "on this spare, unsweetened album (no overdubs or multi-tracking), Waits plays his own trailing piano accompaniment."

Indeed, to maintain spontaneity throughout tracking, the singer-songwriter shared with the television show 90 Minutes Live that "we cut the whole thing like two-track in the studio. It's like uh, so there was no multi-tracking or overdubbing done, so I get a performance in the studio."

Arranger Jerry Yester, who worked alongside Waits and Howe for much of the latter catalogue added that "from all of the sessions I saw after that first album, not much changed in the way that he worked, and Bones was very good about that – because he was from the old days of making records. So there was no labouring the arrangements and doing things countless times – it was one or two takes. So he never got more technical in the studio, past arrangement ideas Bones and Tom might have come up with.

Delving deeper into Bones Howe's production approach by that point in his five album collaboration with Waits, Yester added feeling "impressed with Bones' going for live two-track, and backing up with 16-track. I really liked Bones' ease and comfort in the studio, he did his job so effortlessly. He was just about the most capable engineer I'd ever met, and I'd actually hired him to mix some songs from the Association back when I produced their second album, and we'd worked out of the same studios after that, engineering the Mamas and the Papas and some really fine records.

"Seeing him working with Tom years later, I always felt he was like an older brother to me, whether he knew it or not. I would have been glad to stay on as his producer, but I think its great he did get Bones, because Bones knew all those incredible musicians from the old days making jazz records, and through those relationships, could get those players on Tom's records quickly – and did get all these great musicians from the old days. Bones, being so good at what he was and so knowledgeable at the whole process, he was very good at putting Tom at ease and they were very comfortable with each other."

Recalling some of the band's many magically spontaneous moments, producer Howe recalled that "if you listen to the finished record of 'Burma Shave' – which was a case where Tom had listened to the full-band version and thought it would be better with just he singing and playing piano – when we listened to the records side by side, I said 'I agree the reading is much more poignant with you by yourself at the piano, but I gotta have Jack Sheldon's cadenza at the end – he played this wild trumpet at the very end of it. So he asked 'Well, can you cut it on there?' And I did, and he said 'That's great, it works great, let's leave it.' And that's the way it was, and the way we made so many of these records.

In other cases, the song worked better with the full rhythm section, but we put all the records together on our feet. On 'Foreign Affair', I said 'I gotta have a musette on this record.' So Pete Challey came in with his accordion, and was also a great jazz pianist, so we always had these people who moulded themselves into the recording sessions. Shelly Manne, who I'd known for years, played on a Waits record, and he and Waits loved each other because they were the same kind of people."

When discussion turned to Waits' lead vocal tracking, Tom explained at the time in an interview with journalist Pete Oppel that he felt "my voice is changing, that's why, I'm just going through puberty. I'm a late bloomer, I'm developing a bit of a conversational style, but then I never was an Anna Maria Alberghetti. Those efforts were thwarted by continuous self abuse." Rolling Stone would observe of Tom's vocal style on the record that "his singing again shows traces of that gritty but well-modulated, Fred Neil-like style that made 'Closing Time' so insistent."

Bones Howe revealed from his memory the only difficult moment during the recording of 'Foreign Affairs's vocals coming with Waits' collaboration with Bette Midler, who Howe remembers "drove me crazy when she duetted with Tom on 'I Never Talk To Strangers', because she kept saying 'I need to fix this, that's out of tune', and I said 'Bette, it's the record. And she hounded me for days and days. When you make a record with Waits, it's the record, we're done."

Upon completion and release, among the other affairs the album continued was Waits' own with his adoring music critics. This continued as passionately as ever before, with Rolling Stone affectionately concluding that 'Foreign Affairs' "shows…Waits' voice and ability to write moving lyrics…as he stacks up fresh, filmic images that make you care about this cowboy punk and the small-town girl who hopped into his wreck." San Francisco Weekly would admire the album as a "tender work," and the BBC reviewer highlighted "'A Sight For Sore Eyes', 'Potter's Field', 'Barber Shop' and the title track" as favourites.

Rolling Stone magazine, a dedicated fan of Waits' work to date, continued the critical love affair with their conclusion that "Tom Waits is never less than intent and honest – he pushes to his own slow, heartfelt beat…'Foreign Affairs'…shows that Waits is still the kind of performer who can make us say: 'You must be reading my mail.'" By that point in his career, Tom seemed content with what he proudly deemed "a signature," adding in closing comments to Time magazine that "it's nice to have your own niche… I have my own turf."

"I wrote 'Blue Valentine' in a month. The whole thing." – TOM WAITS, 1979

PART VIII: 'Blue Valentine' (1978)

By 1978, Tom Waits' status was that of a "singer whose cult has definitely grown to a national following," as one major music media magazine – Hit Parader – took note of. Q magazine retrospectively added that four albums into his career, the singer-songwriter "mindful that he was getting stuck in a retro groove…switched from piano to electric guitar for much of 'Blue Valentine'."

Having reached that decision independently of any commercial pressure, Waits – in an interview with Sounds – quipped that "I suppose my style is reflected in my sales figures, but fortunately my record company doesn't stand over my shoulder and tell me what to do. If I wanted that I would've been working in a car wash or something."

Still, he did seem to empathise a bit with the fact that "I'm not easy to merchandise," adding in the same discussion with Hit Parader that he does the majority of his marketing "on the road…(where I spend) eight months a year. That's what I end up doing and that's more of a sales pitch than anything anyone else can do." That said, Tom shared with NME that one area he remained entirely protective of was his live set lists, such that "I don't ask the audience (what I should sing). I don't have any hits. Helen Keller gets more (radio) airplay than I do. I'll do whatever I want on the stage. They don't play me on the radio stations so when I get on stage it's my radio show and I'll do whatever I want."

Tom admitted to Hit Parader on his musical ambitions that, while commerciality didn't factor into his songwriting equation this time out, "I try to make some kind of breakthrough on each album – that's why each album is more difficult to do than the one before. That's why the stories are so important to me, and show some other sides of me. I'm going to try and write with that in mind."

Billboard would later declare Waits' effort toward that end a success once again, noting that "though his world view remains fixed on the lowlifes of the late night, he expands beyond the musings of the barstool philosopher who previously had acted as the first-person character of most of his songs… The result is a broadening of subject matter, a narrative discipline that makes most of the tunes, story songs and a coherent framing for Waits' typically colourful and intriguing imagery."

Seeking a stylistic change-up that became Tom's invitation incorporate the blues into his sound, Bones Howe recalled that – from a production point of view

– "for 'Blue Valentine', Waits wanted to do a blues album, and Tom's blues album is entirely different than, say, a John Lee Hooker album. A Waits blues album is a Waits blues album, and it defies definition." This was true for Waits from a compositional angle, offering of the challenge to music writer Charley Delisle that writing "the album was a huge boulder I had to move. There was pressure, but it was my own pressure. Most people think, 'Oh yeah, he's the guy that writes about winos and hookers.' That is just not true. I've written a wide range of songs about different kinds of experiences. A writer should challenge himself with a variety of subject matter and be able to do that well."

One strain that remained consistent throughout Waits' writing on 'Blue Valentine' was his focus on the dark side of city life, confessing candidly to journalist Greg Linder that "I can't write about 'Dear baby I love you and everything's gonna be alright 'cause we're gonna get married.' It's presented problems in my personal life as well. I've just developed a more and more grim attitude." That attitude, in terms of his success in carving out a niche all his own among the most celebrated singer-songwriters of the Seventies, had been both "a blessing and a curse" as a composer, with Waits adding to Hit Parader that while "its important to have an image, and a signature and all that, and I'm glad I have…but from there I want to build."

Tom demonstrated a creative discipline even as ideas poured out of him, revealing in the same conversation that, once he got down to business, he hunkered down in "a little room in Hollywood where I go – by Van Ness and Sunset, next to the Denny's. I wrote all the songs on 'Blue Valentine' between here and there in three weeks."

Utilising his home town once again as a muse, the singer-songwriter confirmed to Circus that "most of the stories on 'Blue Valentine' took place in Los Angeles in the last few months," adding to Hit Parader that the latter-mentioned regimen was required simply because when "I go out on the road for so long, and I play my songs so much…I have to come home and write new stuff just so I'll have new tunes to take out… I don't write on the road anymore – too busy. Somebody pulling on my coat all the time; get no sleep; different town every night. I'm a real scatterbrain out there – now I just come home to write."

Exploring some of the lyrical territory inspired by LA's urban underbelly, Waits began with 'A Sweet Little Bullet From A Pretty Blue Gun', explaining to Greg Linder that "it's about a suicide on Hollywood Blvd. About a year ago, this 15 year-old girl jumped out of a 17th-floor window with a guitar. Never made Crawdaddy magazine. You never hear those stories."

Turning to '$29.00', Tom offered that the tune was "originally inspired by my neighbour. I live next door to two pimps and one night about three in the morning I heard somebody screaming on the phone. 'Twenty-nine dollars! Twenty-nine dollars! Twenty-nine DOLLARS!! One of his girls had her dress ripped by a trick and she wanted him to reimburse her for the dress and the dress cost $29.'

Continuing, Tom explained that "I heard $29 for an hour and I was trying to watch The Twilight Zone. So I opened the window and I said fuck a whole bunch of $29, and they got quiet. Months later it stayed abreast in my imagination and

I wrote '$29.00'." He told Circus magazine that 'Romeo Is Bleeding' was "about a Mexican gang leader who was shot and died in a movie house in downtown LA" Turning to 'Christmas Card From A Hooker In Minneapolis', Tom revealed to the Star Tribune that "the elements of a story usually come from different places. You put 'em together like a model. No, I didn't actually get a Christmas card, but it's more like an impression of events that have happened."

New Musical Express would eventually note of Waits' powerfully graphic writing on the record that "as an arranger and tunesmith working the cool blue jazz sphere Waits was peerless... His unique power came from contrasting those talents with his coarse gut-bucket growl and mesmerising wordplay. Waits mined the post-war fault line of Kerouac and the Beats, focusing on the loners and losers that littered America's highways and byways."

The Guardian, meanwhile, observed of his craft that "there's something almost Shakespearean about the breadth of Tom Waits' take on modern American life, his astounding capacity to get into the heads and lungs of, inter alia: barflies, hookers, junkies, fairground barkers and burlesque crooners; veteran soldiers with shrapnel-freckled limbs, reduced to selling their tin stars on the sidewalk; Pentecostal thunderers roaring doom; washed-up baseball stars wasted by booze; psychos on a short fuse; woeful optimists losing it in the marinade of their Martinis."

Once his songs were written, Waits set about assembling a band to bring the specific style of music he heard in his head to life. This required him making a complete line-up change, a move he admitted to music writer Charley Delisle "was tough... I'm changing my sound a little. Something different. I've got to keep it fresh. God, it was tough letting those guys go," before adding of his new band that "they are all Negroes. I'm the only spot in the group." As producer Bones Howe recalled, the player swaps had come in part because "Tom had gotten fascinated with second-line rhythm sections, like those in New Orleans. So we had put together some players for the record, and for this rhythm section, he said he had heard this sound in his head when he was creating these songs."

Opting to track the album out of Filmways/Heider Studio B, fittingly located in the heart of Hollywood, Waits sang the studio's historic praises to journalist Stephen Peebles, recalling that "we worked in the RCA building on Ivar and Sunset... The Stones worked there. I heard the Monkees did, too. Oh, yeah, Ray Charles and Cleo Laine recorded an album in that room with Frank de Vol. They did excerpts from Porgy And Bess about 1975-'76. Martin Mull cut his last Elektra LP, the live one, there, too."

Howe revealed of album's sonic evolution that "once the band was in the studio, and starting to do them, they began to shape themselves into that mould. So you hear some things which are more traditional Waits from the records before, and then some things that are completely different in terms of the ways they moved on."

Making no secret of his distaste for the recording process, Tom candidly volunteered to journalist Larry Goldstein that he considered it to be the equivalent of "cruel and unusual punishment. It's excruciating, like going to the dentist." For

Howe, working around Waits' attitude as the pair navigated through recording was a matter of communicating on a level that the producer recalled "by that time, Tom joked that he and I were like 'an old married couple.' I would argue with him about sequence, and say 'Don't you think the rhythm section ought to be such and such or so and so?'

"But we always came to an agreement that we were both excited about. It was never somebody giving up something for the other person, except when it came to the sequences. Sometimes I would be so sure that we needed to open the album with a particular cut, and he would disagree, and we would have this song, drawn out argument about it. I would keep prodding at him and prodding at him, and he would finally say 'Un uh, that's the way its gonna be.' That's the way it was with us. I would make a suggestion, and he would say 'Well, okay, let's try it.' But if he was set on something, then we would do it."

Waits again returned to '$29.00' to offer an example of that process in action with his new band, sharing with journalist Greg Linder that "I've known George Duke since he worked with Frank Zappa and the Mothers. That's where I met George. I used to do a thing on stage with the Mothers. Frank called me Wino Man. Wino Man would come out and tell a little story. Anyway, before George worked with Frank he worked with Cannonball Adderley, and now he's on his own doing a get-your-hands-together kind of funk thing. He's more successful with that.

"So I took George and his group into the studio with me and they got into this sort of funk thing. Hey-ah-doddely-ooh-dow. Hey-ah-doddley-ooh-dow. I said 'NO!' I was the only spot on the stage, if you know what I mean. I told George to play like early Ray Charles and we did a tune called '$29.00'." Rolling Stone would later conclude the recorded results ranked "high among the sentimental sagas that contain Tom Waits' strongest writing."

Recorded live in the studio as with all his previous albums, Circus magazine reported of the album's recording that it was done "with no overdubs. Waits plays electric guitar and acoustic piano." Discussing what he felt his role as pianist was in a blues context, Waits reasoned that it didn't vary much from his past albums, calling himself a "pedestrian piano player" in a conversation with Contemporary Keyboard magazine, where he added of his technique that "I'm a writer, I compose melodies… I don't hardly take any solos; I 'solo' lyrically or with a story-tinged approach to the keyboard."

Joking that when tracking his vocals for the record, "I was trying to sing instead of just growling and grunting," the singer-songwriter told journalist Larry Goldstein that "by the time I get off the road it's all I can muster up." Tracing the R&B roots of his voice to "the music of the Sixties," Tom added in conversation with journalist Nigel Williamson that "when you're trying to find an original voice, you look (in) a lot of different places to discover who you are and find something that's uniquely you. And to do that you take a little bit of something from whatever you can find."

With tracking completed in just six recording sessions, producer Bones Howe reflected back on the end product he and Waits had created in context of the singer's stylistic ambitions. "Every record had its own kind of musical personality, and that was the personality of 'Blue Valentine'. In a way, 'Small Change' and 'Foreign Affairs' are in a period, there's a lot of stuff that's the same about them, but then Tom started getting caught up in this idea of second line and blues."

Released in September 1978, critics like the BBC were instantly impressed with the album. "Waits shakes things up a bit on this one, his most musically diverse album up to this point in his career. It opens with 'Somewhere' (from West Side Story) with the same orchestral sound established on 'Foreign Affairs' but the song lacks momentum, though it's pleasant enough. The second song, 'Red Shoes By The Drugstore', has a predatory drum and bass line with ghostly piano shimmering in and out. 'Christmas Card From A Hooker In Minneapolis' is a jazzy musing with flirtatious piano licks and so the album continues with each track being distinctly different from the others – and yet it works as a whole… It's worth the price of admission for the aforementioned 'Christmas Card'…and the fragile tale of growing up, 'Kentucky Avenue'. That one song puts a tear in my every time. Very good album in my opinion, don't overlook it."

Back home in the States, Billboard took an instant liking to the fact that, throughout 'Blue Valentine', "Waits alters the instrumentation, bringing in electric guitar and keyboards and largely dispensing with the strings for a more blues-oriented, hard-edged sound," further noting that while the singer-songwriter hadn't made "radical reinventions" to his overarching sound, the fact that he'd achieved a "course correction was big news".

Rolling Stone found Waits' new sound pleasing enough to the ear to conclude that "on the whole, though, 'Blue Valentine' is as solid a record as Waits has made." Looking to his future in a business where his star was continuing its slow rise, Tom seemed determined to keep his feet on the ground and head out of the proverbial clouds, reasoning to Creem magazine that "a lot of people end up writing about what they're going through inside the machinery. I think you have to focus on other things, and keep as open as you can to different musical influences. That's what I'm trying to do…"

"I don't know how I'm looked upon in the context of American culture. It has to do with how long you stay around. How long you're allowed to stay around." – TOM WAITS, 1981

PART IX: 'Heartattack And Vine' (1980)

'Heartattack And Vine' was Tom Waits' going electric, a pleasant shock for fans of an artist who volunteered to NME at the outset of the album's recording that "I think I'd like to try some rock'n'roll... I don't really know, I just got this idea in my head to try something a little harder."

He added in an interview with WNEW New York that "I'm really kind of poised on the threshold on some sort of a new direction. I'm working on a new project... (where) I'm looking for something that's a little more refreshing for me." Indeed, the album marked a significant departure for Waits, comparable to Bob Dylan's similar decision on 'Blonde On Blonde'.

In describing how Waits stumbled upon the electrified sound that would define the album overall, longtime producer Bones Howe began by offering that, indeed, "Heartattack And Vine' was an entirely different kind of feel from any album we'd done before." He recalled the genesis of what would become a new signature in Waits' sound for years after coming one day when "Tom and I were sitting in a rehearsal room in the back of his manager's office, and there was a set of drums in there.

"Waits brought in an electric guitar, and started playing, and I hopped behind the drums. So he hit the few open chords to the song, I started thumping on the drums, and he said 'That's the sound of the record.'

One aspect of Waits' sound that had stayed constant throughout his career, as noted by Rolling Stone, was the fact that, "for almost a decade, Waits has submerged his own personality and played this role so completely that he's now a willing surrogate for all the low-life dreamers who don't have his gift of gab."

Confirming to Australian television host Don Lane that, indeed, "most of my songs are kinda travelogues," he explained to the LA Times that, on the surface, his muses included "hobos, prostitutes, people in trouble, the negative machinery I create to motivate myself." He added to Melody Maker that, on a deeper level, "I twist whatever I see, you know. Most of my writing is a metaphor for something else."

Though the outside world was his muse, during proper writing for the album, Waits revealed a far tamer routine to Melody Maker wherein "I usually go to a room and I stay there until I'm done, and that's where my real rewards are." Describing himself to Sounds as "a bit of a workaholic really," Tom added in the same conversation that "I quite enjoy my own company and when I do get time to myself I usually like to spend it alone in some hotel room catching up on my sleep or working on my new project cause it takes a great deal of concentration." Fans would also be surprised to learn that, in spite of his boozy on-stage persona, Waits shared with NME that "when I'm writing I'm usually pretty clean. I don't think it's alcohol that makes the music come out. It's hard to tell. Sometimes alcohol massages the beast, sometimes it doesn't. I kinda subscribe to my own particular madness rather than soak it."

Revealing that his inspiration came in "seasons as a writer", the singer-songwriter shared with journalist Stephen Peebles that in the course of writing material for his new album, he was imploring a bit of a different approach wherein "at this point, I'm trying to learn how to write faster. I just used to brood over songs for months and months. The writing for 'Heartattack And Vine' was more spontaneous." As he began to share the music he'd been writing for the new album with Bones Howe, the producer recalled a trend developed wherein "Tom would write the songs, then we would pick them, and then talk about what they were going to be, and there was always a link backwards to what he had done before, and always something new."

Delving into the writing of specific album cuts, beginning with the album's title track, Tom shared with journalist Stephen Peebles of its inspiration that "I was in a bar one night on Hollywood Boulevard near Vine Street, and this lady came in with a dead animal over her arm, looking like she'd obviously been sleeping outdoors. She walked up to the bartender and said, 'I'm gonna have a heart attack', and he says, 'Yeah, right, you can have it outside.' I thought that was pretty chilly. So I re-named Hollywood Blvd 'Heartattack'."

Bones Howe added of the latter bar that, indeed, "with 'Heartattack And Vine', the way the title came to him, there used to be a bar on the Sunset Strip just east of Western Recorders, called the Ski Room. It was a bar downstairs with a sleazy hotel upstairs, and Tom used to go drink with the characters at the bar, and he would get a lot of ideas from what he'd hear at the bar. So one day he came to me and said 'I was in the Ski Room, and there was this guy sitting at the bar, and he had obviously had had too much to drink. And he kept asking the bar tender for another drink, and the bar tender kept refusing, and the guy finally said, 'You have to give me another drink, I'm a heart attack.' So Tom walked out of the bar, which wasn't at Hollywood and Vine, it was about six blocks from there, but he said 'Heartattack And Vine', and that was the title of the song and album. It was the ultimate down-and-out-in-Hollywood song, without really talking about Hollywood so much."

Discussing the now-legendary line from the title track's chorus, 'Don't you know there's no devil, its just God when he's drunk', Waits shared with NME of its birth that "I was just sitting on the toilet, and there was this spider web in the corner, and I lit a match and a cigarette, and I held the match up to the spider and the spider started crawling up the web. So I got the match closer. I opened up a can of beer, drank the beer, tried to decide whether I should burn the spider off his web or let him go on his way... I figured there must be somebody like that up there: has a coupla cocktails every now and then and there's trouble on Times Square."

Turning to Waits' more familiar ballad territory of 'On The Nickel', Tom – in a discussion with Australian television host Don Lane – traced its real life inspiration to "downtown Los Angeles…(where) there's a place called Fifth Street, it's a place where all the hoboes are, and they call it 'On The Nickel.' There was a motion picture called On The Nickel…and this is a story, kinda a wino's lullaby." Turning to the muse behind several of the album's other tracks in a conversation with journalist Stephen Peebles, Tom – beginning with 'In Shades' – explained that "originally, it was titled 'Breakfast In Jail', but we changed it," then adding of 'Saving All My Love for You' that it was "an old song, about four years old. It was scratched off of another album, I think 'Foreign Affairs'," before closing with perhaps the record's most personalised ballad, 'Jersey Girl', which Tom candidly recalled "I wrote…for my wife, she's from Jersey, well she's originally from Illinois, she moved to New Jersey, and she grew up there, Morristown, New Jersey, and so I wrote it for her when we met."

Recorded in the summer of 1980 between mid-June and mid-July, Waits decided to work once again with longtime producer Bones Howe, Waits confessed in the same conversation with Peebles that initially "I had some plans to explore new producers. I'd moved to New York for about five-six months, wanting to challenge myself with an entirely new environment. But my relationship with Bones has been a very close and personal one. That for me is more important than anything when you're in the studio – to have somebody you can trust and who knows you, knows who you are and doesn't let you get away with anything. I didn't really want to disturb that relationship. But at the time I thought I wanted to change everything. Then I decided that the change was something that had to take place inside of me and with my own musical growth. I wanted to take some dangerous chances, and I felt Bones could best accommodate me."

One personnel change the singer-songwriter did make ahead of beginning recording on the new LP came with his band, which he explained in an Island promo interview was necessitated because "the subject-matter that I was dealing with was caustic enough to require an ensemble that perhaps sounded a little more jagged, so I considered musicians and selected the band with that in mind. It's not Mahogany Rush, but it's the best I can do. I let a drummer use sticks for the first time, instead of brushes. I mean I used to hear everything with upright bass, muted trumpet or tenor sax. I just had a sort of limited musical scope, so I wanted to try to stretch out a little bit on the new one. I think I've accomplished that to a degree. It's all part of an ongoing process."

Elaborating on the specifics of the player shake-ups in the same discussion, Tom shared that "I used my drummer from the road, 'Big John' Thomassie, who's from New Orleans. He used to play with Freddie King, Dr John and Bonnie Bramlett. He's been with me on the road for two years now, and this is the first record he's done with me. Then there's Ronnie Barron on piano, who's also from New Orleans and is someone I've admired for many years. It was a real pleasure working with him. He played (Hammond) B-3 (organ) and piano. Larry Taylor, who's from Canned Heat, is on bass.

"On guitar we had Roland Bautista, who grew up on Slauson Avenue (in Los Angeles), and that was good enough for me. But he's played with George Duke and the Crusaders before and does a lot of session work in LA In addition to the quartet, I had Jerry Yester (producer of Waits' first LP, 'Closing Time', in '73 and frequent string arranger on subsequent albums) write two arrangements, and had Bob Alcivar do another two. Bob worked on 'Foreign Affairs' and wrote 'Potter's Field' with me. He's done some other arrangements and things for me, too. He's also working as orchestrator and arranger on the Coppola project. He's had experience as a film composer himself."

Turning to the technical specifics of tracking the latter musical ensemble, producer Bones Howe recalled that "the production was done the same way we'd done all his albums previously in terms of tracking live to a two-inch reel. We did everything live, because there's an immediacy about tracking live that always worked well for him." A daring approach considering Waits admission to Melody Maker that "it's a little difficult for me in the studio. I don't feel comfortable. It's like so antiseptic, you know. I pull away from anybody who's tried to give me any sort of direction, never had anybody look over my shoulder, tell me what to do. I don't turn it into a party or anything."

To ensure the process of recording stayed focused at all times, Tom revealed to journalist Stephen Peebles that "I moved in there and lived there while we recorded. Everybody thought I was crazy, but it seemed to help me a lot. Our recording schedule was to begin about two every afternoon. I just wanted to stay there because I was writing about one tune ahead of Bones every day. I was writing each night and every day so when the band got there I'd have something new for everybody. So it was valuable for me to be writing in the same environment I was recording in. I'd never tried to do it that way before. It's a lot of work, it's not a party. I don't invite anyone that's not directly involved in the sessions. I sweat bullets for a month and a half, but my relationship with Bones was very healthy during the whole procedure. He had a lot of faith in me that I'd be able to work under those conditions. It would make a lot of producers very nervous to be working against a deadline like that with all that gold riding on it."

Pulling back the curtain on how he and Waits achieved the electrified sound that defined the overarching sonics of 'Heartattack And Vine', producer Bones Howe shared that "in terms of the guitar sound on the album, that's just the way Waits' amp sounds when he plays it. Its got a broken speaker, and how it sounded naturally on tape. Putting these things back in context, you have to think about what was happening then. I bought Tom a copy of an Asia album because I wanted Tom to hear how strong the jazz influences had come into that area of pop music. And he wanted to get away from this kind of pretty piano sound to something more funky, that was part of his purpose. He didn't want to do blues, he wanted to do it funky."

His vocal style of delivery, Tom confessed to NME, came from an inner sense that "I think my voice is ready for it now. I'm ready to scream...yeah, I really feel like screaming." In spite of its ragged glory, during recording, Tom actually made an attempt to clean up his pipes, sharing with journalist Stephen Peebles that "I quit smoking during the recording of the new one. Maybe that had something to do with it. I tried to arrive at some level of personal hygiene. I thought the record deserved that. I just tried to clean myself up a little. I think it helped."

Delving into the recording of the album's individual tracks, Waits began with 'Downtown', recalling to Peebles that the song was "a first take. I was just running it down to the band just to learn it, but it became the record. We tried several other versions of it but this take seemed to be the one that took. I love Ronnie's organ solo. It's real amphetamine. The tune's just a fast story, like a fast news update." In the same discussion, Waits offered of the instrumental 'In Shades' that "I always wanted to put out just a little straight R&B instrumental."

Turning to his tribute to wife Kathleen Brennan, 'Jersey Girl', producer Bones Howe recalled that, from a derivative vantage point, "Tom wanted to do a rip-off of the Boss by putting the bells on the end of the song. Its like a celeste, a keyboard instrument but when its played it sounds like orchestra bells, and we did that as an overdub. 'Jersey Girl' was about his future wife Kathleen, and he was entering his electric period." Quipping in a conversation with journalist Stephen Peebles that "I never thought I would catch myself saying 'sha la la' in a song'," Waits added that he was going for "one of them kinda Drifters feels. I didn't wanna say 'muscular dystrophy' in it or anything, 'cause I didn't think it fit in with the feel of the number. So lyrically I tried to do it straight ahead, a guy walking down the street to see his girl."

Stringmaster and arranger Jerry Yester, elaborating on the R&B influence Waits sought to reflect in the song, offered that "Tom wanted a Ronettes influence in 'Jersey Girl', little elements of the Wall of Sound influence on Tom's stuff, and that is Phil Spector. Tom said 'Okay man, let's do it.' Then I listened back, and I'd gotten an orchestra bells to do the glockenspiel, but I couldn't hear it in there on the playback. It wasn't that kind of song, and Tom was really disappointed with it, he almost got angry at the session and said 'Man, this doesn't sound like Bruce Springsteen.' And I said 'Neither does the song, Tom', and he almost didn't record it. He begrudgingly went over, sat down and recorded it, and I think Bones the next day said 'Tom, I think you need to listen to this again because it's pretty good. Its not what you might have been looking for, but its just as good.' Then Tom called me and said virtually the same thing, 'Listen, I'm sorry about all that, I really like the way it came out.' And I told him I agreed, and it became a great song."

Discussing the song's arrangement, Yester added that "on Jersey Girl, Tom was first interested in a song of mine called 'Brooklyn Girl', and first said he wanted to use it, but then got inspired to write 'Jersey Girl', because Tom doesn't really do other people's songs. So when he was talking about the arrangement, he knew what he wanted, and said he wanted to it to sound like Bruce Springsteen. That sound is what he wanted. He said, 'I'll get you a couple of his albums, I want you to listen to them, I want to get that feel on this', went to Tower Records and when he walked in, unbeknownst to him, Bruce Springsteen happened to be at that same store at the same time!" The moment was so serendipitous that Yester even recalled that "they arrived at the checkout counter at the same time, and Tom had two of Bruce's albums, and Bruce had two of Tom's albums. They became good friends after that."

In discussing 'Ruby's Arms', Waits seemed the biggest fan – in context of the song's various musical elements – of its arrangement, sharing with journalist Stephen Peebles that "I love Jerry's arrangement on it. He used a brass choir and made it sound like a Salvation Army band at the top of the tune. It really got me. It's a little bit like that Matt Monro thing, 'Softly As I Leave You.' I was trying to visualise this guy getting up in the morning before dawn and leaving on the train, with the clothesline outside. I just closed my eyes and saw this scene and wrote about it."

Yester offered his own fond recollection of the song's creation that "Tom really loved Ruby, really loved Ruby. My wife and I were both at that session. Bones I remember on the tape that was used for that session, before we started tracking, said 'Okay, let's get Jerry's child born.' The money I was getting for that gig was paying for my child's birth. The string section was similar to 'Small Change', but had brass also, it was the same group – we did 'Ruby' and followed it with 'Jersey Girl' in the same session. Tom played guitar along with the band."

Upon release in September, 1980, critics would almost universally celebrate Waits' sonic breakthrough, beginning with Rolling Stone magazine's note that "on 'Heartattack And Vine', the patron saint of America's hobo hipsters returns to the sentimental ballad style he abandoned for jazzier, less song-oriented turf after 'The Heart Of Saturday Night'," while the San Francisco Chronicle observed that Waits – who the paper noted had become "a cult phenomenon by the early Eighties" – had successfully "recast himself as rock 'n' roll's ingenious rag man" with a sound that the BBC celebrated as "twisted roadhouse blues-rock."

Spending three months on Billboard's Top 200, critics picked up on an optimism woven into Waits' latest musical offering that Q magazine would note as a "theme of lowlife redemption, of escape," while Rolling Stone magazine offered its conclusion that "in a time when hipness is often equated with selfishness, Waits' woozy, far-out optimism has never seemed fresher."

In the wake of the album's release, producer Bones Howe recalled that the singer-songwriter was at a point where "his life was changing rapidly at that point, he and Kathleen were deeply in love, and he'd moved out of the hotel, and had informed me he wanted to produce his next record himself. We had a very amicable parting. I told him 'you know the kind of record I'll make with you, so if you ever want to make a record like that again, call me and I'll be waiting.' That was the last time that we ever talked about working together personally."

Commenting for his own part on he and Howe going their separate ways, Waits reflected in a conversation with Mojo magazine that "I don't know if I'd call it particularly unhappy, but I was at the end of a cycle there…When you're working with the same producer and you're kind of collaborating on the records, it's a little harder to go your own way. You kind of wanna take everybody with you. For me, eventually I just wanted to make a clean break. Both those records I did with Bones, and I was kind of rebelling against this established way of recording that I'd developed with him. And I was still with Herbie Cohen in this tight little world."

Waits seemed to welcome the season of change blooming in his life at that point, beginning with wife Kathleen, who he candidly confessed to journalist Johnny Black he'd "spent ten miserable years looking for." He added to Rolling Stone of their union that "we met on New Year's Eve. Roy Brown was playing. It was love at first sight. We got married in Watts, at the Always and Forever Wedding Chapel, twenty-four-hour service on Manchester Boulevard… She's my true love."

Waits shared in the same conversation with Black of the couple's honeymoon that, because "my wife's part Irish, we spent our honeymoon crawling up and down the shoulders of Ireland for the last three weeks. Best thing that ever happened to me. We stayed in an old house, used to be owned by William Blake. Radio was busted, so we called down to the guy on the desk but he'd gone to get parts for the radio. Didn't come back for four days. Just great. They live at my level of incompetence. We fit in real well there."

On the professional front, coupled with Waits' new sonic direction, he seemed eager to broaden his stylistic horizons, confessing to Rolling Stone that, by the end of the Seventies, he felt "felt like one of those guys playing the organs in a hotel lobby, making the boom-chicka-chicka sound of a cheesy rhythm machine for emphasis. I'd bring the music in like carpet, and I'd walk on it. My wife, she's the one who pushed me. Finding a new way of thinking – that came from her… She encouraged me to take more risks in my writing." Admitting some nervousness about moving beyond the sound that had come to define his sound for over 10 years with his admission to journalist Bill Foreman that "people want to get you to the point where they know who you are and what you are so they can just kinda bottle it, so you can have one of everything. And it's difficult to grow up in public and be allowed to change and experiment."

His change in musical styles from acoustic to electric gave him the potential to also expand his fan base. For Tom this specifically translated to a desire to grow beyond piano lounges, quipping to NME that "the only trouble with going to heaven is that I'm scared that there's no nightclubs up there. I think I'd rather go down there. I'm sure all my friends are down there. All my heroes… It's taken seven years and I've gone from beer bars to small theatres, so I guess you could say that I'm breaking out of the bars."

One territory where Waits was making progress in growing his fan base was internationally, where he shared with Australian television host Don Lane during a tour of that country promoting 'Heartattack And Vine' that "I have a growing level of popularity throughout the intercontinental United States, Japan, and I travel extensively in Europe, as well. I don't do half bad." Indeed, the same talk show host, in introducing Waits to his studio audience, would note of his progress that "one of the newest singing phenomena's overseas is a 29-year-old, gravelly-voiced singer/poet."

Elaborating more directly on his desire to grow his audience back home in the United States, Waits offered candidly to Melody Maker that, heading into the

Eighties, "I don't want to play beer bars for another seven years...because I don't get played on the radio ever. Marcel Marceau gets more airplay than I do. I heard myself once in North Dakota, that's all. I was in Michigan somewhere and I was listening to the radio, and I called the disc jockey. I said, 'Listen – I just played a concert, sold out a twenty-five hundred auditorium. And I'm bustin' my chops, would ya mind, you know?' He said, 'Who is this?' I said, 'My name is Tom Waits.' He said, 'No it isn't.' Hung up on me... In the States I'm starting to play auditoriums now. Old movie theatres. I like that fine... I'd like to make some kind of breakthrough."

"The project was so interesting and I was new to it. The money didn't matter. Money's not a barometer for me, never has been."
– TOM WAITS, 1982

"For Waits, the movie offered an opportunity to reach a wider audience than the cult following his albums had garnered."
– CITY LIMITS MAGAZINE

"For me, I just like the way his mind works. He's unlearned a lot of things and he's managed to remain very childlike in terms of his imagination. He also has a considerable amount of leadership quality, and that's rare. He inspires the people around him."
– TOM WAITS ON FILM-MAKER FRANCIS FORD COPPOLA

PART X: 'One From The Heart' (1982)

As the Eighties unfolded, Tom Waits was in the midst of an artistic – and arguably personal – period of confusion. He tod Melody Maker in 1981 that, in stylistic terms, he felt he'd "painted myself into a corner. I'd fallen in with a bad crowd and needed a new landscape, a new story."

Waits had been astute in selling his image both live and in song to his fan base over the last decade, but was beginning to feel his life had begun to imitate his art to the extent that he began considering a radical change of course. "I just got totally disenchanted with the music business. I moved to New York and was seriously considering other possible career alternatives...Away for three months, come back with high blood pressure, a drinking problem, tuberculosis, a warped sense of humour. It just became predictable."

Seeking a departure from that uninspiring norm, Waits told journalist Dave Zimmer that opportunity knocked when "I was in New York back in April of 1980. Francis Ford Coppola was there auditioning people he wanted to be involved with the film. Somebody had sent him my records and Francis liked the song 'I Never Talk To Strangers', a duet I'd done with Bette Midler. He liked the relationship between the singers, a conversation between a guy and a girl in a bar. That was the impetus for him contacting me and asking me if I was interested in writing music for his film."

It was just the shot in the arm Waits needed to get renewed musical inspiration. Waits told City Limits magazine that he "got a call in the middle of the night and went over. It was like having an audience with the Pope." While attracted artistically to "the sole process of making music that would adhere to film," Waits admitted it was "a little terrifying (because)...it was still something new to me." The singer added that at that point, creatively, "I needed something to stimulate my growth and development...(and) working with Francis seemed like a good opportunity." Waits' entry into the film world via scoring was a perfect blend of his sensibility for what fitted a character or scenery in a visual context.

Waits opted to team up once again with longtime producer Bones Howe, staying for the time being in comfortably familiar territory where his recording making process was concerned to temper the stylistic chances he was taking. While, initially, he had plans to explore new producers, "I'd moved to New York for about five-six months, wanting to challenge myself with an entirely new environment. But my relationship with Bones has been a very close and personal one. That for me is more important than anything when you're in the studio – to have somebody you can trust and who knows you, knows who you are and doesn't let you get away with anything. I didn't really want to disturb that relationship."

Bones Howe recalled to journalist Dave Zimmer that "it just wasn't happening for him. None of it – neither the producers nor the city itself. New York, New York may be a wonderful town, where the Bronx is up and the Battery down, but Tom Waits was feeling a little lost." Taking his longtime collaborator back to California to begin work on the soundtrack, Howe added in the same interview that "the original meeting that Tom and I had with Francis (where)…he said, 'What I really want you guys to do is go make an album called 'One From The Heart', and then I'll make a movie that goes with it.' In fact, we didn't work exactly that way, because Tom is not the kind of guy who sits down and writes on cue. He needs stimulus and inspiration and time."

Once settled back in California the singer-songwriter prepared to write. Pre-production meetings with Coppola took place at his winery in Napa where "we had musical summit meetings… I'd sit at the piano with a brandy snifter and Francis would try and set up little dramas, to begin a musical dialogue about romance, and I'd syphon out ideas.

"It's very difficult working with someone who has a vision, especially Francis' four-dimensional vision, when you are required to implement it. He'd come in and start to brainstorm musically, skull out things, give me some borders and horizons. But he didn't want to put his hand in my hand. He wants your expertise in your area. In my case, he wanted me to create this pile of music that he could then take and throw up against a wall and see how it hung."

Waits added in a conversation with Mojo magazine that he saw the opportunity as one where he could depart from a musical style he'd begun to tire of. "I think by the time Francis called and asked me to write those songs, I had really decided I was gonna move away from that lounge thing. He said he wanted a 'lounge operetta', and I was thinking, well, you're about a couple of years too late. All that was coming to a close for me, so I had to go on and bring it all back."

Viewing the album as his stylistic swansong ending his first decade of album-making, Tom did his best to summon up one last round of inspiration, confessing in the same discussion that the process felt at times like "growing up and hitting the roof. I kept growing and kept banging into the roof, because you have this image that other people have of you, based on what you've put out there so far and how they define you and want they want from you. It's difficult when you try to make some kind of turn or a change in the weather for yourself. You also have to bring with you the perceptions of your audience."

Francis Ford Coppola, in a DVD interview on the making of the film, shared that he was eager to get away from the dark territory of his previous opus, Apocalypse Now. "That film had been so tough; so thoroughly frightening; so strange in its exploration of morality that I wanted very badly to make a film that was its opposite. Something more like a fable; more like the musical comedies I used to direct in college." Waits' impression of Coppola as a collaborator, as he recounted to City Limits magazine, from the beginning was "incredible. there's no distance for him between imagination and execution. It's devilish. I have an idea, Francis says great, starts working out ways to do it. I'm saying yeah well it's only an idea…next day he's set up the machinery and doing it."

Producer Bones Howe, in helping to flesh out precisely what he and Waits were hearing from Coppola, explained that the director had first become interested in hiring Waits after hearing "an album called 'Foreign Affairs' we had done, specifically a duet on it with Tom and Bette Midler called 'I Never Talk To Strangers'." He added in his same conversation with BAM that "it's a mini-story, a vignette of a guy and a girl sitting at a bar who start talking. She finishes every line by saying, 'But I never talk to strangers.'

"The concept of the music for the film evolved out of that, like it was happening at a piano bar; a lounge act kind of thing. Some of the music had strings added to it later to fill it out, and also to give it a more romantic feeling in places of the film where it needed that 'Hollywood' tug… To write a dozen songs loosely to Francis' specifications was a big order, and was something that Tom had never faced before." Excited by the challenge after the wheels were turning and he saw he would not be left entirely to his own conceptual devices, Waits rolled up his sleeves and got to work.

As writing for the album commenced, Coppola gave Waits some idea of where he wanted the story of the musical to go. "There was a blueprint, a skeleton," the singer-songwriter added in his conversation with journalist Dave Zimmer, adding that "right out front, Francis explained that the story would be changing as the production unfolded. But before I started writing anything, I met Francis in Las Vegas. In a hotel room, he took down all the paintings off the walls and stretched out sequences of events and would spot, in every rough, cryptic notations where he wanted music. It was helpful. I was able to get an idea of the film's peaks and valleys."

For Waits, the departure from his past work came with being in "the position of having to write songs that didn't speak directly for the characters, yet fit into this separate reality of dazzling effects, like a (store) window that almost never touches this world. The songs were supposed to be a sub-text, an interior dialogue, creating a kind of lounge operetta. It was a new experience for me, because in the past, I had always written songs by framing the ordinary, the commonplace and the parade of characters that I came in contact with…Francis wanted the 'cocktail landscape.' So for me, as a composer, it was like being an actor and having to try on different gloves. But it was a good challenge to write for somebody else's approval, to be part of something larger than just the songs."

Topically, Waits delved a bit into some of the themes Coppola was aiming to tackle in the course of the lyrics. "He told me, 'anything you write that deals with the subjects of love, romance, jealousy, break-ups can find its way into the film.' He explained that he would be building certain scenes around the songs, so that the music would be playing a much larger role than background or atmosphere. The film would be like a very carefully designed Valentine, the singers would be like Hera and Zeus, commenting on this small community."

To accomplish that task, Waits told Melody Maker of a process whereby Coppola would play Tom music and verbally detail a scene from the film, thereafter handing over the reins over to Waits. he would then "get the musicians together in a small room and we'd start playing and he'd start conducting in his own way. I'd throw out song titles. Some of it works better than others… I started with a lot of titles, and wrote about 12 different scenes, to be used wherever he wanted them, then I strung them together like an overture for a musical. What he wanted was a glass of music that you could add to or take from. Then we got together and made a scratch tape where we spotted the story for music. I was reworking themes so I got about 175 musical cues to be extracted from the score. It ain't fun doing that." He added years later upon reflection to GQ that the process throughout the writing of the record felt like something akin to "being at a university".

As Waits got down to work, he set up headquarters at an office in Coppola's still under construction Zoetrope Studios, detailing a daily routine to journalist Dave Zimmer that was more domesticated than past projects. It began with his rising "in the morning, have a cup of coffee, read the paper, get in my station wagon and then drive to work along with millions of other Americans. At Zoetrope, I'd sit in a little room in the story department with a piano, a couch, a tape recorder and a view of a Gulf station. Sometimes, to start the wheel turning, I'd just write a stream of consciousness, let it all come out, then sift through and find something to use. I might dismantle a melody, discard one lyric and break a piece off from another song. I'd do that a lot. If one line didn't work in a song, I might stick it in somewhere else. I never threw anything away. Because I never knew, when I was writing, what Francis might end up using. What, a year and a half ago, might have been a scratch track could have conceivably been used in the final cut of the film."

That process of construction, Waits recalled, was consistent atmospherically with the natural sounds going on around him. "When I sat at the piano and first started writing at Zoetrope, I could hear the carpenters outside building the sets for the film. It was like hearing the soldiers drilling. It gave me incentive and was like built-in pressure." The singer added in a separate in a conversation with Melody Maker that the routine "was good for me, it disciplined me, it made me – I had to sit in a little room and they'd ring me up on the phone and put memos under my door – it was like working in an office. Builds character, I think the lock was on the outside of the door, not the inside, they were afraid I was gonna go to Acapulco."

Musically, as he fleshed out the album's musical soundscapes, when it came to arrangement, Tom recalled that "that had been nailed down early on…(because) there were a lot of different arrangements of that music, but I was constantly working with a click track… I had to work with the pace of the click track, so when the music was put against the dancing, everyone would be moving at the proper tempo." Drawing from his natural musicality and understanding of arrangement from the point of view of an experienced songwriter, Waits' longtime arranger Bob Alcivar recalled on the One From The Heart DVD of the singer-songwriter's wildly impressive creative process that "Tom would come over to the house, put his hands on the keyboard, and say, 'Now that's it. He'd say, 'I don't know what the chords are but that's the beginning of the song.' I learned a lot from this, because Tom was doing things that were out of school and had nothing to do with education or music theory. He was just doing it from the heart and soul."

Using the film as a real-time inspiration throughout, both to inspire Waits and the cast and crew, the singer-songwriter shared with BAM magazine that "throughout the making of One From The Heart, the carpenters met the designers, who met the composers, who met the actors – it was like a huge carnival. When Francis started shooting, he played a lot of music I'd written through a PA system for the cast and crew on the set. It took some of the chill out of the cold soundstage."

The intention was to make sure the film and its score were as perfectly synched as possible, "to come up with right musical atmosphere. I worked very closely with Bob Alcivar, the arranger and orchestrator, and Bones Howe, my album producer. And Richard Beggs, who was really the sound sculptor, would sit in a little room, around the clock, with a catalogue of musical cues. Richard was the one most responsible for getting all the music to mesh with the film."

Waits admitted that, unlike writing for his own solo albums, he found writing for film to be a son-of-a-bitch. He found the process challenging quite simply because, for as far and wide as he'd adventured as a songwriter over the years in context of real-live muses, this one was more intimidating. "I've never been in that kind of situation before, doing a film score requires an application to detail I'm not accustomed to. Plus I was working for someone else's approval, which was hard for me at first"

The fact that the songs evolved with the film itself meant the two-year duration over which Waits wrote the album was one where, he explained, "it was necessary at times to take a little sabbatical... I needed to get a little distance from the film periodically." He added in the same conversation with BAM magazine that, to avoid writer's block, "I toured a couple of times, just a few shows back East and in Australia. I wasn't used to concentrating on one project for so long, to the point where you start eating your own flesh." Getting a well-deserved vacation from the office, by going back out on the road, Tom was arguably also gathering fuel for his creative fire from fans who helped encourage him to stay on the musical path he was travelling, even if he felt it was against a transitional backdrop in terms of his future direction following the Coppola collaboration.

When he was back at home working closely with Coppola in crafting the album's compositions, Waits shared with journalist Kristine McKenna that among other lessons he took away from the collaboration, "one thing I did learn from working with Francis Coppola and that whole process with One From The Heart, is that your first idea isn't always right. Francis will wait and wait. He never finishes anything, somebody just takes it away from him, and he continues to make changes up until the very last minute."

Waits entered Wally Heider Studios in Los Angeles in October 1980 to begin recording 'One From The Heart' with Bones Howe. In a conversation on the One From The Heart DVD the producer described an experimental recording approach wherein "everything at that point was 'Try it on and see how it fits.' It ended up being that way throughout the whole film because, in fact, Tom never wrote a piece of music for any specific place in the film. The film kept changing so there was a constantly updated video version being made...Sometimes we would go in the studio and lay down a demo on two-track so that Tom could have a tape to take home and listen to. Often it was just a melodic segment with Tom, on piano, and his bass player. A lot of that stuff ended up being considered for the final film because we couldn't recapture on 24-track the mood that we got the first time through."

'Broken Bicycles' was an example of the latter where "in the film is, in fact, a two-track demo of Tom singing and playing piano, and Greg (Cohen) playing upright bass. It was done at the end of a session where we had recorded other music, and Tom said, 'Let me get this down on tape so I can listen to it.' We didn't even bother to make a 24-track of it because we assumed it would be re-recorded with a huge string section later, which in fact it was. But we ended up using the original two-track because with the big string section it ended up sounding too dramatic."

In addition to the bassist Greg Cohen, Waits rounded out the band with saxophonist Teddy Edwards, trumpeter Jack Sheldon, pianist Pete Jolley and drummer Shelly Manne. Arranger Bob Alcivar recalled in his interview for the One From The Heart DVD that "Tom said that was the sound of this movie. No matter what else was going on, there was always Jack or Teddy."

Tom's vocal co-star for the record, Crystal Gayle, was originally brought to his attention by wife Kathleen Brennan in an early example of the value Waits placed on her ear. Producer Bones Howe recalled in an interview with the LA Times that Kathleen had "heard some of the jazz-flavoured tracks on Crystal's albums and played them for Tom and me...We made a tape of the songs and played them for Francis and he thought the all-American quality in her voice would be perfect for the film."

For Howe, the choice of Gayle was an opportunity to showcase "just how good a songwriter Tom is. He was always known for his lyrics because most people couldn't get through his voice to hear the melodies in his songs. When Crystal sings them, however, you can see just how beautiful they are... Crystal, her voice finally enables people to see (that)."

For his own part, Waits depicted the decision to hire Gayle as "a collective one," adding in the same conversation with journalist Dave Zimmer that "there were a lot of candidates. Bette Midler was originally going to be involved, but there were some scheduling conflicts. So we kept throwing names around. Then, when my wife and I were on the road, we heard Crystal sing 'Cry Me A River' on the car radio. I really liked her rendition of that. So, ultimately, Crystal became involved and she worked out real well. She was nice and easy to work with."

A critic with Bay Area Magazine would take note in his review of the results the pair achieved that, while "Waits and Gayle, as singing partners, may seem like an odd pairing, their voices work off one another perfectly. Gayle draws upon a jazzy, vulnerable part of her vocal talent that is imbued with more feeling than most of her slick pop-country recordings, and Waits – well, his vocal rasp still snaps hard, but it also softens up, touched with sensitivity."

Waits, in the same conversation with journalist Dave Zimmer, revealed that 'Is there Any Way Out of This Dream?' and 'Take Me Home' were written for Crystal Gayle to sing. "'Old Boyfriends' was originally for me, then for her, then it turned into a duet. 'Picking Up After You' and 'This One's From The Heart' were written as duets. I found that it was hard writing for a woman. There are certain words they're uncomfortable with. I can get away with a certain vernacular, while a woman singing it would have trouble. I had to change things around, put everything into her words. It was tough. I felt like I was writing lines for an actress."

The aforementioned 'Take Me Home' turned out to be one of the final songs written and recorded for the album, as Waits recalled that "the musical idea came early on, but the words were some of the last ones I wrote. I tried to sing it and it sounded real soppy, so I gave it to Crystal. She was in town for just this one day. I sat down at the piano, played it three or four times for her, then she cut it. I liked the way she did it."

Billboard would hail Tom and Gayle's rendition of 'Don't Talk To Strangers', the duet Waits originally cut with Midler that had inspired the collaboration between himself and Coppola, as "one of the most beautifully wrought soundtrack collaborations in history." It added of the song's recording that, "along with producer Bones Howe, Waits and Gayle cut their duets largely from the studio floor, live with the small combo-style studio band that included the saxophonist Teddy Edwards, drummer Shelly Manne, trumpeter Jack Sheldon, pianist Pete Jolly and bassist Greg Cohen, among others."

Tracking wrapped in September 1981, and the soundtrack was released the following year. While critics spoke viciously of the film itself in reviews, they singled out Waits' soundtrack as its silver lining, Rolling Stone poignantly noting that the soundtrack was "a smooth-sailing counterpart to a beautiful car crash of a movie." The Austin Chronicle would observe years later that "it's not that old black magic keeping Tom Waits' original song cycle for Francis Ford Coppola's long-shelved One From The Heart in print since 1982."

For Waits, the process of subsequently waiting two years for the film to finish was one he had to keep in a non-traditional perspective from that of the usual record release schedule. Doing his best to keep patience with the long roll-out process, Tom candidly told RockBill magazine that "a film is so huge it's like a small town digging a ditch. It's like sewing a button on a great big sport coat and you can't contact the guy who's working on the sleeves. The guy who's doing the lining hasn't been hired yet. Or he just quit. It takes from the lives of the people who work on it. It's like throwing a rock and waiting (that long)...for it to go through the window."

From the time the soundtrack landed on critics' desks, it stuck around as an instant classic, as reflected by Billboard's conclusion that "One From The Heart is a welcome addition to any soundtrack library to be sure, but also an essential one to the shelf of any Waits fan." Years later, iTunes would agree, hailing the album as "one of its most daring creative cornerstones remains arguably its most satisfying:

Tom Waits' elegantly boozy collection of bittersweet ballads, as voiced by one of the most accomplished oddball soundtrack duets ever — Waits himself and country songbird Crystal Gayle. The songs come wrapped in the lush orchestral production of Bones Howe, which variously serves as stark counterpoint to Waits' typically gruff, if often playful delivery, and as a perfect frame for the oft-bluesy ache of Gayle's diva turns."

For indulging his cinematic musical instincts on 'One From The Heart', Tom Waits would receive his first Academy Award Nomination for Best Musical Score in the process. Waits shared with David Letterman in the aftermath of the nomination his indecision as to whether to attend the ceremony or not. "I went back and forth as...'I'm gonna go, I'm not gonna go', I couldn't make up my mind. In terms of fashion, I don't know, we'd have to classify this as a cotillion. You know, it's a lot of 1959 prom formals and that type of thing... An old clothes horse like myself was in the right place. You really are nominated by people who are in your field and a lot of composers and songwriters and musicians recognised the score from the Coppola film, so it really is flattering."

Accolades, aside, Waits revealed to Melody Maker that, in hindsight, he considered the soundtrack "the most rewarding experience I've had since I started working," in part because it had helped to motivate him in a new stylistic direction that would require a brave departure from his previous norms heading into his musical future. Admitting to Smash Hits magazine that "I've never taken on anything that big," Waits nonetheless "enjoyed it very much," adding candidly to journalist Dave Zimmer that the creative challenge he'd pulled off had Waits in a state of suspended animation.

"I've been sweating bullets since April (1980), I've never worked on anything as challenging as this, having to conceptualise and design the musical fabric of an entire story. But those are the real rewards when it comes down to it – working with someone like Francis who has so much insight and daring. Sitting down with someone like that over a glass of beer, talking about film, exchanging ideas, knowing you're making a contribution – that makes you feel you're really going somewhere."

Indeed, Waits was heading in a new direction by 1982, not just creatively but also personally, having married wife Kathleen Brennan over the two years he'd worked on 'One From The Heart'. This inspired the singer-songwriter to volunteer in the concluding comments of his interview with journalist Dave Zimmer that meeting Brennan had inspired him to "believe in happy endings, now more than ever." Sharing in the same conversation that "I met my wife at Zoetrope, where she was working as a script analyst in the story department," Waits added in another interview with Smash magazine that he knew instantly he'd "spent ten miserable years looking for her."

Having met his soulmate, in life, love and art, Waits' marriage to Brennan would mark the beginning of a period of radical change that would affect all of the aforementioned categories equally as profoundly – most notably in the new music he would make over the next few albums.

Trusting Brennan implicitly from the jump, Tom – seeming to feel instinctively that change was good for him all around – added that upon marrying his wife, "I've also gotten rid of my ex-manager, and a lot of the flesh peddlers and professional vermin I'd thrown in with. My wife and I are taking care of all my affairs now." The true impact of Brennan's influence on every aspect of Waits' life was best summed up by producer Bones Howe, who explained to the LA Times that "she really separated him from everybody in his past. And, frankly, it was time for that for Tom. Kathleen has been very good for him. He was never as wild as many people have said, but he was living in a motel and not really taking that good care of himself. It really was time. She separated him from everybody. Unfortunately, I was in the cut. I was from the past"

Those professional personnel changes seemed to stem from Waits' desire to head in a radically different musical direction with what would become his next studio LP, 'Swordfishtrombones.' So dramatic a departure was coming that Blender magazine would note years later, in their review of 'One From The Heart's "14 gems of cynical, lovesick wit" that "this was the last group of songs in his piano-bar Seventies style, with glimpses of the clamorous, surrealistic jazz he developed on 'Swordfishtrombones' and later albums."

"A blend of wild, raw ethnic and crooning brass, barroom organ and New England schoolmarm piano." – MELODY MAKER

"She's adventurous you know and she picks up a lot of stations that I don't pick up. I get kind of narrow and concerned in making something and giving it four legs and getting it to stand up. She's more interested in what goes inside. She's very feminine and I think that's what works." – TOM WAITS ON WIFE AND CO-PRODUCER KATHLEEN BRENNAN

PART XI: 'SWORDFISHTROMBONES' (1983)

Shortly after finishing his work on 'One From The Heart', Waits – whose creative fires were clearly burning again – announced in a conversation with BAM magazine that he was stepping out into the new musical direction he heard in his head as his own man, having parted company with longtime producer Bones Howe in favour of taking "more of a role as an arranger and be responsible for all facets of conceiving, producing and putting together the entire (new album I'll be recording)... I used to think that after I was done writing and singing, I'd already done all that I was supposed to do. I left the rest in someone else's hands. I didn't want to deal with the rest of the production. Now I'll get more involved."

Waits desire to take the full control of the creative reins stemmed from a broader ambition – as he recalled to Mojo years later – to "to reach a new channel... I know I was anxious to, and sometimes we don't know how to do that. You're like a wound-up toy car who's hit a wall and you just keep hitting it. I was very self-destructive. Drinking and smoking and staying out all night long and it wasn't good for me so I sounded like I had been screaming into a pillow. You know, I needed to shift gears – I knew that I wanted to change but I didn't really know how to do it." Having shed that skin, Waits was itching to re-invent his image as a songwriter, and the bravely experimental direction he was heading would result in 'Swordfishtrombones'.'

Waits admitted candidly to journalist Robert Elms that "I feel I've shaken off an identity that was hindering me for some time. People thought I was some kind of a throwback, a time-warp demented oddity." He added in conversation with Barney Hoskyns that shedding his artistic skin was important in context of the new music he was writing. "The way I'm constructing songs now is different from the way I used to... Because I wrote primarily at the piano, and you write a certain kind of song at the piano. The piano brings you indoors immediately, so those types of songs were all a different shade of colour. Now I'm trying to go outside more, maybe to write more from my imagination, rather than being a chronicler... It's more like collage, maybe. I'll take this and put that there and I'll nail that to the side and then we'll paint it yellow and. it's more like construction... I prefer to think of it in terms of construction, or junk sculpture."

Waits' attempt to re-invent his sound also seemed to stem from his philosophy that "music is constantly reinventing itself," adding that as a songwriter he felt a responsibility to do the same. He had raised the stakes in gambling that fans would embrace his new direction, expressing the candid opinion to journalist Kristine McKenna that because "thematically, you do tend to wind up in a particular, comfortable musical geography," after a decade of one signature sound, "I'm trying to break away from that. I don't want to feel as though I'm knitting something, then unraveling it and knitting it again. And I think I did get beyond that with the new record… I wanted it to be a bit exotic, and to be more like a painting than a photograph. I see it as being sort of an odyssey, and I also thought of it as a wreck collection."

Waits confirmed in the same conversation that the writing of 'Swordfish-trombones' had made him feel alive again creatively as he mined for new musical gems. "I'm in a very exciting period for myself, as a writer, and a lot of the things that break through may go unnoticed, and that's okay too." One challenge Waits had to navigate in the course of constructing his new sound came with the fact that "I don't write year round, I write for a season and then I'm done," adding in his interview with Rock's Backpages that while "I'd like to be able to write through it all…it gets hard, so you say, 'I'm gonna set this time aside.'" One of the singer's primary distractions to the latter came naturally with the fact that "all these things pass through you all the time," setting up a scenario where he could possibly have become overwhelmed in that process.

Tom told New Musical Express that the only solution he'd fashioned for keeping abreast of his flood of musical ideas, came "when (I) sit down to write. It's really just like purchasing a butterfly net. It's going on all the time, it's just that you're going to draw a frame around it now. You're going to reach up and grab some and swallow it. There are times when you're more receptive to it than others. There are times when I feel more musical than others. I used to write a lot on the road, in hotels and stuff, that whole transient quality of my life. I'm not really what you'd call anal retentive. I found that the travelling brought me to a certain place as a writer. Now, I'm working on something that requires myself to stay put. I find it difficult to write on the road now."

Once he'd committed creatively to writing his new record, having been off-season for a while in-between 'One From The Heart' and 'Swordfishtrombones', the singer added in conversation with Rock's Backpages that he plugged back in by "going back to a place where you go a lot, but the season changed and the vines grew over the entrance. and you get back there and you say, 'Well, I'm standing right where I was, how come I can't get back in?' And then you realise that things grew over, so you get through that and then you see the little path and then you're on your way." With his new creative season in bloom, Tom aimed to break what would – for his audience and arguably music listeners in general – be new ground entirely, both from a sonic and stylistic vantage point.

Waits began by offering a very naked look at his raw songwriting process, sharing with Sounds that "sometimes I get up in the middle of the night when I'm still drunk from sleep. I go over to the piano in the dark and just hit random arbitrary notes and like where your hand goes it goes there for a reason. If you put a little baby down at a piano, she doesn't know anything, she likes to hit it over here because there are more black notes, or there may be some missing so she goes down here."

Beyond the piano, in searching out his new sound, the singer-songwriter explained that he'd been "composing on different instruments," adding in the same conversation with RockBill magazine that he'd found that approach "will give you different songs. So, I'm trying to get away from the piano as a compositional device and find something else to write on." Offering a specific example of the absence of familiar instrumentation on his new record and its impact on his creative process, the singer shared with music journalist Kristine McKenna that "there are no saxophones on the record and that's a conquest for me."

Elaborating on his expanded use of varying instruments in the course of composing his new record, Waits began by offering a more thorough musical explanation for why he was leaving his old sound behind, telling television host Steve Taylor that "I got used to upright bass and tenor sax and brushes and guitar and I couldn't hear anything without it for a while." As his ears began to open up to new sounds, Waits spared no potential source of inspiration, volunteering to music journalist Barney Hoskyns that he'd even utilised the city sounds of New York, specifically "construction sounds, for example. I started taping a lot of stuff, but how that'll integrate itself into what I'm doing I'm not certain. I started taping the sounds of machinery a lot and I play it back at night, 'cause you miss it when it gets quiet." Building upon this abstract foundation, Waits added in a conversation with reporter Robert Elms that "when you establish a neighborhood for yourself as an artist it's important to keep challenging that, to move on. So I tried to get a more exotic sound. It's a kind of oriental cabaret."

As a lyric writer, Tom – in typical abstract fashion – explained to journalist Kristine McKenna that, in the course of drawing on his own life experiences for inspiration, "my memory isn't a source of pain. Parts of it are like a pawnshop, other parts are like an aquarium and other parts are like a closet. I think there's a place where your memory becomes distorted like a funhouse mirror and that's the area I'm most interested in." Rather than directly accessing his memory for muse, the singer-songwriter explained to Sounds magazine that he preferred to employ a method wherein he found himself "more interested in how your memory distorts things. It's like an apparatus that dismantles things and puts them back together with some of the parts missing. When you remember something it's always a distorted impression, once the moment is gone the memory is very different to the actual moment itself."

While utilising the considerable musical muscle that was his imagination, Waits still kept intact his basic desire "to see things where the words are more concise so that the picture I'm trying to create becomes more clear," adding in the same conversation with Sounds magazine that, at times, in spite of that desire, with certain songs, he found it was preferable to "be more vague in description and allow the music to take the listener to that place where you want them to go."

In an interview from the Tom Waits Library.com, he quipped that, at the end of any musical day and in spite of all his production and songwriting experimentations, "in some demented fashion, I've tried to knit the songs together." Waits also underscored the importance within his lyrics of trying to "have characters reappear at some point or another so there was some sense of a revue or a follies – that it all had some type of logic."

Arguably one of Waits' greatest gifts as a songwriter – his ability to draw the listener into a feeling of comfort with his sound, no matter how outside the bounds of familiarity – began with those aforementioned characters. Where 'Swordfishtrombones' was concerned, the central character to the album was Frank, who Tom explained in an appearance on the David Letterman Show "really is the central protagonist who came to me in a dream and he spoke to me of many things. So really I was trying to find musical instruments that were more nightmarish or dreamlike."

By employing such a wide range of instrumental options this time out to achieve his desired soundscapes, the singer-songwriter revealed to Sounds magazine that "you can usually get the sounds you want to hear. You can usually find an instrument and alter it in some way... Basically I use things very traditionally, most of the stuff I've used has come from an upright bass, tenor sax and piano. Orchestrally I've worked with arrangers but I haven't really explored or been as adventurous as I would like to be. You really have to be driven along some kind of journey." To accomplish the latter, Waits felt arrangement was key, reasoning with New Musical Express that, to that end, his new record was "a little more adventuresome than ones I've previously made in terms of subject-matter, instrumentation, detail and arrangement... It's sort of like casting a movie. You select the correct players and the arrangements seem to follow."

Accompanying him on that musical journey were a cast of players that Waits shared in an Island Records promo interview included "Victor Feldman on bass marimba, Larry Taylor on acoustic bass, Randy Aldcroft on baritone horn, Stephen Hodges on drums and Fred Tackett on electric guitar. I had some assistance from a gentleman by the name of Francis Thumm, who worked on the arrangements of some of these songs with me. Who plays gramolodium with the Harry Partch Ensemble headed up by Daniel Mitchell. So he worked closely on most of these songs."

Waits told Sounds magazine of his longtime admiration for the aforementioned Thumm. "Francis is an old companion of mine, he is a professor and he also plays the crumelodian in the Harry Partch Ensemble, so it was Francis who interested me in Harry Partch... Partch was an American hobo and the instruments he made were all built from things that he essentially found on the side of the road, not literally but figuratively. He dismantled and rebuilt his own version of the whole concept of music and its purpose, but I just like the sounds he makes."

Waits also complimented jazzman Victor Feldman in an interview with Melody Maker, praising him for suggesting "instruments I wouldn't have considered – squeeze drums, Balinese percussion, marimba – things I'd always been timid about." In sum, according to Rolling Stone magazine, "that band – Smokey Hormel on guitar, Danny McGough on keyboards, Larry Taylor on bass and Andrew Borger on drums – invoked blues, parlour songs, gospel, country and New Orleans rhythm-and-blues, but all with rusty parts and loosened screws."

Waits revealed to RockBill magazine that his new band had helped him open his mind to the out-of-the-box soundscapes he was trying to capture on 'Swordfishtrombones'. "For a long time, I heard everything with an upright bass and a tenor saxophone on. I was very prejudiced and republican in terms of my opinions. Now, I'm starting to hear more. I'm trying to form a band that is a beast you can ride. It's very hard to stop doing things you're used to doing. You almost have to dismantle yourself and scatter it all around and then put a blindfold on and put it back together so that you avoid old habits. I like to have a band that could sound like an automobile accident and also rhumba in an appealing way."

As critics like the New Musical Express would later note upon hearing the recorded results of Waits' sonic experimentations, "musically, the instrumentation is bizarre, almost Beefheartian, incorporating marimba, bagpipe, harmonium and accordion. It also has a cinematic quality, segueing ballads, instrumental passages, raw blues, and the hilarious monologue, 'Frank's Wild Years'."

As he wrapped his head around producing his new sound to tape in the studio, which he'd formally entered in August 1982 to begin recording 'Swordfishtrombones', Tom offered in a conversation with journalist Barney Hoskyns that "lately I'd say my strength is an ability to take something and combine it with something it doesn't belong with, and make sense out of it. I'm trying to find different ways to use an umbrella and get away from just chronicling things."

An important breakthrough Waits would make with this effort that would become a mainstay of his re-invented sound was his success in articulating elements of that sound's radically experimental nature via unusual instruments that Melody Maker would later conclude succeeded in producing a "startlingly original soundscape."

Tom would tell TomWaitsLibrary.com that this was among the greatest thrills he took from his new role as head producer because "it's the first one that I've had a real firm active role in the direction and the landscape of the music and there's a lot of different barometers for how you're doing... I think as long as you're still taking turns and exploring and trying out new things, I think then you're better off."

Speaking on the subject of sonics in the same conversation, Waits added that experimentation with microphone placement also played an important role in capturing live what he was hearing in his head. "I noticed places where I pulled back and other places where I stretched out. It's hard to tell immediately till you look over your shoulder and you move on and you say, oh, yeah, that was the place where I went over there so I could come over here. I tried to keep as much air in there as I could so there's a sense of the room itself. Engineer Biff Dawes and I worked on trying to get a sense of the room, using a lot of different microphones to that end."

Tom and wife Kathleen enjoyed their new-found freedom to engage in out-of-the-box recording for certain tracks on the record, recalling years later in a conversation with Addicted To Noise that "my wife and I used to make multi-track recordings at home. And we'd take two pawn-shop tape recorders and we'd do a song on one. Right away you want to hear some other part, so she would just hold the two tape recorders up together and bounce it over to the other tape recorder and get the two tracks going. And sometimes surprising intervals and textures took place just because of how raw the thing was. Then I read something about John Lennon – that's what he used to do. We thought, 'This is crazy', but we'd play it for people apologetically and we would say, 'This is really ragged and ignore that part', but now I know that John Lennon did it."

He revealed in the same conversation that, once in the proper studio, they worked diligently to keep the same open ear to anything that sounded like it fitted within the fabric of the record's production, Waits reasoning that "you can bring something from a ditch that you found on the way to the studio, they'll put it in the room and circle it like it's a moonrock. They'll tap on it with a hammer. They're like scientists that way, and I like that. Everything is a potential instrument, it depends on how you use it.

'I remember I was doing 'Swordfishtrombones' and somebody took a stool – a metal stool – and started dragging it across the studio floor to move it out of the way. And I said, 'That's really thrilling. Do that again and abundantly and carefully and repeatedly, please.' It sounded like bus brakes on a big city bus. So I like things that fall outside of the spectrum of what we consider traditional instruments and acceptable sound. I love all that." Tom only grew bolder with his ambitions for the album's overall sound as it came to life.

Turning to the creation of a rhythm section that served as the foundation for a sound that Rolling Stone observed said "goodbye piano, hello marimba, trombone, and kettle drum," Waits candidly admitted to RockBill magazine that, in the course of constructing that sound, over the course of his past albums, he'd "always been afraid of percussion for some reason. I was afraid of things sounding like a train wreck, like Buddy Rich having a seizure. I've made some strides; the bass marimbas, the boobams, metal long longs, African talking drums and so on... I listened to some Mongolian stuff when I was getting ready to do this record. It sounded like Tibetan Voodoo. It caught my ear and helped me some."

In addition to using "much more percussion than I'm used to in the past," he was attempting to evolve traditional percussive elements into something new that "imitate things that I'm already used to hearing rather than just being separate so it's more like an organised automobile accident and it has some shape to it but it also relates to the real event itself. Some of the stuff on 'Shore Leave' is like sound effects, the low trombone is like a bus going by and I got a little more adventurous. I'm still a little timid about it but melody is what really hits me first, melody is the first thing that seduces me. 'Underground' had some – I thought it felt like a Russian march, the music to accompany the activities of a mutant dwarf community in the steam tunnels – that kind of a feel is what I was after.'"

Tom recalled in the same conversation that "'Frank's Wild Years' is Jimmy Smith organ, Ken Nordine attitude; 'Gin Soaked Boy' is some of that old New Orleans thing, 'Down Down Down' is more of a Pentecostal reprimand. '16 Shells' – I wanted a chain gang sort of a feel – banging a hammer on an anvil, like a work song. We used brake drum and bell plate and tried to take it outside – certain instruments bring you indoors, other instruments take you outdoors, trying to get that kind of feel on it."

Turning to the album's vocals, the Wall Street Journal noted "represented a departure for Mr Waits, featuring irregular time signatures and barking, raspy vocals," a signature style that Tom quipped to journalist Kristine McKenna "at best" made him sound like "a barking dog, but I think my voice is well suited to my material." A pivotal influence over this new vocal direction, as reported by Rolling Stone, came courtesy of "a new collaborator…(who) helped effect the change." Waits was speaking of wife Kathleen Brennan, now his full-time collaborator as both a songwriter and producer. She played what the magazine termed "a key (role in)…the singer's stylistic shift, encouraging the unorthodox at every turn."

Offering an example of the latter in action in the studio to author Bart Hopkin, Waits recalled that "around 1982, my wife Kathleen encouraged me to try singing through a police bullhorn to make my voice stand out in relief when incorporated with instruments of the same colour. Of course, it's possible to do the same thing with an equaliser, but nothing beats the drama of a bullhorn. My engineer Biff Dawes purchased me my first, and it was love at first sight." Clearly planning to stick loyally with whatever new instruments helped him bring his new sound fully to life in the studio or on stage, Waits said "I never record or tour without it. I also try to buy a new one every year, because they continue to 'improve' upon them."

Discussing the construction of some of the album's specific tracks, which in sum iTunes concluded was "part Captain Beefheart/Howlin' Wolf blues, part field holler, part Salvation Army junkyard band," Waits – in a wide-ranging discussion for an Island Records promo interview – began with the album's title track, 'Swordfishtrombones'. "It has kind of a Cuban nightclub feel to it. It's a story to try and give an overview of a character. We tried it with a lot of different ways. It was arranged differently with electric guitar and drums. We had trombone on it and trumpet and ended up… I had to discard most of what we had done and completely rearrange it just to get it as simple as possible. So that it just kind of rolled and allowed me to tell the story over it without any interruptions."

'Johnsburg, Illinois' was an ode to his wife Kathleen, Waits explained biographically that she was, in fact, "from Johnsburg, Illinois. It's right outside McHenry and up by the ching-a-lings. She grew up on a farm up there. So it's dedicated to her. It's real short. Somehow I wanted just to get it all said in one verse. There are times when you work on a song and end up repeating in the second verse what you already said in the first. So I thought I would be more appropriate if it's just like a feeling of a sailor somewhere in a cafe, who opens his wallet and turns to the guy next to him and shows him the picture while he's talking about something else and says: 'Oh, here. That's her' and then closes his wallet and puts it back in his pants. It relates in some way to 'Shore Leave' in the sense that it talks about Illinois. So thematically I was trying to tie it into 'Shore Leave.'"

Of the latter song, Waits added that, in its writing, he aimed for "kind of an oriental Bobby 'Blue' Bland approach. Musically it's essentially very simple. It's a minor blues. I tried to add some musical sound effects with the assistance of a low trombone to give a feeling of a bus going by, and metal aunglongs, the sound of tin cans in the wind, or rice on the bass drum to give a feeling of the waves hitting the shore. Just to capture the mood more than anything of a marching marine or whatever walking down the wet street in Hong Kong and missing his wife back home."

Lyrically, Waits recounted in the same conversation the visual muse of "working in a restaurant in a sailor town for a long time. It's Porkcola National City. So, it was something I saw every night. It was next to a tattoo parlour, a country and western dance hall and a Mexican movie theatre. So I imagined this Chinese pinwheel in a fireworks display spinning, spinning and turning and then slowing down. As it slowed down it dislodged into a windmill in Illinois…and then looked down on us. A home. Where a woman is sitting in the living room sleeping on chairs with the television on. When he's having eggs at some grumulant joint, you know, thousands of miles away."

In an example of New York City being heard as an influence come sonically to life on the record, Waits highlighted 'Underground' in the Island promo interview, recalling that he became inspired when "I originally saw this…theme for some late-night activity in the steam tunnels beneath New York City. Where allegedly there are entire communities of ladies and gentleman living under difficult circumstances beneath the subways. When I was a kid I used to stare in the gopherholes for hours and hours sometimes. I tried to think my way down through the gopherhole and imagine this kind of a 'journey to the centre of the earth'-kind of thing… It was originally an opportunity for me to chronicle the behaviour of a mutant dwarf community and give it a feeling of a Russian march. People banging on steam pipes, thousand boots coming down on a wood floor at the same time. That chorus of men singing, kind of a Dr Zhivago feel to it."

Feeling that the recording came out similarly to "the way I originally perceived it," Tom added in the same conversation that to achieve the sonic extreme he was after, "I abbreviated some of the scope and wanted bass marimba to give it kind of an exotic feel. So, you get the note and you get that kind of a tall wood clang with the attack."

Turning to the album's wildly imaginative and experimentally-arranged instrumentals, beginning with 'Dave The Butcher', Waits explained that "I ended up playing on the B-3 organ. Well I wanted that carnival feeling on it. Kind of a nightmare alley with Tyrone Power and John Blundell. Kind of a monkey on wood alcohol. It was originally inspired by a gentleman who did tremendous amounts of religious things in his house and worked at a slaughterhouse. I was trying to imagine what was going in his head while he cut up load of pork loin and got completely out of his mind with a meat cleaver. I don't think it's going to get a lot of airplay. Unless we put a nice vocal on it."

Waits explained in a conversation from the Tom Waits Library.com that the song's title character, Dave, was reminiscent of his working-class stars of songs past, with his latest creation working "at a slaughterhouse in Ireland. He wore two different shoes, an Oxford and a boot, and his house was filled with religious items and crucifixes and he worked at a butcher's shop. I tried to imagine what was going on in his head while he was cutting up a little pork loin. I wrote everything very close together, all in about two weeks so the songs have a relationship – that's the one I wrote yesterday, so today I'll hitch this one to that one so you usually try to leave an end of the one you wrote before open, so it can attach on to the one you're writing next, rather than just a random, arbitrary collection of tunes.

"I tried to get 'em to knit. It's not entirely successful as far as a libretto, it's just one guy who leaves the old neighbourhood and joins the Merchant Marines, gets in a little trouble in Hong Kong, comes home, marries the girl, burns his house down and takes off on an adventure, that kind of a story."

Of another instrumental, 'Just Another Sucker On The Vine', Tom explained that "it's myself playing the harmonium and Joe Romano on trumpet. I tried to give a little 'Nino Rota' feel to it. Kind of like a car running out of gas, you know, just before it makes the crest of a hill and it starts to roll back. I tried to picture two Italian brothers in small circus arguing on the trapeze. Doing the dozens on each other and throwing insults as they cross each other in the mid air. Or the feel of a band on the deck of Titanic as it slowly goes under. The title is really kind of a lyric to it, it's like you know…Actually I originally planned to write a lyric called: 'It's more than rain that falls on our parade tonight.' But I thought it was more effective as an instrumental and it also sets up 'Frank's Wild Years'."

The central character of the story, 'Frank', would become the lead star in the broader story arch of Waits' next few studio albums. The singer recalled he was inspired by a "Charles Bukowski…story that essentially was saying that it's the little things that drive men mad. It's not the big things. It's not World War II. It's the broken shoelace when there is no time left that sends men completely out their minds. So this is kind of in that spirit. Little of a Ken Nordine flavour. Ronnie Barron alias Reverend Either from New Orleans, Louisiana, on Hammond organ and Larry Taylor, originally with Canned Heat, on doghouse (bass). I think there is a little bit of Frank in everybody."

Waits added in a separate interview pulled from the Tom Waits Library.com that, lyrically, he was attempting to depict "crumbling beauty; Frank is a little bit of that American dream gone straight to hell. Frank is more of a commentary on real-estate brokers and insurance investigators and defence attorneys, That fear, that button down, 8 o'clock, the whistle blows, Bermuda shorts approach to life. I've never liked Chihuahuas."

With '16 Shells From A Thirty-Ought Six', the singer-songwriter explained that while "originally I tried it just with organ and bass, then I was afraid to add too much to it 'cause sometimes you get a feel that's appropriate. If you try to heap too much on it then it crumbles into the strain… I tried to get a 'chain gang work song' holler. Get a low trombone to give a feeling of a freight train going by.

"It's Stephen Hodges on drums, Larry Taylor on acoustic bass, Fred Tackett on electric guitar, Victor Feldman on brake drum and bell plate and Joe Romano on trombone. I wanted to have that kind of a sledgehammer coming down on anvil. Originally I saw the story as a guy and a mule going off looking for this crow. He has a Washburn guitar strapped on the side of his mule and when he gets the crow he pulls the strings back and shoves this bird inside the guitar and then the strings make like a jail. Then he bangs on the strings and the bird goes out of his mind as he is riding off over the hill.

"I tried to make the story a bit impressionistic but at the same time adding some very specific images in there. I worked a long time on this. The feel of it was really critical. I added snare and we pulled the snare off 'cause it made it shuffle too much. I liked the holes in it as much as I liked what was in them. It was a matter of trying to get that feeling of a train going."

On the autobiographical 'Down, Down, Down', Waits recalled its inspiration being literally stranded "in Arizona on Route 66. It was freezing cold and I slept at a ditch. I pulled all these leaves all over on top of me and dug a hole and shoved my feet in this hole. It was about 20 below and no cars going by. Everything was closed. When I woke up in the morning there was a Pentecostal church right over the road. I walked over there with leaves in my hair and sand on the side of my face. This woman named Mrs. Anderson came. It was like New Year's Eve... She said: 'We're having services here and you are welcome to join us.'"

Taking shelter in what he recounted as a truly surreal environment, Waits added his memory that "I sat at the back pew in this tiny little church. And this mutant rock'n'roll band got up and started playing these old hymns in a broken sort of way. They were preaching, and every time they said something about the devil or evil or going down the wrong path she gestured in the back of the church to me. And everyone would turn around and look and shake their heads and then turn back to the preacher."

Waits added in the same recollection that he had consistently been struck by the irony of his experience when on "Sunday evenings they have these religious programmes where the preachers they are all bankers. They get on with these firing glasses and $700 suits. Shake their finger at America. So this is kind of my own little opportunity at the lectern."

'Town With No Cheer', Waits explained, was "basically a folk song". He added that, when his wife first heard the song, she first construed from its message, "'Oh gee, you must have loved her very much.' So I said: 'Wait a minute. This is not a love song. This is about a guy who can't get a drink!' It's about a miserable old town in Australia that made the news when they shut down the only watering hole. We found an article about it in a newspaper when we were over there and hung on to it for a year. So I said: 'Ah, I'm going to write something about that someday', and finally got around to it. That's a freedom bell upfront just trying to get a feel of a ghost town, tumbleweeds and that kind of thing."

Waits further shared with Melody Maker his memory from the song's recording that "Anthony Clark Stewart played the bagpipes, looked like he was strangling a goose, had to record him separately... I was trying to do a bit of an adventure, do some type of 'Beggar's Opera' in a way, with songs that had some kinda relationship to each other, whether it was later on in the story, or in some kinda discombobulated sequence. Thematically, I put in the instrumentals to try and provide connective tissue." The ground he would cover on 'Swordfishtrombones' was the first of many remarkable evolutions of that talent he would achieve over the course of subsequent albums.

Tom explained that the song 'Gin Soaked Boy' was reminiscent "of a Howlin' Wolf feel. It's Fred Tackett on electric guitar, plays good slide. Tried to get that 'rrrrr'-thing. Tried to get the vocal sit way back to recreate the recording conditions that existed prior to advanced technical capabilities. We had it recorded by one round microphone. So, your dominance on the track depended entirely on your distance from the microphone. Also get a room-feel. So Biff Dawes miced the room with several of these contact mics... So it got a real sense of the air of the place. It has a bit of an old feel to it."

One of the album's wilder rhythmic adventures, 'Trouble's Braids', saw Waits using the instrumental's fabric "to get the image of trouble being this little girl. Pull on trouble's braids. He should chase you around and about a guy who's in trouble. Our hero is at this point being pursued by bloodhounds. So he stays away from the main roads." The players on the track were "Victor Feldman on African talking drum, Stephen Taylor on parade bass drum and Larry Taylor on acoustic bass. It has a bit of a Mongolian feel."

Side one closer 'In The Neighborhood' found Waits going for a "Salvation Army feel. All things signed. Have a drinking song. I was trying to bring the music outdoors with tuba, trombone, trumpets, snare, cymbals, accordion. So it had that feeling of a Fellini-esque type of marching band going down the dirt road. And with glockenspiel to give it a feeling of a kind of a demented little parade band."

Album closer 'Rainbirds' was "myself at the piano and Greg Cohen on acoustic bass. It's a real pleasure to work with him. We have a mutual intuition and it's really good to hear him again. Francis Thumm helped me with a glass harmonica introduction. It's kind of an epilogue to the story. After he floats down the stream on an old dead tree. It's kind of…you know… It's a morning you hear the birds and it starts to rain and he's off on another adventure somewhere. I wanted to close the side with an instrumental to give the hero room to breathe. Yeah, that's all…the end."

Though by this point he'd penned several songs that became successful for other artists, Waits still avoided any conscious attempt to write hits, arguing to New Musical Express that "a hit single means that you make a lot of money and a lot of people will know who you are, and I don't know that's so attractive. I don't see the importance of having your face on a lunchbox in Connecticut. I don't see how that fits into the grand scheme of things as far as being something to strive for. And it rears its ugly head. It makes you a geek, and you don't want to destroy the very thing that makes it possible for you to do what you do. A lot of people are looking for affection and acceptance in the form of this anonymous group of people thinking they're wonderful."

For as satisfied as he was with the finished product, Tom didn't find the same reception from his label heads. "The album was made for WEA (Warner/Elektra/Asylum)," he told journalist Chris Douridas, "and Joe Smith heard it; he didn't know what to do with it. He looked at me like I was nuts. At first he said, 'Produce your own record, go ahead, make your own record, you should be producing your own record.' So I said, 'Okay, good.' I made about three or four things and brought 'em in and he heard 'em and he said, 'Well, I dunno…' Then (I) made a whole record, and played it for him, and he said, 'I dunno if we can put this thing out or not.' So Chris Blackwell (at Island) heard it, and I left WEA through a loophole in my contract and I snuck out. Chris Blackwell loved the album, said 'We'll put it out.' So that's what happened. He was very in tune with it. Blackwell has great ears. Because he liked what I did, so I guess that means he has great ears!"

Blackwell, for his own part, recalled that before meeting the singer-songwriter to discuss the possibility of jumping ships, "I didn't know Tom's albums well, though I'd always loved 'Tom Traubert's Blues'. I loved the aura he projected his presence, his extraordinary intelligence and his musical originality." Meeting Waits and wife/manager Kathleen in early 1983 at a Los Feliz, Los Angeles cafe, Blackwell recalled that "Tom didn't speak much. Most of the conversation was with Kathleen. Frankly, she played a big part in my decision to sign him." His new label had succeeded in selling a stylistically diverse roster of records ranging from Bob Marley to U2. Waits was a fantastic opportunity for Island to prove once again its chance-taking instincts. The label allowed Waits the artistic freedom to create 'Swordfishtrombones', and would be richly rewarded for so doing.

Waits explained to New Musical Express why he made the decision to leave his longtime label. "I was at Elektra for over ten years and while I was there I spent a considerable amount of time on the road and blowing my own horn. They liked dropping my name in terms of me being a 'prestige' artist, but when it came down to it they didn't invest a whole lot in me in terms of faith." Still, Waits added in a separate conversation with Rock Backpages years later that, while on the label, regardless of how he was marketed as an artist, "Asylum were really very good to me."

Critics and fans alike acclaimed 'Swordfishtrombones' on its release in September 1983, agreeing with the New York Times that Waits had "reinvented his music, trading pop-folk arrangements for lurching, clattering backups that are as unkempt as his voice," while Melody Maker called it "his finest, most consistent album to date." Spin magazine ranked it the Number 2 album of all time, and Mojo championed it as "one of the pivotal albums of the Eighties," adding along with many journalistic counterparts that the record represented "an American melting-pot music such as had never been heard before."

Seeming at peace with the chance he'd taken with 'Swordfishtrombones', Waits argued in a conversation with journalist Robert Elms that "I would rather be a failure on my own terms than a success on someone else's. That's a difficult statement to live up to, but then I've always believed that the way you affect your audience is more important than how many of them there are." Tom's audience ate his new sound right up, along with a growing chorus of critics over time, including NME, who hailed Waits' new music for "shifting gloriously in mood" while iTunes noted more recently that with the new album at the time – marked "a nearly brand new approach…(that takes) a decisive step into the guttural underground to which he'd always paid a sentimental homage."

Melody Maker offered perhaps the most eloquent observation about Waits' "bizarre progress" over the course of 'Swordfishtrombones', while Tom – for his own part – concluded in an interview with BBC Radio 1 that the LP represented the recorded results of his quest as artist to "try and continue to explore new musical geography, you know? Consistency is the hobgoblin of little minds. And you hope you're moving onward and upward and into something different. It's just an attempt to chronicle things in a more impressionistic way. And I think musically, you know, I made some small private breakthroughs. But you know, the next thing will be a you know, a different alp. But some of the stuff in this new one I like. But usually the things that you are most fond of are the songs that you have yet to write."

"On 'Rain Dogs'…(Tom) didn't really know whether people would like his new direction. So he was really driving himself very hard, putting a lot of pressure on himself – productive pressure that went into perfecting the music." – GUITARIST MARC RIBOT, MOJO MAGAZINE, 1985

"Every day was a different day, we were always trying different things, different players positioned in different spots throughout the main studio live room playing different instruments, and it was not really traditional in any sense. It was a lot of times making sure we got the right guitar sound working with the right piano sounds with the right drum sounds, placing the room with the right room mics."
– ENGINEER BOB MUSSO

"A Tour-de-Force!" – ITUNES

PART XII: 'Rain Dogs' (1985)

If 'Swordfishtrombones' introduced the world to Tom Waits' sonic re-invention, the great leap the singer-songwriter achieved with 'Rain Dogs', came with delivering what Rolling Stone magazine concluded America had "seemed to be missing: a consummate...artist with a boundless range and the uniqueness of Mark Twain."

Tom's talent for telling the tales of the everyday man and ability to couple those lyrical narratives with soundscapes that gave them a visual fabric grew leaps and bounds on 'Rain Dogs' as he continued to take chances in the studio.

Transplanting his vivid narrative from the West to the East Coast, the New York Times would later observe that album-wide, "Mr Waits is (lyrically)...obsessed with America's low-life – the bars, the broads, the booze, the touts, the sleaze. His voice is variations on a gargle, half-conversational mutterings about life's disappointments and dreams. His songs are cast in a folkish, bluesy idiom, though by now he's moved away from electric guitars and rock drums into a sort of vaudevillian instrumental mélange dominated by cheap horns and accordion (the eloquent William Schimmel, perhaps today's best-known accordionist, classical and otherwise)." His former hometown's LA Times would conclude "the move appears to have been good for him" based "on the evidence of his new album."

Though he'd relocated his lyrical landscape from the streets of Hollywood to that of New York, Waits continued his fascination with writing on behalf of the underdog, confessing to Sounds magazine that "I'm still drawn to the ugly; I don't know if it's a flaw in my personality or something that happened when I was a child. It's like when you look out of the window what's the first thing you notice? My wife says I look down, that's what's wrong with me. That's why I see the spit. I don't know – it's what you choose to take from your vision." Waits constructed soundscapes that were as authentic to his surroundings as possible throughout the album's production, tailoring each to the song he was trying to create in the studio.

Waits shared with CBC Stereo (Canada) that he had specifically branded the New York breed of underdog as "a rain dog", defining this as "people who sleep in doorways. People who don't have credit cards. People who don't go to church. People who don't have a mortgage, y'know? Who fly in this whole plane by the seat of their pants," adding to the LA Times that "after it rains, dogs often can't find their way home and they wander around the streets, so rain dogs are the lost people who sleep in doorways... You see a lot of that In New York. But the geography of your ideas is usually much different than the places you're living."

Personalising the narrative, the singer-songwriter, in a discussion with the San Diego Union-Tribune, delved further into its subtext, explaining that at its root, "the album is kind of my impression of a lot of things that have happened to me since I moved to New York, particularly the summer in New York when half of the city sleeps outdoors in a doorway and so many of them are completely deranged. The place really does take on a rather surreal quality... The contrasts in this city are so devastating, in terms of colour, fabric, economy, tragedy and comedy – all crying in the very same beer. It really gets very direct. At first, it drives you crazy, and you try to retain what you had when you came here. You end up laughing at things that appalled you at first. You end up having to get some on you, in order to survive." Feeling he had the respect of his listeners as an authentic voice in speaking for the latter living muses, Waits was ambitious in his desire to depict his newest surroundings in as real terms as he had on past albums.

The same discussion saw him quip that, in the course of conducting his real-life research, "the whole city is like your bathroom. People have to get so crowded in together that they erect invisible walls around themselves. You have to keep moving. They keep pulling things out from under you. It's like an emergency ward. You come out of your door, and a guy literally falls into you, having a stroke. A woman wearing nothing but a blanket, bald as an egg, is singing 'Strangers In The Night' in the middle of 14th Street." Waits shared with music writer Peter Silverton that he tied all these observations together into characters which became "all the people on the album knit together, by some corporeal way of sharing pain and discomfort."

Conceptually, Tom explained to CBC Stereo that "at first I thought there was some place where all these people were held – imported and domestic... place where they were all hooked up. I'm not sure, there does seem to be... for me there does seem to be some connection. I wouldn't say it's a linear story, it's more like an aquarium." Elaborating on his aquarium analogy, Waits added in a conversation with Rolling Stone that "there are distinctive lines of demarcation, but for the most part it's like an aquarium. It's almost overwhelming. Words are everywhere... All you have to do is just look out the window and there's a thousand words."

Pulling inspiration quite literally out of the air as song ideas came to him, he recalled to journalist Elissa van Poznak that anywhere he wandered throughout the city, "it's raining songs. I can't find enough things to catch them in. And words, in New York there's words everywhere just throwing themselves at you so you never have to worry about words."

Waits decided to locate himself in the heart of the city's Lower East Side, explaining to Beat magazine that "I think the place that you write stuff usually ends up in the song. I wrote most of 'Rain Dogs' down on Washington St. It's a kind of rough area, Lower Manhattan between Canal and 14th St, just about a block in from the river. I started sharing a rehearsal space with the Lounge

Lizards. I had nights there in this boiler room and a Siamese cat would go by sounding like a crying baby, every night. And there was a drummer down the hall. It was a good place for me to work. Very quiet, except for the water coming through the pipes every now and then. Sort of like being in a vault…a place that was quiet except for the water going through the pipes."

Tom told Spin magazine his recollection that "New York is really stimulating. You can get a taxi and just have him drive and start writing down words you see, information that is in your normal view: dry cleaners, custom tailors, alterations, electrical installations, Dunlop safety centre, lease, broker, sale…just start making a list of words that you see. And then you just kind of give yourself an assignment. You say, 'I'm going to write a song and I'm going to use all these words in that song.' That's one way. Or you can get in character, like in acting, and let the character speak."

Waits shared details of his writing process with Time Out magazine. "I make notes, write some things down. But you never know how it's all going to fit in until you finally sit down and say, now I'm writing, now I'm working, now I'm gonna make sense of all this pandemonium. It's like anything else. It's the relationship between things where the meaning lies, that's what you try to look at. New York has made a difference but 'Swordfish' and 'Rain Dogs' are not really a switch, more a combination of imported an domestic influences, I guess. An attempt to do something more private, demented, exotic." Building on the new experimental ground he'd broken sonically with his last LP, Tom was even more ambitious this time around, seeking to bring the city's mania to life in that of his own studio soundscapes.

Tom offered a more in-depth explanation of that process to radio host Michael Tearson, elaborating that he used the city sounds as his rhythm track. "When I'm writing I kinda give myself a downbeat and say: from this moment on the things that happen to me and the things that I see will go somehow fall into this hole I'm digging. And the things that I'm dreaming, the blue shoes that fell off the green tractor, and the…broken window that came out through the yellow floorboards, that fell through the ceiling and I just kinda put it all together and from one moment on. So, it's like when it's raining, and you can't find enough things to catch it in. Y'know when it's not, you can stand out in the middle of the street in a dress and a funny hat and nothing's gonna make it rain."

In the same conversation, Tom shared of his natural compositional process that "when you're writing the ideas somehow seem to come to you and when you're not, they don't. Y'know? It's just always been like that for me. So I go through periods of spells." Waits emphasised the mystery inherent in that process. "With music, it's difficult to talk about the writing of it. It gets so pedantic. It's all made out of smoke. When you really think about it, it's invisible. And you're afraid it's not going to come and sit next to you anymore. and that keeps you doing it. 'when I'm writing I have sort of waking dreams. I try to go inside, go through a window someplace.'"

When he was in his creative state, turning the latter-mentioned ideas into songs, he revealed to journalist Elissa van Poznak that, unlike past albums, "I'm trying to get more on schedule – when you work you suspend all logic, the world becomes an aquarium, things are tumbling and floating by and you ordain them to have new meaning. Certain things float to the top, including you, but then you have to drain the pool and answer the phone and fill out applications and go to the post office. I kind of vacillate back and forth between the two states. It's like being on medication, a balancing act, and a lot of time for me goes into getting ready to do this whole thing. It has its own drama, what it does to your life because all of a sudden things that are part of your scope and you never noticed will figure in going to the shoeshine, the Port Authority, the steam coming out of the manhole, the guy on the horse, the news. You drag these things home from your day and put them somewhere and you have three weeks to make something out of it. I give myself deadlines, if you don't it's just life, life going on. So you say, okay, use red, yellow and black. You get involved in the ritual."

The city broadened his mind to new musical influences, and Waits explained to Sounds how he intended to translate those to tape. "In terms of discovery and ideas. I'm trying to get away from that jazz thing. I live where the Nigerian overlaps Louisiana now. I'm trying to listen more to the noise in my head. My writing process has changed. Like when it's rainin' – again! – you have to make sure you have enough things to catch it in. I'm realisin' the possibilities in arranging, exploring. I usually just try to design something that has purity of purpose. Some are just sketches, some are more developed."

As they developed, Waits reasoned to radio host Michael Tearson that "songs should have their own anatomy that suits the story," explaining the visualisation process in a separate discussion with music writer Gavin Martin. "Sometimes I close my eyes real hard and I see a picture of what I want; that song 'Singapore' started like that, Richard Burton with a bottle of festival brandy preparing to go on board ship. I tried to make my voice like his – 'In the kingdom of the blind the one-eyed man is king' – I took that from Orwell, I think." When the source of a song's character was biographical, Tom told the LA Times that "when you're talking about yourself, it all comes down to the way that you do it. There are passages in the songs that refer to my life, but they aren't anything anyone else would pick up on."

In bringing those characters to life, Waits reaffirmed his gift for incorporating what the LA Times deemed as a "staggering vocabulary of slang," praising the singer-songwriter as "the Shakespeare of hipster jive. Waits is a master of the sort of colourful colloquialism that you only hear at the race track, pool hall or in jail." Waits himself told the paper that "this stuff is not a dead language... A phrase like 'walkin' Spanish' is pretty common. It means to fly by the seat of your pants or walk the plank. I listen and I hear people talk this way."

Musically, Tom composed most of the album's songs on "guitar and I rented a little pump organ. It's a little harmonium, and I've been playing the accordion a little bit... It's interesting to write on instruments you don't understand. You know, I pick up a saxophone and bang on a drum or trombone. Anything that I'm unfamiliar with, that is always good for your process."

Waits began with 'Downtown Train', a fan favourite that went onto become a

Number 1 hit for Rod Stewart and was "kind of a pop song. Or an attempt at a pop song.' Of 'Blind Love', "my firstborn country song I think," Waits shared the influences he was channeling in its writing that "I like Merle Haggard and those guys y'know? Those roadhouse guys, I like." Crediting his wife and co-writer Kathleen as muse on 'Hang Down Your Head', Tom recalled that "Kathleen was whistling that and I said: what the hell is that? And she said: Oh I don't know. So I made it… I put it down and took it in the studio. While I'm writing and while I'm recording, everything you seem to pick up during the process somehow ends up in there. You know, it's like a big vat. You know, you just start throwing things into it."

Turning to 'Clap Hands', the singer-songwriter told radio host Michael Tearson that "I just kinda embedded a nursery rhyme: 'Shine, shine, a Roosevelt dime/ All the way to Baltimore and running out of time.' I just tried to imagine all these… these guys going up the A-train. All the millionaires in tuxedos shoveling all the coal into the… Everyone's hanging out of the window, y'know? Just kind of a dark little kind of a Ralph Steadman drawing."

In an Island Records promo interview, Waits explained that 'Walking Spanish' originated "an expression they use when you don't want to go somewhere. It's 5:30 in the morning and the baby just woke you up screaming and you drag yourself out of bed, you're walking Spanish. Somebody says, 'Listen, buddy, give me all your money', and your hand goes back around toward your wallet, you're walking Spanish, you don't want to go. Walking the plank, basically; walking Spanish is walking the plank."

In the same discussion, Tom touched on 'Bride Of The Rain Dogs', recalling it as "an instrumental rendering of the lead cut". 'Cemetery Polka', he elaborated to music journalist Gavin Martin, was "a family album. A lot of my relatives are farmers, they're eccentric, aren't everyone's relatives? Maybe it was stupid to put them on the album because now I get irate calls saying, Tom how can you talk about your Aunt Maime and your Uncle Biltmore like that? But Mum, I say, they did make a million during World War II and you'll never see any of it. It's time someone exposed them." 'Gun Street Girl' was "is about a guy who's having trouble with the law and he traces all of these events back to this girl he met on Gun Street right there on Center Market right in Little Italy there."

Tackling 'Big Black Mariah', Waits recalled that "originally (Mariah)…was the woman that ran some kind of a cathouse in New Orleans I guess and every time it got popped they figured she was the one that blew the whistle so the paddy wagon pulled up out in front and down through the years they started referring to it as the Black Mariah. Now it's the hearse or whatever."

Tom compared the Manhattan-inspired instrumental 'Midtown' to the sonic equivalent of "what it's like to get stuck behind a van or when you thought you had a brilliant idea. You were gonna cross at 29th St and you were gonna hit West St and make it all the way up. You get behind a bakery truck and you're there for like a year."

Waits' first task in bringing his latest musical opus to life began with finding the right engineer to help translate what he heard in his head to tape. "To get the sound that you want," he told Cutting Edge magazine, "you have to really use an engineer who understands what you're trying to do. It's like getting a haircut you know? Take a little of the top and leave the sideburns and, you know? Block it in the back, you know? It's actually how you talk to your barber, so... Musicians like to be told what you're looking for." The man who wound up with the gig was engineer Bob Musso, who recalled that "right before I worked with Tom, I'd worked with Mick Jagger – which had been of course a career highlight – then I got the call saying 'Tom Waits wanted to do a record in New York.'"

Recalling the pair's first meeting, Musso noted several important life changes the singer was in the midst of at that time. "I actually met him at a Times Square donut shot where the hookers all had the names of the donuts, and he was totally cool. I asked him if he wanted to go get a drink afterward, and that's when I found out he had stopped drinking. We decided to work together, and it started off great." As Waits unveiled his latest collection of songs during pre-production, Musso recalls him saying that the songs were going to be a little different. "When I asked 'How so?', he said 'You'll find out.'"

As the two began hunting around for the right recording studio in which to bring the project to life, Musso recalled it was Waits who finally settled on RCA. "After speaking to him a few times before we got into the studio, he had mentioned we were going into RCA and that he would be using a lot more studio musicians than on past albums. The main studio was absolutely gigantic; they used to film the Tonight Show from this room: they would put a full audience, a full Tonight Show band, all the camera and production crew and the stage in the studio, then they'd close off the other half. That's how big it was."

Waits clearly required a big studio to accommodate the city of sounds he heard in his head, but engineer Musso had no idea heading into production what exactly that sound would be. "I didn't know if it was going to be one of those older type of records, like 'The Heart Of Saturday Night' or a jazz record, or something altogether different." Waits explained to the LA Times that "I produced the record because I didn't want to argue with anyone... Recording is like getting a haircut. Before you know it it's too late and then you have to wait for it to grow out and look stupid in the meantime. The only difference is records don't grow out."

As Bob Musso explained, "Tom really did not want to respect any traditional recording rules." The engineer was careful to add that "Tom had a really, really good general idea of the craziness that we could put on the normal songs to make it the way he wanted, and most of the time, it actually worked really, really well."

Waits' opinion of the technical process of recording, as offered to the LA Times in 1985, was that it had become very sophisticated. "There are dozens of different sounds you can easily incorporate into your work at the touch of a button... But in order to feel like it's my record I have to feel like I went out, found it, killed it and drug it back myself. I like to get in the bathroom and hit a bunch of drawers with a two-by-four and get down on my back and sing into a pipe. It makes me feel more involved."

Preferring a more simplistic approach, Waits quipped to journalist Elissa van Poznak that he preferred Musso to "just gimme the basics. I'm overwhelmed by technology... For me it's very basic like I'm making it out of wood but technology, being in the studio, is very abstract. It's a battle. Keith Richards was talking about that. He said you have to go in there with a stick, a drum and something you heard in a bar. You have to carry the idea with you." Waits' plan of attack heading into the recording of 'Rain Dogs', he told You magazine, was to tale "some chances. 'Swordfishtrombones' was done in Los Angeles. It was much more relaxed, much more leisure-oriented."

Waits was chasing a sound that Rolling Stone magazine would conclude "conjures a brilliantly fleshed-out landscape." He was helped by a supporting cast of musicians he characterised as "some people that I really liked very much," adding in the same conversation with CBC Stereo that the band's ability to experiment made "the whole process...very enjoyable." The LA Times would report that "stellar cast of contributing musicians "included John Lurie and Robert Quine, the album is lit with exotic instrumental seasonings – a wheezing Farfisa organ, marimbas, accordion – that place it in the land that rock forgot."

Offering a more intimate look at the roster of players, engineer Bob Musso recalled that "he had some great musicians in mind for the sessions. I turned him onto a couple some as well, including Marc Ribot – who I'd worked with before and thought was really good – and Michael Blair, who was one of the guys I played with in a Buddy Holly show. I recommended him because I knew Michael was big on playing hubcaps and experimental types of percussive sounds. Tom liked Michael, so that worked out really well."

Tom told You magazine that this "experimental direction" with arrangements that were both "original and striking" required him to exhaust himself in the details. "If I want a sound, I usually feel better if I've chased it and killed it, skinned it and cooked it. Most things you can get with a button nowadays. So if I was trying for a certain drum sound, my engineer would say: 'Oh, for Christ's sake, why are we wasting our time? Let's just hit this little cup with a stick here, sample something (take a drum sound from another record) and make it bigger in the mix, don't worry about it.' I'd say, 'No, I would rather go in the bathroom and hit the door with a piece of two-by-four very hard.'"

Percussion played an important role in giving Waits' musical imagination its dancing legs, he revealed to Rolling Stone. "I'm more interested in things that make noise... I had a piledriver by my window last summer that worked all day, every day and Sundays, and I started making tape recordings of it, and my wife says, 'Jeez Christ, not only do we have to listen to this unnatural sound, now at night he finally knocks off and you have to play tapes of it!"

He confessed to journalist Gavin Martin that what sent him sailing off in that abstract sonic direction was "getting lazy... I guess I'm just more curious... I'm just trying to find different ways of saying the same thing. I used to hear everything with a tenor saxophone, I had a very particular musical wardrobe. I've opened up a bit more." Bob Musso remembered that "one day we were trying all sorts of stuff, and nothing was working. At the end of the day, he came up to me and said 'Bob, sometimes I need to walk around the block to realise I'm back where I started and I should take one step in the other direction.'"

That other direction took Waits' fans into another rhythmic realm that Rolling Stone called "junkyard orchestration". Delving with author Bart Hopkins into some of the subtexts of his new organic, rhythmic fascinations, Waits volunteered that in the course of making 'Rain Dogs', he was "also drawn to dumpsters. They have a better sound than any bass drum or timpani, so I took a '4 Cubic Yard Debris Box', the kind with two hinged tops, welded the top shut and used a cutting torch to make a two-foot diameter hole in the centre of the side panel. I then attached seven very choice strings from a salvaged upright piano and stretched them across the hole, fastening them to the surface with two welded bridges.

"You can play it with a silver dollar or a guitar pick, or bow it if you're man enough, and you can also use a wine bottle for a slide – the sound is train-like and huge, like trash day with a purpose. I call it the Strata Dumpster or the Dumpstalele (distant cousin of the uke). I am paying more attention to the sounds produced by dragging chairs across the floor. Metal folding chairs with the missing rubber knobs in empty rooms or on bare linoleum can't be beat; they turn the whole room into a resonator. Drag a ladder, high chair or stool across the floor – some will sustain a note that reminds me of bad bus brakes."

Waits shared in the same conversation the guerilla tracking techniques he employed to capture the latter to tape. "I have a series of recordings I made of the peculiar rhythms and inner voices available from close-micing old upholstered spring rocking chairs. The rhythms are machine-like in their cyclical pattern of metal squeaks and chugs. The springs give the feeling of a printing press, typewriter or rusty cuckoo clock. You can vary your tempo depending on how fast you rock, and the older the chair the more interesting the rhythms will be. Windshield wiper blades on older automobiles are a great source of unusual rhythms and found sound. You can achieve some scary impossible harmonics with rusty blades on a hot day with a dry window."

Offering the album track 'Singapore' as an example of his experimental percussion playing to a successful tune, Waits shared with KCRW FM DJ Chris Douridas that "I always remembered that in the studio the drum sound that we used was a two by four attacking somebody's chest of drawers and the whole song played and all the backbeats were played with a two by four hitting the chest of drawers repeatedly and on the last bar of the song the whole piece of furniture had collapsed and there was nothing left of it and the song was over... That's what I think of when I hear the song. I see the pile of wood and it excites me. Michael Blair was the percussionist It wasn't a very expensive chest of drawers – it was just one that we'd found out on the sidewalk."

Blair was required to adapt to any rhythmic imitation Waits sought to recreate on tape, as well as accommodate mechanical sounds that the artist might have incorporated into a given soundscape. Engineer Musso recalled an example of the more experimental end of that production in action. "We had Michael in one of the small closets off of Studio A in the old RCA studios. He was playing a two by four that he had in his hand, and he was hitting a wooden drawer out of a dresser.

So imagine taking a wooden drawer, turning it over, and hitting that with a two by four in a really small closet. I miced it with a room mic, an RCA 44 ribbon mic that was about 10 feet away.

"In general, during tracking," he continued, "I used a EV RE 20 on the kick drum at times, a Sennheiser MD 421 on the toms, a pair of Neumann U 67s tube microphones as overheads, and AKG 451 on the hi-hat, and a Shure SM57 on the top and bottom snare. I like the SM57 for a lot of reasons, one being I know the mic really well and how to take advantage of the proximity effect (the closeness of the mic to the drum) if I wanted a fat drum sound. I also know that it's very directional and has a lot of side (rejection), so I can take the bottom snare mic and, while pointing it at the snares underneath about an inch and a half away, I can still point it away from the kick drum."

Turning to the album's snare sound, the producer explained that "I get a very good isolated snare sound, with very little kick drum in it because of the technique of actually pointing the two 57s away from the kick drum. And of course, I have to flip the phase on the bottom microphone. They're generally just good mid-range microphones, they don't have a whole lot of top and they don't have a whole lot of bottom, and that's the snare drum. The drums were in the open for the most part, on carpets, but in the open. I ended up using an old trick one of the RCA engineers taught me, where sometimes we took the Neumann U47 tube mics, and sometimes we took the RCA ribbon mics, and put them on these stands and cranked them up about 30 feet, then put them through a Neve 1066 pre-amp EQ into a Neve 2254 compressor and then smashed the tar out of it. 20 to 1 ratio, with the limiter and compressor both on, and the meters not moving. When we blended that in with the close mics at a certain volume level – that's the Tom Waits drum sound on 'Rain Dogs'."

Noting in its review of the album that "the music's percussiveness is startling," Rolling Stone would add that it was "perfectly suited to Waits' ever-deepening voice." The singer-songwriter shared with journalist Pete Silverton that while "vocabulary is my main instrument," in bringing the album's rain dogs fully to life," he'd discovered that with technology ever-advancing, "a lot of things can be obtained later in the recording process."

To accommodate Waits' preferred recording approach, Bob Musso shared that, as the duo tracked, "we would always record a vocal track, and a lot of times, he'd listen to it, think about it, and sometimes we kept it, and sometimes we'd go back and do vocals again. We did a few different things depending on whether it was a live take or an overdub, and I learned a bunch of old school tricks from my Atlantic Records days, and one of the things we did was take one of these Altec 666 salt-shaker mics, and put that through a Poltec filter (which is a passive hi-and-low pass filter with very steep bandwidths), and the combination of that mic – which doesn't have a whole lot of bandwidth to begin with – through the Poltec filter which gave Tom an even more twisted vocal sound. Just to be safe, because that was such an extreme sound, we usually had another microphone right next to it. Sometimes it was the ribbon RCA 44, sometimes an 87, sometimes the SM58. So as a rule, I always had two mics, just in case the weird sound was too weird."

Waits had, by that point in his recording career, abandoned his all-night recording sessions, preferring to begin recording by "about 10 in the morning. I was working in midtown. I had to fight all the traffic and all the other commuters. The hardest thing was just getting to the studio. After that I was all right."

Another conventional aspect of the recording process for 'Rain Dogs' was the technical layout of the studio, as engineer Bob Musso recalled. "RCA Studios was a very old, traditional studio... What they had was a great room and great mic selection."

Turning to the album's guitar tracking, Musso began by enlisting Marc Ribot to play lead guitar. Waits felt Ribot's approach was consistent with his experimental recording philosophy, sharing with Jim Jarmusch that "he's big on the devices. Appliances, guitar appliances. And a lot of 'em look like they're made out of tinfoil and, y'know, it's like he would take a blender, part of a blender, take the whole thing out and put it on the side of his guitar and it looks like a medical show...that look. And the sound seemed to come from, the way it looked and the way it sounded seemed to be the same. (He works with) alternative sound sources, he turns his guitar into an adventure."

As the New York Times, noted in their review of the LP, Ribot "helped Tom Waits refine a new, weird Americana." Ribot, for his part, comically recalled in a conversation with Options magazine that "'Rain Dogs' was my first major label recording, and I thought everybody made records the way Tom makes records... I've learned since that it's a very original and individual way of producing...he brings in his ideas, but he's very open to sounds that suddenly and accidentally occur in the studio."

Elaborating on Waits' approach to collaboration, the guitarist added in the same interview that "he works initially from a groove... He had this ratty old hollow body, and he would spell out the grooves. It wasn't a mechanical kind of recording at all. He has a very individual guitar style he sort of slaps the strings with his thumb... He plays guitar and he'll start communicating to his band what he wants the groove to be by rocking back and forth, and the band gets the message. He almost never said 'Play this' or 'Play that', but he'll keep going in what he wants until people come up with an idea that he's happy with.

"His basic way of working is editing. Waits doesn't dictate, he gives his musicians a lot of room to develop. He starts from a dramatic concept. He thought of the whole thing theatrically, and talked about the guitar as a character – adding a certain guitar part he'd talk of as bringing another character on-stage, like a director. I like his instruction on one tune: 'Play it like a midget's bar mitzvah.'"

Waits, seeming to appreciate Ribot's willingness to dive headlong into whatever direction the singer-songwriter's creative winds were carrying him, shared that, in that spirit, "he also gets himself whipped up into a voodoo frenzy. He gets the look in his eye that makes you want to back off. Y'know? It's like, 'Goddamn!' We were in some after hours place in Holland, in the corner, there was no stage, it was a club with normally no live music. We just got into the corner and plugged in and started to play. And everybody just pushed the tables and chairs back and it was real wild.

"Ribot banged into a speaker box, and there was a bottle of whiskey on it, and it tipped over, and it was full, and it just kept spilling out onto the floor, and he was getting under the stream of liquor, which was splashing onto the floor, and liquor was going everywhere, and you looked at his face and it was like an animal, he'd been, like worked up – whipped up into a place where he was gonna do something."

Ribot's sound, according to the engineer, was "jazzy and pop and quirky, and it was really his style of playing through a Fender Reverb. I miced him with a 57 and 421 with an 87 about a foot away, and that was it. A lot of it was what he did with the guitar itself. From my recollection, a lot of Marc Ribot's tracks were live, I think there were one or two overdubbed parts, but most were cut live during the basic tracks."

Rolling Stones guitarist Keith Richards joined Tom on 'Rain Dogs', following his collaboration with Waits on 'Swordfishtrombones' two years earlier. His playing inspired Rolling Stone (the magazine) to note that "Richards' energetic rocking rescues Waits' bluesy affectations. You have the core of what could have been the most consistent and wide-ranging record Waits ever made." The singer shared with music writer Michael Treason his admiration for the legendary guitarist. "I always loved his songs and his voice... He's a real animal. He's a real gentleman... I really was just lucky, they were coming here to finish up a record to mix an album. So I just got lucky. I thought: 'What have I got to lose?!'"

The dream moment came, he told Mojo, when "I was in New York. I remember somebody said 'Who do you want to play on the record? Anybody.' And I said, 'Ah, Keith Richards' – I'm a huge, huge fan of the Rolling Stones. They said 'Call him right now.' I was like, 'Jesus, please don't do that, I was just kidding around.' A couple of weeks later he sent me a note: 'The wait is over. Let's dance. Keith.' And I was ' Oh Jesus.' Shy? *Entirely* shy."

Tom had been expecting "a big entourage like a Fellini movie, you know – people that don't speak English, a lot of fur. And they just tumbled out of a limo. He comes in laughing, shoes all tore up. He stands at 10 after 7, if you can imagine that. Arms at 5 o'clock, legs at two o'clock, with no apparatus, nothing suspended. He's all below the waist. And if he doesn't feel it, he'll walk away. I was just flattered that he would come. It's kind of like a rite of passage or something."

The singer-songwriter added in an interview with the San Diego Union-Tribune of the session that "we played until about four in the morning, went through a bottle of Rebel Yell. Sour mash. Lighter fluid. He has a guitar valet. And it's unbelievable. Goes everywhere with him. Like a twisted version of 'Arthur'. It was quite astonishing to behold. It was really a great experience for me."

Waits felt made Richards' style of playing fitted his own sound so well because, he told Spin magazine, "I had this sound, I didn't know how to identify it, and I used to say, 'That Keith Richards-type style thing.' There was something in there I thought he would understand. I picked out a couple of songs that I thought he would understand and he did. He's got a great voice and he's just a great spirit in the studio. He's very spontaneous, he moves like some kind of animal. I was trying to explain 'Big Black Maria' and finally I started to move in a certain way and he said, 'Oh, why didn't you do that to begin with? Now I know what you're talking about.' It's like animal instinct."

Richards played on another song, 'Union Square', and did so in an animated fashion where "he leans so far forward, he must have a string attached to the back of his neck and it's run up and it's being held to the ceiling and it keeps him from falling flat on his face. It's unbelievable. He had these old shoes (that)...looked like a dog chewed 'em up...and he looks like a pirate. He's a killer."

Waits came to understand that, when Richards' wasn't performing, he was a very down-to-earth personality. "I didn't realise it at first, but then I met his father and understood. His dad looked like Popeye. He had the little corncob pipe and the wink in his eye – oh man, I was real nervous and trying not to be afraid, but he's real regular, a gentleman, and we had a lot of fun."

Richards, for his own part, explained in his memoir of the duo's history and creative chemistry that "Tom Waits was an early collaborator back in the mid-Eighties. I didn't realise until later that he'd never written with anyone else before except his wife, Kathleen. He's a one-off lovely guy and one of the most original writers. In the back of my mind I always thought it would be really interesting to work with him."

The teaming of Waits and Richards would be, for Waits' fans, one of the album's highlights. Detailing his set-up for Richards' gear, engineer Bob Musso – who coincidentally had worked with Richards' bandmate Mick Jagger prior to entering the studio with Waits – began by offering that "of course Keith Richards was all overdubbed. Keith is a real professional, and he was great to work with. He was in a great mood, and I thought he sounded and played great. He pretty much did one or two passes on the songs that he played. He came in with his own gear, which included a great old Telecaster and a great old Fender Tweed amplifier; he played, and it was a blast, He was a gentleman and a real nice guy, very humble.

"I miced him with an SM57 and a Sennheiser MD 421 up close, and then an 87 back about a foot to 18 inches, and I would usually get a blend of all three microphones onto one track." The engineer added that "I really liked the upright bass sound on that record. One of the things we did was take a Neumann KM 84, wrapped it in foam, and actually stuck it inside the bass. There was a direct signal off the bridge pick-up as well, but the actual, main part of that bass sound is because that microphone is inside that bass."

Musso recalls that "most of the basic tracks were done at extremely low volumes, so imagine that everyone could hear the acoustic upright bass in the room, even if I hadn't miced it, that's how quiet people were playing, so only the overdubs were really loud. We worked song by song, and Tom would set up so that pretty much a good 70 to 80 per cent of the foundation of the song, sometimes including the vocal, would all be part of the basic track. So there was overdubs, but not really a whole lot, and that is part of the vibe that's great on that record."

Waits spoke to CBC Stereo (Canada) about some of the specific players that helped accent the album, beginning with Robert Quine on 'Blind Love'. "He saved the song for me. I was about ready to dump it. Quine...plays with Lou Reed. And he came in and gave it that Jimmy Reed, kind of a little bit of (bluesman)

Jimmy Reed in there. And I was just 'Goddamn, that's all right, 'cause I didn't know what the hell to do with it.' It just had a bass and a guitar. I figured 'Well maybe we ought to open this up and put a little story in here.' You know, a little spoken part. And I thought I just played it a little straight. I thought it came off real straight." He added in of 'Anywhere I Lay My Head' that the song was "a gospel thing, the Uptown Horns played on that."

Musso recalled that Tom maintained a boundless open-mindedness throughout overdubbing to achieve what the LA Times would later celebrate as "an exquisitely detailed song cycle of impressive range. 'Rain Dogs' includes mournful country laments, linking bits of incidental music, off-colour nursery rhymes, shaggy dog stories and gut-bucket rhythm and blues." In creating that range of sounds, the engineer offered candidly his memory that "it was trial and error – 'Let's try this', 'No, that didn't really work, how about that?', until we found the right instrument.

"I always had a few microphones set up – sometimes 414s, U87s, U47s, RCA ribbons. And I'd just audition a different mic in different positions away from the percussionist, and sometimes Michael Blair would have a hub cap, or a Chinese gong, or some other pieces of metal he was hitting together. A lot of times it was about finding the right instrument sound in that regard, rather than the micing technique. Tom had a really good idea of what he wanted as far as that goes. I tried to help him out as much as possible not to make any obvious wrong turns from an engineering point of view if I saw any, and he took my advice into account for the most part, and sometimes he didn't."

The album's horn parts, Musso recalled, "were overdubbed, and most of the time miced with 87s or 67s, and occasionally – depending if it was a crazy bass saxophone, I would use a RCA 44 maybe 15 feet away, just overly compressed, and it's just amazing how close that horn would sound… Sometimes Tom sang then a phrase, and then he would let the horn section figure out the actual two or three parts they would be playing around that phrase. Other times, he might say something like 'I want to make this kind of bold and expressive, imagine you're walking around with your chest out – play it like that.'"

Past albums had seen Waits' piano central to the sound. But this time, as he told radio host Michael Tearson, on some songs, " I didn't really feel compelled to sit down at the piano at all. I played a little guitar and I had… The piano always brings me indoors y'know? And I was trying to explore some different ideas and some different places in the music." Tom added that he liked beginning with the ivories because "the piano always feels like you know where you are."

For those tracks where Tom did play piano, his engineer explained that "a lot of times it was just one mic inside, I believe they had an upright and a grand piano there, and we went back and forth between the two, and I didn't want to use any incredible modern beautiful stereo micing technique, because it's just not Tom Waits in my opinion. So I was going for more of an older, dirtier street sound on the piano, so I even think I used some ribbon mics at times, just to give it that older sound. And sometimes we just dropped the microphone in the upright and went for it. The upright mic would have been 87, or a 58. For the grand, it would have been a pair of 67s."

Musso recalled on the vocal front that "when Tom wasn't happy with his original vocal take, then we went back and just concentrated on vocals". Offering an example of one of many new directions he took with his voice as an instrument on 'Rain Dogs', the singer-songwriter recalled in a conversation with author Bart Hopkins that "around 1982, my wife Kathleen encouraged me to try singing through a police bullhorn to make my voice stand out in relief when incorporated with instruments of the same colour. Of course, it's possible to do the same thing with an equaliser, but nothing beats the drama of a bullhorn."

He traced his discovery of the instrument to engineer Biff Dawes who, Waits recalled, "purchased me my first, and it was love at first sight – I never record or tour without it. I also try to buy a new one every year, because they continue to 'improve' upon them. I find the older Eighties models (the Falon is available at Radio Shack for about $29.95) superior; they're warmer to the ear. Also interesting to explore are the ones made for children, that can change a voice from monster to spaceman to robot. I found humming through them can give you a sound much like Blue Cheer's guitar sound on 'Summertime Blues'."

Tom had another interesting instrument in his armoury which he bought in 1985 from two teenage surfers in Westwood, California. "The Chamberlin is an early-Sixties analogue synthesiser that stores all of its voices (over 60 in total) on tape loops, and with a series of pulleys and chains and springs plays an eleven-second 'memory' of prerecorded sound stored on the tape. Then a spring snaps it back to the beginning, and it's ready to play again. It's a keyboard instrument, and I believe I own one of the early prototypes, because the 'preset' instrument menu is written in longhand.

"It contains some of the most haunting sounds I have ever encountered, including an operatic human voice (both male and female), portamento trombone, pizzicato violin, chimes, gong, squeaking door, thunder and rain, train whistles and chugs, acoustic bass, cello, clarinet, applause and various birds and dogs. The Rube Goldberg mechanism inside is as fascinating as the curiously strange sounds it holds in its tape bank."

Sharing some of his favourite recording memories from the making of 'Rain Dogs', engineer Bob Musso began by singling out 'Downtown Train', later a hit for Rod Stewart. "We were pretty deep into the project, and the record company is calling me trying to figure out when we can really wrap it up and finish the mixing, and we hadn't finished recording the vocals yet. I remember we'd worked all day one day on vocals, and one of the last songs we were recording was 'Downtown Train'. It was really great because it was kind of the end of the day voice for Tom, and had really the right character and expressions and the Tom Waits enunciation and flow; it was just perfect."

The producer added that "once we'd recorded this lead vocal I really thought it was the one. So Tom was like, 'Well, I don't know Bob, its good but I think I could do better.' So I said, 'Alright, why don't I make a cassette for you, you take it home and listen to it overnight, and if you think you can do it better we'll come in tomorrow and give it another shot.' So I set up a rough mix on the board at RPM – no EQ, just a little reverb – then asked the assistant to press record on the cassette machine, said goodbye and went to another session I had booked."

The next morning, Musso recalled, his assistant revealed that he and Tom had spent another few hours after his departure trying to get a better vocal take. "We listened back to the cassette of the rough mix from the night before, he looked at me and said 'Nope, I don't think I can make that any better, that's the one.' And I said 'Tom, all we have is a cassette recording of it', and he says, 'Well, let's use it.' So I made a transfer of the cassette onto half-inch tape, and that's the reason that song is so noisy on the record."

On 'Big Black Mariah', another highlight vocal moment for Musso, the engineer recalled that "Tom wanted that hard, swinging attitude from the rhythm section, and he got it. His vocal was right there accenting the pulses of the rhythm section. And it was one of those vocal performances that was an overdub that I thought was really, really great, and he just totally nailed it. For me, his vocal really makes that song." As was the case with many of Waits' most interesting successes in experimentation, his singularly unique and powerful vocal style is as central as any of its other ingredients.

By the time attention turned to mixing, the team had moved shop from RCA to RMP Studios, working on a Neve 8068 console, in an atmosphere where Musso felt, "toward the end, Tom really wanted to do it his own and he wasn't really listening to anybody, but it worked out really well. I think he does that on purpose because he's really trying to do something new – that's part of his experimental quirkiness, but it was not necessarily an organised musical experiment, if you want it call it that. It was just Tom's way of working as he explored this new sound."

One influence that remained quietly constant throughout the entirety of recording was that of Tom's wife Kathleen Brennan, whose input the engineer characterised as consistently "pertinent, and I think that if there was any advice that she gave him, it was not in front of me, because I didn't hear it. I didn't hear her say anything except 'That sounds good.'"

As with every of the prolific artist's LPs, there were the invariable leftovers. 'Bethlehem, PA' was one of those cuts, Waits explaining to Spin magazine that "it's about a guy named Bob Christ There were a couple of others... I end up dismantling them. It's just like having a car that doesn't run. You just use it for parts. It took a long time to record this album, two and a half months. The recording process has a peak, and then it dissipates. You have to be careful that it doesn't go on too long."

Waits shared with journalist Gavin Martin that, in contrast to former label Elektra, he was content to continue his relationship with Island Records. "I'm happier to be on a small label," he said, describing the label's founder/owner Chris Blackwell as "artistic, a philanthropist You can sit and talk with him and you don't feel you're at Texaco or Heineken or Budweiser. There's something operating here that has a brain, curiosity and imagination."

With 'Rain Dogs', Waits had created what the BBC would later hail as "probably his finest album." A chorus of critics concurred, Rolling Stone agreeing that Tom's latest offering ranked "among the best work Waits has done." Mojo found the album "ambitious and immensely satisfying," while Spin declared it a "clattering and martial masterpiece" that the New York Times would hail as "the best pop record of 1985."

Indeed, 'Rain Dogs' made many such lists, making Number 21 in both New Musical Express and Rolling Stone's Albums of the Eighties. Downbeat concluded that the album represented "Waits' most solid work to date," adding their observation that "it's a more focused and satisfying affair than his more experimental album of 1983, 'Swordfishtrombones'."

Time Out magazine was so impressed by the album's stylistic range that they hailed Tom Waits as "one of the great songwriters of his generation." Waits himself candidly volunteered that "I think I'd like to take a crack at a wider audience, but with that comes responsibility. If you're too big you get self-conscious, if you're too obscure you feel nervous. So it's hard…"

"I've been saying that it's a cross between Eraserhead and It's A Wonderful Life."' – TOM WAITS, SPIN MAGAZINE, 1987

"On this album I tried to take each song individually and create its own world." – TOM WAITS

PART XIII 'Frank's Wild Years' (1987)

Tom Waits approached his twelfth studio LP with a determination to broaden his sound even further, heading into the outer expanses of the stylistic galaxies he'd already thoroughly explored over the course of 'Swordfishtrombones' and 'Rain Dogs.' Indeed, critics were taking close notes on this continual creative metamorphosis, NME observing that "post 'Swordfishtrombones', we have a different Tom Waits, a singer who has reinvented himself, broadened his scope and opened his eyes and ears to a whole new world of received and reconstructed music... 'Frank's Wild Years' completed a period of transition and cleared the way for another step...(into) ever-increasing theatricality."

GQ continued the theatrical reference, pointing out that "the music Waits is creating these days makes the most sense when thought of as some new, bastard form of opera." The singer-songwriter felt coming full circle in that musical transformation "closes a chapter," elaborating to the New York Post that "I guess somehow the three of them seem to go together...'cause Frank took off in 'Swordfish', had a good time in 'Rain Dogs' and he's all grown up in 'Frank's Wild Years'. They seem to be related – maybe not so much in content, but at least in terms of being a marked departure from the albums that came before. In that I produced all three of 'em, so I feel closer to 'em. I got some stuff out. I didn't get everything out that I wanted to but I made some minor little breakthroughs for myself – things I wanted to hear."

Rolling Stone began to unravel the mystery of 'Frank's Wild Years' by explaining it was "based on songs from a musical play Waits wrote with Brennan; first staged by Chicago's Steppenwolf Company, it was about a rough'n'tumble lounge singer freezing to death on a park bench, recalling his life in hallucinatory fashion." 'Frank's Wild Years' would prove as animated and mentally provocative a listening experience as any of his past works, illustrating Tom's genius as it sang through yet another convincing voice.

Waits explained to Musician magazine that alter ego Frank O'Brien was "quite a guy. Grew up in a Bird'seye-frozen, oven-ready, rural American town where Bing, Bob, Dean, Wayne & Jerry are considered major constellations. Frank, mistakenly, thinks he can stuff himself into their shorts and present himself to an adoring world. He is a combination of Will Rogers and Mark Twain, playing accordion – but without the wisdom they possessed. He has a poet's heart and a boy's sense of wonder with the world. A legend in Rainville since he burned his house down and took off for the Big Time."

Waits added in a discussion with journalist Dave Hoekstra that the album/play's plotline "picks up where the song leaves off (Frank has torched his house, along with Carlos the chihuahua he despised). This guy comes from a small town and he went to Vegas to try and be a big-time entertainer. Eight years later he's penniless, it's 30 below and he's wearing a pair of Bermuda shorts in East St Louis. And he's about ready to have a stroke. He falls asleep on a park bench and he dreams himself home."

Musician magazine explained that "'Frank's Wild Years' takes the form of a reminiscence, the story of a guy who decided to let fantasy navigate his life's course (in the original song, he escapes middle-class bondage by torching his house). It's a kind of American Dream." Albeit an American Dream as seen through the eyes of Tom Waits' alter-ego, a persona the New York Times noted at the time "has many antecedents, from the populist sentimentality of Weill and Saroyan to Edith Piaf, William Burroughs and such southern California rock vanguardists as Captain Beefheart and Frank Zappa. Mr Waits sometimes appears entrapped by his obsessions."

Tom told the New York Post that the music had preceded the play: "They were songs first, they lived outside the story." In elaborating on the roots of Frank's motives throughout the record, he explained that, at heart, "It's really a simple story of a guy who is very near suicide, who has been allowed to kind of walk back through his life before he goes under. And he has a chance to turn the ship around, set a new course for himself. That's really all it's about."

Elaborating on the character's own cathartic journey back through the forest of his past, Waits offered that "It just represents somebody who decided to make a change in his life, and in order to do that you have to cut some of the strings that are holding you there, that's all. And then he came back looking for some answers, because the road that he took led him down some very dark paths. So he came home to kind of purge himself and confess and look for some reasons to keep going. It's like going through your past looking for answers, that's all."

Tom cautioned that, by the end of the album, "he's no hero, he is no champion," adding in the same discussion with music-writer Rip Rense that "he was really a guy who stepped on every bucket on the road. His friends kind of pull him out of it, and tell him he's got plenty to live for. In the end, he wakes up on the bench, ready to start again." Starting fresh was a theme Waits had readily and continually embraced throughout the albums that made up the trilogy concluded by 'Frank's Wild Years'.

Reflecting to Musician on how his songwriting approach and process had changed during that period, Waits described it as a journey. "You don't know where it's going to take you, the people that you meet and the changes your life will bring. I can say I wished I'd jumped off earlier, but I don't know if I actually jumped off anything or else, you know, just redecorated. But I know that the last three records are a departure from what I was doing; I'm very aware of that. I don't write the same way."

Waits traced that change back to "a time (that comes)...when you get to an impasse and you have to break the vertebrae of your previous approach and reset it." He added that, as he sought to recalibrate Frank's fortunes, "I started thinking that I really had put governors on most of my ideas. I had surveyed a very small place to work from and write about... Before, I felt like, 'This song is me, and I have to be in the song.' I'm trying to get away from feeling that way. I'm trying to let the songs have their own anatomy, their own itinerary, their own outfits."

The impasse, Waits confessed to the New York Post, meant that "it's hard for me to listen to my earlier stuff. I mean, a lot of people write for a long time without being recognised. By the time you do emerge, you have this network of roots that can be thought of as your own private repertoire; what you build everything else upon. Well, I kind of got it all out there on top and I kind of wish sometimes it was private; that I was standing on the shoulders of something that was impossible to see. It's good, though, to be able to grow and explore publicly, and have people be part of that process and let you move around and change hats; live in different countries. I'm just starting to use my own musical heritage – all filtered through the lens of your own experience in time. That's what I'm trying to do with the music."

Waits told Mojo that, with 'Frank's Wild Years', "I wanted to find music that felt more like the people who were in the songs rather than everybody being kind of dressed up in the same outfit." For fans keener on his earlier material, Tom offered that while "the people in my earlier songs might have had unique things to say and have come from diverse backgrounds," he felt ultimately a change of stylistic fashion was necessary at that point in his career because, by then, "they all looked the same."

Tom explained to Playboy that, to channel his latest inspirations, "I try to make an antenna, a lightning rod out of myself, so whatever is out there can come in. It happens in different places, in hotels, in the car – when someone else is driving. I bang on things, slap the wall, break things – whatever is in the room. There are all these things in the practical world that you deal with on a practical level, and you don't notice them as anything but what you need them to be."

As Tom absorbed his various inspirations from the outside world, they filtered through him in such a way that. "when I'm writing, all these things turn into something else, and I see them differently, almost like I've taken a narcotic. Somebody once said I'm not a musician but a tonal engineer. I like that. It's kind of clinical and primitive at the same time."

Tom found song ideas coming to him easily because inspiration was "really all around you all the time." The challenge came in "framing it. You gotta catch it – make sure your umbrella is upside down." The singer-songwriter told the LA Times that, when writing for 'Frank's Wild Years', "I get in the car, I just start to drive, and my mind wanders... I am not a photojournalist I do not do reportage. You tell someone stories – they come from a lot of places, dreams and memories and lies and things, things you found and heard and saw and read and dreamed and made up."

Waits explained to Playboy that "I've learned how to be different musical characters without feeling like I'm eclipsing myself. On the contrary, you discover a whole family living inside you." Describing the vernacular he developed for that 'family' specifically in the context of Frank O'Brien, he told NME that "what happens is that you sorta evolve a language. I got my own shorthand," adding to journalist Bill Forman that, though he drew from the real world around him in building the world around Frank, "usually you hide what everything represents. You're the only one who really knows. I don't so much chronicle things that happen to me as kind of break down the world and dismantle it and rebuild it and look at it that way. Pieces from a lot of different places."

As much as Waits tried to control the shaping of Frank's wild years, he confessed to the New York Post that "I'm starting to find that songs find their own logic." He explained that he nurtured each of his songs as gently as he would his own children in terms of letting them grow into their own distinct selves. "When we listen to them, we don't push them in a logical fashion. We let them go in some other place. They have their own kind of Joseph Cornell collection of images. So sometimes a lyric comes to me; I try to deliberately find things that don't particularly have a meaning at the moment. Then I write 'em down, then I think about 'em. Then I understand 'em...Songs can be about anything. If you master the art of it, you can aim at anything."

Waits once again co-wrote with wife Kathleen Brennan, sharing in the same conversation with the Post his feeling that "we're great together, it's a real even exchange" and elaborating to Playboy that "she encourages me to go into areas I would not go, and I'd say that a lot of the things I'm trying to do now, she's encouraged." Quipping to WXRT Radio that, as a team, "she's responsible primarily for the libretto and I'm responsible for the music," the pair billed the album as 'Un Operachi Romantico in Two Acts', which Waits told journalist Gary Tausch was "something Kathleen and I came up with. But it's not like I'm studying opera or anything. This is just one of my own demented adaptations of things I've seen and heard and remembered. Actually, what I like most about the old recordings of opera is the scratches as much as the music."

Many of the LP's musical ideas, Tom revealed to Musician magazine, came from "the mistakes – most things begin as a mistake. Most breakthroughs in music come out of a revolution of the form. Someone revolted, and was probably not well-liked. But he ultimately started his own country." For Waits, the heart of that creative revolution began when he started "trying to get my music to be more like what goes on inside my head," explaining to City Limits magazine that "for a long time I wrote in a very restricted world. I gave myself limited tools to work with. It got to a point where my life and what was really going on in my head what I was really hearing, was very different from what I was writing."

The style of music he was writing for 'Frank's Wild Years' saw Tom "pay attention to elements, I want to try to bring different colours in." In spite of its complexities, he insisted in a discussion with the Chicago Tribune that "the songs themselves are basically very simple...they're like field hollers and jail poems and Irish folk songs in terms of structure – this isn't (modernistic, atonal Austrian composer) Schoenberg or anything like that. If you stripped these songs down you could play them on a guitar; there hasn't been any deep, radical departure from my approach to writing."

Tom told the New York Post that, in the course of adapting the album's music from stage to studio, "the whole approach to each one, in terms of getting them to have their own character, changes. When you have a band on stage, you can't radically change from song to song – the instrumentation, that is." One outside influence on his writing for the project, specifically the title track, that Waits suggested to WXRT Radio came courtesy of "Ken Nordine, who's a real hero of mine. I love his thought process and his word jazz and his stories, they're like movies for the ears."

As with his past few albums, Tom was keen to credit his wife for her contribution, informing journalist Rip Rense that "we worked side by side on it. I'm getting to the point where I can take chances, I think. It's hard when you're a producer, and you're writing and performing. You need somebody you can trust standing on the outside to kind of push you into the water."

Delving into the writing of some of the record's specific cuts as they tied into the broader storyline, Waits – in a conversation with the New York Post – began with 'Train Song', explaining it was "kind of a gospel number. Frank is on the bench, really on his knees and can't go any further. At the end of his rope on a park bench with an advertisement that says 'Palladin Funeral Home.'" Trying to escape the hopelessness of the 'Cold, Cold Ground', Tom said of the song that it was "the only real Marty Robbins-influenced number on there. Just kind of a harkening back to his earlier times; a romantic song thinking about home, and all that."

Of 'Yesterday Is Here', the singer-songwriter recalled in the same conversation that "the title was given to me by Fred Gwynne. He had the title, and didn't know what to do with it. He said 'It's yours; see what you can make of it.'" Waits credited his wife Kathleen for changing "the melody on that. It was almost like a Ray Charles number before. All of a sudden we ended up with Morricone. Wanted to get some of that spaghetti-western feel. 'Today is grey skies/Tomorrow is tears/ You'll have to wait till yesterday is here."

Tom confessed that where, on previous albums, he used to be frightened of the studio, his wife's encouragement and his own ambitions had helped him discover in recent years that "there's a lot you can do if you don't allow it to intimidate you." Explaining in the same conversation with music writer Bill Foreman that he viewed the studio as "a laboratory," Waits was careful to note that by no means did he consider himself a sonic scientist, volunteering that "I'm still very primitive in the studio. It's not a science and I don't approach it that way. And I don't necessarily have a way of working now that I bring with me every time I record. Mainly I try to keep things spontaneous and live, full of suggestions. Keep it living."

Tom offered to Playboy that, in the process of bringing his songs to life in the studio, "you fashion these…ideas into your own monster. It's making dreams. I like that." Waits' vision of that musical monster arguably looked something like Frankenstein in his willingness to be "very crude" in the course of creating, explaining that "I use things we hear around us all the time, built and found instruments – things that aren't normally considered instruments: dragging a chair across the floor or hitting the side of a locker real hard with a two-by-four, a freedom bell, a brake drum with a major imperfection, a police bullhorn. You know, I don't like straight lines. The problem is that most instruments are square and music is always round."

The singer-songwriter explained to the New York Post that, in contrast from the stage version of the songs, as he produced, he was "trying to (change)...the way they're arranged and recorded, tamper with the way they're perceived," adding that "in the studio I can make them sound as if they're coming over a crystal set. You can shape them like they're made out of wire... While in the studio, it's made of smoke, you can just move it around. If you strip the songs down, they're very simple." One area of recording where Waits had embraced the increasingly advanced multi-track recording technology now available to him came in his admission to Musician that "a lot of this stuff is 24-track; I finally allowed that and joined the twentieth century, at least in that regard."

Another aspect of his recording process that had changed was highlighted in Musician magazine's observation that "much of what separates Waits' past three albums from his early career...is the way he's expanded his musical palette, from solo piano man to chief alchemist for a gang of complementary dispositions. Those cohorts include guitarist Marc Ribot, percussionist Michael Blair, bassist and horn arranger Greg Cohen, Ralph Camey on saxophone and William Schimmel on a variety of equipment, from accordion to Leslie bass pedals. Waits' instruments include pump organ, guitar, Mellotron, even something called the Optigon."

Stylistic changes notwithstanding, the singer-songwriter stayed loyal to his players, confirming to WXRT Radio that, indeed, "most of the band members were on my last record: Greg Cohen, Michael Blair, Ralph Carney and Morris Tepper on guitar. So it's a real good group...(and) William Schimmel is our accordion player, he plays accordion, pump organ, piano." Keeping his band on their talented toes throughout tracking, Waits shared with journalist Bill Foreman that one of his favoured tricks was to have band members "sometimes (approach)... an instrument you're unfamiliar with," offering that often "the discovery process is good." Painting a picture of this experiment in action, Tom recalled that "I had Ralph Carney, the sax player, on several cuts where he played three saxes at once. And then Bill Schimmel playing the pedals, Greg Cohen playing alto horn."

Waits had finally assembled a band that could cover the wild spectrum of styles from his rainbow of musical colours. In the process, he was offering fans a gallery of songs that collectively embodied a sound Rolling Stone would celebrate as featuring "everything from sleazy strip-show blues to cheesy waltzes to supercilious lounge lizardry given spare, jarring arrangements using various combinations of squawking horns, bashed drums, plucked banjo, snaky double bass, carnival organ and jaunty accordion (the last provided by Los Lobos' David Hidalgo on two tracks)."

In the course of communicating over several albums with the same players, Waits, in a discussion with Option magazine, explained he felt he developed a "musical shorthand...after a while you can tell them with a nod, or you just get in the mood and they know that it was wrong and you don't even have to tell them why." That telepathy between band members and Waits as leader came from what Tom felt was their very own "way of communicating. Just like a director talks to an actor, you have to know how to say the right thing at the right time to the right person that will have meaning to them."

He expanded on that unspoken language in greater depth to Musician magazine, explaining he had surrounded himself "with people who can know when you're trying to discover something and they're part of the process. Keith Richards had an expression for it that's very apropos: He called it 'the hair in the gate'. You know when you go to the movies and you watch an old film, and a piece of hair catches in the gate? It's quivering there and then it flies away. That's what I was trying to do – put the hair in the gate."

Waits suggested in conversation with fellow music legend Elvis Costello that he loved paying attention to "the stuff that people are doing in-between takes...you have to always be aware of what's happening in the room at all times. Because as soon as the camera's not on and the tape's not rolling. The amount of time it takes to discover something, sometimes you discover it on the first moment, sometimes it takes two weeks to find it... It's music by agreement, to a degree."

Pushing his players to take out-of-the-box chances came to be a signature of his new sound. Tom, in the same conversation, reflected an ambition for chance-taking, wherein during recording "you look forward to the brilliant mistakes. Most changes in music, most exciting things that happen in music, occur through a miscommunication between people 'I thought you said this.' Poetry comes out of that too. It's like song lyrics, Kathleen always thought that Credence Clearwater song 'Bad Moon Rising' – she always thought, 'There's a bathroom on the right.' That's outside, a song about that, because that happens all the time – you go to a club, 'There's the bathroom on the right.' But I love those mistakes. I salute them and encourage them."

Delving into the creation of some of the album's most colourful tracks in the studio, Tom began with album opener 'Hang On St Christopher', recalling his fondest memory of the song's recording in a conversation with the New York Post that "it was really great to see Bill Schimmel, classically trained at Juilliard, on his hands and knees, playing the pedals of the B-3 organ with his fists. Working up a sweat. It was worth it just for that. Has kind of a little bit of a North African horn action going on – that's Ralph Carney and Greg Cohen. I think it moves along rather well. Kind of mutant James Brown."

Waits elaborated to Musician magazine on the song's creation, recalling that he took the "Leslie bass pedals and (raised) them up to a kitchen table so you can play them with your fists. Which is what we did in the studio... I'm trying to put together the right way of seeing the music. I worry about these things. If I didn't, it would be easier."

Turning to the 'North African' horn parts featured on the track, he shared that "that just happened in the studio... I think in music the intelligence is in the hands. The way your hands rub up along the ends of a table. You begin to go with your instincts. And it's only dangerous to the degree that you only let yourself discover the things that are right there. You'll be uncomfortable and so you'll keep returning to where your hands are comfortable. That's what happened to me on the piano. I rarely play the piano because I find I only play three or four things."

Discussing the recording of 'Straight To The Top (Rhumba)' with the New York Post, he said he was aiming to reflect "a little Louis Prima influence there. Louis Prima in Cuba. A little pagan. Not so Vegas – more pagan. Like a guy who is obviously not going straight to the top, but the fact that he feels as though he is makes you almost believe that he might be; that somebody like that is going to burn a hole in something – but certainly not the business. Probably himself. We used the Optigon on that... It's one of the early organs created for home use. Where you have a program disc that you put inside the organ, and it creates a variety of sound worlds for you to become part of. Like they have the Tahitian/Polynesian number complete with birds and waterfall. And you can be a 32-piece orchestra – instant adagio for strings, you know. There's a cabaret setting, a little jazz thing with a kind of Charlie Byrd feel to it."

The singer-songwriter shared of 'Temptation' that the song "started out real tame. I added a bunch of stuff to it, and it started to swing a little bit. Now it sounds practically danceable to me. The whole thing was sung in falsetto... The song was there; it obviously needed an injection of some kind, so I tried to sing it in a new way. If you have enough time to live with a song, you can find it." Of 'I'll Be Gone', Waits explained it as "kind of a Taras Bulba number. Almost like a tarantella. A Russian dance. The guy is speaking further of his departure – 'In the morning, I'll be gone.' The images...nitroglycerin, the pounding of hooves, women in the tent. Tomorrow we ride. It's an adventure number. Halloween music...from Torrance. Ritual music. Part of a pagan ritual we still observe in the Los Angeles area."

Speaking of 'Telephone Call From Istanbul', Waits recalled that the song "started as a title, then became just a junkyard for one banjo and drums there. Got a little eastern slant on it," adding to journalist Bill Foreman that "I usually don't like to isolate the instruments. On that song, I pulled out the Farfisa and then just put it in very hot at the end, just so it sounded kind of Cuban or something." On 'Please Wake Me Up', the singer-songwriter credited wife Kathleen with starting "out with the melody on that. It's just a little lullaby of some kind. With Mellotron, baritone horn, upright bass." Discussing 'Way Down In A Hole', Tom recalled that "we wrote that one real fast; it was practically written in the studio. Checkerboard Lounge gospel...that's Ralph Carney on three horns simultaneously... Here, Frank has thrown in with a berserk evangelist"

Tom cited 'I'll Take New York' as a track that "frightened me a little bit," specifically the section "toward the end when the ground starts to move a little bit. We just riffed on that in the studio. I described the mood of it, and everyone seemed to understand it an we got it. I think it's the closest thing on the record to a nightmare. Guy standing in Times Square with tuberculosis and no money; his last post card to New York. It's deranged." Composed first-hand from eye-witness research living in the heart of the city over the past few years, the song was "Frank's nightmare experience of New York."

Musician magazine commented of album closer 'Innocent When You Dream" that the song sounded like "a whisper from the hollows of a broken man's memory. It's a strange, funny and soulful saga, spiced with a cauldron of musical surprises Waits stirs together with shamanistic skill." Waits identified it as the track that tied the entire album together, "the song that got him started; that he went out on the road with, and this is a reprise. The 78 RPM (revolutions per minute) quality is to give it an epilogue feel."

The singer-songwriter explained the idea's genesis to journalist Bill Foreman. "The '78 version' of that was originally recorded at home on a little cassette player (the Tascam 244, the one with the clamshell holster). I sang into a seven-dollar microphone and saved the tape. Then I transferred that to 24-track and overdubbed Larry Taylor on upright (bass), and then we mastered that. Texture is real important to me; it's like attaining grain or putting it a little out of focus. I don't like cleanliness. I like surface noise. It kind of becomes the glue of what you're doing sometimes."

Waits, in a discussion with Musician magazine, seemed to find an amusing irony in the fact that "there's something in the fact of a studio with instruments you've spent thousands of dollars renting, to walk over to the bathroom and the sound of the lid coming down on the toilet is more appealing than that seven-thousand-dollar bass drum. And you use it. You have to be aware of that... I like picking up instruments I don't understand. And doing things that may sound foolish at first. It's like giving a blowtorch to a monkey. That's what I'm trying to do. Always trying to break something, break something, break through to something."

In that spirit, Waits shared with journalist Bill Foreman the desire "to stay open to as many choices as I can. It can be 13 bass players, it can be recorded outside, it can be done in the bathroom. There's a lot of ways to skin a cat. Being in the studio is like organising noise. I just had to learn how to know exactly what I wanted and not be satisfied until I heard it. It's a journey, it's like being a scavenger." Highlighting another percussive arena where the singer-songwriter had grown bolder in recent years, Waits confessed to WNEW New York that, prior to his recent studio efforts, "I was terrified of drums for a long time and now I'm less frightened of percussion than I used to be," adding to Option magazine that "it used to terrify me, the idea of drum machines, and now I've figured it still comes down to who's operating it."

One player from the band Tom felt was an invaluable asset to creating the latter soundscapes was guitarist Marc Ribot, who, he explained to journalist Bill Foreman, "prepares his guitar with alligator clips, and has this whole apparatus made out of tin foil and transistors that he kinda sticks on the guitar. Or he wraps the strings with gum, all kinds of things, just to get it to sound real industrial." Ribot, in turn, appreciated the artistic freedom he was allowed as a player during tracking, telling Option magazine that "he let me do what I hear. There was a lot of freedom. If it wasn't going in a direction he liked, he'd make suggestions. But there's damn few ideas I've had which haven't happened on the first or second take."

While listeners were impressed with Tom's increasingly adventurous soundscapes, Rolling Stone noted that it was "Waits' gravel-pit voice, from which he digs a number of distinct characterisations, that remains the most striking instrument." Crediting his ever-burgeoning film career with informing his skill as a vocalist, Tom shared his feeling with the New York Post that "in some way, acting and working in films has helped me in terms of being able to write and record and play different characters in songs without feeling like it compromises my own personality. That I can be different things in the studio that I can separate myself from the song... On this album, I've learned to try to approach each song like a character in a little one-act play. I don't feel like I have to be the same guy in all the songs. So in each one I set the stage for myself and I try to approach it in whatever way I have to in order to be living in the story. You know, method singing."

Waits had allowed each vocal performance to take on its own character, "trying to get away from feeling that way, and to let the songs have their own anatomy; their own itinerary; their own outfits." He shared with Bill Foreman that the effect made him "feel more like I'm building some kind of a little world for myself, my own territory."

He gave the voice of his alter-ego, Frank O'Brien, a fresh sound, one which iTunes noted found Waits "singing in a strained voice that has been artificially compressed and distorted." The singer revealed to journalist Rip Rense that this had been achieved by singing "all my vocals through a police bullhorn. Once you use a bullhorn, it's hard to go back. There's something about the power it commands and the authority it gave me in the studio."

Waits added in the same discussion of the significance the bullhorn played in tying the whole project together. "When I finally discovered what a bullhorn can do to your whole sound, it was a big moment for me. I'd never sung through a bullhorn. I'd tried to get that effect in other ways. I tried cupping my hands, singing into tin cans, using those seven-dollar harmonica microphones, singing into pipes and there it was. A battery-operated bullhorn available at Radio Shack for $29.95." Waits arrived at the bullhorn after trying "to stimulate that sound in a variety of ways," explaining to Musician magazine that those included "singing into trumpet mutes, jars, my hands, pipes, different environments. But the bullhorn put me in the driver's seat. There's so much you can do to manipulate the image, so much technology at your beck and call. But still you gotta make choices."

The result Waits achieved from "his recent vocal experimentations," in the opinion of GQ, "may very well lay the groundwork for the next innovations in singing. It's not that many singers will ever cop his technique of crooning through a police bullhorn as he does on 'Frank's Wild Years'. But Waits has been pushing and bending his vocal instrument the same way that the computer chip and MIDI (an electronic-instrument 'language') have allowed musicians to reinvent 'playing'." Elaborating on other experimental vocal innovations he discovered in the course of tracking his latest LP, the singer-songwriter shared with the same publication that "I've tried singing through pipes and trumpet mutes, singing into drinking glasses, cupping your hands, things that have been done before. You can call up a lot of these sounds through technology, but I'm discovering that if I find something myself and nail it to the wall, then it's mine." Ultimately, Tom – as he told the New York Post – seemed to find the greatest satisfaction from the organic aspect of the bullhorn because "it makes me feel like I'm making the sound rather than finding the sound through EQ and whatever."

Waits also appeared to have discovered another voice he was excited about incorporating into his new album's sound in the Mellotron, telling the New York Post that he loved the instrument because "the pump organ really has lungs. It actually breathes. I think I like the physical action of playing it; the sound it makes. It's always a little sour; always a little off. Each one has its own personality, and I have several of them now. The Mellotron, I've been hearing about over the years, and I've always been afraid of it. You know, when you hit a key, you actually get that particular note taped on a particular instrument. So when you hit the note, it feels like you're tapping somebody on the shoulder and they begin to play. It's very real. Dream real. Most of the instruments on the tracks, though, can be found in any pawn shop. I haven't completely joined the 20th century."

Waits added in a conversation with journalist Bill Foreman that "I've always liked the Mellotron. The Beatles used it a lot, Beefheart used it a lot. They're real old and they're not making them anymore. A lot of them pick up radio stations, CB calls, television signals and airline transmitting conversations." He added that the old-school nature of the instrument was challenging because "they're very hard to work with in the studio, they're unsophisticated electronically. So it's almost like a wireless or a crystal set."

In the same discussion, Tom also sang the praises of "the Optigon...(which is) kind of an early synthesiser/organ for home use. You have these discs that give you different environments – Tahitian, orchestral, lounge – and then you apply your own melodies to those different musical worlds. It comes with a whole encyclopedia of music worlds." Tom shared his hope with Musician that in the long run, "I'd like to see the accordion back at the vanguard of the world of music where it belongs."

Upon release on 17 August 1987, 'Frank's Wild Years' would be received critically as "Tom Waits at his rosiest," in the glowing opinion of Alternative Press, who further noted that "the best part about 'Frank's' is that it (is) no rock record. It's truly a musical with Waits' avant, freakish touch, including the hitting of some off-colour notes and Victrola-like warbles to add a touch of dementia to the mix." Mojo magazine highlighted the album's "genius flashes", while the New York Post celebrated the record as "a dreamy saga of fate and resurrection."

Having brought Frank's journey full circle with the release of 'Wild Years', Tom candidly revealed to Playboy regarding his future musical ambitions that "I don't know if I turned a corner, but I opened a door. I kind of found a new seam. I threw rocks at the window. I'm not as frightened by technology maybe as I used to be. On the past three albums, I was exploring the hydrodynamics of my own peculiarities. I don't know what the next one will be. Harder, maybe louder. Things are now a little more psychedelic for me, and they're more ethnic. I'm looking toward that part of music that comes from my memories…"

"You think you're a victim of your musical environment. To a degree you are." – TOM WAITS, 1987

"I feel a lot more like a conductor then a character." – TOM WAITS, NPR, 1988

PART XIV: 'Big Time' (1988)

Not quite finished with Frank following the release of 'Frank's Wild Years' a year earlier, in 1988, Waits reincarnated the character once again for a live album whose genesis TV Guide candidly described as "a bit confusing: in 1986, Waits and his wife Kathleen Brennan developed a play, Frank's Wild Years, from the song of the same name on 'Swordfishtrombones'. The play was produced in 1986, with Waits in the lead role (the beginning of his interest in theatrical productions), by Chicago's Steppenwolf Theatre. Waits devised new music for that show, which became the basis for the album 'Frank's Wild Years'. Big Time is not a film adaptation of the play Frank's Wild Years, but a concert film from Waits' tour following the release of the album 'Frank's Wild Years'."

Clarifying exactly what inspired the concert film, Waits shared with NPR that he'd "been threatening it for a long time and my wife finally said: 'Well, I guess it's time we get something here that we can look at after you come back from the road.' 'Cause you rarely come home with anything that you get some snapshots and some reviews but I guess it gives me a chance to capsulise some of the songs on the last three albums."

Crediting Kathleen Brennan as "the only one who really pushed to have a film done," Waits elaborated on his aforementioned motivations in the same Island Records promo interview. "I'd get home from the road, and I wouldn't have any pictures of the band or anything. We'd talk about it like something that didn't really happen. It was the first time that we pursued pulling it together."

Waits explained in a conversation with WNEW New York of the influence Brennan had had over the direction of Waits' music in their almost 10-year relationship. "She opened my eyes to a lot of things, and my ears. You know, opera, Rachmaninoff, Prokofiev, John McCormick, gypsy music, makeup secrets, that type of thing. Kathleen's a writer, and we collaborate on some songs, stories, a lot of things." Delving further into talents of his wife's that he felt enhanced his own creative process, he shared with Graffiti magazine that he was helped lyrically by the fact that "she's an avid reader and she tells me about the things she's read and I feel like I've read them. She's extraordinary. She's the brains behind the pa, as they say. She can catch a bullet in her teeth. And she's also a great writer: short stories. Paints, too."

Offering fans an inside look at the couple's collaborative process, Tom revealed to Interview magazine that "when we write songs together. I fight her all the time because she's usually right and I feel compelled to, Kathleen has great musical instincts...because she's a woman; she has four-dimensional ability. You get very linear sometimes in music; you know the logical steps." Ultimately, Waits seemed to feel most grateful for the fact that, as an artist, "Kathleen has helped me to feel safe in my uncertainty. And that's where the wonder and the discovery are."

Though already well-documented through his promotional interviews for 'Swordfishtrombones', 'Rain Dogs' and 'Frank's Wild Years', in the course of promoting 'Big Time' Waits reflected proudly on the progress he felt he'd made in shifting the soundscape of his music to better reflect what he candidly explained in an Island promo interview in 1988 as "more like what goes on inside my head. For a long time I wrote in a very restricted world. I gave myself limited tools to work with. It got to a point where my life and what was really going on in my head what I was really hearing, was very different from what I was writing... You get to an impasse with your work and you have to do something about it. You can't go forward and you can't go back, and sometimes you fell like you have to break all your vertebrae and then reset 'em. That's what I tried to do, a little bit at a time. It's a nose job."

Elaborating on the same musical metamorphosis to NPR, Waits reasoned that "at a certain point you feel as though you need to find some new territory for yourself, I think that's natural." He also clearly felt a loyalty to see Frank come full circle in his journey, adding that "I'd kind of stayed with a small piece of geography for some time I'd stayed with the same producer in the studio, so the last three records, the last four records I produced myself. So I started taking responsibility for all those things which I thought was an important thing to do."

Within the 21-song opus that composed 'Big Time', his label noted "one hears the echoes of avant-garde American composer Harry Partch, blues man Howlin' Wolf, Frank Sinatra, Argentinean tango master Astor Piazzolla, Irish tenor John McCormack, Kurt Weill, wild man Louis Prima, Mexican norteno bands and a Martini tumbler of Vegas lounge singers." Explaining to Rolling Stone magazine that he and Brennan's goal in filming the concert was "to avoid...having a concert film that felt like a stuffed bird. I tried to film it like a Mexican cockfight instead of air-conditioned concert footage. Some of it felt like it was shot through a safari rifle. You forget about the camera, which is what I was trying to do. But when you see yourself in concert, it rarely looks like the way you feel when you're up there. It's shocking sometimes to see yourself up there."

The process of bringing those characters to life from song to stage for Waits was one he explained to Interview magazine where "it's a matter of pulling the play into the song; once I separated the music from the story I felt compelled to put some optical illusions in the songs. Some were more susceptible than others, but I was trying to make them more visual... It's never done as a linear piece of fiction. It was just a way to try and create some kind of other dimension and stability. Concert film is a bit of an orphan because you're filming something that happened live."

He quipped to disc jockey Gary Tausch that "you could say ('Big Time') is a concert film…(because) it was all shot in one day for about a hundred bucks and on-stage, with a band. I mean there's some other footage in there." The film was shot over the course of two live concerts in November 1987 at the Warfield in San Francisco and Wiltern Theatre in Los Angeles. Featuring a band TV Guide noted was "a small but tight ensemble who supply a broad range of sounds to flesh out Waits' tales of small-time life," Tom praised his band to journalist Steve Dollar as seasoned "veterans of other groups, with a great sense of adventure… I'm running the show, but I'm not the police. My wife just said 'Huh!' Everybody's allowed to bring forward ideas. Every group has its own anatomy."

Elaborating on his band's individual members' contributions to that anatomy, Tom explained that "Marc Ribot has a very strong pygmy industrial violence, but also a very strong gypsy side to him. So he goes from Django to Hendrix. And I like that range. Greg Cohen has a lot of cruise-ship experience. Sorry, Greg. He's worked a lot of lounges. He's been in bands since he was seven years old in the garage with his brother. Ralph Carney has a very Chinese approach to music. He'll play four or five saxophones simultaneously. He also plays organ and just about anything. He's very adventurous, creates his own labyrinths and catacombs. He's worked with Pere Ubu and his own group in Ohio…Tin Huey. He lives in Brooklyn. Michael Blair plays in Latin bands and worked in a lot of salsa bands and also has a real industrial side to him. Willy Schwarz is a real authority on Egyptian music."

Expanding in greater depth on his band members' talents as it related more directly to bringing his sound to life on stage and screen, Waits explained to Interview magazine that, at the heart of it all, "it has to do with the chemistry of the people that you work with. Mark Ribot was a big part of the thing 'cause he has that kind of barbed-wire industrial guitar, Greg Cohen is solid; he plays both upright and electric bass. Ralph Carney plays three saxophones simultaneously. Bill Schimmel doesn't play the accordion, he *is* an accordion.

"They enjoy challenges. Michael Blair will play everything. He plays every instrument in the room and then goes looking for things to play that aren't instruments. They all are like that, and it's like a dismantling process – nothing carries its own physical properties by itself. You can talk to them like actors, and they'll go with the drug, and that's what I like. You have to really know your instrument; you have to understand the power of suggestion to be able to do that. I can literally talk colours."

An example of the latter in action was, Tom explained, that "I can say, 'We want kind of an almond aperitif here' or 'industrial hygiene with kind of a refrigeration process on this', and they say, 'Yeah. I'm there. I'll go there.' And that's exciting. Like Mark Ribot – we were playing after hours in a club in Copenhagen I think it was, and he knocked over a bottle of some foreign liquor; it was spilling all over the floor and he's splashing around in the liquor, jumping up and down playing the guitar, yelling. 'Play like a pygmy, play like a pygmy.' And everybody knew exactly what he meant. When you find who you communicate with on that level, it's very exciting, because they'll go anywhere with you. And they were all the best part about the movie Big Time."

Discussing the one track from the album that wasn't culled from previous Island releases, 'Falling Down', Waits explained disc jockey Gary Tausch that "that was cut in the studio. That's a song I was doing on the road but we never got a good take of it. So, I got home, rather than bring a band out from New York to Los Angeles, I worked with people who were already there: Larry Taylor and Fred Tackett and Richie Hayward, so we put that on there." Beyond the latter studio cut, Waits remained as experimental as ever, with director Chris Blum observing that even throughout the live performance of Big Time, "Tom uses musical instrumentation as sound effects. He sometimes uses sound effects as music."

Waits explained his wife's influence over his keyboard sound to Interview magazine. "She's a bit pedestrian at the piano, which is good because playing the piano is like being in a truck – you may be able to go some places in it, but you don't have this weightless ability to do any kind of flying or dipping or plunging. She doesn't let the piano stay in the room. She goes out the window with it, and that's what I love: it's very beautiful."

In the same interview he gave further background to his newest studio adventures. "Lately I like to get inside the piano with timpani mallets and lie across the strings and bang on them, because after a while the hand has a memory, and when it goes somewhere, it knows what to do – how to wrap around something, or what to do on the keyboard. And you have to kind of give it a stroke. You have to put an electric fence around it so it doesn't go where it wants to go, because the hand has an intelligence all of its own, almost separate from you."

One form of keyboard Waits had employed on all of more recent albums was that of the Mellotron, confessing to Elvis Costello in a conversation with Option magazine that "I love that thing so much. I just used one yesterday. (Its owner) guards it with his life because it's such an exotic bird, it's a complete dinosaur, and every time you play it it diminishes. It gets old and eventually will die, which makes it actually more human. You're working with a musician that is very old, he's only got a couple more sessions left. It increases the excitement of it... Those Mellotrons, the first time I actually played one, it really thrilled me. It's like you touched somebody on the shoulder, every time I touch you on the shoulder I want you to play a note. It was that real."

Reflecting following the release of the film in September, 1988, Waits confessed to Rolling Stone that, while overall he was happy with the result, "now that it's completed...here's always something you want to change after it's over." Critics by and large were dazzled by the results, with IMDB.com noting that by "bringing his unique sense of humour to this bizarre and original piece of movie-making, Tom Waits takes the audience through a musical journey with his jazzy, quirky, bluesy tunes presented as you would never, ever, ever expect."

Billboard felt Waits had achieved a breakthrough for those in his audience who felt his was "challenging music," noting that it was "made somewhat more accessible in a live context. Waits' performances tended to be somewhat over the top on the studio versions of these songs, but before a live audience his theatrics seem more appropriate." From a derivative vantage point, the Washington Post noted that "the music itself is often intriguing, with echoes of Brecht and Weill, Astor Piazzolla, Rudy Vallée, gospel, cabaret, blues, the kitchen sink. Waits' piano and Willy Schwarz's accordion often evoke entrancing textures, and the band has a supple, amiable grace."

While Waits for his own part quipped to Interview magazine that Big Time, in essence, was "Swabbie night at the Copa shot through the lens of an African safari rifle…basically an action film," his label Island proudly elaborated with a more mainstream summary that declared that "Big Time throws Tom Waits' skills as a mime, actor, storyteller, and verbal sleight-of-band artist into startling relief. In round-robin fashion, the viewer meets an ever-shifting rogues' gallery: the brimstone-spouting preacher beating the Devil 'Way Down In The Hole'; the wisecracking guy who drives his piano like a truck through the film; the smarmy white-jacketed lounge entertainer taking a nightmarish journey 'Straight To The Top' the silk-robed theatrical jack-of-all trades whose reveries shape the action of the film; and a masterly singer who may or, in the context of the film's dreamy logic, may not be Tom Waits himself."

Time Out magazine perhaps offered the best critical assessment of Waits' achievement, noting that throughout the film, "musical, visual and verbal puns abound; elements of vaudeville, burlesque and soulful balladry are orchestrated by what is evidently, for all the downbeat, offbeat imagery, a fantastically energetic imagination. A concert film unlike any other." Following the release of an entire new generation of music for his ever-diversifying fan base, it was clear Waits' gambles had paid off due to the genius he evolved in real time with his growing adventurousness as a producer and artist, something that promised to grow only bolder with the arrival of the Nineties.

"I don't think the record's as scary as I would like it to be."
– TOM WAITS, 1992

"This is an album with all its edges not only exposed, but proudly displayed." – REFLEX MAGAZINE

"I do believe songs will come to you more if they know you've sacrificed something for them. I don't want that to sound like some kind of bullshit psychic spirituality, what I mean is…music doesn't like everybody. Everybody likes music, but music doesn't like everybody." – TOM WAITS, 1992

PART XV: 'Bone Machine' (1992)

Having become the master of his own sub-genre by the time of 1992's 'Bone Machine', Waits reasoned in a conversation with The Guardian that, by that point in his 20-year-plus career as a songwriter, "if you're an artist, you feel there's a shorthand you hope you've developed with whatever the process is."

The music Waits produced with that talent had nevertheless continued to reinvent itself, Reflex magazine critic noting that, indeed, "at least twice during his 20-year career, Tom Waits has managed to forge a fresh genre without becoming mired in it."

Having firmly established his own sub-genre by the early Nineties, Tom Waits – based on the avant-garde ground he'd laid musically throughout the Eighties – was now considered one of the godfathers of the underground alternative rock scene. With the coming advent of grunge, Waits would find himself suddenly 'fitting in' to a mainstream that had a suddenly-open ear to his sound. He would watch his record sales rise, his music video rotations get heavier on MTV, and suddenly – for the first time in his career – release a studio LP that would win him a Grammy!

Having his technique down to a science, Waits shared with journalist Peter Orr that "some things are best written fast. And you can still spend a lot of time developing it," admitting in a separate conversation with journalist Peter Silverton in context of the five years that had passed between studio LPs that "I don't know how long it's been…(but) it takes a while to get started. I collect ideas and I usually got them on me somewhere. It's just a matter of getting them all in one place. The songs came kind of fast. I f you think you've got one in you, you take a fly at it…

"It's a bit like taking a pill. If you're doing it right, there's nothing in the world that's as thrilling. Songs are really simple. You hold them in your hand…You have to make yourself some kind of an antenna for the songs to come to you. So you have to make yourself a kind of a musical yourself. You have to be of music and have music in you; some way for songs to continue to want to live in you, in or near you. You gotta be real quiet sometimes if you wanna catch the big ones."

One immediately noticeable aspect of Waits songwriting as he continued to evolve was the ever-more complex and experimental soundscapes he'd begun developing with 'Swordfishtrombones' seven years earlier. It was an aspect of his songwriting that Tom conceded in his conversation with Peter Orr had resulted in "recording not being simple for me as it once was. I used to go in and sit at the piano and sing the songs and leave. I was afraid to do anything else." To get him past his fear, Tom quipped to Musician magazine that "there's only one reason to write more songs, it's what Miles Davis said. Because you're tired of the old ones." Always motivated by his desire to break new ground, Waits would indeed do just that on 'Bone Machine'.

The album's title, he told journalist Derk Richardson, was inspired by the fact that "we're like bone machines... Most machines take on a certain kind of human quality, even a bicycle, particularly an old bicycle that's been ridden a lot, even when nobody's on it. I like that aspect of machinery. I saw a picture of a bottle-making machine and a guy working it, back in the Twenties. It made 40,000 bottles in 12 hours, and there was something very human, something very animal about it; it looked like some kind of creature with the skin burned off. I like those sounds. I wanted to explore more machinery sounds."

He elaborated in a conversation with journalist Seth Nielsen that, initially, "'Bone Machine' started out as just a title. Let's make something that sounds like it could be part of a group of songs that were entitled 'Bone Machine'. Let's come up with songs that...(sound) kind of skeleton music; this is like horror, like music from a horror movie."

His final reflection on the title was made to journalist Rip Rense. "What's a bone machine? Most of the principles of most machines developed in the machine age were principles that were found in the human body. Originally, I was going to take sounds of machines I'd recorded, and add a really strong rhythmic sense; I was going to try to build songs out of the rhythms. But then it didn't really develop that way. The stories kind of took over. So it's more bone than machine. Bone Machine...We're all like bone machines, I guess. We break down eventually, and we're replaced by other models. Newer models. Younger models. Bone Machine."

He confirmed to The Face magazine that his new LP represented "a darker view" than previous releases. He defended that creative vantage point by offering that through that "darker lens of things, I seem more and more comfortable there. They're perfectly legitimate areas for songs. Songs live there." Arguably inspired because he'd found a way past the aforementioned fear of writing without piano as his central instrument, Waits added his discovery within exploring into this new territory that "a great many songs live there. So that's where I've been digging lately." By departing from the compositional comfort zone of the piano, Tom was allowing his musical mind the freedom to dig into the proverbial garden – or arguably in his case graveyard – to raise the spirits of new sounds he needed to succeed in crafting its next life.

As he began to visualise the album's songs in his mind, Waits shared with radio host Chris Douridas that, at that point in his career, he'd come to "like songs with adventure in them. I think that's what everybody's looking for: songs with adventure and, you know, acts of depravity and eroticism, and shipwrecks, murder...experiments and expeditions into a world of sound and stories.

I mean, particularly with percussion, I was more interested in percussion in these Bermuda Triangles of percussion, that you find and sometimes you drop off the edge of the world."

Though Waits joked with journalist Bill Dolan that when writing for 'Bone Machine', he liked "to turn on four radios at the same time with different stations and listen to the collision," the implied confusion was deliberate as Waits – by this point in his 20-plus year career as a recording artist, seemed to feel he'd developed his skill for attaining whatever song he was chasing down in his head, offering to Pulse magazine of that process that "I like to think wherever I aim this thing, I can hit it. You get to where if you really know how to shoot it, you can pick anything off. But a lot of songs don't want to be caught, and they do get away. If you want to take them alive, you have to have something other than a conventional understanding of music. It's like anything else – what you put yourself through in milking it is what comes back to you, in direct proportion."

As Waits' creative energies began flowing, he offered to Telerama that he had no shortage of ideas as "there's so many thousands and thousands of things for songs to be about," adding more specifically to journalist Derk Richardson that – in a departure from past albums – "I have some new categories…The end of the world, that's kind of a new category for me." As he began to hone in on the thematic heart of the album, he explained to the Village Voice that he centred in on 'Bone Machine' because it felt "like a signpost up ahead," which – as he followed it – he found himself writing "songs real fast, and the best ones just come out of the ground."

That proverbial garden of creative seeds was fertile for Waits once what he "was aiming for when I started writing songs for the album" started to reveal itself, recalling to journalist Michael Fuchs-Gambock that, at its core, the album thematically "really is all about bones, cemeteries and dirty blood. And maybe also about how tomorrow I might have a drink, even though the world's a desolate place."

He told music writer Derk Richardson that, as his creative spirit began floating through the aforementioned imagery in his mind, the singer would "just pick a topic and drift, that's my favourite part," Tom added that things got less enjoyable once Waits began developing specific song ideas, adding in the same conversation that there were times within that process where "I get real cranky about the songs…I get mad at the songs. 'Oh, you little sissy, you little wimp, you're not gonna go on my fucking record, you little bastard. No way are you going, and we're leaving in about three days and you're not going with us, 'cause you're a sissy and a wimp.' And then songs start to get like, 'Oh, God, we can't go.' Toward the end it's always good to whip the songs a little bit, scare 'em, then make fun of them. And then they change. You come back the next day and they're better behaved."

As if raising the composition from infancy into a full-grown song, Waits, elaborating on his process for raising the songs on 'Bone Machine', explained "a lot of times…(you're) listening and thinking, 'What does it need?' Some of what goes into song-building is almost a medical Frankenstein process.

What does it need? It's very beautiful but it has no heart, or it has nothing but heart and it needs a rib cage, or whatever. I'm usually good at the medical questions about music. Eventually I'll probably just be a medical consultant in music. I'll be called in to look at sick songs and I'll either say, 'Put the sheet over it', or 'Operate'. I'll have a little bag with my saw. Sometimes you have to break the leg and then reset it. I'm good at that. It's painful…(but) you gotta be willing to go through some discomfort. I like breaking songs, breaking their backs. I like songs with scars on them – when I listen to them I just see all the scars."

Lyrically, the singer-songwriter explained to the Guardian that as he approached tackling that aspect of his latest LP, he had the advantage of "(loving) words. Every word has a particular musical sound to it which you may or may not be able to use. Like for example 'spatula', that's a good word. Sounds like the name of a band. Probably *is* the name of a band." As the songs began to take shape in the visual gallery of his musical mind, Waits – elaborating to journalist Rip Rense – shared that, "to me, these (songs) are like movies for the ears, and if you can make a little painting for the ears with a few words, well, I like words. I like cutting them up and finding different ways of saying the same thing.

"To me it's more what they sound like, because ultimately you're going to have to put them in the soup and decide whether it's a tomato or a bone. That's just how you do it. You have to do it with your writing. I get into a spell, and it all comes easy. I don't labor over it. I go inside the song. I think you make yourself an antennae for songs and songs want to be around you. And then they bring other songs along."

As he navigated that lyrical landscape, Tom shared with Image magazine that, in the course of developing these themes conceptually, "there are things you are drawn to, and will always be drawn to, and they'll keep happening and you'll keep writing about them, as if this time I'll solve it. But I think the best songs are riddles that you try to discover what you think about them while you're writing them. And then the deeper the riddle, the longer you'll sing the song. And then, some songs, like Bob Dylan said, are best written in a very peaceful place and sung in turmoil, and then other songs are the other way – they're written in turmoil and sung in a peaceful place. They really do have a lot of power and they really do help you sometimes."

Aiding Tom in his journey was co-writing captain and wife Kathleen Brennan, who co-wrote eight of the album's 16 tracks. Her husband, argued in an KCRW FM Radio that the two were a good creative pairing because "she spins the chamber and I pull the trigger and sometimes the other way around. She's got a wonderful sense of rhythm and melody and she doesn't subscribe to the traditional co-ordinance of music. She's more like a kid in her approach to it so she's really changed the way I hear music and we wrote a lot of the songs together."

Favouring an approach that he explained to friend and filmmaker Jim Jarmusch involved songs he and Brennan "most (wrote) with just a drum in the room, and my voice, just hollering it out," adding of that collaborative process in a conversation with journalist Steve Orr that "we went into a room and wrote together. We came up with a list of about 60 ideas for songs, and maybe 19 will make it."

He revealed to Pulse magazine that, for as much progress as they make together, he and wife Kathleen with certain songs began "with nothing sometimes." In contrast to his prior method of composing alone, collaborating with his better half is "a different kind of thing, writing songs with someone. But hey, we got kids together, we can make songs together."

Describing the way he and his wife pushed and pulled one another into new territory musically, Tom began by explaining that "I fall into a groove too easily. I get in there and say, 'Oh, here's my place.' It's like a shovel handle. Even on the piano, my hands are at the same place every time, because your hands have an intelligence that's separate from your own. But sometimes you need somebody to say, 'No, put 'em over here and try this', and she does that. She calls me on all that stuff. 'Oh, this again, oh Jesus! Oh, here's the hundredth one of those.' But, oh yeah, I beat her up, too. Not literally. I don't really beat her up, don't misunderstand me."

Waits and Brennan became so immersed in their creative process that Tom later told Image magazine that, as a consequence, "I don't know who wrote most of what. Most of them, we just started out going back and forth. When you have kids, it's easier. You fight about so many other things, that writing a song is like... Well, you still fight about what it should be. Oh, I think it should be six feet long and have blue hair and a bunch of nails sticking out of it. And she says no, it should be chrome. Chrome thing in shape of a pear, and it shouldn't have any hair. It's a cynical song; the kind of stuff you'd like to say to an old girlfriend at a party. Who are you this time? Are you still jumping out of windows in expensive clothes? A thing you'd like to say to anybody who maybe raked you over the coals."

The singer additionally offered his opinion that he and wife Kathleen's chemistry worked well because of his feeling that "to collaborate with someone, you have to come from totally different backgrounds. Otherwise one of you is unemployed in the collaboration," adding in the same interview with journalist Bruna Lombardi that "she's a lapsed Catholic. She's from Illinois. She grew up on a farm. So she has... Her background in music is from her own. She invented herself. From church music and Irish music. She has her own mythology. It has changed the way I hear music, because when I started working with her, I think she changed the way I hear things and see things. The way I hear music."

Trusting his wife's instincts implicitly, Tom's nature as a songwriter had evolved with his sound in the process of taking her on as his collaborator over the years, arguing that he was happy to do so because "I think we complement each other."

Waits felt his wife was of great aid in covering the biblical realm, offering to friend and filmmaker Jim Jarmusch that he respected her strength in this area because "she has a real daring – and also sometimes when you sit down and write by yourself you find yourself falling into the same patterns that you've been falling into before. You develop these little cow paths through the music that are well worn by other journeys, so sometimes it really helps to be working with somebody that wants to go to a totally new place.

"She has a lot of biblical imagery that she keeps coming back to. She still knows all of her novenas and Hail Marys, the whole bit. But they give her a very deep sense of questioning and spirituality."

Even the couple's children got in on the creative action in the course of writing 'Bone Machine'. An Island Records press release reported that Waits and Brennan's "daughter contributed the word 'strangels', meaning 'strange angels', to 'The Ocean Doesn't Want Me'.

Waits explained to journalist Rip Rense that the song was inspired by a story in "one of the local papers up here printed two photographs. One was a picture of a woman on the beach holding a bottle of beer and a cigarette, looking out at the ocean. And the next picture was the same day, a couple hours later, of her floating face-down in the brine, the beer still in her hand. And the photographer had walked past her and heard her say under her breath 'the ocean doesn't want me today.'

"He just clicked a picture. He went all the way down to the end of the jetty, turned around and came back, and then he spotted her floating in the surf. So it's a little suicide note. See, the riptide is raging and the lifeguard's away, it's like I can make my break now. Strangels. Like strange angels. (Daughter) Kellesimone said that. So if you have strangels, then you can have braingels. Those are the angels that live in your head."

Another collaborator of Waits' on the record was legendary Rolling Stones guitarist Keith Richards, a longtime friend and a writer the singer-songwriter shared with Image magazine he was excited to work because "he writes songs in some ways similar to the way I do. Which, you know, you kind of circle it, and you sneak up on it. It was a real joy to write with him. You can't drink with him, but you can write with him. It was really a joy.

"I felt like I have known him a long time, and he's made out of very strong stock, you know. He's like pirate stock. He loves those shadows in music. And he's totally mystified by music, like a kid. He finds great joy in it, and madness and abandon. And it's still there, very much, for him. He looks at the guitar, and his eyes get all big, and he starts shakin' his head. He's made out of something that music likes to be around.

"I mostly play drums, he plays guitar. He stands out in the middle of the room and does those Chuck Berry splits, y'know, and leans over and turns it up on 10 and just grungg! I mostly just play drums. He plays drums, too, he plays everything. It was good. I'm just recently starting to collaborate in writing and find it to be really thrilling." Richards' rock'n'roll voodoo melded well with Waits' mysterious musical mojo, allowing the pair to create a magic together in the studio only musicians of their rare virtuosity were capable of pulling off.

Revealing that, as a writer, the legendary guitarist was "all intuition," Waits elaborated in a conversation with Derk Richardson that, as Richards worked on developing song ideas, "he's real like voodoo about it. He circles it. He's like an (vulture), smelling it, kicking dirt on it. He's real ritual about it, real jungle. I had an experience writing with him for several weeks and it was really thrilling.

"He's written so many different kinds of songs. You identify him with that really dirty guitar and that gang-like stance, like a killer at a gas station – 'Oh man, we better not stop for gas here' – and then you realise he's a real gypsy.

We had some wild times. You can't drink with him – just forget about it, you'll be leaving early, he reduces you to something very embarrassing. You'll be the table – they'll put drinks on you. He toughens you up."

The collaboration proved prolific enough to produce "almost an album's full of songs," even though only one made the final album. The same was true for Waits' own collection of songs initially written for the album, such that, as he and wife Kathleen approached the conclusion of writing for the LP, he shared with Image magazine "a lot of the songs had more verses than we could use. It's better than not enough." Of those new topical areas covered across the record's lyrical landscape that did make the final cut, Waits to journalist Rip Rense – "there's a little Revelations mixed in there. A little biblical material – new area for me. The Bible is a new world for me."

When attentions finally turned to recording, Waits began by revealing that "recording can sometimes be a violent operation," elaborating in his conversation with journalist Peter Silverton that "I think recording studios sometimes can be like a slaughterhouse, where you have some ideas you want to try and wrestle with. Many times you end up with a lot of feathers. A dead bird and a mouthful of feathers. It's not easy for me. Music is like a living thing. You don't wanna murder it… You don't wanna splatter it all over the walls. You wanna go into certain worlds; you wanna go into a teardrop or go through a hole in the crack in the plaster."

Happier than ever with his career and his collaborators, Waits was ambitious to "go someplace you've never been before and sometimes those journeys are successful and sometimes you're left with just dead bodies all over the meadow. Sometimes you realise you didn't bring enough supplies, you're outta water. But I love the process of it all."

Waits' recalled to television host Chris Douridas that, as excited as he was to get started, he and his team had not got off on the right foot. "We worked at it for a couple days in a real studio, and I was really upset, just depressed. This room sounds awful, and I said, 'No music will ever grow in this room.' I was furious. I was so, I was so…I was down."

Imploring a predictably abstract approach to solving his sonic problem Waits next recalled in his conversation with Douridas that "I went 'round looking around the place, and I said, 'What about this room over here, I bet this room sounds good', and everybody laughed. I said, 'No, really, what's wrong with this room here? Feels better. Hot water heater, a door, a window, table, a chair, some maps on the wall. Get all these crates outta here, and let's do it right here, just run the wires down the hill.'

"Everybody said, 'Oh, sure'. And they did, and we got in there, and everything started to come together, so it was good, was good the project had a flat tyre on the first day, cause outta that we invented a new place for it to happen."

Quickly dubbed Studio C, or alternately 'The Waits Room', the singer-songwriter added to Village Voice that the discovery was truly a relief because "the room felt great. It wasn't built for recording and I think maybe that's why… I told them, 'We want to work down here. It's got a better sound.' I think they were a little bit embarrassed. They were like, 'We have a room up here that we sank about half a million dollars into. At least give it a try.' I said, 'Well I did. I spent a whole day up there and it sounded like dog meat to me.' But that's how any discovery happens. And it (the room downstairs) has all the natural requirements of a great sound room. It's got wood walls, a wood ceiling and a cement floor. It's not sound proofed, so the world comes in. I think that was good for this record."

Reasoning that sonically, the room suited his ear because "I'm more and more inclined toward texture," Waits added in the same conversation with Musician that "you can't get texture with this whole bio-regenerator flesh approach to recording. It gets a little too scientific for me. But the great thing about DAT is that you can record anywhere now. Because the room becomes a character. And fortunately, we stumbled upon a storage room that sounded so good – plus it already had maps on the wall. So I said, 'That's it, we're sold.'" Studio chief Mark Rennick added in a conversation with reporter Charles McDermid that "(Tom) gravitated toward these 'echo' rooms and created the 'Bone Machine' aural landscape."

Waits added that, because of that "the good thing about recording in a rural environment, you find things from the shop that you can use – you can mike and drag into the room." To accomplish his out-of-the-box approach to recording the new album, Waits paid a loud and clear compliment to his recording staff, explaining to Image magazine that his highly – experimental soundscapes' creations were in part possible because "I've got great engineers – Tchad Blake and Biff Dawes and Joe Marquez – and they can get a great sound out of anything. They don't flinch. If you say you want to put a mic up that bull's ass over there, and you want to slap him on the stomach, they'd say, 'Well, uh, I guess we could use a 57.' They wouldn't look at you twice. They'd say get the rope out and get that bull down here."

Offering friend and filmmaker Jim Jarmusch the example of the latter in action, Waits recalled that "Tchad Blake, my engineer (on 'Bone Machine')…got into India, a street, and stand in a fish market with his mike on, and record the bicycles, the bells on the handlebars. Ching-a-ching! Ching-a-ching! And the chings are coming in and ching-ing out, and it's a wonderful movie for the ears. You can just reach out and like, you can see the fish. Whoa! And trains, I've got a lot of trains on tape. Real chugs that are like a rhythmic chug, you just can't believe it. Like you pee your paints. And the ting ting ting as the bell's coming up."

Correctly noting in their review of his latest LP that "essentially, Waits now extends his creative process to the very mechanics of recording," Reflex magazine's observation was confirmed in a conversation with KCRW FM that, indeed, "I'm becoming more and more to the point where I think the sound is married to the music." Waits was arguably pioneer of the craft – as he revealed to journalist Bill Dolan – of "when you're recording…(as) you're always looking for something that sounds better than the stuff you brought in there."

Elaborating on some of the recording equipment he employed during the recording of 'Bone Machine', Tom told music writer Peter Orr that "I do have a fondness for pawnshop tape recorders – you know, equipment you might find at a swap meet. I've always liked that. You can make a record anywhere with DAT now. You can make a record literally in your bathroom, and go right to 24-track with it. It's changing everything. My theory is that music doesn't like to be recorded, so the more you can do to go out in the field and find it where it is, or take it to a place where it's more comfortable than in a studio, the music is more prone to actually staying on the tape. While you're recording it, you're dealing with a living thing."

Tom delved into the complexities of that process of deconstruction and re-creation by offering that, by and large, he and Brennan were flying by the seat of their pants on instinct in the studio, in that "you're making it, you're changing it – you might be tearing its wings off, you don't know, because you're working with something you can't see. So a lot of times you can be very irresponsible in a studio. That's why the best people to record you sometimes can be very naive about it, and it comes out great, instead of having some guy say, 'Oh, we'll do this to it, we'll do that, we'll bring it over here and nail it to this piece of wood.' A lot of times what you end up doing is catching the clothes that music was last wearing. The music is slippery. Like in the cartoons when you grab for a character and you get his underwear. A lot of what you're hearing on record is music's underwear, not the music."

Waits revealed in the same conversation with Dolan that weather also affected the sonics of the album, recalling that "I think it rained the whole time we were down there! And I think the room changes when it rains. The air is charged with something different. A lot of rooms that I recorded in were like laboratories with a ventricular decapitator emergency room." An influence that hung over the entirety of recording, Waits added his recollection to journalist Steve Orr that "it rained all the way through the sessions, and they dragged cable down from the control booth into this little room. And then the room sounds different depending on the weather – I guess because of the air density. I'm more particular about those kinds of things, sound detail."

One aspect of Waits' routine unlike his younger years as a single bachelor musician was that he recorded in daylight hours. He joked with Bruna Lombardi that "my recording sessions are always at ten o'clock in the morning. Everybody hates it but me. But I think this is the best time cause everyone's clean and everyone is empty," adding in an interview with KCRW FM that "I love it in the morning…We recorded everything about 10am. Everybody's fresh. Nobody has any residual music (from the day before)."

As recording got underway, Waits and his production team worked to create a sound that Entertainment Weekly would ultimately conclude "is like going through an amusement-park fun house: you never know when you're going to be shocked, thrilled or just plain unnerved by some startling image or sound." The singer continued the trend he'd begun on 'Rain Dogs' of constructing his own percussion instruments to match what he heard and saw in his musical imagination.

He explained to Pulse magazine that "I'm exploring more and more things that make a sound but are not traditional instruments. It's a good time to do it, too, because there's a lot of garbage in the world that I can use that is just sitting out there rusting. I can't believe it. I think something is gonna come out of this garbage world we're living in, where knowledge and information are becoming so abstract and the things that used to really work are sitting out there like big dinosaur carcasses, rusting. Something's gonna have to be made out of it that has some value."

To achieve that end, Waits sought out the best in the business of fashioning original, one-off instruments, recalling in a conversation with KCRW FM that he enlisted the expertise of "people who design, build and perform on their own inventions. Para ventricular decapitators and that type of thing. Harry Partch lived in Petaluma for a while and he was always hitting something that wasn't really an instrument but all the instruments that we know had to go through this evolution. There's skin and metal and wood and glass and wind.

"Basically you're dealing with the same physics that they were dealing with then but because the world is changing and people are finding that there are a lot of recyclable items that are fascinating sound sources. There's a guy up there named Tom Nunn in San Francisco. He built something called a T-Rodimba and another thing called the Bug. It's a 3/4 inch plywood sound base and these enormous metal rods that come out of it. It sounds like – it's like metal and wood, somewhere in the middle of metal and wood. It has a great sound. So I'm always listening for that stuff."

In the same conversation, Tom explained that "it's fun because when you start recording it's difficult because you want to hear something you've never heard before. We've integrated some farm machinery into the sounds that we've found on this record. Some of it found its way onto the record and some of it didn't." Waits added in his conversation with the Village Voice that he made great use of "metal objects, alternative sound sources like a crowbar. I'm listening to more things that are like that lately. I don't know if it has anything to do with living in the sticks or what. Going into a hardware store, looking around and saying, 'Goddamn!'"

The sounds Waits created on 'Bone Machine' would startle listeners, beginning with critics like Image magazine who noted in their analysis of the album's sonics that "musically, the record is his most daring. Few of the sounds on 'Bone Machine' are predictable; most everything has been devised, designed – and, in the case of percussion, sometimes invented – to frame, decorate and embellish the tales being told and thoughts being expressed. The noises are an unending surprise; the songs clang and float, waft, rave and slither."

Those results, Waits reasoned in a conversation with music writer Rip Rense, stemmed from the fact that "I have a lot of very strong rhythmic impulses, but this is not my world. I just pick something up and I hit it, and if I like the sound, it goes on. So sometimes my idiot approach serves the music." Offering an example of that ear for the abstract, Tom reasoned that "it's like the chest of drawers with three legs. I can be the four books that are stacked up to keep it from toppling over. I like things that weren't intended to be instruments being used as instruments. Things that have never been hit before. So I'm always looking for those things; things that have been out in a field somewhere, or that you find in the gutter. I'm always dragging things into the studio."

The New York Times would agree with Waits' method, concluding in their review of the album that "instrumentally it sounds as though it were recorded using debris: instead of Waits' former snake-pit orchestra of swamp guitar, honking saxophone, wheezing accordion and pump organ, the songs here are constructed on a percussive skeleton of bangs and thwonks, like someone hitting the different surfaces in a junkyard with a pair of sticks. Beyond rhythm, Waits adds little adornment – shafts of piano, bass and pedal steel guitar – and the whole album crackles and hisses as if coming out of a transistor radio."

Delving into some of the specifics of capturing those aforementioned sounds to tape, Tom explained to Pulse magazine that, as each song was produced, "getting it to make sense in the studio is always something different – how it's miced, what kind of room it's in. You're always up against the physics of it. I'm interested in that. I get into absurd arguments with myself about sound and the texture of it, all these things that keep you up at night that just drive you nuts, which is why I'm glad that this record's finally gonna be released: get it out of my house! But I love the process, I really do. I like having music going through my fingers."

When he felt any given song was heading in a wrong direction, Waits – likening his production process to the title of the LP itself – reasoned in the same conversation that "if you don't like the way something is going, you can totally change the bone structure of a song, or three or four songs in the way they all work together. The thing I hate about recording is that it's so permanent. Ultimately you have to let it dry, and I hate that, 'cause I like to just keep changing the shape of 'em, and cut 'em in half and use the parts that I didn't want on that one on another one."

At times, Waits compared this process to feeling "like you have to save the life of a particular song or if it's just not gonna make it," adding to journalist Steve Orr of the latter that "you have to find a way. A lot of times you go beyond what you know in order to save it. You summon something other than you technique and experience... So I do that to songs sometimes: 'Fuck you. You never were anything. I've spent all this time and money to make you into something, and you're nothing. You'll never live around me.' Then you hear the song start to rattle. 'Oh, don't give up on me.' Okay, we'll try.

"Sometimes songs make it for a week, and then they're dead. You take 'em on the road, and they just die. Other songs you keep singing, because they're riddles. You keep singing them because you never understood them, and you keep trying to understand them. So I think it's good to write songs that have puzzles for yourself, that don't necessarily have immediate meaning to you."

While he argued this process was "the part that drives everybody crazy," unlike many of his alt-rock peers, "I like to get in there with the songs and eat them up and push them around and explore all the variables. Sometimes it sounds Irish and then you tilt it a little bit this way and it sounds more Balinese and over here it sounds more Romanian. I like that part of working with music; you can find yourself in a different latitude and longitude." In the course of navigating those creative coordinates, Waits added that "there's a lot of different coordinates for rhythm, and when you start exploring rhythms, you find that maybe it sounds Chinese, and then you realise it's just kind of like banging sticks on the ground, it's just something that comes naturally and you don't necessarily have to put it in a particular country. Some of these things come out of your own rubber dream."

One element of this building and rebuilding process Waits singled out as among his favourite was the art of arrangement – creating musical collages that, he shared with journalist Peter Orr, was a process he loved. "You take a song and arrange it 10 different ways. Totally refigure it. Also what happens in that type of a journey is you run into all kinds of things – rhythmic things, international borders of music where you explore rhythms and so forth. I have a good time doing it. People can go a lot places with just a brain, if they do it correctly."

Tom collaborated with his band over the course of the album's recording, explaining to Telerama that translating the sonic concept for 'Bone Machine' as he'd heard it in his head always began with "a suggestion you could give to a small orchestra and you could tell them – let's see if we can make ourselves sound like a bone machine. I guarantee you that the people I work with would know exactly what to do, Some would sound like a machine and some would sound like bones and we would put them together and we would have a bone machine. It's a musical suggestion.

"I feel like a farmer at the opera with these guys. They play everything from John Cage to Mozart and everything in between." Tom added that because his players were so rounded in their talents, and capability of going wherever he needed them to musically, "what happens to me is I feel like I have to find a common language. I don't read music. So you find a way to communicate. It's good… If I find my own way to speak to them, everybody understands. I'm enriched by being with them."

Waits, in a conversation with KCRW FM, revealed that "I usually like things that have struggle involved. Particularly with percussion. I think drums play a lot better when you're mad. I think unfamiliarity is good for your development, the mystery of musicianship. It's important to keep that alive. I like to do it with the band. I say let's try this thing once all together and now let's switch instruments and let's get really off balance here and see if we can play it again with no co-ordinance and no centre of gravity at all. Let's try it like that.

"Or you take it and say let's cut the band in half. Half you guys play the song now, the other part of the group here, I want you to play it too but a little bit behind the beat so we get that kind of wobbly kind of Titanic feel. I think suggestions to groups are really important things that you say to them before you go into a song. I like to work with people who respond to those things."

With abstract rhythms now such a central part of Waits' sound, he explained to Thrasher magazine that he felt the beat was at the heart of any of his songs, such that "we all have a drum in our chest from the moment we're born. I think music where the tempo is faster than the heartbeat excites you and music that is slower than the heartbeat calms you down. We all have a constant rhythmic beat going on, whether or not you hear it, it's continuing. You feel it all the time whether you acknowledge it or not."

Wife Kathleen was again playing an important influence over the direction Waits was taking his new record. He shared with journalist Bruna Lombardi that she had helped to make the singer-songwriter "maybe more rhythmic, more fearless, more percussive. Making instruments: 'make your own instrument, you don't have to play that if you don't like that! Make one yourself, make one that sounds better.' Like this sound (shakes something standing beneath the two). 'Put that in a song! What do you want? Have courage! Be bold. Be like a wizard. Be like doctor Frankenstein. Make what you want. Wait for the storm. Put the wires on his neck and he'll get up and walk.' And I believe it."

As he fleshed out the album's rhythmic soundscapes, he shared in the same conversation that "I try to nail a lot of different things together. I'm more and more getting interested in rhythm. I like to really kick it hard. I like to play the drums until my knuckles bleed, until I pee my pants. Throw myself against the wall." He added to journalist Bill Dolan that, practically speaking, in the studio, even though "I'm not a drummer. I just like to hit things. I find it reasonable pleasing for myself. You can go crazy trying to communicate certain details of what you want to a drummer. So, I started hitting them myself."

Beyond the conventional drum, Waits recalled to Image magazine that among his customised percussion "I had a couple of things built. The thing that's called a conundrum, it looks like a big iron crucifix, and there are a lot of different things that we hang off of it. Crowbars, Tijuana sabres and found metal objects that I like the sound of. It's a sideline of mine. People have been doing that for years. If you don't like the sound of the drums, you hit the music stand or the chair, or the wall. Or put the microphone in the bathroom and slam the toilet seat down. This is older than dirt, you know. If the room is right, you can get a great sound out of anything."

Elaborating on the construction of the conundrum to radio host Chris Douridas, he added that "Serge Etienne built that, a friend of mine. It's just a metal configuration, like a metal cross. It looks a little bit like a Chinese torture device. It's a simple thing, but it makes… It give you access to these alternative sound sources. Hit 'em with a hammer. Sounds like a jail door. Closing. Behind you. I like it. You end up with bloody knuckles, when you play it. You just, you hit it with a hammer until you just, you can't hit it any more. It's a great feeling to hit something like that. Really just, slam it as hard as you can with a hammer. It's good therapeutic, and all that." The effect could be heard on 'Earth Died Screaming'.

Waits recalled in a conversation with Pulse magazine of its creation that "we got sticks and we tried them everywhere. I wanted to try and get some of that sound of pygmy field recordings that I love so much, and we couldn't get it. We tried different places in the room, different microphones, nothing. Different kinds of sticks, sizes of sticks.

"Most of those field recordings that you hear were all recorded outside. Alan Lomax – all that stuff that he did was all outside. He also was interested in capturing sounds that will no longer be with us. Songs of the junkyard, songs of machinery and things that we take for granted that they'll always be around us that we will always keep hearing that are vanishing. I love letting the words into the studio rather than trying to shut it out with soundproofing."

Preferring as organic and open a creative environment as possible while making the album, Waits added that "we didn't record this in a soundproof room. We had airplanes to deal with and cars and the world. So – we better stop – wait for that train to pass. I like dealing with that, it puts you in correct perspective on what you're doing. You have to stop for an airplane. It's good for the music. You might say, let's let the airplane be in there. There are no airplanes on here but there are some things that happened that you can hear if you listen carefully. Helicopters and that stuff. I've always been curious why they haven't considered sending musicians out into space. Because there's all this talk about contacting other life forms and discovering other cultures in space and I've always wondered why they hadn't created a spacecraft where you could have speakers on the outside of it and have musicians inside playing and have them just out there in space playing. Sound never ends, it never disappears. Once you set those things in motion they get more difficult to hear but they never actually go away."

The epic song, which Waits would later single out to Pulse as "one of my favourites," also featured Primus bassist Les Claypool, who Waits explained in a conversation with Thrasher magazine "came up and played on 'Earth Died Screaming'. He was in between fishing trips at the time. He's great, he's got such an elastic approach to the instrument: a fretless, spastic, elastic, rubberised Plasticene approach. He's like a funhouse mirror."

In addition to the aforementioned guest players, Waits enlisted the help of bassist Larry Taylor. "Larry's great. He used to play in VFW veteran's halls with Jerry Lee Lewis, where he would take a violin pickup and wrap it in a hanky, and drop that into the piano hole. That would be the mike. Larry would play over by that hole, and whatever came out of the speaker was the bass. He's a very intuitive musician. And right after we finished the record, his bass broke. Which I thought was great. It just couldn't take it anymore."

Of his eclectic keyboard choices in the course of creating what Rolling Stone concluded were "(trampled) melodies with an ear for twisting clichés. The music matches Waits' hollers with plenty of upright bass…over-the-top percussion… (and) late-night piano," Waits explained to the Village Voice that he considered the piano "a percussion instrument…it has 88 sympathetic strings. I found a soundboard and strings of a piano that had been destroyed by a heavy-metal group. They had blown it up with some dynamite. I think it was just for fun. And they only left the soundboard so I started banging on that with some drumsticks. Just leaned it against the wall and whacked it."

Elaborating on some of the other keyboards utilised in the course of creating 'Bone Machine', the singer began with the Chamberlin, "the first keyboard sampling instrument… It's a 70-voice tape loop, it's a tape recorder, an elaborate tape recorder with a keyboard… It changes the physicality of your approach to the instrument because the keyboard is not easy (to play). It goes down too far, your fingers get stuck down there and can't get back up… The Chamberlin has a full sound effects bank that's thrilling. It has the sound of Superman leaving the window. It has storms. It has wind, rain and thunder. There are three keys right next to each other. What I have is a prototype, so its got whatever he discovered. I've got one Mellotron and one Chamberlin, and the Chamberlin I have is a prototype. So it's made with found electronic objects…(I used them) on two songs, on 'Earth Died Screaming' and 'The Ocean Doesn't Want Me'."

For most listeners, the most powerful musical element of Waits' new album was, as always, his voice. iTunes concluded in their review of his performance that Waits' "singing is even more tortured and extreme and his lyrical obsessions have curtailed their surrealism to focus on mortality's eerie call." To invent descriptions like the aforementioned, Tom revealed to Pulse magazine of creating his singularly unique style that "what I like to try and do with my voice is get kind of schizophrenic with it, and see if I can scare myself or go from one song to the next and see if I can like turn my head around on my body so my vertebrae cracks. Or I put on lipstick and start screaming into a tin can. Oh, yeah, I'm happy with my voice as an instrument. I quit smoking and nobody noticed. Or I say, 'I lost my voice, I have no voice', and they say, 'I didn't notice.' That really hurts."

Alternative Press rated the singer's "apocalyptic howl" as "Waits' strongest calling card positively bowls you over," and the singer himself seemed biased entirely toward his newest vocal incarnation, underscoring the latter by sharing with KCRW FM that – at that point in his singing career – "my early records, I can barely listen to 'em. I sound like a kid. I said boy, what are they doing recording a guy that sounds like that? Now I've gotten to the point where it feels comfortable and I can do things with it. I guess that's my real instrument, my voice. I can push it around and find different things it can do."

Amazon.com Essential Recordings noted that "this is Waits' most harrowing album ever, thanks not only to such heartwarming sentiments as 'What does it matter, a dream of love or a dream of lies/We're all going to be in the same place when we die' but also to the ravaged, shamanistic croak with which he delivers them." Melody Maker paid him a broader compliment in the context of storytelling that "Waits doesn't prettify, he just simplifies, as the best storytellers must…shows his roots in the spirituals of black American slaves, gospel, Leadbelly's blues and the Depression folk of Woody Guthrie…weird and wonderful."

Waits commented of his technical strengths as a singer during an interview with KCRW FM. "Nobody ever said (I was right on pitch, but)…I get good grades. You know I can sing like Pavarotti if I want to but I find I feel more comfortable the way I do it. But on a good day I can sing like opera." Rather than opera, some critics – like Stereo Review – concluded that "'Bone Machine' is minimalist music from hell, played on the bones of sinners and sung through the rusty, ravaged, and perhaps even channeled voice of the devil, who shovels coal through Waits' dreams."

Billboard concluded that Waits' voice produced "a chilling, primal sound made all the more otherworldly (or perhaps, underworldly) by Waits'…often-distorted roars and growls." In addition to his own voice, Waits again utilised the Chamberlin

2000, explaining he loved the instrument because "it's stunning, really. I have like 70 voices on the instrument, from horses to rain, laughter, thunder, seven or eight different trains, and then all the standard orchestral instruments. It's a good alternative if you don't like the sound of the more conventional state-of-the-art instruments – sometimes it's like they've had the air sucked out of them."

Another of Waits' consistent strengths – as always – in the course of creating 'Bone Machine' came with his songwriting, which Waits explained to the Guardian, dealt "with violence and death and suicide and the end of the world, and they're all strung together like old vertebrae." That collection, according to Spin, was "a shining collection of tunes" that Billboard added matched "the evocative power (of his voice)…is Waits' songwriting, which is arguably the most consistently focused it's ever been. Rich in strange and extraordinarily vivid imagery, many of Waits' tales and musings are spun against an imposing backdrop of apocalyptic natural fury, underlining the insignificance of his subjects and their universally impending doom."

Referring to the creation of some of the album's highlight tracks, Waits began with his Keith Richards collaboration 'That Feel', saying to Musician magazine that "it's great to have somebody to write with. It's still really a mystery why songs come around and then leave. Keith is always pondering these same questions; he's extremely down-to-earth and very mystical at the same time." Turning to 'Murder In The Red Barn', Waits explained its meaning to journalist Rip Rense. "For some…it is said, murder is the only door through which they enter life. I guess that's true. It's just a story about a small-town murder. How everything gets covered up. And the weather changes everything. Pretty soon you stop talking about it, and you don't even remember it anymore, and you move on. I don't know what else to say about it. I like it."

Another song close to Waits' heart on the record, 'Whistle Down The Wind' – was dedicated to an old friend of the singer's, Tom Jans, who Waits explained "died in '83. A songwriter and friend of Kathleen's and mine. From the central coast of California, kind of a Steinbeck upbringing in a small town. We dedicated it to him. He wrote 'Lovin' Arms'. Dobie Gray recorded it, and also Elvis did it. He used to play with Mimi Farina. It was written about another friend, but it was the kind of song that Tom Jans would have written. He was there in spirit."

Of 'Goin' Out West', Waits reasoned of its muse that "when you live somewhere other than California, you do have this golden image that everything will be all right when you get here, no matter how twisted your imagination. Orange trees, bikinis, sunglasses. It's like a guy that gets out of jail and he's going to out there and shake things up, show 'em what a real man's like." The singer-songwriter added in conversation with journalist Steve Orr that when he started working on it, "I figured, let's do a rocker. We'll just slam it and scream. And my wife said, 'No, this is about those guys who come to California from the Midwest with very specific ideas in mind.' That's how the line about (movie actor) Tony Franciosa fits. There are people who come to California with less than that to go on. A phone number somebody gave them, you know, for a psychic who used to work with Ann-Margret: 'And if I meet him, maybe I can get somewhere, maybe if I play my cards right…'

Waits explained to journalist Rip Rense that, originally, "I was going to throw ('I Don't Wanna Grow Up') out. I wasn't going to record it, but Kathleen said, you've got to finish that. I said no, that's cornball. Then in the studio it took on another life, because we put it through a Marshall amplifier and turned it up real loud, and then it felt better. It's like you could hear it at a carnival. Little county fair Buddy Holly kind of thing going on there. It's fast. The best ones come fast. They come out of the ground like a potato," adding to KCRW FM of its origins that "this happened real fast, a real fast song. Kathleen said, 'Oh, that's a great one.' I said, 'Gee, this is a lame song. This was written too fast. This is the kind of song you write in the car.' But sometimes those are the best ones."

Expanding on his songwriting as it had evolved, Tom offered that "my theory is the best songs have never really been recorded so we're all listening to used music. We're listening to things that made it through but there's so many songs that have never made it cause they were scared of the machine and wouldn't allow themselves to be recorded. The trick is to get it in there and not bruise the gin. Don't hurt the song when you record it.

"This happened real fast. We only did it a couple of times and we just slammed it. We said, well, we better not do this again cause it'd just sound stupid. This was the version that we did and there was only one of them. We said okay, that'll do, you can go, you can come on the trip. I haven't played that song live. That's a good one to have. It's a sing along, it's like a hootenanny."

The musical genesis for 'A Little Rain', the singer recalled to journalist Rip Rense, actually began with wife Kathleen. "She had this melody, and I saved it from the fire. She has all these Irish melodies. Then we read one of those terrible articles in a newspaper about a kid in a van that went out of control and went over a cliff, and they all died. Goes through some different time periods. Starts out with the ice man's mule, then it goes to the dancing on the roof with the ceiling coming down, and ends up in the van. So I think it comes forward in time, a little bit, with the images. But it's a song you can add another verse to, if you want."

Turning to the cryptically-titled 'Dirt In The Ground', Waits began by explaining that the song's title came courtesy of a line from his longtime saxophonist Teddy Edwards. "That's his line. That's what he used to tell girls in the lobby of the hotel. Trying to get 'em to come up to his room. 'Well, listen, darlin', we're all just goin' be dirt in the ground. So that kind of explains itself. There were some verses that we left out. It was getting too long. One of them was Mata Hari was a traitor, they sentenced her to death/The priest was at her side and asked her if she would confess/She said, 'Step aside, Father, it's the firing squad again/And you're blockin' my view of these fine lookin' men/And we're all gonna be dirt in the ground…'

"That's what people say that were present, that just before the firing squad opened up she opened up her blouse a little bit, and then she winked, and then they took her down. Ralph Carney played the horns, and he gave it those low Ellington kind of voicings – bass clarinet, tenor and the alto together."

Elaborating on saxophonist Carney's role in bring the song to life musically, Waits added his memory to journalist Seth Neilsen that, indeed, "Ralph played all the saxes on that. I think he has kind of an Ellingtonian sound he got on that, with the horn section. I just play a very simple piano. I tried to sing in my high, my Prince voice…ha. I can only do that once or twice and then it's gone. If I try to sing like that on the road every night, forget about it. So when you're in the studio, you're taking better care of your voice, you can do things like that."

Turning to 'All Stripped Down', Tom candidly volunteered in his conversation with Rense that "it's about death, but it's also a sexy thing, too. It's like Jerry Lee Lewis. Walk a line between Jesus and girls… Maybe it would be more of a Jimmy Swaggart approach. Because they say that's what you have to do before you can get into heaven. You have to be all stripped down. You can't go to heaven with your body on. You just go up there with your spirit. I guess it's going to be like a mayonnaise jar with some smoke in it. So I save jars. You want to save different sized jars for different family members. I think it's like a Prince song." He told Image magazine of the song's challenging recording process that "we recorded it at home. I have this tape recorder at home that I love so much. I recorded all these really rough tapes on it and loved the grit that I got. And I was really trying to find the same feeling in a studio. That was the challenge."

Of 'Jesus Gonna Be Here', Waits – in an interview with KCRW FM – revealed its authentic inspiration as having come from real-life street preachers, who he recalled he "used to hear them in downtown LA all the time, the guys on the corner with their own sound systems in the briefcases and the microphones. Heavy traffic. They always picked five o'clock when it's really busy downtown. It usually seemed like the most important thing that was going on but it was also disregarded by everyone. It used to make me really – I would always stop and listen 'cause when you have something to say and it's important to you and no one's listening it's a lonely place and it takes a lot of courage and it takes a lot of conviction. Sometimes it just elevates you."

Tom elaborated that in "knowing that nobody's listening – there's a freedom in that. You can say anything you want when no one's listening. If you're raging in a room where nobody cares what you say you can say anything you want. I love those guys. Plus the sound systems were really – I love the sound of the little broken speakers… (Musically), this was done real simply, it's just guitar and bass and that's it – in a small room. I never played upright bass before. It was one of those trades, Larry took the guitar and I took the bass. You can hear the helicopter on that."

Discussing the inclusion of ballads, once a signature of Waits' earlier albums, he admitted in the same radio interview that "I go back and forth between – I like to hear family heirlooms thrown against the wall and also I like a lot of different kinds of sounds." Waits added that "when I first started writing songs I loved harmony and melody but I'm changing a little bit. But I still have the other side of me, the old drunk in the corner who had too much wine starting to get a little sentimental."

Waits told Pulse magazine that the decision to complete mixing the album was never an easy one, simply because "you don't really finish – you just stop. You just keep painting it and doing things to it and eventually you have to stop."

When that time finally did arrive, Waits singled it out in a conversation with KCRW FM as his favourite time in the record making cycle, reasoning that "you think that you're gonna be happier when it's done but you're not really. You're happier when you're in the centre of it and it's really an expedition, it's a journey and anything can happen.

"I think leadership is best when you're lost. The captain is blind but you can never let the crew know that or they'll lose confidence in you. I love exploring sound and I lose myself in it and I work with people who love to vanish into these things. The songs are simple. They're small and they have three legs and you hope they move forward."

'Bone Machine' was an instant smash with critics on its 8 September 1992 release, earning 'Best Albums of the Year' rankings from the Village Voice (Number 9) and Spin (Number 13). Musician magazine's compliment that the record was "one of the most singular-sounding albums to come along in some time…'Bone Machine' should be counted among (Waits') best efforts." The San Francisco Chronicle, on reviewing the album, concluded it was "an investigation of sound…(that) breaks new ground," while Billboard declared that "all of ('Bone Machine')…adds up to Waits' most affecting and powerful recording." Rolling Stone magazine paid Waits perhaps his biggest critical compliment with their note that "albums this rich with spiritual longing prove the validity of that effort, no matter the odds."

It was awarded a 1992 Grammy for Best Alternative Album but, for Waits, those lasting impact of his record upon listeners, as he explained to Telerama, came from the fact that "with music…you're working with something that's invisible and has great power over you and people believe that every sound that you make never goes away. Sound waves never disappear."

Commercially speaking, Waits did admit to Musician magazine that it was important to him that the record "do well…I want it to," adding that while "I seem to have a wide reputation, my records don't sell a lot. A lot of people seem to have bought one record or they heard one record a long time ago and got me down, so they don't have to check in anymore: 'Oh, that guy. The one with the deep voice without a shave? Know him. Sings about eggs and sausage? Yeah, got it.' But you send 'em out there, 'cause it's true that things kind of land in your back yard like meteorites. Songs can have a real effect on you – songs have been known to save lives."

Across the critical board, there was agreement that 'Bone Machine' was "absolutely gorgeous in its idiosyncratic genius" – as noted by iTunes – in a review that further observed the record as "a highlight in a career with many peaks." Waits shared with radio disc jockey Gary Tausch that he could only "listen to this for a while," adding that "I'll be listening to this for a while and then I'll stop… (because) then you start listening to things you can't hear which is the music that you're gonna do next."

Discussing the prospects of what his next studio LP might sound like, Waits would only tell journalist Steve Orr that "I hope it's very different – but I'll tell you, real departures usually require some traumatic change in your life.

Something that really bends you, you know? Most times you think you're being adventuresome, but you really never left your backyard. People move in steps. Nobody grows overnight. I would like to really go out there – really out there – but I can only go a step at a time."

For the moment, Tom seemed to be content with where he'd arrived as an artist, offering his closing feeling to filmmaker and friend Jim Jarmusch – who he would collaborate with that same year on a film score to Night On Earth – that his next few years would be musically-prolific ones simply because "it's been a good period. So I'm anxious to start work on another original album of new songs. I've got backed up with material for new songs…"

"I run hot and cold. I like melody, and I like dissonance. I guess maybe it's an alcoholic personality. I get mad, and I cry." – TOM WAITS

PART XVI: 'Night On Earth' (1992)

Any introduction of 1992's Night On Earth, which Tom Waits scored, must begin with an examination of the film itself

"Jim Jarmusch's delirious new comedy," the New York Times explained, "explores a primal urban relationship, that of man and taxi driver, in situations in which woman is sometimes man and sometimes driver. The cab itself is the world temporarily shared. It's also a distinctive cocoon (each taxi in the film has its own special purr or knock) from which one of the parties will emerge if not changed, then at least shaken up, or, in one case, no more sure where he is than when he got into the cab."

This rise, according to Rolling Stone magazine, was aided and "abetted by the haunted bleat of Tom Waits' vocals and the spare elegance of Frederick Elmes's cinematography," allowing Jarmusch to create "the world whizzing by those taxi windows – a thing of beauty and terror."

Waits rapport with director Jarmusch began on a personal level, Waits recalling to journalist Jonathan Valania that the two had met years earlier "around the time of 'Rain Dogs'. He stuck out. His movies were like Russian films, like nothing anyone had ever seen before. For me, they were like the hair in the gate. You know when you used to go to the movies and a big hair would get stuck in the projector, and you would sit there and watch that piece of hair? You would lose the whole plot for a while. So, he was the hair in the gate."

By the early Nineties, the pair's creative collaborations already included Waits' co-starring in 1986's Down By Law with Oscar winner Roberto Benigni and Ellen Barkin, and 1989's Mystery Train alongside Steve Buscemi and the Clash's Joe Strummer. When he got a call in 1991 from Jarmusch, rather than being for another acting part, the subject of film scoring came up.

Waits recalled that John Lurie, who he regarded as "the master of film music… (who) did Jim's last two pictures…was busy," adding in the same conversation with Reflex magazine that he took the challenge on because "sometimes it's good to work with limitations; you make something from what you have. Sometimes you need the drama of having to create this thing in an hour. It's not something I have at beck and call. I have a special rapport with Jim."

Having been an actor within Jarmusch's cinematic vision of how film was made was certainly of benefit heading into the writing of Night On Earth's score, which

Jarmusch hoped in connection with the film itself would cause the "audience (to)…just slip into it as an imaginary world that is not very obviously taking place right now. I mean, black and white does that by nature for people." The singer was clearly a fan of the way Jarmusch painted the world in his films, and that visual fabric aided Waits in composing the music.

He explained to KCRW FM that "Jarmusch is a very good friend of mine. We have a rapport. He's Dr Sullen. We work really well together. We're going to do a video when I go back up home for 'I Don't Wanna Grow Up'. I love Jarmusch. He's a great observer of human nature and loves the details. I'm big on details. It's great to work with someone you have that kind of shorthand with."

From the director's vantage point, he explained to NME that conceptually, he desired a departure from what he felt was a running trend at the time where "it seems like people use music, especially pop songs, in films these days to drive a sequence, something that's not really important in the film. And instead I use them with very static shots, and let the song really interact with the characters, the way that people listen to music."

As Waits incorporated these notes into his pre-production writing for the record, the director – who shared with Time Out that "Tom and I have a kindred aesthetic, an interest in unambitious, marginal people" – felt Waits' Tom's natural preference for writing songs which incorporated "imagination, memories, nightmares, dismantling certain aspects of this world and putting them back together in the dark" fitted well with the vision he was expressing.

Continuing, the director reasoned in the same conversation with the TomWaitsLibrary.com that "songs aren't necessarily verbatim chronicles or necessarily journal entries, they're like smoke. It's like it's made out of smoke, the stuff that makes a song, usually a song will remind you of something, take you back somewhere, make you think of somebody or someplace. They're like touchstones, like a mist."

Clearly inspired by the film's nocturnal theme, Tom quipped to Rolling Stone that he was inspired as such because "the moon beats the hell out of the sun." On a more serious note he revealed that his true inspiration for the project was rooted in his belief that "there's something illusionary about the night. If we were sitting here in the afternoon looking out that window you wouldn't be able to see the reflection of the kitchen and the cook. And you wouldn't know what's in that parking lot across the street. So your imagination is working overtime. And the night is music."

As he completed writing for the album, Billboard reported he did so once again with wife/collaborator "Kathleen Brennan…(contributing) three songs with lyrics…(and a score that brings) an appropriately international flavour to his mostly instrumental score for Jim Jarmusch's globetrotting taxicab movie. As in all his music of the time, Waits' chief influence is Kurt Weill, and using horns and accordion among other instruments he re-creates Weill's creepy, catchy style in 16 short tracks running almost 53 minutes."

Heading into the studio, Tom lined up an eclectic band that featured Josef Brinckmann on accordion, Matthew Brubeck on cello, Ralph Carney on trumpet, saxes, clarinet and pan pipes, Joe Gore on guitar and banjo, Clark Suprynowitz on bass, Francis Thumm on harmonium and organ and Waits himself on vocals, pump organ, drums, percussion and piano. In selecting the players, Tom explained it was a requisite with each of them that they spoke his unique musical language in such a way that they could communicate it musically onto tape precisely as he heard each instrument playing in his head, explaining that "you can't see music, so sometimes talking about it is difficult. So you use metaphor. When you're speaking to musicians, you use images."

Waits' favourite go-to instrument in the course of tracking the score was the Chamberlin 3000, which he loved utilising because "its got a variety of trains, it's a sound that I've become obsessed with, getting an orchestra to sound like a train, actual train sounds. I have a guy in Los Angeles who collected not only the sound of the Stinson band organ, which is a carnival organ that's in all the carousels, the sound from that we used on Night On Earth, but he also has pitched four octaves of train whistles so that I can play the train whistle organ, which sounds like a calliope. It's a great sound."

Tom explained that "a lot of the first, earliest experiments in sound, in creating illusions with sound and manipulating sound happened with mediums that created this matrix of pipe configurations in their homes. Mediums that were doing séance work, contacting the dead, and they would outfit the room where they would conduct the séance with this whole matrix of pipes and things they could send voices into and have come out in unusual places. All of a sudden the sound of an old man snoring would come from under your chair. And you're in a dark room holding hands, and this was all an elaborate ruse to convince you that the spirits were visiting the room."

Upon completion, the soundtrack album was released by Island on 2 April 1992. Billboard noted in their review that "Waits performs in a calmer, more melodic way than those on some of his recent albums. Still, this soundtrack is very much in the style of Waits' 'Swordfishtrombones', 'Rain Dogs', and 'Franks Wild Years' albums."

Assessing the score's impact on the film overall, the New York Times concluded that it "transforms (Night On Earth)…into something haunting, mysterious and newly true." Waits enjoyed the collaborative spirit of Night On Earth so much that he would dive right from the Jarmusch project into another collaboration, this time with play director Robert Wilson and legendary Beat writer William S Burroughs on the score for a live theatrical production of The Black Rider…

"**The songs flow into one another, creating extended dreamlike sequences.**" – ITUNES

"**Tom Waits has made a career of obliterating artistic boundaries.**" – SPIN MAGAZINE

PART XVII: 'THE BLACK RIDER' (1993)

For his fifteenth LP, Tom Waits chose to follow up 1992's 'Bone Machine' with an even more ambitious branching-out of stylistic studio pursuits, working with what iTunes termed "two challenging avant-garde artists, avant-garde theatre director Robert Wilson and novelist Williams S Burroughs" in a collaboration that would come to be known as The Black Rider. Explaining what initially drew him to such a creative teaming, Waits told Mojo that "working with (Burroughs) was just a chance to be up on the wire without a net and you really find out what kind of resource you have. Because you're with someone who has a whole community inside of them. It was very heavy."

He found working with director Robert Wilson equally as impressive, revealing to the San Francisco Chronicle that "I've worn glasses ever since I met him. He's like an inventor, you know, and he throws down the gauntlet for your own imagination." Teaming with two equal geniuses for a meeting of collective minds would produce one of the decade's most provocative recorded operas.

Offering a description of the collaboration's genesis, Wired magazine explained that "The Black Rider, which premiered in Hamburg in 1990, tells the tale of Wilhelm, a clerk who makes a deal with a dark horseman in order to win his love, a forester's daughter, in a shooting contest using magic bullets. Wilhelm wins the match, but accidentally slays his bride with the same bullets: He goes mad." While Melody Maker warned even Waits' most open-minded fans to "roll up for ringside seats and prepare to be amazed, astounded and bedeviled," concluding upon listening to the album that "this ringmaster has no living equal."

Rolling Stone magazine pointed out that "this odd, operatic collaboration with Burroughs and Wilson does not completely fit in with the whiskey-and-bar-stool concept of Waits' previous albums," but was eager to clarify in the same time that "it does continue his intriguing expansion into more surreal realms. His dervish-like approach to The Black Rider makes you gawk like a freakshow spectator in fear, fascination and delight."

From the outset of the project, Waits figured he was "writing music for a cowboy opera… Four principal characters, all the rest will be carrying spears. One of these oblique pieces, based on a German folk legend. I'm not even sure how it's all gonna hang together yet. All these ideas are very easy to come up with, then the work begins. It's like the guy who sits down and writes at the top of the page:

Rangoon 1890, and then tries to get a budget for it, y'know. I don't know what we're up against, but I'm very excited about it."

An even greater thrill came with the opportunity to meet one of his lifelong literary heroes in William S Burroughs. This involved a journey into the heart of the Midwest, as he told Mojo magazine. "We all went to meet William in Lawrence (Kansas), Greg Cohen and Robert Wilson and myself. And we talked about this whole thing. It was very exciting, really. It felt like a literary summit. Burroughs took pictures of everyone standing on the porch. Took me out into the garage and showed me his shotgun paintings. Showed me the garden."

As he and Burroughs got to know one another's arguably competitive worlds of weird, Tom shared with San Francisco magazine his memory that, among other interests, "Burroughs loves firearms and reptiles and…(has these) shotgun paintings. He would finish a painting – he painted on plywood – and then he would stand back from it with a 12-gauge shotgun and shoot a hole in it with buckshot. And then he'd say, 'That's done', and in a way, ironically, he gave life to it, with all these splinters coming off of it. And around three, 'cause it was almost cocktail time, he'd start massaging his watch, as if maybe he could get that big hand to move up there a little faster."

Admitting to the New York Times that, initially, "he was scary when I met him," as both artists let their guard down, Waits shared that "he let everyone be a part of his whole creative process. As the group began to brainstorm song ideas together, Tom told Mojo, ideas began to bloom. "We'd talk about the story and all these songs just started occurring to him. 'Take off your skin and dance…'"

Waits confessed to the Chicago Tribune that "writing songs for other people is just mortifying at times. You stand by and watch other people completely butcher them… Sometimes they're completely elevated. But I figured I could improve upon most of them," In the course of collaborating with Burroughs, Waits sought to maintain "a democratic approach to sound expedition," reasoning that such a creative journey was "always a mystery…(in terms of) where you're going to wind up.

"But the best thing is to work with people who respond to suggestions, just like you would tell actors. You have to know something about them, and you have to share some common desire for mystery and danger, and then you can say things to them that they will take you someplace. We'll all go someplace together."

As the pair made headway with their writing sessions, Burroughs shared his own memory with the New York Times that "when Tom was here in Lawrence, and we were sketching out the basic structure of The Black Rider, he had some very good ideas. I had the idea of comparing the magic bullet in the original German story to heroin. Once you use one, you'll use another. Tom said, 'Yeah, and the first one's always free', and of course that went right in." Tom recalled his favourite aspect of collaborating with Burroughs was the constant river of creativity that flowed from the legendary author. "Burroughs is like a metal desk. He's like a still, and everything that comes out of him is already whiskey."

Tom shared with the Orange County Register that "he wrote most of his words at his place in Lawrence (Kansas), and he'd send piles of material. Our dramaturge (would) edit and paste and cut and find the right spot for everything. Burroughs was just coughing up all this stuff, not writing in any linear way. Sometimes I would take something he wrote and turn it into a lyric. Sometimes we'd collaborate, like in 'Just The Right Bullet': 'To hit the tattered clouds you have to have the right bullets' – that's all Burroughs. 'The first bullet is free' – that's me."

In adapting a score to director Robert Wilson's theatrical version of The Black Rider, Tom – in a discussion with San Francisco magazine – described the challenges of working with an entirely different artistic perspective wherein, he explained, Wilson "makes these dreamscapes up onstage, and you sit out there in the dark and you start hearing what could possibly be the accompaniment to what you are seeing. But to do that, you have to kind of fall into this liquid dream that he's making for you."

Wilson described his collaborative relationship with Waits in an interview with the New York Times. "Tom and I are very different men… Tom and I dress differently, have different styles; I tend to be cooler, more formal. But nevertheless, I think we're emotionally tied somehow. In my work, the emotion is sometimes hidden or buried, and Tom's music has a very deep emotional centre for me. I immediately liked it when I first heard it; I liked it very much. And Tom knows theatre; it's in his blood. We can talk. I can ask him about how things look on the stage, and that really helps."

As he got deeper into pre-production writing with Wilson, Tom told Paste magazine of the director's working method that he was "more like an inventor, a real visionary, and he's meticulous about what he wants and doesn't want. It's not a democracy. That's why what you're seeing is a very specific vision from one man's mind – you're not seeing a collaboration."

The singer-songwriter added his memory to NPR that "when you meet him you think this guy's with aerospace or he's some kind of a medical guy. He has that feeling around, there's a certain precision to the way he speaks and works and I thought it was very different then my own approach which was more like I guess more like falling down the stairs compared to Bob. But somehow the fact that we were very different seemed to come together."

In spite of the director's sometimes-singular vision for the theatrical aspects of the production that The Black Rider score would accompany, Tom added in the same conversation that "everyone trusts him so much – he's like a professor, like the best professor. For me, in all my years in school, (there was) nothing like Wilson. Like you'll always remember a particular teacher? I'd say Wilson is my teacher. I mean, I didn't go to college. But there's nobody that's affected me that much, as an artist." Inspired by the director much in the way an actor would be on Wilson's stage, Waits rolled up his sleeves and dug into the adaptation. it was reminiscent in ways of his collaboration with Francis Ford Coppola on One From The Heart over a decade earlier.

The New York Times reported that "in Hamburg, Mr Waits and Mr Burroughs worked separately, at night, bringing their results to Mr Wilson's rehearsals the next morning." As they shaped the album's songs, Waits revealed a natural translation for him as a composer between his own animated imagination and the action of live stage performance, reasoning to the Times that it worked because "to me, everything is really music – words are music, every sound is music, it all depends on how it's organised.

"In terms of an actor's choices, all behaviour is fair game, so why isn't all sound considered music? I really like the physicality of music-making and the possibility of human error. As much as you rehearse and perform it, the music never really wants to stay the same. You can make it do that, but then what you've got to do is respect the moments when it escapes your control."

The nature of their compositional process affected the way songs developed, as the singer-songwriter recalled in the same conversation. "Because of the way we worked, the recordings naturally tended to be kind of crude, like work tapes, and I didn't realise at the time that a lot of these recordings would eventually be released. Which was great for me. I've always struggled with that; as soon as I think we're doing something for real, it just freezes me up." Tom confirmed that, indeed, "my favourite recordings tend to be those kind of uninhibited moments in music that had no idea that they were music."

Tom opted to incorporate their aforementioned crudeness into the natural sonic fabric of the record, recalling to Spin magazine that these recordings "were made under the circumstance of where I try to get myself creatively, where I say to myself, 'This is no big deal, this is not the national anthem, if it doesn't happen, that is all right.' It doesn't care what you are doing when it comes together. Sometimes you go in the studio with a fist and you have to trick yourself, because often it finds you when you don't want to work.

"You're driving along and you have to pull over and put your sandwich in your lap and get out a piece of paper, and you have to write a thing. But there's the thousand times when you've sat there with the same empty piece of paper in a house with the window open and the birds are singing and fucking nothing. Sometimes you can't do it, and you have to trick yourself because it's not about making a fist; it's about opening your hand."

Once he migrated from the Music Factory in Hamburg to Prairie Sun Studios in Cotati, California, Waits undertook a overdubbing process of "add things to make them sound more crude." Elaborating on his method for layering crude on top of crude, Tom shared with friend/director Jim Jarmusch that "most of them were recorded very crudely in Hamburg in a studio, and then we brought 'em (home). So some of 'em are real crude, which I like. I like to hear things real crude, cruder. I think if I pursue it, I don't know where it'll take me, but y'know, it's getting more and more like that. I just like to hear it dirty. It's a natural relation to where we are in technology, because things swing in and swing back. That's normal. And I like to step on it, scratch it up, break it. I wanna go further into that world of texture."

Offering in the same conversation the recording of 'Gospel Train/Orchestra' as an example of that world of texturing in action, "that train thing…came from taking nine pieces and improvising something really quickly, like lining up children and having 'em march and scream out some word. 'Real quick, we gotta make it happen right now', it was like real fast sketch, which is real hard to do when people come from (high) music, because that's high music.

"People who play in all those symphony orchestras, like some guy who plays contra bassoon, it's rare that he's gonna get to do anything. Where it's just free, do something free, y'know, with structure and planning, but very spontaneously from the depths. That's something you don't really get from an orchestra, so I loved doing that. It gave everybody a great feeling. You know that expression '(orchestra) go out to the meadow', when you leave the room, you leave the music, everyone is just like a ship, a strange ship, and everyone feels essential to it…I love that. And those are the things I keep looking for in the studio, and how to do it."

Recruiting longtime arranger Greg Cohen, Waits and his band created an instrumental world the New York Times would conclude was "by turns gloomily nocturnal and nightmarishly lively, scored for banjo, bass clarinet, cello, French horn and other instruments not generally heard in contemporary pop music. Strains of vaudeville, rock, waltz and cabaret weave in and out with a hurdy-gurdy regularity."

Waits' studio cast of musicians included the usual carnival of genius, beginning with Ralph Carney on sax, Bill Douglas on bass, Kenny Wollesen on percussion, Matt Brubeck on cello, Joe Gore on banjo, Nick Phelps on French horn, Kevin Porter on trombone, Greg Cohen on bass, percussion, banjo, viola, Don Neely on saw, Larry Rhodes on bassoon, Francis Thumm on organ, Henning Stoll on contrabassoon, Stefan Schäfer on bass, Volker Hemken on clarinet, Hans-Jorn Braudenberg on organ, Linda Deluca on viola, Gerd Bessler on viola and Christoph Moinian on French horn.

Tom explained to the Orange County Register that the players worked well together because most "were either from classical music or they were playing in a train station. At first there was a little conflict in the orchestra. There were folks that didn't read (music) and folks that had played in the Berlin Symphony; they were a little uppity. I like unusual sound sources. I remember at the time I had a circle of friends from this more experimental musical world, and so I tried to write some of that into it. There were Stroh basses and cellos. The sound is captivating. And of course they look really cool, too."

Even though his studio band included seasoned session pros, in tackling some of his and Cohen's complex musical arrangements, Tom likened those aspects of the album's recording to managing "a ship of men", adding that, because of the variety of line-ups that occurred from song to song, tracking was "different every time. There's always a collective unconscious that happens in a group if the soldiers are open to confrontation. Sometimes you have to confront your own limitations and smash them and go on. That's when you end up in a place that's new. And I have to do it myself."

Waits reasoned that, creatively, he responded to "working with people that maybe you are a little bit intimidated by. You want to challenge your own limitations. I still have a very crude approach to music. I don't read music and I don't write traditional notation. I developed my own crude shorthand or hieroglyphics that I can respond to if I'm writing on a plane or train or in a car, and I'm not around an instrument, just use your voice.

"But it's also helpful to sit down at an instrument you have no history with, and then you approach it more like a kid. There's no right and wrong about it, and it frees you from it. But then the other side of that is that the fingers also have an intelligence, and places that they want to go. Before you get there they've already gotten there, so it's…like writing sitting at a typewriter. Sometimes it's just you and the machine."

One of the highs of recording The Black Rider was "a session…where we took just viola, double bass and cello, and we created a pointillist kind of ant colony, it just happened very spontaneous and thrilling," Waits used it as an example of why "conceptually, working with suggestions is usually the best way for me. We made up a train, a monster.

"Sometimes it's good to combine high music with low music, orchestral guys with guys that play in the train station. Then, through the conflict of background you go to a new place. And there's a lot of orchestral guys who rarely get an opportunity to just, to abandon their history on the instrument, just play free, go to a totally free zone, and you fall into these Bermuda Triangles of rhythm, melody. And lately those are the places that I like to go to."

On the more frustrating end of the spectrum, in the same conversation Tom shared that "there are certain variables that are possible to control, but that's what frustrates me when I'm in there all the time, because… I've taken fingers off. I'm not proud of it, but it's just part of… One accordionist I worked with just eats the music. He eats the music, and you find him, it's all over his shirt, down his chin, it's just been murdered… Accordionists will sometimes take a part and they'll just play the hell out of it until it's dead. But y'know you're always fighting those things, the same thing on a film set. You've got to turn it around."

While not the stage/film production's director, Waits was the captain of The Black Rider as a musical ship, and with that title came the daunting responsibility of "navigating through strange places. I've had these terrible dramas about the expedition, and they remind me of music, of operations where sometimes you lose a patient, and I'm despondent over it, I'm so fucking mad about it."

When attention turned to the album's vocal tracking, the most exciting moment was Waits' collaboration with William S Burroughs on 'T'aint No Sin'. Waits began by explaining to Rolling Stone of the song's importance that it was "his reference point for the whole play. He was looking rather skeletal himself and singing that tune was a Halloween moment…"

Waits told San Francisco magazine that, on the track, Burroughs "plumbed the depths of so many levels of hell. Burroughs is kind of like a demonic Mark Twain. He's like the real dark heart of America. Comes from the Burroughs Adding Machine family, you know, and he threw off all the shackles of his inheritance and struck out on his own. Like they say, when you're in hell, keep going. So at times he was much more in the realm of Philip K Dick in science fiction.

"Anyway, very inspiring. And I was very romantic about all the Beats when I was first coming on the scene myself. And that voice. My favourite thing is, 'That's the way the cookie crumbles, that's the way the stomach rumbles, that's the way the needle pricks, that's the way the glue sticks.' That stuff really killed me."

Tom Waits had succeeded in channeling his shared muse into a living, breathing beast that was the perfect companion to Burroughs equally-as-ragged voice as heard on the record.

Delving into some of the signature out-of-the-box instrumental moments that wound up on the album, Tom told Spin magazine that, in order to completely open his musical mind to the abstract, he felt it was important first and foremost not to "bring your ego to the process. You just shake hands with your instrument. Sometimes music will like you better if you are more innocent, it will want to say around longer. I'm disorganised and I lose some lyrics, and I think, 'Well, maybe I was supposed to lose the lyrics so I have to write another.' That's why I love to bring in new instruments I found somewhere, I love ghosts in the machine.

"You lose things. 'What happened to that trumpet? I thought we had that trumpet! Do we have to do it again? We can't, he's gone. The trumpet player is in Vienna. We can't reach him. I guess there's no trumpet on this thing, then. Maybe it's better without the trumpet. It is! I never really liked the trumpet. I'm actually glad we didn't find the trumpet player because then we would have felt obligated to put the trumpet in there. Now I can tell the trumpet player I didn't take the trumpet out; don't get your feelings hurt, we just lost it.'"

Offering a specific example of the oddest instruments that wound up on The Black Rider, Spin singled out "the waterphone from Waits' collection of exotic instruments. It looks like two pizza pans welded face together with a length of rope-wrapped muffler pipe fitted to the centre. Varying lengths of steel rods are staggered around the edges. When water is poured down the muffler pipe into the pizza pans you draw a bow across them to achieve deep-sea, science-fiction-movie sounds."

By the time the fog cleared and the team emerged from the studio, Rolling Stone would decide that Waits, as an artist, had "grown consistently stronger, more ambitious and less self-conscious. The Black Rider continues that tradition. Its songs offer the morbid excitement of a ride on a decrepit old Tilt-a-Whirl. The rich, dizzying tunes incorporate graveyard fright noises, bizarre piano sounds and creepy sci-fi whistles into traditional, orchestrated Fiddler On The Roof-style melodies…The 20 tracks, written for director Robert Wilson's revision of The Black Rider, back the twisted Faustian tale with dark and wickedly funny melodies…A clanking, tin-can beat lurches through the material like a frantic Ichabod Crane, while disturbing violin and contorted blasts of French horn trudge along like drunken, determined sailors."

Entertainment Weekly, meanwhile, felt the record showcased Waits' "penchant for disturbing mood music" that Wired added was "all Waits…the music, shifting among haunting instrumentals, tender ballads, discordant symphonies, and old-world dances." For as clearly impressed as critical reaction had been, when the record reached the ears of executives at Waits' label Island Records, he recalled a more confused reaction to Rolling Stone magazine, one where as a consequence, "they didn't do much with it. But you know, people don't know what to do with recordings from theatre experiences. People don't know what to do with them if they buy 'em. They wonder, 'Should I have seen the show?

And if I haven't will it make sense?'"

Ultimately, the album made enough sense to NME to conclude that "with records as challenging, tuneful and blackly comic as The Black Rider, Tom Waits threatens to come as close as anyone since Brecht to piecing together a cross-cultural jigsaw that doesn't fall apart."

"I don't have a formal background. I learned from listening to records, from talking to people, from hanging around record stores and hanging around musicians." – TOM WAITS, 1999

"I have a hard time listening to my old records, the stuff before my wife." – TOM WAITS

"Iconoclastic, eccentric and hugely talented." – NEWSWEEK, 1999

"I'm not in the music business, I'm in the salvage business. I salvage people, music, places, furniture…the things that other people have thrown away." – TOM WAITS, 1999

PART XVIII: 'Mule Variations' (1999)

In 1999, Tom Waits was approaching the 30-year mark pioneering a style of music that had become not just a sub-genre all its own, but one that Rolling Stone magazine – in a cover story titled 'The Resurrection Of Tom Waits' – pointed out "was critically respected…(and among peers, as) his songs have been covered by Rod Stewart, Bruce Springsteen and the Ramones, among others."

It continued by saying he participates in outside projects of exquisite taste and eccentricity," citing a few recent examples to highlight the fact that, while Waits had been out of the spotlight, he hadn't been on vacation from recording music altogether, appearing on select releases including "a tribute album to the late Moby Grape singer and guitarist Skip Spence and the recent experimental-music collection 'Orbitones, Spoon Harps & Bellowphones'."

Tom was taking a hiatus from the spotlight to focus on raising his three children. In his absence, Newsweek studied his legacy, reasoning that approaching the Millennium it had "made him one of the most deeply admired songwriters in pop today. To the post-boomer generation, he's more Dylan than Dylan himself." Offering a more pointed insight into why Waits' sub-genre had resonated as the years went on, the publication added their observation that "Waits' melting-pot approach to Americana, his brilliant narratives and his hardiness against commercial trends have made him the ultimate icon for the alternative-minded."

Waits' sound had found its way into the ears of a new generation of alternative rockers whose embrace of his back catalogue had put the reclusive singer-songwriter in a position where stardom, as USA Today observed, was suddenly "stalking…pop music's trend-upsetting, fame-retardant eccentric. The singer-songwriter, long admired by peers and worshipped by discerning cultists, is losing his grip on mainstream anonymity as the public finally gets wise to his unconventional and long uncommercial wisdom."

Mojo observed that this latest studio LP, was "coming out at a time when Waits' musical influence has never been greater – when the Nick Caves and PJ Harveys of the world are carving careers out of the man's crazed Bible-belt imagery, and when everyone from Beck to Sparklehorse to Gomez is trafficking in his mangled country blues." The risks he took had finally paid off for the artist in the context of a wider listening audience.

Crafting the sonic blueprint for his newest musical offering began with a study of his last LP in context of "doing the finer, closer work…(of standing) back from it to see how it all works together," adding in the same conversation with Mojo that "then when it's all over you have to decide if it has four legs and a tail or what…When I was done with 'Bone Machine', we listened back and we were like, 'Oh, man, everybody's got problems on this record.' But the whole arc of it you don't really get a sense of it until it's all completely done."

Waits added to USA Today that he had taken a five-year break from the studio because "I went through a period where I was embarrassed by vulnerability as a writer; things you see, experience and feel, and you go, 'I can't sing something like that. This is too tender.' Maybe I'm finding a way of reconciling that… I'm married, I got kids. It opens up your world. But I still go back and forth – between deeply sentimental, then very mad and decapitated."

Waits and Kathleen Brennan began with a title. Waits quipped to New York Rock that "my wife called me a mule. She once said, 'I didn't marry a man; I married a mule!' I kept thinking about it. It was in the back of my head. I think it makes a good title for an album… She didn't call me a mule for nothing. But I'm rather consequent in my stubbornness. I think they're pretty straight animals. They don't listen to anybody else."

Translating the title into musical terms, Tom explained to journalist Brett Martin that "ever since Robert Johnson wrote about an automobile, it's kind of been rock's most popular vehicle…Halfway through a record you start riffing on something, and titles emerge out of the work somehow. Some of the songs had what we started calling a rural quality. They're kind of sur-rural – a combination of surreal and rural." Waits' focus heading into the writing of 'Mule Variations' was introducing the next generation of his alt-blues-folk sub-genre to fans old and new as the Millennium approached.

He again planned to record deep in the Northern California countryside at Prairie Sun Studios. The singer told the Austin Chronicle that the album's songs reminded him of "(Bach's) Goldberg Variations, only these are 'The Mule Variations'. People don't write as much about animals as they should. Perhaps they will now in the future… I don't know what people are going to think 'Mule Variations' are… (We'd written) the song, 'Get Behind the Mule', we'd done it several times. We did a Chinese version, and we did a cha-cha version, and a raga version – and acappella. And at one point, somebody mentioned that we had all these different variations on the same song: we had these mule variations. So we started referring to the record as 'Mule Variations', but in kind of a humorous way…it's just one of those titles that stuck."

As with his last decade of songwriting, Waits and his wife "co-wrote most of the songs together. We like writing together. It's a family thing. We have more fun with the record before it comes out. Then everybody hears it. Until then, it's like a family record that only we've heard." Waits told USA Today that "its an adventure. You've got a, flashlight, I've got the map. You, hold the nail, I'll swing the hammer. You wash, I'll dry."

Waits offered in the same conversation that "my wife has dreams and is…

clairvoyant and female. I write more from the news or what I see in my field of vision. I'm boots and hats and pocketknives. She's filled with musical and lyrical surprises. She's a joy to work with… She encouraged me to take some giant steps." Those included a variety of expansions into new stylistic territory that the singer recalled came courtesy of Kathleen, explaining in the same conversation that "my wife loves ethnic music, tangos and polkas and waltzes, Bavarian bands and mariachis and Balinese stuff."

Waits detailed his wife's own musical background to journalist Bret Kofford. "She's more refined than I am. I'm more throw it against the wall… Yeah, I like the little part, too. My wife's like a cross between Eudora Welty and Joan Jett. Kathleen is a rhododendron, an orchid and an oak. She's got the four Bs: beauty, brightness, bravery and brains." He added in a conversation with music writer Jonathan Valania that Brennan was an "excellent pianist, plays contrabassoon, classically trained. Used to play recitals with all the relatives around, and she would start the nocturne and then go off and everybody would cock their ears like the RCA dog: 'That ain't Beethoven any more.'

"She's free-floating. She doesn't seem to be pulled in any one direction. You see, we all like music, but what we really want is for music to like us, because it really is a language and some people are linguists and speak seven languages fluently, can do contracts in Chinese and tell jokes in Hungarian." Waits told KCRW FM that he was so inspired by his wife that he desired at some point to "do a whole record of her dreams. She has amazing dreams and it's just remarkable and I think they should all be turned into songs."

Waits revealed some of the inner-mechanics of the couple's collaborative routine to Artist Choice magazine. "We have a good way of working together. It's telepathic and compatible, it's pugilistic, it's fascinating. She's a great collaborator." He elaborated to KCRW FM that "the way Kathleen and I work, she'll write a line, I'll write a line, she'll say that's a terrible line. You've written that song 700 times before, what do you keep writing the same damn song for?

"She writes in journals all the time, just a constant log going of all things happening in the world and so she has this enormous wealth of material that is compiled mixing dreams with the kids' stories and magazine things and things you cut out of newspapers and remembered… We have a big stack of newspaper articles that we're getting ready to go through. Which is a good thing to do. Particularly for songs. 'Cause there's so much in the paper that you see, you read, you forget, you'll never see it again."

As they began fleshing out the musical ideas that would define 'Mule Variations', Waits recalled in a conversation with LA Weekly that "Kathleen and I came up with this idea of doing music that's surreal – it's surreal and it's rural. She'll start kind of talking in tongues, and I take it all down. She goes places – I can't get to those places." As partners along that path, Tom told Mojo that, at times, "when you're making songs you're navigating in the dark, and you don't know what's correct. Given another five minutes you can ruin a song."

He added in the same conversation that, in this respect, his wife was "an incandescent presence on all songs we work on together," Waits saw his wife's role as guiding light in inspiring him musically to the extreme that "I rely on her to be like a seeing-eye dog… In my case, she has the extraordinary ability to invent and sustain a mood."

Waits explained to Performing Songwriter that, at this stage of the writing process, he relied on his wife's background as an editor. As he saw it, "I'm the prospector, she's the cook. She says, 'You bring it home, I'll cook it up.' I think we sharpen each other like knives. She has a fearless imagination. She writes lyrics that are like dreams. And she puts the heart into all things. She's my true love. There's no one I trust more with music, or life. And she's got great rhythm, and finds melodies that are so intriguing and strange. Most of the significant changes I went through musically and as a person began when we met. She's the person by which I measure all others."

Tom told journalist Greg Quill that "I write when I feel the urge, when unemployment looms, when there's a death in the family. These are triggers. 'Songs are just layin' out there like fish in the water. When you're ready, you just wade out and bring 'em in.' But one thing I've learned: You've got to be real quiet if you want to catch the big ones." That process occasionally proved difficult when writing from home "when I'm trying to get to get the kids to be quiet so I can think."

To work around that distraction, he shared with KCRW FM that "the quietest place for me is in the car driving on the road 'cause at home if I go into a room and close the door the kids all want to know what I'm doing in there and then when Kathleen and I are in there together writing then they really go crazy. It's like geez, the whole bottom just dropped out – what are you guys doing in there? It's funny – but the car is a better place really."

In conversation with journalist Mick Brown, Waits added that, to avoid missing anything, "I've got a tape-recorder that I carry round in my pocket; I record in the car, play it back; you bang out a rhythm on a chest of drawers with your fist in a motel room, record that. So in a sense I'm always recording things. It's like people that draw… I say, what do you like? When you're going to draw, do you like to start out with a piece of paper that's already scribbled on and find a little place down the bottom to do your drawing? Or do you like to get a nice clean, white sheet of paper? Which do you prefer? 'Oh I want a clean, white sheet of paper.' Okay, well right now I can't hear; I'm trying to make up some. I need to have the auditory equivalent of a clean, white sheet of paper."

The origin of songs, he revealed, "is usually very different than anything you would probably imagine. They come from all kinds of places, not necessarily my songs. They're just songs…You're not really sure what you're doing when you start and you figure it out on the way. You find some kind of a motif… I like it when you still try to discover what it is. That's the exciting place for a song for me, when it's completely undeveloped and raw and could go in five different directions. What's he building in there?"

Waits shared in a discussion with Performing Songwriter that other songs "just kind of start with something amusing. Something amuses me and I let it pass through my mind, along with a lot of other things. Hundreds of melodies and ideas go through your head when you're not writing. You just let them wash over you. When we start writing, we put up a little dam and start catching them. It's the old butterfly net theory," adding in the same conversation of his vetting process for these ideas that sometimes as you make up songs…you just get up in the morning and start singing something on the way to work. You don't know why, and maybe it's worth remembering, or maybe it's not."

As he sifted for nuggets of gold throughout his musical mining process, the singer-songwriter added to KCRW FM that "what I like about the songs when you're writing them is you don't even know them yet and they're really ill-formed and they haven't really been turned into anything yet and they can go anyway. I seem to want to keep them that way as long as possible 'cause nobody knows them but you. So they're like your own personal songs." Once he'd given them away to the world, there was no doubt Waits' latest offerings would be listened to, and in the process studied, by curious ears for generations to come.

While Waits had clocked up 30 years as a songwriter, he readily admitted to disc jockey Bret Saunders that "you write a lot of songs that just kind of pass through you and… I don't know where they come from, they kinda come from all kinds of places. You build 'em out of things you see and remember and find and felt before and feeling now… I don't know who you're writing for. Sometimes you just write 'em for music.

"You have songs that you remember and loved and you just kinda parted the whole thing. You leave in the little things for folks to discover later and you know they're kinda like containers. Songs are really just containers that you put things in. Some songs you sing them once and you'll never sing them again. Other songs you sing for years and still try to figure out what it is, what it means. Another time, you may hear a song that you haven't heard in 20 years and it may break your heart because you've changed."

Waits told the Star Tribune of the struggle he faced at times trying to find a happy musical medium between melody and dissonance, "the kind of polar opposites I carry in me," adding that it felt like the equivalent of "two dogs fighting all the time. I think I have two audiences out there: people who want to hear me go out there and just scream and stomp and talk about liquor. And people who want me to get very tender and sentimental and sensitive and vulnerable. It's all part of it."

As he wrote the record, Waits explained to journalist Rip Rense that the blues was "where I keep coming back to. As an art form, it has endless possibilities, as an ingredient or a whole meal. Definitely part of the original idea was to do something somewhere between surreal and rural. We call it sur-rural. That's what these songs are – sur-rural. There's an element of something old about them, and yet it's kind of disorienting, because it's not an old record by an old guy."

Waits drew on that style lyrically as he worked through ideas for the record, explaining to Time Out New York that, as stories, "songs have to be anatomically correct. They need to have weather in them and the name of a town and usually something to eat – in case you get hungry." He collected details of any given song's lyrical landscape with a view to "stitching them all together. You know, lines come to you all the time. People say them every day. But they're always in the context of something else. So we all say things that are fascinating without knowing it. It's like looking for interesting shapes of stones…like picking stuff up off the ground."

When it came time to name the characters he and wife Kathleen had constructed for 'Mule Variations', Waits used "real people. They all come from history, or my history. Or letters received, or things read, or half-remembered." He added in an interview with Sonicnet that "these are people who inhabit the geography of the imagination and American history and the Salvation Army. And the stalactites of my mind. They inhabit letters and books. Some are actually blood relatives. Some are old neighbours. Some are people whom I've never met."

Newsweek would note that the "cast of characters" that populated 'Mule Variations' included "the dreamers and wanderers and no-gooders from albums like 'The Heart Of Saturday Night' in 1974 and 'Rain Dogs' in 1985" while adding that, along with their composer, this cast seemed "to have a new sense of purpose. They're searching for stuff, be it an answer, a home or just a creed they can live by."

Delving into some of the specific characters that – as always – were for the most part inspired by Waits' real-life observations, he began with 'Georgia Lee', sharing with music writer Rip Rense that the song was inspired by a real-life murder Waits' read about locally in the paper, wherein "the girl's name was Georgia Lee Moses. It's been over a year. They had a funeral for her. A lot of people came and spoke. I guess everybody was wondering, where were the police, where was the deacon, where were the social workers, and where was I and where were you?

"Now that she's gone, one thing that's come out of it is that her neighbour has opened her home as a place where teenaged girls can come, where latchkey kids can come and hang out after school till their parents get home. A lot of kids are raising their parents. You usually run away because you want someone to come and get you, but the water is full of sharks."

Turning to the inspiration for Big Jack Earl in the song 'Get Behind The Mule', Waits recalled to journalist Jonathan Valania that he was the "tallest man in the world. Was with Barnum & Bailey. If you see old archival photographs, they used to put him next to some guy that was like a foot tall. Big hat, tall boots. That's why Big Jack Earl was eight-foot-one and stood in the road and he cried.' Imagine a guy eight-foot-one standing in the middle of the road crying. It breaks your heart."

In the same song Birdie Joe Hoaks, he shared with the same journalist, was "this gal, 12 years old, who had swindled Greyhound. She ran away from home and told Greyhound this whole story about her parents and meeting them in San Francisco. She had this whole Holden Caulfield thing, and she got an unlimited ticket and criss-crossed the US. And she got nabbed. They took her bus pass, for starters. I don't think she did hard time.

"Me and my wife read the paper and we clip hundreds of articles, and then we read the paper that way without all the other stuff. It's our own paper. There is a lot of filler in the paper and the rest is advertising. If you just condense it down to the essential stories, like the story about the one-eyed fish they found in Lake Michigan with three tails, you can renew your whole relationship with the paper."

Waits explained to the Austin Chronicle that Evelyn's Kitchen mentioned in the song 'Pony' was a tribute to "my Aunt Evelyn, who passed away during the making of the record. Her and my uncle had 10 kids and lived in a place called Gridley. I guess I've been far away from home, and have thought about her kitchen a lot and that a lot of people feel the same way when they've been far away from home. I dreamed about getting back home to her kitchen. That's why we put her in there – a tribute to Evelyn. The other people are just different people I've come across over the years – known, heard about, read about."

'Get Behind The Mule' was the track that inspired the album's title. Waits told Performing Songwriter that "that's what Robert Johnson's father said about Robert, because he ran away. He said, 'Trouble with Robert is he wouldn't get behind the mule in the morning and plow,' because that was the life that was there for him. To be a sharecropper. But he ran off to Maxwell Street, and all over Texas. He wasn't going to stick around. Get behind the mule…can be whatever you want it to mean."

'Lowside Of The Road' was inspired by a factual incident involving another blues pioneer, Leadbelly. Waits explained he "involved in a skirmish after a dance one night on a dirt road, late. Someone pulled out a knife, someone got stabbed and he went to jail for it. He was rolling over to the low side of the road. I seem to identify with that. I think we all know where the low side of the road is."

Turning to 'Cold Water', the singer-songwriter told Jonathan Valania that "I have slept in a graveyard and I have rode the rails. When I was a kid, I used to hitchhike all the time from California to Arizona with a buddy named Sam Jones. We would just see how far we could go in three days, on a weekend, see if we could get back by Monday. I remember one night in a fog, we got lost on this side road and didn't know where we were exactly. And the fog came in and we were really lost then and it was very cold. We dug a big ditch in a dry riverbed and we both laid in there and pulled all this dirt and leaves over us like a blanket. We're shivering in this ditch all night, and we woke up in the morning and the fog had cleared and right across from us was a diner; we couldn't see it through the fog. We went in and had a great breakfast, still my high-water mark for a great breakfast. The phantom diner."

'Filipino Box Spring Hog' had its origin in real life. "When we lived on Union Avenue in LA, we had parties. We sawed the floorboards out of the living room and we took the bed, the box spring, and first dug out the hole and filled it with wood, poured gasoline on it and lit a fire. And the box spring over the top, that was the grill. We brought in a pig and cooked it right there."

'Take It With Me' was inspired by "the old expression 'you can't take it with you'… we wanted to turn it on its ear. We figure there's lots of things to take with you when you go. We checked into a hotel room and moved a piano in there and wrote it. We both like Elmer Bernstein a lot. My favourite line is Kathleen's. She said 'all that you've loved is all that you own.' It's like an old Tin Pan Alley song."

In a wide-ranging conversation with the Austin Chronicle, Waits explained that, with 'Pony', "we wanted to have it bare and by itself, like those Lomax recordings, those Library of Congress recordings that I love so much. You try to find the right sound for the record. The whole challenge of recording is to find the appropriate environment and atmosphere for the song. What suits it. And that's kind of what you spend most of your time doing. Where should we record this? How should we record this? It worked – on that one it worked."

In the same interview, he credited wife Kathleen with 'Black Market Baby', recalling that by the time it was presented to him for input, "she had it almost all finished. She says, 'She's my black market baby, she's my black market baby, she's a diamond that wants to stay coal.' I thought she said cold. That was almost finished the minute that she said that. Just kind of filled it in."

Waits summarised 'Picture In A Frame' as a "simple song. Sometimes I listen to Blind Lemon Jefferson or Leadbelly, and you'll just hear a line or a passing phrase. The way they phrase something sounds like the beginning of another whole thing, and they just use it as a passing thought, kind of a transitory moment in the song. But it sounds to me like it could have opened up into another whole thing. I heard that title, 'Picture In A Frame', in another song. I don't even remember what the song was now. And I thought, that's a good title for a song. So I made it about Kathleen and me."

'Take It With Me' was another sentimental number from the album inspired by Waits' love for his partner. He candidly volunteered to Newsweek that it was, for him, "a very vulnerable song. We wrote that together, Kathleen and I, and that felt good. Two people who are in love writing a song about being in love.'"

Waits' latest ballad was particularly touching for its reflection of the distance they'd travelled together in reinventing his life both professionally and personally over the past 20 years in a way that had given Tom, by his own admission, the career he'd enjoyed.

On the less touching subject-matter of 'Jesus' Blood', the singer shared with radio station KBCO-C that this song was discovered "through a documentary on songs that people remembered from their childhood. And they interviewed a lot of homeless people in England. And they went under to the bridges and out to the beach and downtown and found people and asked them what are the songs they carry with them, what are the songs that mean something to them. And there's a lot of people (who) have lost everything and maybe all they've got is these memories and these songs and this was one that they found. So (British classical composer) Gavin Bryars orchestrated it; it was called 'Jesus' Blood Never Failed Me Yet' and he made a record with that title."

As he and wife Kathleen finished writing for 'Mule Variations', Waits reflected in a conversation with the Austin Chronicle that "all the songs develop in a different way. Some of them happen and they're finished in five minutes. Others you work on over and over again and change them and develop them and let them evolve. Every song is different. I usually sit down and write a collection of songs. It's like fishing, you know. You just go out there and wait sometimes. That's what David Lynch said. He said, 'You've got to have a very comfortable chair and you have to be very quiet if you want to catch the big ones.'"

Ultimately, Waits told music journalist Gil Kaufman, the pair "wrote 25 (songs and)…16 of them made the record and the others go in the orphanage. You line up these guys and you tell them, 'Okay, now go out and bring dad home some money.' There's a relationship between the songs because they're written around the same period of time."

Waits worked as closely with his wife on the recording of the album as he had its writing, telling Audio Media magazine that she had been his biggest champion since his decision a decade earlier to produce himself. Before that, "I'd never worked without a producer, so it was exciting. I always thought that the producer knew more than the artist did, but Kathleen encouraged me to trust myself and explore many musical styles."

By the time of 'Mule Variations', Waits had learned that his role "when you're producing a record and you're also recording it yourself" was to focus on the latter task above all others, reasoning that "a lot of people divide those jobs. You have to decide what your role is going to be. You farm out or subcontract the rest of the job. I don't always do my own electrical work at home, I usually hire an expert. So we hired professional musicians – and I don't know if I can honestly consider my part of that group. I am like the creator of forms and I sometimes get my own way."

Waits felt that, to keep his musicians inspired throughout, "the main thing is to have people working with you that will succumb to the power of suggestion. The whole thing is kind of a hypnotic experience, and when you say you want musicians to play like their hair is on fire, you want someone who understands what that means. Sometimes that requires a very particular person that you have a shorthand with over time."

He returned once again to the familiar surroundings of Prairie Sun Studios, which Addicted To Noise described thus: "Looking around the main recording room, you begin to feel what it is about this place that appeals to Waits – besides the outdoor plumbing, of course. The main space is referred to by Prairie Sun staffers as 'The Waiting Room.' It's a square, barren concrete bunker, perfect for dragging the odd piece of metal across the floor to create just the right kind of clatter. An adjacent room is an explosion of brilliant colour. Filled with various instruments and amps, the room's ceiling and walls are hung with random rectangles of spray-painted cardboard featuring vaguely agrarian themes. In the entrance hallway there's a dusty soda machine and the skeleton of an early-Eighties video game."

The magazine further observed that "nearby is a room that contains a lonely vintage keyboard strewn with empty lyric sheets. There's also the gnarled bit of driveway just outside the door that was so inviting. At various times, Waits has asked his band members to drag their instruments outside and try tracking a few things. This is a man who is comfortable with relocation as one would expect, given the fact that his career has taken Waits to some unexpected places." Engineer Mark Rennick told journalist Charles McDermid that the studio was as happy to have the artist as he was to be there, sharing that "what we like about Tom is that he is a musicologist And he has a tremendous ear. His talent is a national treasure."

As he had with 'Bone Machine', Waits bypassed the state-of-the-art Studios A and B and headed straight downstairs to what studio staff a decade earlier had unofficially dubbed the 'Waits Room' prior to updating its moniker to 'The Waiting Room' in 1999. He shared with journalist Jonathan Valania that his innate approach to experimental record producing "makes it more like an expedition". The singer-songwriter added to the Austin Chronicle that "sometimes you just reach for something when you're working on a song. That's why I like to have maps up on the wall when we're recording, because it always feels like we're off on an adventure. And I like to refer to the maps."

Long-serving engineer Jacquire King explained to Audio Media magazine that Waits' studio consisted of "a small room of 12ft by 15ft and a 15ft-high ceiling. There is no acoustic treatment, just a concrete floor, and big double doors that open right into the driveway by which you enter the ranch. Almost all of Tom's parts, including the vocals, were recorded in that room. 90 per cent of the recording took place in the barn, which is about 50 yards from the control room, so we needed to have a good communication set-up. We had about 20 Neve 1073/1272-style outboard mic pre-amps in the barn, so that the mic signals bridged the 50 yards and came into the desk at line level."

Waits' affection for the studio was split between its basement room and its surroundings, which Waits reminded Performing Songwriter consisted of "a chicken ranch out in the sticks. What's nice about it? In between takes, you can pee outside. That, for me, is the reason I keep going back. I'd say that's probably one of the more attractive qualities. In fact, they ought to put it in their brochure. That's what keeps me comin' back, that and Clive Butters, who is the ranch foreman. Who is also now a member of the Boners."

LA Weekly would conclude that "what makes Tom Waits most valuable and continually attractive to succeeding generations of listeners…is – apart from his heart and his humour – his restlessness, his perfect willingness to destroy the lab for the sake of the experiment." Celebrating the aforementioned creative sentiment, Tom reasoned with USA Today that, for him as both an artist and producer, "recording is a mad adventure and the studio is a laboratory. Like anything creative, the unpredictable stuff is what's interesting. I'm getting more eccentric in my recording."

Waits viewed the latter perspective as "just the natural course of recording," adding in conversation with the Austin Chronicle that – within the context of the way he worked – "inevitably, someone will look around the room and find something that, when they hit it, sounds better than their cymbal or better than their bass drum. You might use the Dumpster in the alley – get a bigger sound than your bass drum. So you go ahead and do it. You put a mic in it and you use it. That's just kind of part of the whole evolution and forward development and movement of recording itself. You know, from being curious and inquisitive and blasphemous or investigative. That's just part of recording."

Delving further into the deep sea of experimentation that guided his explorative recording process, the singer-songwriter revealed to Exclaim that while "the surface of a song is important to me…you can't get away from the fact that you still have to write a song. You can't just rely on the texture or the technique you use to record it. I do like to experiment with all that. What's interesting about working with great engineers is that if you stop by the side of the road and drag something out of the ditch, throw it in the truck and bring it down to the studio, these guys will circle it like it's a moon rock. They'll mic it, hit it with a hammer and find out the most expeditious way to approach it. Move it around to different parts of the room."

He wanted 'Mule Variations' – as he had with every record since 'Swordfishtrombones' – to work with sound engineers who by nature were "more like scientists. They get very subjective about the whole issue of sound. But you don't really know when you're going in what you're looking for. Sometimes you find it while you're there."

Waits sought to take advantage of every creative aesthetic available to him including the farmland itself, quipping to USA Today that, to his eye and more importantly ear, "one man's garbage is another man's clothes. I just like to open up the variables. Most people isolate the music. I am slowly trying to integrate it."

He explained to Performing Songwriter that they went outside for one song and set up in the driveway. "You use directional microphones. They look like rifles, and they use them for field recordings. The engineer found them at a flea market. So if you set up right outside with the dogs and chickens, airplanes and trucks, it's amazing how your surroundings will collaborate with you, and will be woven into the songs. So I find that a lot of times, where you're trying so hard to keep those sounds out in a studio, that it's surprising when you actually allow them in how they become part of the tune."

Waits shared with Blues Revue that he heard his music come to life, before he ever laid anything to tape. "Recording mostly happens inside your head. When you get to that point it doesn't really much matter where you are because the song really is the landscape. It has a lot to do with what you've been listening to and what you've been absorbing."

Soaking in the natural environment around him while he crafted the album's outer-atmospheric soundscape, Tom reasoned to journalist Chris Douridas that "after a while I guess you get more natural about it like the way people work with a camera knowing there's a machine there that's capturing everything but there is something I think that's kind of like a pasteurisation process that takes place when you record that takes out a lot of the nutrients in the music sometimes if you don't approach it right. You kind of have to sneak up on it or it has to sneak up on the music."

Waits' principal engineer Jacquire King offered fans a further behind-the-scenes look at Waits' sonic preferences in conversation with journalist Paul Tingen. "I think Tom definitely feels that analogue has a better overall sound, although I don't think he looks down on digital. For this album he wanted to experiment with playing loops, and the possibility of changing the arrangements on the songs. I suspect he'd been hearing from friends and associates how powerful Pro Tools was and wanted to check it out. But the overall sound of the album is analogue.

Pro Tools is just a component."

The engineer revealed that Waits utilised the then still relatively new digital recording platform for "some loops, such as Tom's metal dressing bashing on 'Big In Japan', the Optigon keyboard sound on 'Lowside Of The Road' and the vinyl needle sound on 'Black Market Baby'. On 'Filipino Box Spring Hog' I actually changed the arrangement of some of the overdubs, although the drum and vocal performance are true to the take. In the latter track there were also some small voices that Tom had recorded into a small toy sampler for kids, and that I sampled in Pro Tools, just like the turntable elements. All this was manipulated in Pro Tools and then laid back to tape."

Waits explained to Performing Songwriter that – regardless of the medium – "we go through the usual sturm und drang about it in the studio. Is this done? Or is it dead? Certain songs we'd record five different ways, and then not even use them on the record. They didn't make the cut. We ended up having to take nine songs off the record. We had 25 songs. We had enough for two records – I think, a little too much material to digest. I don't know what will happen with those songs. Probably come out in some form or another."

The LA Times homed in on the new album's "harsh, experimental touches," the Toronto Star adding their observation that "these references to ironwork and internal combustion reflect both standard Waits imagery – his fascination with cars and mechanics is well chronicled in song – and the nature of the music he has been making in the past few years, music that sounds as if it were composed on and for found instruments. Scrap metal, rusty bedsprings, crashing bricks, cardboard boxes, hubcaps …you name it."

The same review concluded that the sum of all these elements produced "a very clever construction, musically valid since all the extra-musical bits and pieces – those other than piano, guitar, banjo and the occasional sardonic sax or trumpet – are chosen for their pitch and harmonic qualities. What's more interesting is that their hard tones and industrial textures, enhanced by turntable-scratched loops and synthesised, computer-generated samples, create a soundscape that embraces both astonishing bleakness and stark beauty, a sort of post-apocalyptic wasteland rendered in sound by a primitive savant wielding tools that have lost their proper application."

Waits shared with disc jockey Chris Douridas that his use of experimental, one-of-a-kind instruments was part of a broader local tradition. "Up where we live there's a lot of people that build their own instruments and that's Harry Partch country up there where we are. He lived in Petaluma for a long time and there seems to be a little enclave of his niche – artists up there that build, instrument builders and sculptors and all that.

"There's a very interesting guy who lives in Ohio, his name is Q Reed Ghazala and he made something called the Photon Clarinet that is a box with a light-sensitive patch on the top. The tone responds to the intensity of light so, if you aim a flashlight at it, it goes crazy and sounds like you just threw a lobster on a campfire. Then if you bring the lights down it goes kinda hoooooo augghh – down in here. He takes apart toys and puts them back together and they're never the same. There's a lot more conventional guys up there that do like stuff from a hardware store. It changes the way you see a hardware store when you start hearing these instruments. You go into a hardware store and you start thinking, God, I wonder what that bucket sounds like over there?"

Discussing the influence of the late inventor/composer Harry Partch, who died in 1974, Tom shared with the LA Times that "I'm drawn to anybody who kind of creates his own world. He once said, 'Once there was a boy who went outside. That was me. I went outside of music.' He seemed to be as affected and influenced by Chinese lullabies as he was by things he saw written on water tanks on the side of the railroad. He put disparate elements together."

Waits elaborated on his deeply rooted respect and admiration for Partch's influence to journalist Mikel Jollett. "He was a great forgotten American composer. Like everybody else, I'm captivated by his story. Like how I assume people became captivated with my story. He was a hobo and he found things on the road and turned them into instruments. He created his own instruments, created his own scales, his own music, his own paradigm really. In that sense, I don't rival him. He was very eccentric. He had these industrial water bottles that he called 'Cloud Chamber Bowls'. You hang them from the ceiling and hit them with a mallet... He did things that no-one had ever done and I like that."

Other 'outside' instrumental influences included a live rooster on 'Chocolate Jesus', with Tom quipping to the Austin Chronicle of its inclusion on the track that "hey, a rooster will never crow when you're crowing. They wait 'til there's some clean air. They wait 'til you're done and then they get the best spot. Which I've found about recording outside. Most people are afraid to record outside because they're going to have too many collisions with the natural world. But I've found if you do go outside, everything collaborates with you, including airplanes. And movies – they make movies outside. You have to wait, sometimes, for a train to pass or a school to let out or whatever. Dogs, kids, trains, cars, planes, and chickens will kind of find their own place if you do go outside."

"You texture and layer them," Waits elaborated to Performing Songwriter. "You do it by taking things away and adding things until you have just the right feeling for where you're going. It's like a room in your ears," adding to the LA Times that "I am attracted to things that fall outside of the practical domain of music, I like hearing the orchestra tune up. That for me is the show."

Turning attention to Waits' more straightforward operations in the studio, engineer Jacquire King recalled to Audio Media magazine a routine wherein "we were usually tracking him with at least one other person, most of the time an upright bass player, sometimes a drummer. His vocal performance and his piano or guitar, plus the bass, are the basic take. What you hear on the album are often first takes. Tom rarely did more than two or three takes in a row. If he felt it wasn't coming together, he'd switch to piano or guitar and try a different approach, or to another song. We were always trying to capture a mood and atmosphere.

"If there was a mistake, or a lyric that was rewritten, we would punch it in on the basic take. We never did vocal comps. Tom came in with finished songs, and would then try different ways of executing it. He will try something, and maybe a week, or years, later he will try it again in a different way... It was a matter of sonically trying to realise what he was trying to do, and do it very quickly. I would say that Tom is very articulate in the studio, and he will instruct musicians in what to play, but he will also allow them to come up with things. It's a little bit of both."

In the course of fleshing out the album's songs, Waits added in conversation with the Austin Chronicle that "when I'm in the studio, songs really are, at their best, like little movies for the ears. I'm in charge and I'm producing them and casting them and directing them. It's much more interesting to be able to be responsible for the whole thing, instead of just your little bit."

The singer-songwriter explained in a discussion with Addicted to Noise that he often shaped arrangements over multiple takes. "You record one song and you may end up doing seven or eight versions of the same song. You've got the cha-cha version, spoken word, a little Cuban thing, you record it inside, you record it outside. I did want it to have somewhat of a field recording mood to it 'cause I love those Library of Congress tapes. I always loved the fact that they were grainy documents of raw music."

Guitarist Smokey Hormel recalled to Audio Media magazine that, with 'Chocolate Jesus', "Tom kept telling me, 'It sounds too pretty, I'm going to open the barn door.' And so he did! You could hear the dogs in the background and see the people walking by on the road below. It was very rustic and homey. You forget that you're playing into a $20,000 microphone."

In the same discussion, Waits explained of the spare instrumental 'Pony' that "we wanted that particular one bare and by itself, like Alan Lomax's Library of Congress recordings that I love so much. You try to find the right sound for the record. The whole challenge of recording is to find the appropriate environment and atmosphere for the song, to find what suits it. And that's what you spend most of your time doing. Where should we record this? How should we record this? On that one it worked."

Fan favourite 'Big In Japan' was written, Waits told journalist Rip Rense, "in Mexico in a hotel, and I only had this little tape recorder. I turned it on, and I started screaming and banging on this chest of drawers really hard, till it was kindling, trying to make a full sound like a band. And I saved that. That was years ago. I had it on a cassette, and used to listen to it and laugh. It sounded like some guy alone in a room, which it was, trying his hardest to sound like a big, loud band. So we stuck that in the front."

Waits offered the image to Performing Songwriter of seeing "myself in the harbour, ripping up the electrical towers, picking up cars, going in like Godzilla and levelling Tokyo. There are people that are big in Japan, and are big nowhere else. It's like going to Mars. It's also kind of a junkyard for entertainment. You can go over there and find people you haven't heard of in 20 years, that have moved over there, and they're like gods. And then there are all those people that don't do any commercials, they have this classy image. They're hawking cigarettes, underwear, sushi, whiskey, sunglasses, used cars, beach blankets."

Waits, as usual, enlisted an A-list band of players, to create what NME later concluded was his very own unique brand of "quite batty, often fabulously so.... mutating jazz, blues, parade music, show tunes, fairground banter, immigrant songs and beatnik spiel" to life. "Music, by nature, is a collaborative endeavor – it's social. My wife (Kathleen Brennan) and I wrote the songs together, arranged them and produced them in the studio with great musicians like Charlie Musselwhite, Marc Ribot, John Hammond, Larry Taylor, Greg Cohen, Andrew Borger, Smokey Hormel and Christopher Marvin – Lee Marvin's real son – plays drums."

The album also featured Chris Grady on trumpet and Ralph Carney and Nik Phelps on reeds. While some of these players were new or borrowed additions (as in the case of Beck's longtime guitarist Smokey Hormel), others – like bassist Greg Cohen had been with Waits for a long time. "Greg plays with all kinds of people now. He's excellent. We have a longstanding relationship and Greg plays percussion, he plays everything, he plays alto horn and guitar. I like multi-instrumentalists. Marc (Ribot) plays trumpet too. And he's got all these bizarre things he does to his guitar to give it that dental sound that I like so much."

Ribot told Mojo magazine on that "the skill of being a musician in 1999, when anybody can buy a sequencer and play more accurately and faster than any musician possibly could, primarily has to do with being able to intuit what the songwriter wants. The songs are in all different shapes when he brings them in the studio. Often, he hasn't completed the lyrics. I've seen him working on finishing lyrics before he's doing the final vocal. But the studio is an instrument in itself, and to be really good at using that instrument – like Waits – you must be willing to throw aside preconceptions in favour of what actually goes to tape well. Waits' records are very studio-oriented without being technologically oriented. There's a lot of awareness of recording history, what sounds were used 20, 30, 40 years ago, which is part of his dramatic idea."

Waits explained harp-player Charlie Musselwhite's presence on the album to journalist Bret Kofford. "He brings about 300 harmonicas, microphones. And he's up for anything. Some stuff adapt to that cross harp, but the songs that we tried it on did. On 'Chocolate Jesus', just before the song starts you can hear him talking into the mic. He says, 'I love it.' That's my favourite part of the song."

Waits explained to journalist Barney Hoskins that "I hadn't thought of using harmonica before. Somehow it suited the material, being more rural...Charlie has a tone like Ben Webster and he developed that over a long period of time. He can play just one note and break your heart."

Turning to guitarist Smokey Harmel's recruitment, the singer-songwriter told Hoskyns that the recommendation came courtesy of bassist Larry Taylor. "So Smokey came up to the studio and brought in these West African instruments that he played on 'Lowside Of The Road.' They're these strange instruments made out of branches and gourds."

Quipping to the Dallas Observer that the more uptempo numbers on the album were "a beat quicker than the heart", engineer Jacquire King detailed Waits' drum-micing set-up in the studio to Audio Media magazine, beginning with "a D112 on the kick drum, 421 on the toms, SM57 on the snare and on some songs AKG TL2s as overheads. Room mics for the drums were a pair of 87s and a pair of Neumann 582s, and often we'd open the doors from the live area into the echo chamber and put a SM69 there. We also used the 582s as room mics in the medium sized room."

King explained that "the upright piano was recorded with a 414 or a 451, and often put through the Sony reel to reel mic pre-amp." Waits added in a conversation with music writer Rip Rense that "piano have to be in the right room. Most studios are designed to keep the outside world out, and they rely heavily on baffling and carpeting and all kinds of architectural devices on the wall to shape sound waves and whatnot. I don't go in for it, myself. We've got a concrete room with a wood ceiling, and we got a great sound. We just brought the piano from home and moved it in. I gave it to Kathleen a long time ago for a birthday present. It's a Fischer from New York. We use it to catch the big ones."

Waits recruited white bluesman John Hammond to play on the album, and detailed their shared history in a conversation with music writer Bret Kofford. "I used to open up for him, when I first started playing clubs. Don't let him open the show for you, because everybody will leave after he gets done. He's so good. He sounds like a big train coming. one guy. He gets those chops down so strong... John is an exceptional in and I admire him. He asked me to produce the record and I said to myself, 'Jesus, how could I say no?' Except I don't know what that means, to produce a record. 'You mean stand around and drink coffee while you play?'"

As the team tracked the record's bass and guitars, engineer Jacquire King recalled that "acoustic guitars were miced with a KM84 or 451, guitar amps were either SM57 or 421, bass amp with a 47, and acoustic bass with an M49, 47 or 552, routed via a Neve 2254 compressor." Unsurprisingly, the band employed some out-of-the-box recording techniques that included Waits instructing guitarist Smokey Hormel to "open the barn door" because the guitar part he was playing on one song sounded "too pretty", adding to Newsweek that once he did, "you could hear the dogs in the background and see the people walking by on the road below. It was very rustic and homey. You forget that you're playing into a $20,000 microphone!"

Attention turned to Waits' legendary vocals, which the LA Times noted had taken on "increasingly harsh touches, causing his singing to be described over the years as everything from a 'scabrous rasp' to a bark." Waits seemed amused by the various critical depictions of his voice over the years, joking with the Austin Chronicle that "I'm the gravelly-voiced singer. Invariably, that's how I'm referred to. There have been lots of descriptions of it. Gargling with various cleaning products, that type of thing. They're trying to be funny. I'm okay with that."

Alternative Press, in their five out of five star review of the LP, noted that Waits' "marvellously expressive voice sounds richer than ever....but (Tom's) greatest strength is in his interpretive skills." To take maximum advantage of the latter mentioned skill, Waits shared with Telegraph magazine that "when I'm recording music I can be uninhibited and I can sing a song seven different ways. There are actors that can do that with a director: the first take is like some kind of rant; the next take is a prayer; the next take is like some old black man. They can go through all these different moves." Engineer Jacquire King shared with Audio Media magazine that "Tom's vocals were always recorded with an M49, through a Neve mic-pre and Teletronix LA2A tube limiter, although we often altered the sound of it afterwards."

Waits' first studio LP in over six years saw him throw everything into a recording process that, Newsweek concluded, produced "the kind of gnarled eclecticism that has become his hallmark" and Billboard noted "delivers what fans want, in terms of both songs and sonics." The singer-songwriter explained to journalist Edna Gunderson that, of everything he tried to incorporate during the album's recording, only bagpipes didn't work. "With all due respect, forget about it. It's hard for (bagpipe players) to play with anyone other than another bagpipe player. And even that is a challenge because they have their own scales. And they're so loud. I ended up telling them to play far, far away."

Once attention turned to mixing, Waits wanted to make sure "you're not recording the bone and throwing away the meat. It's very easily done." Jacquire King revealed that "mixing is done very quickly, some songs were mixed in an hour, others took a few hours. There were a couple of songs where the mixes were too complex to do them in one pass, and so we recorded them in segments to the half-inch."

King added in the same conversation that "we applied EQ, compression, natural reverbs, some analogue slap-back delays, guitar pedals like Zoom or Sansamp or the Smokey, usually running things live. Tom was always present, helping out with the mixes, usually adjusting levels. He would never adjust EQ or effects or ask for a specific effect, but always had requests in terms of mood, tonal quality or distortion on his voice."

The engineer added that "He often wanted things to sound more old-timey, like a phonograph, so we sometimes filtered off low and high end. I also used a Neve 33609 bus compression over the stereo mix. But we were always going for a mood, and never concerned with cleaning things up. We happily left all the creaking of the piano stool and pedals, for example, like at the beginning of 'Picture In A Frame'. What you are listening to is not all overdubbed and clinical, but a real performance that happened in a very small and intimate environment. We wanted it to sound like that and therefore kept all the mics and channels wide open."

Waits told the Austin Chronicle that, in settling on the 16 songs that made 'Mule Variations' final cut, "We took it song by song. It started out with a group, and then we kind of strip things away and add things, and it's more elimination. We started out with a certain group, but it did change." Waits elaborated to New York Rocker that "sometimes I didn't even use the songs I wrote. Sometimes we recorded as much as four or five different versions of one song before I decided that I wouldn't use it."

As Waits prepared to release the album, he had chosen to begin the millennium on a new label. His decision to leave Island was because – first and perhaps most importantly – "it started changing a lot…(after former owner Chris) Blackwell's (departure)," adding in the same conversation with journalist Jonathan Valania that "for me, it's about relationships. And when Blackwell pulled out and started his own company, I lost interest."

He took his time in choosing a new label, eventually settling on Epitaph who, Waits quipped "needed a parental figure over there." He explained to the Austin Chronicle that "my contract ran out with Island, and I was in between trains... (and) they put together a very impressive proposal. I was between labels. They're young and hungry and do an excellent job. We just did one record with them. Probably do more. You know, it's owned and operated by musicians. It's just a real good place for us right now. They like unusual challenges. A lot of the larger labels, you find yourself falling between the cracks sometimes, if what you're doing doesn't have a wide, broad appeal. They're kind of eccentric like me. That's what I like about it."

Elaborating on the freedom the label's truly independent spirit afforded him, Waits – in a conversation with journalist Michael Barclay – explained that "I could do anything over there and they would celebrate it and get behind it. Those kind of situations are rare. I could do can-cans and torch songs and Indian ragas and Cuban stuff and midget wrestling, and they'd say, 'Great!' I'd say, 'And I only want to play one gig, in Buenos Aires in a place that holds four people.' They'd say, 'We love it! When do you want to start?' Kathleen and I felt more at home there. Plus, they're musicians. They're forward-thinking; they're not part of the plantation system. They respect artists, and they pay them. I really think they are the way things should be."

Waits also confessed to being motivated by the younger members of his family, recalling to Mojo that "my kids listen to some of the (Epitaph) bands. See, I'm at the age now where if you wanna find out what's happening, you ask your kids: 'Check this out, Dad.'" According to Newsweek, his new label "signed Waits partly out of a belief that his ethos resonates with its roster of skate punks and headbangers."

Waits had been discovered in the Nineties by a whole new generation of teenagers digging back through their parents' record crates. Without a doubt he was among the most original and provocative artists of his generation, leading him to connect with a new generation of fans. And those fans appreciated him that much more because of how rarely he released new music.

Tom recalled that what impressed him most about Epitaph was that a musician – Brett Gurewitz, formerly guitarist and songwriter with Bad Religion – had started the label. He added in the same conversation with Mojo that "most record guys came from the garment industry, so this makes it a little easier to communicate. I don't mind them coming in the studio. The boss, Brett Gurewitz, is great. First thing you see when you walk in the Epitaph office is an enormous engine from some muscle car. They have good taste in cars, good taste in barbecue and good taste in music. Wayne Kramer told me everything on Epitaph was 160 beats a minute, so he was glad to have some company... I signed with Epitaph on the basis of mutual enthusiasm."

The singer-songwriter added to Blues Revue that he saw eye to eye with Gurewitz because "Brett's an innovator and a visionary and an iconoclast He's very fair in all ways. He's not a gouger. They see themselves as more a service industry. You make music and they put it out. They're not part of the long tradition of the rape and pillage of artists, and the servitude. You get a lot of respect there." Ultimately, Waits felt his new home at Epitaph was "frankly...more like a partnership," in contrast to other meetings he took with prospective majors who, he recounted candidly to the LA Weekly, "start looking at you like they want to lift up a part of you and look underneath, you feel like they're smelling meat."

Waits paid his new label head the closing compliment in Rolling Stone of confirming that he would re-sign with the label, after the one-off deal covering the release of 'Mule Variations'. "Not to generalise about large record companies, but if you're not going platinum you're not going anywhere."

Released on 16 April 1999, 'Mule Variations' would help Waits' recording career explode into a new renaissance commercially as the decade turned. It debuted in the Top 40 of the Billboard album chart for the first time in years, delivering what the LA Times concluded was "a work that contains some of the most personal and affecting music he's written in a distinguished three-decade career." USA Today noted that "Waits' music has retro credentials, fierce individuality and a backwoods ease that deliver a perfect tonic for pre-millennial tension." Mojo magazine would pay the album the honour of ranking his album Number 1 on their 'Best of 1999' list, and made Rolling Stone's Top 500 Albums of All Time list in 2003.

Billboard seemed most impressed by what they proudly hailed as "a hell of a record", taking further note of the fact that "Waits is still writing terrific songs and matching them with wildly evocative productions." Rolling Stone, for its part, observed that 'Mule Variations' "continues 'Bone Machine's experiments in artfully scuffed sound (though, regretfully, doing away with the first-take immediacy of the earlier record), Waits has found DJs this time to help him build his sonic doghouses, with scratches, hisses and gabbling field recordings. And Waits, as producer, has made his lurching stomps sound like they were deep-fried before they reached the mastering plant."

Selling half a million copies worldwide, 'Mule Variations', from Entertainment Weekly's point of view, "restores the humanity – and a more traditional sense of song craft – to his music," complimenting the artist as "the last of the classic American tunesmiths." Tom would confess to the LA Times of his newest batch of ballad-heavy songs that "I guess they are a bit more vulnerable than before, I don't know. Maybe I feel more at peace with myself, more able to talk about these things without being afraid of what people are going to say. Maybe I was too vulnerable before."

Waits' post-Seventies career had seen him become more and more himself on record, no matter if it went against any popular trend. In the process, Tom had carved out his own niche that had grown in not just acceptance but also popularity.

Agreeing wholeheartedly, Melody Maker stated boldly and quite matter-of-factly that "nobody else makes music quite like this," while the Telegraph magazine commented of the album's blend of musical styles that "'Mule Variations' sounds like a reconciliation of all the various musical styles that Waits has explored over the years, as if the songs have been hammered together from the skin and bones of American myth: scratchy Delta blues, Sixties R&B, vaudeville rants and Salvation Army band hymns."

Rolling Stone homed in on the presence of blues on the album, concluding that "what Tom Waits does to the blues is something like what newspapers do to bright colours — in the way that a picture of the Sistine Chapel's ceiling ends up looking like roast beef in the morning edition, Waits' arty, seasick imagination turns a rural American song form into a garish, surreal fantasy." Hailed as "exquisitely paced" by the San Francisco Chronicle, CMJ magazine would champion the album as "one of his finest efforts yet." The album would be nominated for two coveted Grammy awards, one for Best Male Rock Performance and one for Best Contemporary Folk Album, which it won.

Commenting on his Grammy win to music journalist Bret Kofford, Waits said that while the acknowledgement was welcome, "it doesn't really drive me. Grammys are kind of like the Food and Drug Administration. People like to be USDA-approved, with the little sticker on it and everything. It's safer. It's kind of people formulating their tastes for what they like. They like the company of others. But it's a good thing."

What seemed of greater importance to Waits was that he was as happy with his critics with the fruits of his creative labour, offering to Addicted To Noise that "it's satisfying to make a record. Once you come out and have the songs go out there. Actually, there's a period when nobody's heard the songs and that's nice too. It's just a family record. Everybody knows the songs and nobody else has heard them. Then you send them out there. To finish something, it's cathartic."

"Music's what I love. I find myself doing it whether or not there's going to be any result or product at the end of it." – TOM WAITS, 2002

"They're both strange little operas in the sense the word 'opera' really means work, and believe me it was a lot of damn work."
– TOM WAITS, 2002

PART XIX: 'ALICE' (2002)

When Epitaph announced in 2002 that Tom Waits had "jumped right back into the studio and began working on not one but two new albums," they reflected an ambitious path undertaken by few artists. Indeed, some might have questioned if the label could support the commercial investment required up front to finance the release of two albums simultaneously. Thankfully Waits, having built and maintained his own sub-genre over the past 30 years, was a risk worth gambling on.

Guns N'Roses had successfully pulled it off a decade earlier with 'Use Your Illusion I & II', both of which sold millions of copies worldwide. But Bruce Springsteen's attempt to repeat that success with 'Human Touch' and 'Lucky Town' had failed miserably, earning some of the worst reviews and album sales of his life.

The results completed a trilogy of projects Waits had been collaborating on with filmmaker/playwright Robert Wilson. USA Today.com explained that the first LP, 'Alice', embodied "a shadowy and vivid rumination on insanity...(that) was based on a play about Victorian writer Lewis Carroll's obsession with the girl who inspired Alice In Wonderland. It opened in Hamburg in 1992 and ran for 18 months."

Elaborating on Carroll's obsession, GQ magazine added that 'Alice' was "based on a real-life story of a middle-aged Victorian minister who fell in love with an enchanting nine year-old girl. The little girl's name was Alice. The minister's name was Reverend Charles Dodgson, but he is more widely known by his pen name (Lewis Carroll) and for the surreal, not totally-made-for-children children's story (Alice's Adventures In Wonderland) he wrote as a valentine to the girl he adored."

Waits told journalist Dan Cohen that the album's songs "all sprout out of that root", adding in the same conversation that they were "all different ways of saying the same thing. I guess the deal was that when he was writing (Alice's Adventures In Wonderland and Through The Looking Glass), photography was reasonably new, and it was just the phenomenon of the chemical reaction to the images on the film. People were seeing photographs for the first time. I think they were mystifying, almost ghostly – to be able to capture emotions or moments between moments."

He offered a more in-depth analysis in a conversation with USA Today. "It's a hypothetical situation," he mused. "I'm imagining a whole Victorian atmosphere and someone like himself, who had this obsession and compulsion. He was mystified by this peculiar, sparkling little girl. I'm trying to explore the nature of obsession, not just in his frame of mind but also as it applies to any love affair."

Waits told the Austin Chronicle that the record itself almost never happened. "When we were doing the songs, all the tapes were in my briefcase. My car was broken into and someone stole the work tapes of the show. They realised they had something that might be worth some dough so they ransomed it and I paid $3,000 to get it back. Not a lot of money, was it? I was a little insulted… I think they wanted fast cash and no arguments. Along the line, the tapes got copied and the bootleg got out. At the time, I wasn't interested in recording anything at all. I was taking a break from the whole damn business, so it went south."

Almost a decade would pass between the kidnapping and Waits' dusting off the project and taking another look at it. "I stuck it all in a box and stopped recording for a while," he told USA Today. "When I did start again, I wanted some really fresh material, so I did 'Mule Variations'. Then I got back to 'Alice'. You don't want songs to go bad on you, and you don't want to waste them. A good butcher uses every part of the cow. So I either use them or cut them up for bait to catch other songs."

As usual, Waits' behind-the-scenes motivator was wife Kathleen, who "kept dripping on me…encouraging me to go ahead and record 'em. You know you need a little kick in the pants." Waits quipped in an interview with journalist James Nicholas Joyce that he finally agreed through "a combination of the Chinese water torture and the general enthusiasm and encouragement. And it finally happened."

Knowing he had gems in that treasure chest, Waits recalled that once he had dusted off the tapes and given them a listen, he found "all the same stuff, you know. It's like giving away a box of clothes and then you get them back, you know. 'Hey, those pants, I like those pants, that shirt. I always liked that shirt.' I never really recorded them, you know, we just did rough demos and then you give the songs to someone else to do. And they either do them in a delightful way or they particularly butcher them and you're not having much say one way or another about it. Except that we were involved in the production and you make suggestions. But essentially I can't do it for them. There's a place where the singer and song kind of become inseparable, so they became orphans for a while and then I got them back. And I was glad to get them back. I had forgotten I liked the tunes."

Waits was working on sister LP 'Blood Money' simultaneously, explaining to Australian Weekly that "they're completely different, unique collections of songs… 'Blood Money' is perhaps a little rougher. 'Alice' is more like taking a pill, I guess. They're completely different trips, but they both pretty much came out of the oven at the same time."

Like musical twins born minutes apart, Waits latest offerings had stylistic similarities, but Tom was trying to make it 'Alice' "music from another world, songs from a distant place inside." He added that, as he began the process of digging down into his endlessly creative well, he felt that if a song "really wants to be written down, it'll stick in my head. If it wasn't interesting enough for me to remember it, well, it can just move along."

Waits explained to music writer Patrick Donovan that his ideas "evolve, and they're kind of shaped like stones, or they migrate like seeds. I'm fascinated with that. Blues is a fascinating art form. They're like Jello moulds. They're containers, you know. I don't know how you classify them. But a craft is like anything else. You make a choice as to what you're going to include and exclude. My feeling is that all songs should have a little weather in them, and the names of towns, something to drink and eat, names of streets and some place to go."

Waits explained his innate melodic preferences to Entertainment Weekly. "I like beautiful melodies telling you terrible things… I don't know why. It's a curse. After a while it becomes a steady companion. It's not something you distinguish. Is it my thorny, dark, oozing side, or is it just the way I see the world?"

Wife/collaborator Kathleen Brennan was well suited to be his creative co-pilot because, he told journalist Gavin Martin, "she does everything blood, spit and polish… She's fabulous, ominous and hilarious. We used to play a game called Let's Go Get Lost. We'd drive into a town, and I would say, 'But, baby – I know this place like the back of my hand, I can't get lost. And she'd say, 'Oh hell you can't, turn here, now turn here. Now go back, now turn left, now go right again.' And we'd do that all night, until we got lost, and she'd say, 'See, I thought you knew this town?' Now you're getting somewhere, now you're lost. That's a good metaphor for how we collaborate."

In the same conversation, Tom explained that "we talk about what we're doing all the time. The way we work is like a quarrel that results in either blood or ink. You find you may not have known how you felt about a particular sound or issue or phrase or melody until you are challenged to expand or change it. If it's a successful collaboration, you end up with more things in there than occurred at the outside. But, hell, we got kids. Once you've raised kids together, you find songs come easy."

The pair had been together in every aspect of their life for so long that, by that point, there was nothing either one kept from each other in their creative collaboration. From Waits' perspective, this meant she was a brutally honest critic. "I can run things by and she'd say 'That's a lot of bullshit, you've been doing that for years. That's really corny. That's really cliché.' And it's good so we kinda sharpen each other like knives. And it seems to work out like that."

Tom quipped to the New York Times that "Most songwriters are probably writing one or two songs over and over again in one way or another. Kathleen said that with me, it's either Grand Weepers or Grim Reapers."

In addition to collaborating with Brennan, Waits also included input from avant-garde stage director and playwright Robert Wilson, which Waits confessed to the Sydney Morning Herald "was like being in a slave galley." Waits was quick to qualify that context by offering that it was because of Wilson's eccentric genius that the collaboration proved challenging at times. "He's a deep thinker, a man who chooses his words very carefully and is not to be trifled with. We found out we were very different, but there was something that that we both understood about each other which was a good thing. If you're too much alike, there's not much you can learn from each other."

Waits added his feeling that, creatively, Wilson operated something akin to "a scientist, medical student or an architect – he has that quality when you first meet him. He also probably has an attention deficit disorder, dyslexia and probably a little compulsive disorder syndrome, too. I must have recognised aspects of myself in him. He seems almost autistic as he's compelled to communicate, but has the limits of certain known forms of communication, and he's gone far beyond in developing others.

"In theatre, he's developed a whole language for himself and those he works with...right down to the way he has people move. He's compelled to create a world where everyone conforms to his laws of physics. He has everyone move real slow, because you can't grasp the full drama of a movement onstage that happens in real time, it won't register with you. It makes you think about the simplest movement, the act of getting out of a chair or reaching for a glass." Waits added to Time Out that the director expects the same work ethic from all his collaborators. "Wilson's a challenging guy, makes you dig really deep...and he's dyslexic and has an attention deficit disorder, just like me, so he's found a way to communicate that is very powerful... I think he thinks of words as like tacks on the bedroom floor in the middle of the night when you're trying to make it to the bathroom."

As the team worked through the writing and re-writing of the album's songs, the BBC would note that ultimately "Wilson, Brennan and Waits have conjured a vivid impressionistic portrait of dark obsession and childhood innocence." Waits told NPR radio that the title track "is like a private moment. It's like sitting in a chair, by yourself, thinking about someone."

'Poor Edward', Tom explained to journalist Claire Barker, "is about Edward Mordake, one of those early last century characters. It's a true story about a man who had a woman's face on the back of his head. It's kind of a sad story, it eventually drove him to madness and suicide, so it has an operatic feeling to it. I tried to get into the mind of that man, but at the same time it's a metaphor for any kind of obsession or compulsion that might be impossible to control."

'No One Knows I'm Gone' was a song the singer-songwriter admitted to USA Today that "I made up. I really don't know what that means. I pictured her going down the rabbit hole, and I like to imagine what it's like down there. I'm sure it's different for everybody that's dead." 'I'm Still Here' was based on a biographical recollection. "The story is...I guess it was Oxford University had a celebration. And they wanted Alice, the Alice of Alice In Wonderland...to come and speak in front of the class. 'Cause by then she was in her eighties. So she came all the way from, wherever she came from, and it was a long journey, and she got up on stage and she walked up to the microphone, banged on the microphone and said a few words to the class. And this was kind of a hypothetical song that we created to cover a situation like that. It's just kind of an odd situation to imagine a story with a little girl who is like nine years old, and then to see her as a grown woman walking out."

Turning to 'Table Top Joe', Waits shared with Richard Kingsmill that, "the Eck brothers were twins. One was normal size anatomy and the other, Johnny, his body stopped at his waist. He was called 'The Man Born Without A Body.' But he played the piano and had his own orchestra. He was a big hit in Coney Island. Anyway, they had an act together on stage were he would saw his brother in half. And, of course at the end of the procedure Johnny would come out of the box and walk off stage on his hands to the thrill and astonishment of the viewers. Anyway it's just like a tip of the hat. I nicknamed him 'Table Top Joe' cause he used to be on a pedestal."

In the end, as with any of the hundreds of songs in his catalogue, Waits treated his latest batch of material as "these vessels containers of emotional information," reasoning in the same conversation with Inpress magazine that for his listeners, the record was "like getting a letter from me, maybe. It's understandable. Just like we were saying before, when you join your experience with the elements that are there inside the song in this kind of potion. That's why people say, hey, that's my song, man. Or you say with your girlfriend, that's our song. Because it IS your song. you know. Until these songs come out, they are only our songs, no-one's ever heard them. It's kind of like your kids' drawings on the refrigerator, because they're ours."

Opting to record both 'Alice' and its sister LP 'Blood Money' simultaneously offered Waits certain advantages, chiefly because "its a lot of work to go into a studio." He told the Chicago Tribune that to "mobilise a lot of people and equipment... I figured once we got in there, let's do another one while the motor is running. Eventually, no one will care what day they came out on. If it's a good idea, I'll take credit for it. If it isn't, I'll blame it on somebody else."

There were also added challenges in his chosen approach, as he explained to music journalist James Nicholas Joyce. "The trouble when you do two records at the same time is giving them their own distinct profile and colours and textures. And so that's a challenge. And the reason that no-one does two records at the same time and puts them out on the same day is that it's too much damn work. You know, you got two sets of musicians, you got two covers you got two mastering dates."

Waits told disc jockey Richard Kingsmill that getting a keeper song down on tape was never a sure thing. "We're assuming that the technology is such that we can capture anything that we want on tape and I don't necessarily think that it's true. I think there's something about a machine, repeating it over and over again. I don't know, it's like, it's more like hunting you know? You have to go out there with a scope and three days worth of food. You have to be really quiet if you wanna catch the big ones you know? It's not as easy as you'd think. Even though everyone goes to the studio with the same equipment basically. Like most tape machines, instruments and... But it's a pretty interesting laboratory. A lot of things are discovered while you are there. The best things are discovered while you are there."

As Waits worked in the studio, he offered from a producer's perspective that he felt "songs are domesticated, complacent little creatures who will never get out in the wild again," adding in the same comments to USA Today that "I like my songs raw, with the pulp and seeds. Those are nutrients." Talking to journalist Robert Lloyd, he expressed his feeling that "the trick to recording them is to capture something and have it be taken alive. So there's always a trick in the studio."

Waits, as always, employed his signature out-of-the-box approach to creating sonic experimentations rooted in his love for "bringing things in that I've never recorded before." Tom told The Onion that "we tried to find a Theremin for 'Alice', but we were unable to find anyone locally that was really accomplished... We found the granddaughter of Leon Theremin. She was really amazing. You would imagine someone like that would have some really sophisticated instrument, but she brought this thing that looked like a hotplate with a car aerial coming out of it.

"She opened it up, and inside, all the connections between the circuits were established with cut-up little pieces of beer can wrapped around the wires. All the paint was worn off but, when she played it, it was like (virtuoso violinist) Jascha Heifetz. They're doing experiments with the Theremin now. The sound waves you experience when you play it have therapeutic value." The album's broader instrumentation included Stroh violin (a violin affixed with a brass horn), cello, viola, piano, upright bass, clarinet, marimba, saxophone, trumpet and drums.

GQ would comment that "Waits uses his voice as if he were singing tormented lullabies to somebody who's dying, or leaving forever, or growing up too fast," while Rolling Stone would declare of 'Poor Edward' that "Waits devours the victim's name with Shakespearean relish, stretching it out in a malignant growl, like a burned-out coroner showing you the dead body with a tired sweep of his arm. Waits' ravaged voice surrendered all pretensions to melody ages ago; his throat is now pure theatre, a weapon of pictorial emphasis and raw honesty."

Tom explained to NPR that by that point in his career, he'd developed what he described as his own "musical vocabulary. You find the appropriate sound for the correct tune and mess them up. Yeah, you know I like to scream and I can croon, all that stuff." Journalist Gavin Martin was told that, as he worked through bringing each of his song's characters to life, "when you sing, you're kind of acting. The whole act of singing is like a big question you're asking, something you are reaching towards, wondering about or ranting over. In 'Alice' there's a lot of images and reflections, like a fever dream or something. Songs are sometimes at their most satisfying when they confuse you – you don't listen to them for information. It's not like you read a recipe on a box of macaroni. If you listen to a song, you're asking to be confused or mystified. You're asking to go get lost."

As he developed each song's individual personality, Waits explained to journalist Mikel Jollett that "My thing is more mutating things," elaborating to music writer Robert Lloyd that he had "a ball with just the sounds. It's kinda thrilling to invent a language and not know from one word to the next what you're gonna say. You have no idea what you're gonna say. It's free, it's a free feeling... It's called sub-vocalising. I guess maybe it's part of the evolution of language. It's going backwards. Back to when sounds had just basic shapes to them and had yet to be applied to anything truly meaningful."

Waits offered that, within that process, "you go through a series of emotions. You're angry, you're compassionate and you're sad. You go through a whole range, but you're doing it with eh.. just shapes. 'Ein-choin, fein-mon tein-shein fun-ka', you know? 'Hidde-minga, balle-minga, bolle-monga, kille-monga, bille-monga.' It's really a language. Sid Caesar used to do it all the time. But it's actually therapeutic. You ought to try it. If you're angry: don't say words, just say shapes and sounds."

Waits revealed that "one of the songs on there, that's on 'Alice', 'Kommienezuspadt'…there are a few words in there that have real meaning but the rest of it is just pure gibberish. But a lot of people when they hear it the say: 'Ghee I didn't know you spoke Rumanian', or 'I didn't know you spoke the odd dialect of Finland.' I have been known to tell them that I DO speak those languages, but truthfully I don't."

At the end of any day's work, Waits was as weathered as an auto mechanic covered in grease after a day working under an engine, describing his physical appearance as one where "my knees are all skinned up and my pants are wet and my hair's off to one side and I feel like I've been in the foxhole all day. I don't think comfort is good for music. It's good to come out with skinned knuckles after wrestling with something you can't see. I like it when you come home at the end of the day from recording and someone says, 'What happened to your hand?' And you don't even know. When you're in that place, you can dance on a broken ankle."

By the time he reached the mixing stage of recording, Tom confessed to Australian Weekly that while "it was a lot of work," the effort was ultimately rewarding "by the time you're done…(because) you'll never listen to it as many times or as closely as when you're working on it. You have to be in a certain frame of mind. It's like acting. You have to be making certain choices about how to approach the song. Sometimes it's hard to know when you're done."

Waits quipped that the, for him, that process was over "when they take it away from you – that's when you're done." Addressing the inevitable B-sides that didn't make the final cut, the singer-songwriter offered to the Onion that "there's always a bunch of them that don't make the boat. That's normal. You just stick 'em all together later and put 'em out by themselves."

Upon release on 4 May 2002, the album was an instant hit with both fans, debuting at Number 33 on the Billboard Top 200. GQ noted in their review of the LP that "the good people at Waits' label, Anti, struck a bit of genius when they decided to release these two albums simultaneously. Because the contrasts of 'Alice' and 'Blood Money' perfectly highlight the two aspects of Waits' musical character that have been colliding in his work for decades." Alternative Press's nine out of 10-star review of the LP pointed out "had gained a reputation as Waits' 'lost masterpiece'," adding that "that claim proves well deserved." In the UK, where Waits maintained a loyal fan base, the BBC praised Waits' latest offering as "arranged and performed to perfection", while NME celebrated the album as "a shimmering, mournful gem".

The critical celebration continued Stateside as Spin magazine awarded the album seven out of 10 stars, and USA Today noted that "the achievement underscores his cult's ferocious appetite for the twisted beauty, sonic alchemy and uncommon sense of Waits' music." Rolling Stone observed that "this is fertile darkness for Waits, who excels at putting a human face on the bizarre and finding redemptive cheer in flophouse woe."

"I heard better stories in the AA meetings, to be honest with you."
– 1992

"Most people in showbusiness are mining the strangeness that's inside of them." – TOM WAITS, 2002

PART XX: 'Blood Money' (2002)

By this point in his career Tom Waits had the luxury – as he explained to Australian music journalist Iain Shedden – of "pretty much (doing) what I want... If I did disco or parlour songs or anything, it wouldn't matter. I don't feel chained to anybody's affectations of what they think I should do. I'm in a unique position."

'Mule Variations' had sold over a million copies worldwide, reaffirming the artistic freedom he had worked so boldly to secure over the past two decades. This, he suggested to Time Out, had earned him the right to ignore trends and "go my own way. Try not look at it as a business. I'm kind of on my own quest, and I'm still able to make a living, so I'll keep doing it."

Waits used that creative capital to bring full circle a collaboration that he'd begun a decade earlier when he and wife Kathleen Brennan had first teamed with Robert Wilson on The Black Rider. The Star Tribune explained of the proposed new album that its roots were "based on an 1837 German play about a soldier, driven mad by army medical experiments and infidelity, who murders his lover. The music often is pretty, but the lyrics tell terrible tales."

Waits told journalist Gavin Martin that initially "we were going to call the album 'Woyzeck', but...nobody knew who he was." It was wife Kathleen who finally came up with a far more accessible and catchy title. "She said, 'Let's call it 'Blood Money' and that made sense. The guy's a lowly soldier who's offered money for medical experiments which contribute to his loss of balance and sanity."

The singer-songwriter credited his wife with having first introduced him to the play. "I didn't know anything about Woyzeck. Kathleen knew more than I, but I didn't really know the story or anything. I was just told the story in a coffee shop in Boston over eggs a few years ago. You try to create some sort of counterpoint for this story, but you're still dealing with song logic. When people listen to songs... it's like a form of hypnotism that goes on during the listening process so you're taking it up through a straw. It's like a separate little world in the world. You go in there and then you pop back out. Those musicals always sound so corny when somebody stops and thinks of something and goes back to life."

Tom offered to USA Today that "its a story that continues to surface in Europe. Wilson told me about this lowly soldier who submitted to medical experiments and went slowly mad from taking medications and herbs. He finds out his wife is unfaithful. He slits her throat and throws his knife in the lake, goes in after it and drowns, and then his child is raised by the village idiot. I said, 'Okay, I'm in. You had me at slit her throat.'" Waits explained that "its a proletariat opera. The child is left to be raised by the village idiot, this real witch of a woman. So it's got, you know, all the things you'd want from opera."

Waits delved deeper into the story's arch in an interview with Clare Barker, explaining that the play was a departure from his norm of writing "about things that you understand and have compassion for. You don't write about worlds that you don't inhabit yourself." That said, Wait's historical talent for dark lyrical narratives and musical soundscapes took the songs on 'Blood Money' on a "descent into madness that ends in murder and suicide," as he explained to Nigel Williamson, adding to Uncut that, as he wrote the album, "the songs aren't really a linear narrative; you couldn't understand the story from hearing them. They might have been part of a theatre piece to begin with, but if you are going to do a record it has to stand alone. You have to get beyond the original concept; it's like making a movie out of a book."

For this album, the root of his music began "just with the sound. And somehow the meaning finds the sound and they join, and you get over it. That's the way I do it anyway." Waits told music journalist Patrick Donovan his feeling that "songs live in the air and they appear at all times. If you're a songwriter you like music, but what you really want is for music to like you. You want to be an aerial, or an antenna, for songs to locate you, and they do. They're everywhere." Tom suggested to the New York Times that, through his music, he felt "you do give voice to people who don't have songs written about them or don't have a chance to tell their story, and it's actually good to get all those people out of my head. Download and make room for some other stuff."

The singer-songwriter, continuing this discussion, shared that "sometimes they're coming so fast there's not enough to catch them in, and other days you have to do a rain dance for it. You wait. I've got tape recorders all over the house. I can scribble notes on a napkin." Tom added that he'd developed a more organic approach wherein "what I've really done is learn to exercise my memory. If I have a melody in my head, my challenge is to keep it in my head all day. And then try to sit down to dinner, forget it and then go back in the car and see if I can remember it again. I think if this is a really good melody it'll never leave me. Some you lose. A lot of them get away. Those are the best songs, the ones that got away."

Waits explained to journalist Nigel Williamson why his records often took a dark turn. "I like to hear a beautiful melody telling me something terrible, Kurt Weill was the master of that. 'Mack The Knife' has a beautiful melody… But he's talking about this terrible crime. And that's so out there. It's really revolting and revolutionary and nobody knew what to make of that. It changed popular music." Admitting to USA Today that "I thrive on pain and discomfort," Waits added that, as a songwriter, "I like misunderstandings. I think I have an auditory processing problem. I like when I hear a song from a radio far away and I mishear it. As it limps across, it gets interrupted by the tractor or an airplane or the wind."

Waits shared decision-making with his wife, as was now customary. "I trust her opinion above all else. You've gotta have somebody to trust, that knows a lot…

It works. We've been at this for some time now. Sometimes you quarrel, and it's the result of irritation, and sometimes it comes out of the ground like a potato and we marvel at it. She doesn't like the spotlight. She's a very private person, as opposed to myself."

He felt the pair worked well together because "we kind of sharpen each other like knives." Waits added in the same conversation with journalist James Nicholas Joyce that "sometimes we quarrel. But for the most part we kind of try to make each other better by not allowing each other to do anything we consider to be mediocre. Even though of course it's inevitable. But when there's two people working on something, it's always different."

Tom added to Time Out that while, understandably, "it takes a long time to trust somebody long enough to let them stand up to you and tell you what they think," his belief in her creative instincts had paid off Waits felt in part because "she has an amazing imagination and is someone I trust immeasurably."

GQ magazine's cover profile of the singer homed in on Brennan's influence over her husband, observing that "she's the most mysterious figure in the whole Tom Waits mythology... She's everywhere, but invisible. She's private as a banker, rare as a unicorn, never talks to reporters. But she is the very centre of Tom Waits – his muse, his partner and mother of his three children...his wife says that all his songs can be divided into two major categories – Grim Reapers and Grand Weepers."

The BBC paid Brennan the compliment where 'Blood Money' was concerned that "credit should also go to Kathleen Brennan, as Waits repeatedly states, describing how her initial inspirations are then realised by his musical instincts. This time round, those instincts lead him in predictably unpredictable directions, employing bizarre instrumentation and some inspired arrangements."

Waits explained to disc jockey Richard Kingsmill that, in deciding to jointly track the records, he "went in there with over 30 tunes and I just recorded a big mezzo... They weren't done separately, they were done in the same studio and there was a lot of the same musicians as well."

His intention was to keep his talented band – which included bluesman Charlie Musselwhite, reedman Colin Stetson, bassist and guitarist Larry Taylor, marimbist Andrew Borger, and others – freshly focused on the projects' respective differences. "Most of the musicians drove up (on a) two-hour drive from San Francisco, and I instructed them that they were not allowed to listen to any music in the car on the way up, and I wanted them there by 10am, so they were clean, you know? Their heads were clean. And we could start fresh."

He told music writer James Nicholas Joyce that, even though he and Brennan kept the broader vision in sight, "you can't really rule with an iron fist in the studio, you're really trying to capture something. It's more like sneaking up on a bird. So you really have to be careful and you have to choose your companions very carefully... I don't make them do anything, you know. It's like casting: you usually choose people that you have some kind of shorthand or rapport with."

In the spirit of that spontaneous approach to recording, Waits explained to friend/filmmaker Terry Gilliam that he sought to surround himself with players who are equally as adventurous and willing to "go anywhere, and then use metaphor… I go in with a certain number of experimental musical instruments. I try to use unusual sound sources, so that I'm putting on record things that may have never been used as an instrument before, and (songs) always get an unusual texture from that."

Waits continued his junkyard scavenger hunts for sounds to turn to treasure during his record-making process. "The first thing you do is look around at the studio when you get there, to look and see if there's anything anybody left there from the session before that you can use, you know. Or if anyone left an upturned trash-can that you can use. And then you evaluate all the equipment."

In the same conversation with James Nicholas Joyce, Waits recalled that "we had a lot of vintage microphones, there were microphones that I'd only ever seen in Hitler documentaries. All these bizarre compressors. And the engineers came in there and said, 'this is too much.' But when it comes down to it, your real gifts are the ones that you bring with you. Hopefully the tunes are strong enough, and I worked with really good people. You know, I try not to rehearse the song to death. In fact, we rarely rehearse it. We say, let's try it and then roll. And invariably, you get it on a first take. Or at least you get something you can use even if you have to do a little cutting and pasting. But I think songs are like anything else: once you get used to them or once they get used to you there's a certain level of complacency that you arrive at. So you want to continue to press forward with the element of surprise. And that's usually when it's new, when it's fresh."

Tom shared with Time Out his open-mindedness to trying anything that might help achieve the sound he heard in his head. "My feeling is, to a certain degree, all sounds are music, and of course it's your job to decide what you think's appropriate for the project and what's not." Offering an example of that philosophy in action, Waits added that "if you realise that, when you hit this furnace with the leg of a chair as hard as you can, you get a better sound than you do on your drum set, then you're going hit the furnace with the chair.

"I like my music with a little bit of grind and grime and rind; I like it with the pits and peel. I remember those early Bob Dylan bootlegs that were so difficult to hear – the quality of them was so bad that it actually added to the mythology. It's like when you listen to an old Caruso 78, and you hear the scratches and it sounds like he's trying to reach you from the bottom of a mine, and you feel like you want to help him."

To make his own music reflect both those elements as well as an ingredient all his own involved trying to "put things in songs that will explode later," offering to USA Today that. through careful arrangement, "they're set for a certain time. You light the fuse. Oh, that's not really a good image these days. Let me rephrase that or I'll have somebody following me. As soon as the songs hear the crack of that rifle, they go running for cover. But I've usually got three days' worth of food and a scope. You want to avoid recording the feathers and throwing away the bird, I guess. You do want something to be living in them. So you sneak up on them. Because the recording process involves putting something through a machine, you have to wonder what falls down into the filter. Sometimes we pull out that lint and make other songs."

GQ magazine noted a consistent feature of every song on the album – in one form or another – came with "Waits love…(for finding) strange and resonant objects hidden deep in piles of garbage, objects he can rescue and turn into new kinds of musical instruments." Elaborating on this favourite feature of the recording process, Tom told the Boston Globe that he liked "playing instruments that aren't necessarily instruments, incidentally. It puts you in touch with a whole evolution of things in a way," adding to GQ that, in the course of that evolution, "I like to imagine how it feels for the object to become music: imagine you're the lid to a fifty-gallon drum. That's your job. You work at that. That's your whole life. Then one day I find you and I say, 'We're gonna drill a hole in you, run a wire through you, hang you from the ceiling of the studio, bang on you with a mallet, and now you're in showbusiness, baby!'"

Turning to his percussive preferences, Waits told the New York Times that the process began with "certain sounds that I am attracted to… I always like things that sound like they're trying to reach you from far away, so I feel like I need to lean in and give them some help. I like clank and I like boom and I like steam. I thought that would be a good title for a record: 'Clank, Boom And Steam.' Clank, boom, pssssst! There's something kind of locomotive about it, coal-driven."

He had broadened his musical pallet to include accent rhythm elements, a mainstay feature since 1985's 'Rain Dogs'. He recalled to Nigel Williamson that "at a certain point I got interested in unusual sound sources. I'm still fascinated by that. I started bringing things into the studio that I found at the side of the road to see what they sounded like. I started wondering what would happen if we deconstructed the whole thing. I like things to sound distressed. I like to imagine what it would sound like to set fire to a piano on the beach and mic it really close and wait for the strings to pop. Or drop a piano off a building and be down there waiting for it to hit with a microphone. I like melody. But I also like dissonance."

Waits explained to journalist Dan Cohen that it was necessary to look at being in a studio as "kinda like being in a submarine – after a while I think you go through a certain amount of sensory deprivation. You're looking for something you can't see, can't smell, can't taste, you can't touch – so it's kinda like going in there with Jacques Cousteau gear looking for a paperless piano at the bottom of the lake."

Waits' favourite instrumental example of the latter in action seemed to be a 1929 Pneumatic Calliope, which the singer explained to USA Today was "ear-bleeding loud. It has all these pipes that look like radiator hoses. If you call the whistles 'pipes', by the way, a calliope player will hang up on you. I loved it. You can scream when you're playing it and not be heard. I'd like to see more of it in popular music."

His scavenger hunt, he told the Chicago Tribune, took him to "Iowa, actually, back of a flatbed truck. It was a small, red-suspender band, their sleeves held up with elastic, wearing straw hats. Greg Cohen, who's married to my wife's sister and has been my bass player for many years, asks if it's for sale. 'Absolutely.' So he gives me the phone number. Says his wife would kill him if he purchased a calliope. So he decided to let my wife kill me, instead. I paid two grand for it, and it needed work…a background in car repair would be advantageous because it's all hoses and pipes."

The instrument was so large that Waits added to journalist Dan Cohen it took "six guys to pick it up put it in the back of an El Camino. Don't ask why, but for some reason all these calliope people live in Iowa – there's a whole coven of calliope people. They congregate like circus people who have settled in Tampa, Florida… But (the calliope) is very loud, it's designed to be heard from five miles away. So if you can imagine that, but you're sitting next to it." It reflected the distance Waits was willing to travel to attain the sounds he heard in his head.

One instrument that was decidedly absent from much of 'Blood Money' was the guitar, a previous Waits staple. "Kathleen said, 'Let's try and solve some of these problems without guitar. The guitar is so versatile. There's so many times when you hear a guitar that it pulls your focus, and there's a certain normality to it. I like to hear things that are a little more conflicted sometimes." Having now forsaken both the guitar and piano – mainstays of past compositional constructions – Waits described the process of flying blind as something "like a little tease or a challenge for yourself. It's like, let me see if you can walk to the corner with a blindfold."

Even with the absence of guitars, the Times concluded in its rave review of the LP that "the music drags hymns and parlour songs, blues and ballads into a sonic menagerie that, on the new albums, includes Swiss hand bells, calliope and a four-foot-long Indonesian seed pod." Spin magazine offered its own musical observation in a glowing review that "from the fantastically sinister mock-tango instrumental…to the hilarious whiskey-bar soundtrack…this album has an edge and forward motion."

Turning to the tracking of the album's vocals, Waits told journalist James Nicholas Joyce that "I like syncopation. I like to use my voice like a drum, you know. I counterpoint and all that. And then of course I sub-vocalise, because I'm dyslexic, attention deficit disorder: I'm always making sounds for the sake of making sounds. Before you have words you just make sounds." Tom added to USA Today that "I make a lot of sounds that don't have any meaning, and slowly they form into words, and the words form into meaning. I start from inside, just kind of hollering out odd-shaped sounds as a musical ingredient."

A discussion with music writer Robert Lloyd elicited the admission that "I do actually dance when I sing. Don't we all? I sing and dance. I guess I'm part of that whole tradition on a certain level." In all the excitement, Waits confessed to NPR that, at times, when pushing his voice for the sake of the song, there were times when "I've hurt it, I have worried. But I have a voice-doctor in New York who used to treat Frank Sinatra and various people he said: 'Oh you're doing fine, don't worry about it.'"

As Waits and Brennan neared the end of production, they had a longstanding studio tradition for when a song wasn't working which, the singer-songwriter shared with journalist Elizabeth Gilbert, went something like "Doctor, our flamingo is sick". GQ magazine added that "it is at difficult moments like these that Kathleen will show up with novel ideas. (What if we played it like we were in China? But with banjos?) She'll bring him a Balinese folk dance to listen to, or old recordings from the Smithsonian of Negro field hollers. Or she'll just take the flamingo off his hands for a while, take it for a walk, try to put some food into it."

Even when the pair did know they had a keeper on their hands for the final track listing, Tom reasoned to journalist Robert Lloyd that "you don't always know when a song is finished. And I'm not sure if a song *is* ever finished to be honest with you. You know they're constantly evolving. It's like-jump rope songs, you know. When are they done? They are never done. You know people are always changing them, changing the tempo, adding new verses, getting rid of old verses. So I mean, when you are ready to record there is a certain finality to that."

The latter decision wasn't made for Waits and Brennan until final mixing was completed, and while mixing 'Blood Money' they liked to leave themselves as many options as possible, such that "we did different versions" of each song… With songs, when you're working on them, you never listen to them as many times and as carefully as when you're working on them. It's like this kind of fantastic voyage inside the corpuscles of the songs at once it's up and running and off, you don't visit it with the same intimacy as when you are working on it. So for us, we did…different mixes and different arrangements of the tunes and finally, these are the versions we selected."

Once they'd handed the album into Epitaph along with sister release 'Alice', Waits gave Terry Gilliam his opinion that the label was "an unusual place. It's a bit of an asylum for damaged artists, I think. Because it's also very just and sane and fair. You know, you take your suit to the cleaner's and you actually get your suit back."

'Blood Money' moved 32,000 copies in its first seven days on sale from 4 May 2002, reaching Number 32 on Billboard's Top 200. Fans agreed that 'Blood Money' "was unequivocally inspired, unique, and impossibly good," the BBC adding in the same review that "only Tom Waits can do this." USA Today felt the album was both "graceful and intoxicating," and Alternative Press argued that Waits' latest offering "worked perfectly".

GQ would praise the album as "rich, complex and mysterious", while Q hailed Waits' "tunes and rhythms" for being "at their jauntiest", Mojo magazine concluded that the album made "for an extravagant headphone experience", while Billboard topped even that praise, saying that the album was an "elegant, stylish, and nuanced work". Waits seemed satisfied that he'd delivered his audience exactly what they wanted to hear, reasoning in a conversation with disc jockey Richard Kingsmill that "I've got folks out there that listen to me…and that's what I'm sending these out there for. The fans, people that follow my career and all that. Interested in what I have been thinking about. And these records are like a letter or a newsletter, or a chain letter or something. We'll see how they do…"

"Recording for me is like photographing ghosts." – TOM WAITS

"His new record 'Real Gone' on Epitaph's Anti subsidiary is an amalgam of earthy funk, beatnik howl and backwoods river bottom blues." – THRASHER MAGAZINE

"She hates the spotlight, and I get a kick out of it."
– TOM WAITS ON WIFE/COLLABORATOR KATHLEEN BRENNAN

PART XXI: 'Real Gone' (2004)

The BBC summed up Tom Waits' standing after 35 years in the business by saying, "Waits has never played the music-industry game. Every few years he emerges from his family home in 'Nowhere, California' with a new album, written with his wife Kathleen Brennan. He does a couple of interviews, he plays a few gigs and then he disappears again. And yet he remains one of the most influential and revered artists alive."

His influence and longevity was attributable to a globe of loyal foot soldiers that hit record stores album after album – whether a year had passed or 10 – to support whatever new direction he had adopted in that particular cycle of stylistic re-invention. The San Francisco Chronicle illustrated that loyalty in action with their report in 2004 on "his zealous cult following" and their routine of "stampeding the stores the week of release", resulting in "his past three albums…(all making) mid-chart premieres. Never destined for MTV stardom, Waits can nonetheless make releasing a new album a cultural event."

Part of the secret behind that success was the fantastic expectations for new sonic surprises his fans had come to expect on each new studio LP. By the time of 'Real Gone', Time Out regarded Waits as "an artist at the peak of his powers, digging deep, reaching back and pushing ever on", further noting that "what makes him so unusual is that he has maintained this position over two decades." Tom shared candidly with the LA Times that "part of my compulsion is I'm unable to repeat myself in certain things. Other people are nervous when they have to digress or deviate from the scripts, and I'm compelled to change things all the time."

Having earned the career capital by that point in his career to "do what I want", Waits was careful to clarify to Time Out that "I don't think of that as something unique or bizarre. You can pretty much make your own way in the world, make your own rules. Of course, it's easier to ride on the road that's already there, but sometimes you need to make your own road." Speaking from a compositional angle, he added in a discussion with Irish radio host Dave Fanning that his purpose for continuing to enter the studio at that point in life revolved primarily around his desire "to make some new tunes because you're tired of the old ones… (That's) the only that makes you go back (the studio)… There's no other reason to do it you know. Otherwise you just make one record and you'd be done with the whole business."

This time around, Tom opted to enter a musical territory that the Telegraph magazine accurately depicted as "Waitsland. He has staked out this surreal, archaic American territory as his own and given it an utterly distinctive sound – gruffly romantic, beautifully written ballads interspersed with a weird, fractured, clanging music of his own invention." Describing his production philosophy to Mojo magazine, he quipped that "I used to think I was making movies for the ears – writing them, directing them, releasing them. Kind of making a fiction in a non-fiction world. Taking the real world and then getting rid of certain things that I didn't want to be there and adding certain things that I hoped would have been there. I was overly maudlin and romantic and I really hadn't grown up. I still very much lived in a fantasy world."

His co-creator of that fantasy world, wife Kathleen Brennan, had remained throughout their 25 years of collaboration the one who consistently "encouraged me to look at songs through a funhouse mirror and then take a hammer to them." Waits happily added to radio host Vicki Kerrigan that "she is my muse," adding in the same discussion that "when you write songs together it's kinda like shooting off firecrackers.

"Sometimes you feel like you're doing too much lighting and not doing enough throwing. Sometimes you feel like you want to be lighting and holding and throwing. You want to get the whole pack and go out to the driveway by yourself. But without (a good partner) you get to be like the emperor's new clothes. You need someone to tell you that you're about to walk off a cliff. Like somebody spotting you on the high wire."

Trusting his wife as a safety net, Tom reasoned in a conversation with Zembla magazine that "if you're doing a highwire act, you've got to have someone on the ground, right? You need someone around to tell you when you're full of shit and I'd rather have my wife say it than someone in the newspapers. I watch her back, she watches mine."

As the pair began planning 'Real Gone', Waits – speaking to Mojo magazine in a metaphorical context of a recipe he and Brennan were whipping up – reasoned that "you want it to be fresh in some way. I don't want to repeat myself. It's always a little bit of something old and something new – except I don't record with great frequency so, with the times that's gone between records, you can't avoid having gone through some changes. I think you get more confident with your process – even though you're trying to change the process, you know? Because I don't cook the same way every time."

He offered fans a bit of direct insight into their writing routine when speaking with Magnet magazine. "We just throw out lines, it's like dreaming out loud. When we're writing, we kinda go into a trance." As song ideas began to arrive, Tom revealed to the BBC that their origins remained as mysterious as ever. "I don't know where they come from. Some of them you make up, some of them you build like contraptions and some of them, you know, just find you. Sometimes songs want you, they wanna come to you."

Tom conceded to Zembla magazine that, in seeking inspiration, "nothing comes out of nowhere. Nothing comes out of your hair. There's always a story that happened before it emerged in you. By the time you see something new in the garden it had a long history getting there. The same is true of tunes. It's really about the migration of seeds. That's how music changes. And I'm always interested in volunteering in the garden, you know. Pour a little extra water."

Elaborating on the organic aspect of this process, Waits shared with the LA Times that "sometimes things just do naturally come together. You just have to know how to draw a frame around it." As song ideas began to collect, while some immediately stood out from the crowd, Tom explained to the San Francisco Chronicle that, often, "the best ones come out just like a litter. I usually start with two tunes, put them in a room together and they have kids. There are usually two songs that are the parents of the rest. That's my theory."

Tom told Irish radio host Dave Fanning that "I think I've gotten a lot younger in a lot of ways. I certainly write songs a lot faster, you know we write 'em a lot acappella." He explained some general rules-of-thumb about the songwriting process to Paste magazine. "People who make songs don't go to school to learn how to do it. You sit down next to the record player and you write down the words and try and figure out these changes, and that's how everybody does it."

Expanding in a discussion with the Ottawa Xpress, he added that open-mindedness was key. "The trick (is) not to make things too personal. It's the art of it. If you're going to write about something that's current, then when it's no longer current the song will have no value. How do you photograph your driveway and make it seem like the road of life? Why would people buy pictures of people they don't know? You have to shape it, make it recognisable. If you're going to write a song about the war, you better make it about war itself, not just about some story in the newspaper. Well, that's just my way."

Turning specifically to the songs on 'Real Gone', the singer-songwriter told the Ottawa Xpress that "words are already music all by themselves... My theory is that all songs have to have weather in them, and the names of towns and streets, and something to eat. People in songs, you can't just stick 'em in there and not give 'em something to eat!" . Waits viewed each character/song as part of a world "you are creating...and you are asking people to enter that world – you gotta give 'em something to do once they get there... Folk expressions and names of towns, names of people – that's musical to me. I hear them at family gatherings, or from books. Some are made up...sometimes they just come to you. You could make up a name right now: 'Norberry Ellen and Coriander Pyle had 16 children in the usual style.' It's a trick. A place you gotta get to. It's more like daydreams... and you're doing incantations and talking in tongues."

Tom next explained to Thrasher magazine that "when you're making words for songs, the first thing you do is just make sounds. 'I waa for miiiles and miiiiiiles and woosh auck through mordor.' You're just making sounds. And then you listen to that back, and you try to get it to explain what it's trying to say to you. Sometimes it sounds like, 'It's something about a sewing machine', or 'Jeez, it's something about going to get my medicine.' So, I get mystified by the spontaneous incantations. It's a perfectly valid musical approach to me. I consider anything that makes a sound valid. It's just how it's orchestrated and how it's organised."

Finding himself at times "under a spell" during this creative exercise, Tom reasoned to Mojo that when "writing songs, you're the instrument. You know, you're really working on yourself." Highlighting some of the particularly poignant jewels he and Brennan obtained from this process, the Guardian would single out 'The Day After Tomorrow' as the "most remarkable of all: an unadorned song about a soldier writing home: 'I'm not fighting for justice, I am not fighting for freedom, I am fighting for my life and another day in the world.' Its power comes not from sonic shock value nor pertinence to current events, but from its uncanny sense of timelessness: it sounds like it could have been written at any point in the past 50 years, without seeming in any way hackneyed – an incredible trick to pull off."

Offering insight into exactly how he pulled that trick off, Tom told the LA Times that the song's composition was an extension of a requirement for any songwriter, specifically that "you have to be able to write about what goes on around you. Pick up a newspaper, write a tune. That's all I was trying to do. Not like I'm making speeches at the UN. But there's nothing but war in the papers now. The whole world's at war." Billboard would eventually hail the results as "one of the most insightful and understated anti-war songs to have been written in decades."

'Sins Of My Father' was another album high point the LA Times would celebrate as "part revelation, part East Of Eden, and part backroom political culture framed by the eve of the apocalypse" adding that it was "hunted, hypnotic, and spooky". Waits told Magnet that "'Sins Of My Father' is political. 'Hoist That Rag' is. There's a bunch of soldier songs…(On 'Sins Of My Father') I'm talking about my father, I'm talking about your father, I'm talking about his father. The sins of the father will be visited upon the son. Everybody knows that."

One of the album's lighter lyrical numbers, 'Circus', was quite literally about "running away with the circus…a thing I used to think about in school…. I remember George Burns once said that after he saw some vaudeville show, he realised he wanted to get into showbusiness as soon as possible. What is it about that? Some grand old tradition, I guess. Usually it's filled with people who are in some way fractured or bruised or chipping. It's the old irritation-in-the-oyster-making-the pearl. You think you're going to the circus looking at the show people? They're looking at you. You're just an extra in their show that night. Your being there is twofold – to be entertained, and as background noise, part of the strange pattern of faces in the crowd. Of course it's highly romantic the way I put it. It all has to do with what you leave in and what you leave out."

Waits' process for creating the basic bed tracks that made up 'Real Gone' was chaotic by conventional recording standards, with Telegraph magazine reporting that the album "was largely recorded on four-track tape in the farmhouse bathroom." Tom told Zembla magazine that he felt "the acoustics are great in there. I moved instruments in there, a four-track recording rig. When I went into the studio we set one in an empty schoolhouse near Sacramento. I had all these raw tapes that I made in the bathroom and I was hoping to replicate them, but the studio sounded nothing like my bathroom at home. Not even, the bathroom in the studio sounded like my bathroom. So it was really disturbing and kind of disconcerting to find out that you can't recreate what you've already done. Some things only happen once. And you can never recreate the conditions under which they happen. So I ended up using the tapes I brought and the musicians played over them."

Detailing the technical end of that process, Waits recalled to Skull Cave that "I took a little four-track, had a 58 microphone and just clapping sounds wonderful. You know, rooms are instruments as well." To that end, when Waits was first hunting down the ideal recording acoustics to accommodate the sound he heard in his head, he offered to the BBC that "we couldn't really get the sound in the studio as good as it sounded when I was doing it at home," leading to his quest to find what he shared with Magnet magazine at its most basic was "a place that might have an unusual sound."

Waits concluded to radio host Vicki Kerrigan that "I think I like the rooms that weren't designed as studios, just like I like certain sound sources, unusual sound sources that become experimental musical instruments."

In contrast to past decades where Waits had lamented the arduous process of recording an LP, his opinion had shifted 180 degrees with his declaration to Harp magazine by the time of 'Real Gone' that "I like recording you know. I guess that's my favourite thing." That had become his position in part because, following the pre-production process, "I have a pretty good idea what it's going to look like. I have a vision about it, you know. I wouldn't call it scientific but there's certainly much more of a plan involved."

He was quick in the same conversation with Skull Cave to clarify that "beautiful accidents happen all the time, sometimes changing the course of the tune. But that's part of the whole process too. Being open to and paying attention to the possibility of that happening."

Revealing just how rugged his process of discovering those beautiful accidents got during recording, Tom shared with Telegraph magazine that, as a rule, "I get all banged up in the studio. At the end of the day I want to feel like I've been to work. You have cuts on your hands, you don't know where they came from. You're bruised up and sweating. I love it," adding to the Globe And Mail that, as a result, "the songs on 'Real Gone' are real beat up, and it took a lot of care and attention to get them that way."

Waits quipped to the San Diego Union Tribune that, as a producer, "what happens with me is, I heard the needle being mashed down and those great mics being trashed, and it creates an energy in the music. It's like somebody wincing. It's like scratching off the linoleum or breaking a window, and you still feel it." Expanding on that process of experimenting, the singer-songwriter conceded to Mojo that, by nature, "what I do is kind of abstract – I work on things that are in some way invisible. Yeah the room's filled with instruments, but to process things that are invisible."

Waits told Harp magazine of the new ground he'd covered in sonic experimentations throughout the writing of 'Real Gone'. "I made a tape…called The House Of Sound. I took 24 tracks, and did something different, completely unrelated, on each adjacent track. There was screaming, there were rhythmic things. I'd bring the parts up and down one or two at a time, and it was always different, depending on which rooms you entered. And then we'd go into the common room, with everything happening at once, and it was like an orchestra tuning up. Somebody's playing scales, somebody else is going over a passage they trip up on, and the mash-up of all the sounds is amazing."

Philosophically, Tom explained to friend/musician Elvis Costello, this sonic carnival of sound was as natural a part of his native creative process as any other element. "It's like translation. Anything that has to travel all the way down from your cerebellum to your fingertips, there's a lot of things that can happen on the journey. Sometimes I'll listen to records, my own stuff, and I think God, the original idea for this was so much better than the mutation that we arrived at. What I'm trying to do now is get what comes and keep it alive. It's like carrying water in your hands. I want to keep it all, and sometimes by the time you get to the studio you have nothing."

Tom seemed to feel he had an endless well of inspiration at his disposal, reasoning in his conversation with The Tribune that, to his ear, "any sound is music already, and sometimes I just make up sounds and don't know what they mean. Then I play the sounds back and listen to them like a foreign language. And I say: 'If this was a foreign language, how would I decipher it? And pretty soon, I realise certain words are starting to form. What are they saying?

"When you listen to other artists' records, you think: Did he say 'medicine' or 'mason?' All songwriters listen to records and try to figure out what key it's in. Or: 'What voicing is that? I can't find it on my guitar.' And then it's (like) your dissertation and part of your cycle of learning." From an overarching production vantage point, Waits explained to Mojo that, "in the studio my job is to locate that mood, enlarge it and then put everybody in the middle of it. You want them to dance like there's nobody watching. You want them to be talking in tongues."

Waits broke new ground to get precisely the sound he heard out of his head and onto tape, choosing to generate beat-boxed rhythm tracks into a tape recorder in his bathroom at home. "Most of (the record) was written acappella. I started with these mouth rhythms, making my own cycles and playing along with them. That's fairly new. Sometimes when you just do sounds into the tape recorder, you don't realise it, but you're channeling something." Explaining in the same discussion with Magnet that he tracked the album's bed rhythm tracks utilising only "a Fostex four-track with a Shure SM58 (microphone) in a really small bathroom with about a four-second delay and overload the hell out of it," Waits added to Thrasher magazine that what made the bathroom "an excellent-sounding room" was "the configuration of the tiles and the architecture."

Once Waits found the sound fitted what he heard in his mind, he added to the LA Times that "I was determined to kind of go all the way that way. I'm all by myself with a tape recorder and trying to sound like a band. It's not tape loops, you know. I would do it for three and a half minutes. When you can't find the sound you're looking for, you make one up. Mine are very crude, like me." Offering to the San Diego Union Tribune that the heart of his trick to this type of tracking involved putting "a mic up to your mouth and overload it in a Pignose (miniature amplifier), and you can make those sounds in front of a bank on the sidewalk. What I do with it is very crude (compared to) the people who do it, the pros."

Tom explored the science of creating that sound in conversation with the Rock's Backpages website. "I'm more like a rhythm guitar that I play with my throat. It adds texture and corn starch to the existing tracks. They're weren't loops, because loops start feeling like wallpaper after a while – you know it's coming around again and your mind has no need to probe any further. But when you're trying to communicate with a drummer and you don't play the drums, the first thing you do is use your voice to illustrate what you want."

Waits described his unique style of beat-boxing as "mouth rhythm" in a conversation with Telegraph magazine. "It's old. Pygmies do it. You ever hear any of that stuff? Sounds like birds and hogs. Amazing. They also do this thing where two people go into the water and they play the water. Kla-boom-splash, just the sound of your hand slapping the water and going in but all very rhythmic and controlled. Then of course the Ramayana Monkey Chant, oh man, those guys. Chacka-chacka-chack-chack-cha...But it's like a thousand men sitting in concentric circles in Bali, telling a story about when all these monkeys came out of the trees and saved the tribe and they offer up this chant as a way of thanking the monkeys. It's a wild, wild piece of music. It'll scare the kids."

As he applied it through his own creative interpretation, the singer-songwriter added to Thrasher that, in essence, what he was producing were "incantations or talking in tongues... If I'm by myself and I have a tape recorder I make drum sounds. 'A-boom-Ch-Aaack, A-boom-Ch-Aaack,' you know? I do it for three minutes and I have a song." The Guardian would conclude that Waits had transformed "his technique into something impressively horrifying," adding that "his impersonations of drums now come interpolated with tortured guttural hacking noises," while the San Francisco Chronicle would note that "the tracks groan and clang with a burglar's bag of strange percussion instruments and other mysterious, almost stray sounds. Waits gets his barnyard soundscape by overloading tape, slamming vintage microphones with information and singing the often bizarre 'mouth rhythms' that fill the backgrounds of his songs."

As he shaped these skeletal elements of the album's broader soundscapes, Waits explained to Harp magazine that "I didn't want things to be so perfect. I did it for four minutes just like you'd do a drum part, get all sweaty, and that way it would feel like I was really inside the tune, with everything sliding a little bit." He added in a conversation with Mojo that he remained conscious throughout the beats' creations never to think of them as "a loop. The trouble with a loop is once your mind realises it's a loop it stops listening to it, just like you stop looking at the pattern on that tablecloth. There's no reason to continue to stare at the pattern. So every three or four bars you have to do something different.

"I was making sounds that weren't words but once I listened back I could actually determine certain syllables. It was like going back in time with the language where the sounds came first and slowly shaped itself around items and experiences. I'm one of those people that if I don't have my knees skinned and a cut on my hands, I don't really feel like I've had much of a days work. That's where the title came from – the blues thing, like I'm really gone."

Waits recalled to radio host Vicki Kerrigan that because "we couldn't really replicate them in the studio, we just used the crude sounds themselves and then built around them." A group of studio veterans seasoned in Waits' style of recording was assembled, the San Francisco Chronicle highlighting "longtime associate Larry Taylor on bass, a journeyman whose resume extends back to Sixties boogie kings Canned Heat, and drummer Brain, who used to bang away behind San Francisco thrash-punk band the Limbomaniacs, but most recently has been playing with Axl Rose in the current edition of Guns N' Roses. Bassist Les Claypool of Primus, who also plays on three tracks from the new album, introduced Brain to Waits.

"On guitar is downtown New York avant-gardist Marc Ribot, who adds a lot of funky, Cuban-flavoured playing to the spare, gritty sound. Ribot, who has recorded with Elvis Costello, played on Waits' 1985 landmark 'Rain Dogs' and did some overdubs for 'Mule Variations'."

Delving into why many players in this line-up had become his mainstay band over the course of 20 years of recording, Waits – in conversation with the San Diego Union Tribune – offered that they "gotta be able to drive! Oh, you mean me? What I look for? A certain amount of bravery is essential, as far as avoiding the obvious, and people who can sleep anywhere and eat with their hands. You have to develop your own language with them. Mainly, when musicians meet they have to sniff each other, like dogs, and find out what they know, who they've met. Nobody goes to school; it's more like: 'What have you heard? And how have you integrated it into your own work? Can you speak seven languages?'

"I like multi-instrumentalists myself and I am usually interested in how it sounds to have everybody switch instruments. When somebody is playing music on an instrument they're unfamiliar with, you always get interesting results. The fingers always want to go where they've been before, so the entire discovery process (comes) by 'unfamiliar zing' yourself with the new keys or surfaces or strings. Sometimes the things you haven't played on before sound the best."

The album would be a group effort wherein "we all decided democratically what belonged on it, what would be advantageous, what would detract, you know, The same we do all the time making a record, you know? You know half of the stuff you bring in, and the other half you find when you get there. So, you know, you go in the studio with medical professionals. That's the secret."

Elaborating on the inner-workings of that diplomacy in action, the singer-songwriter told the San Diego Union Tribune "you allow for a certain amount of discussion. You trust the people you're playing with. There's a certain kind of telepathy you develop after a while. I didn't realise he hit that sizzle cymbal just once; that's Brain. He was playing several sizes of hand drums, a bass drum and a lot of ethnic drums. My theory is if you don't bring it (to the recording session), you'll definitely need it. Silence is a huge part of music. It's essential. I'm always interested in what's not there and I like it when things are implied and things are left out. So I brought in Brain, Ribot and Larry Taylor. It was the right group because they're intuitive and telepathic."

The one element of the album everyone in the band agreed upon was that of Waits' beat-boxed rhythm tracks. "I came in with all these mouth rhythms, beatboxing, that I recorded in my bathroom at home. And they said: 'That's cool, don't touch it.' You're asking for their opinion. I care more about their opinions than the public's, because they're in the kitchen with me. I appreciate the honesty of musicians; it means they are in there with you, and they are concerned about how they'll sound and what they can contribute."

Another element of his record-making process where his band made significant contributions came with the aforementioned 'happy accidents'. "Music moves forward through its mistakes, that's what I like to do, you know, play pin the tail on the donkey now and then with songs and instruments. Because in a sense you're learning something and you're being told what to do. Most musicians are rebellious in one way or another and a lot of them won't do what you ask them. Or they'll nod and say they will and then at that part of the song say: 'Fuck it', and not do it.

"My son's like that. I'd say: 'Hit the floor tom with a mallet, and the snare drum upside down with a regular stick.' And he'd say: 'Yeah, right.' All he heard me say was: 'Take out the trash.' We started with a rock-steady beat on 'Sins Of My Father', and Larry Taylor said: 'I won't play that reggae shit. I don't play that (rock-steady style).' He's played with Jerry Lee Lewis, Canned Heat – he's played with everybody – and he said: 'I won't do it, man!' I said: 'Come on, Larry!'"

Elaborating on why he felt bassist Taylor fitted so naturally within the fabric of his instrumental sound over their 20-plus years of working together, Waits told Skull Cave that their mutual creative intuition ran as deep as Tom starting "sentences and he finishes them. And he's played with anybody. You know he played with Jerry Lee Lewis and…Canned Heat for a number of years. His brother was in the Ventures, did you know that? And he's done a lot of blues over the years of course. But he's very versatile and a joy to work with."

Waits shared the same unspoken musical language with longtime guitarist Marc Ribot. "Somebody like Marc I think is just as comfortable with, you know, industrial noise guitar as he is with uh…you know, legato, you know, very lyrical styles as well. So, you know, he's really someone who does a little plumbing and he also does some electrical. You know, he's well rounded and speaks 17 languages. You know? He eats with his hands. You know? Brave, strong and courageous."

Ribot's innate sense of adventure as helped bring his bold visions to life on record. In a discussion with Rock's Backpages, Waits hailed the guitarist as "really indispensable if you're looking for diversity and electromagnetism. It's so difficult to be a unique and distinctive guitar player, and he's in a category all his own." Offering the San Diego Union Tribune an illustration of just how electrified Ribot could become in the studio, Tom recalled that "With Ribot you have to be a little careful, because if you say you want a little feedback, you might get an automobile accident. It's always interesting finding somebody who, you know, they know just as much about pygmy music as they do (about bluesman

Arthur) 'Big Boy' Crudup or Memphis Slim or Gavin Bryars. He also is adept with industrial music or noise."

Son Casey's addition to the band on 'Real Gone' expanded the family connection. Adding the ingredient of a child's creativity seemed a logical move on all fronts, with Waits quipping to Time Out that, after all, "it's just the family business." Adding in the same discussion that "I'd been trying to get Casey to put his own band together, but I don't know, in the studio with your kids can be kind of sketchy."

Tom added in a conversation with Skull Cave that "the thing about with your kids in the studio is that you give 'em instructions but.. You know it's hard to tell your kids what to do whether you're working or you're at home… So for him it was kind of like listening to your dad telling you what to do. But, you know, we got over that and it turned out good."

To help keep his son on the same page with the rest of the band, Tom joked with radio host Vicki Kerrigan that he occasionally relied on the fact that "he got paid. He wasn't just doing it because like we were going on a family trip… He's a drummer and a percussionist…and it turned out good!" Explaining in the same discussion that he felt there was an artist advantage to the generational gap in band members' ages, Tom recalled that "the spread in ages was good. Because there was…Yeah, my bass player, he's in the Sixties and Casey is 18; it was a good balance."

One arena where Waits took advantage of his son's diversity as a music listener from his own tastes showed up in the form of Casey's turntable scratching. As Tom shared with the San Francisco Chronicle "All that stuff gets played around the house because that's what happens when you have kids. You stop dominating the turntable. I haven't had that kind of sway around here for years. 'Put on that Leadbelly record one more time, Dad, and I'm going to throw a bottle at your head.'" Ultimately, Waits found the experience to be "great and weird at the same time," adding in the same comments to the LA Times that watching the next generation of Waits come to life musically "was both euphoric and embarrassing – for him. I mean, playing with your dad." He paid his son the further compliment that "I learned a lot more from him than he learned from me."

The process of tracking his lead vocals saw Waits, for the first time, recording over the top of rhythm tracks created from his own voice. He began by explaining the technique he applied to Harp magazine. "When I do it, and then sing over it, it's like harmonising with yourself in a way. There's already a rapport… The voice seems to sound different when there are all these other vocal things around it. We got at a whole different energy in the rhythm."

Waits revealed to Skull Cave that "most of these were first takes and most of these were live vocals," adding to the BBC that, as he layered his leads, he kept constantly in mind that his voice – as much as any other on the album – was "an instrument" he sought to keep as experimental as any other element of the album. Harp magazine would comment of Waits' "vocal instrument" that it came to life on 'Real Gone' as "a broad-spectrum assault weapon: Sometimes when he sings, extreme high harmonics resembling the squeaks of a church mouse are audible, way in the ether.

"Running beneath them is a saw-tooth snarl in the upper-mid range that sounds like paint being scraped from a ceiling. Along with that comes a touch of battery-acid bray, then down low, in the bass range, the formless howl of a marine animal. You hear him sing several of the demanding vocal things from 'Real Gone' – the brutal 'Hoist That Rag', the more mannered 'Sins Of My Father' – and there's so many textures coming through at once it sounds like Waits multi-tracked himself."

Waits ventured once again as outside the box – in the context of the traditional recording studio – as often and ambitiously as possible. This exploration at its roots had begun years earlier, he told the Ottawa Express, when "I moved out to the sticks, I felt like an unplugged appliance. It gets really dark and really, really quiet. Now the quiet is part of the music, and so are the trucks going by. I let those sounds into the recordings... I like to feel like the world is collaborating with me."

In that spirit, Waits shared his feeling with the Sydney Morning Herald that "everything's valid. All sound is music to someone. That's my theory. It's just how it's organised, whether it's pleasing to your ears or mine." Elaborating on this philosophy as he applied it organically, Tom gave the Globe And Mail his opinion that "everything has equal value for me. If it's something you found on the side of the road on the way to the studio, that to me is worth as much as an oboe, or a bassoon, or the toilet seat. I like two radios on at the same time, or a song coming out of a car as it's driving by. I like things that have been beat up a little bit."

By allowing such experimentation to take root in his creative process, Tom shared that among his more interesting results, "I wrote an orchestral piece once for a squeaky door, a Singer sewing machine and a washing machine set on the spin cycle." Another unusual string instrument on the album was the 'Bastarda', that had shown up on tape courtesy of Les Claypool. "It's like an electric stick with four strings, like a bass without a body. 'Real Gone' is definitely not a record filled with bizarre, left-wing sound sources. The idea was to go in and do something that was going to be bread and water, skin and bones, three-legged tables, rudimentary three-minute songs. That was the idea."

Critics like the BBC highlighted what they felt was "a real surprise on this new record – for the first time in 30 years, there's no piano." Explaining why he opted to abandon the piano completely during the recording of his latest record, Tom reasoned in a conversation with the Ottawa Xpress that "piano is indoors, and this is an outdoor record. Sometimes when I use piano, it brings me indoors when I don't want to come in yet." Nonetheless, to ensure he had all potential points covered on the instrumental map, the singer-songwriter added to Magnet that, at the outset of recording, "I moved the piano into the studio, and we never touched it. We put drinks on it. I put my coat on it. Before you know it, I couldn't even see it. It just became an end table."

As production wrapped, Tom told Mojo that he deferred to wife Kathleen to "make up the title", proudly adding in a discussion with Magnet magazine that "I was going to call it 'Clang, Boom And Steam'. She said everyone's going or really gone, and there's a lot of leaving on the record. It's almost hard to get laughs these days; we are living in such a dark place." Critics picked up on the darker lyrical tone in their reviews of 'Real Gone' upon its release on 3 October 2004. It cracked the Top 40 of the Billboard Top 200, the legendary publication hailing this latest offering as "another provocative moment for Waits," praising "the stellar achievements of his risk-taking vision and often brilliant execution."

Uncut declared that the album was "scarily magnificent", noting that that throughout, "Waits is still taking more risks than most US' singer-songwriters' of his generation." The Guardian, for its part, felt upon review that "there is plenty that is remarkable about 'Real Gone'. There are dense concoctions of unlikely musical influences. There is line after line of hugely entertaining opulent imagery... As the song and the album ends, you are left more certain than ever that Tom Waits is entirely out on his own."

That alternate musical universe, or sub-genre, was a world the LA Times argued "he's long occupied musically," and one the Independent concluded delivered without disappointment every time, making 'Real Gone' their "album of the week, any other week of the year."

"What I do is kind of abstract. I don't work on cars, I work on things that are, in some way, invisible." – TOM WAITS

"By now, we know Waits is a master storyteller, one who prides himself in narratives from an underclass of misanthropes."
– SAN FRANCISCO WEEKLY

PART XXII: 'Orphans: Brawlers, Bawlers And Bastards' (2006)

For most artists, the release of a 'B-Sides And Outtakes' LP comes in place of a new studio album, either due to writer's block, a band hiatus or a last album due under a label contract. None of these applied to Tom Waits decision in 2006 to treat fans to a three-LP collection of what he – in a term of affection – chose to title as 'Orphans: Brawlers, Bawlers And Bastards.'

The Chicago Tribune would celebrate the record as "a defining statement, the kind of album that summarises and culminates an era in which Waits evolved from a saloon balladeer into a sonic adventurer, the writer not just of resonant songs but of surreal mini-movies for the mind." The New York Times concluded that this "jumble of past and present suits a songwriter who has long abducted vintage Americana – blues, ballads, rockabilly, hymns, saloon songs, Tin Pan Alley – and dragged it into sonic dark alleys of his own."

Tom recalled that the genesis for the project began after discovering "a lot of songs that fell behind the stove while making dinner, about 60 tunes that we collected. Some are from films, some from compilations. Some is stuff that didn't fit on a record, things I recorded in the garage with kids. Oddball things, orphaned tunes," adding to music writer Ethan Dawes that "these are just parallel projects we were doing while making records, you start workin' on something then someone pulls you off the tractor and asks you to do somethin' else. They're just things I've been through and ongoing things. Something for a movie or a compilation record, things that normally wouldn't wind up on the same record, just some satellite projects."

He was motivated in part out of a fear that "I didn't want to lose these songs. I don't have a big archive, I've just got some tapes I keep in a drawer along with my hair oil, some pizza and bug spray. And like pictures in a family photo album, I'm not sure if these songs will mean anything to anybody else but me," adding to journalist Katherine Turman that the latter concern made the whole process "kind of overwhelming. Mainly, I was afraid I was going to lose all this stuff because I don't really keep good records.

"I don't have a big vault or a real organised room with all my stuff. I don't know. Maybe like you, I imagine, when I want something, I can't find it. And when I don't need it anymore, I find it… Some of it I never had the original or the DAT or the multi-track or even the half-inch. I just did it and then, you know, sting 'em and go. I'm starting to get more archival as I get older."

Waits underscored just how rare some of the previously unreleased material was when he revealed to Katherine Turman that "a lot of the stuff I bought from a guy in Moscow who had this stuff on a CD that he'd collected. It was weird: black-market stuff from a guy in Russia," adding in a conversation with Now magazine that "I end up buying some of the songs…for big money. This is a guy who's somehow got hold of these tapes. A plumber! In Russia! I'm talking to him on the phone in the middle of the night, negotiating a price for my own shit! I'm not kidding.

"'Poor Little Lamb'…there's probably 12, 13 things on there that this Russian guy had. That's the weird thing. It's the Internet now, you know? I had no DATs on these, I had no multi-tracks. I don't have a vault. He had recordings of these songs, good recordings. These were recordings that had come off the desk at one session or another, and then I didn't get the DAT of. I did the project, and then these got lost and there was only one copy and someone got hold of it and made two copies and he sold them to somebody!"

Once he had the full archives in hand, the singer-songwriter recalled in the same conversation that there were "about 25 songs are from other collaborations," adding to Pitchfork that the process was "like having a whole lot of footage for a film. It needs to be arranged in a meaningful way so it will be a balanced listening experience. You have this big box with all these things in it and it doesn't really have any meaning until it's sequenced. It took some doing. There's a thematic divide, and also pacing and all that. There are different sources to all these songs and they were written at different times. Making them work together is the trick."

He and wife Kathleen sat down and began plotting possible track listings, Tom telling journalist Mick Brown that "it was hard to sequence because the tempos were different, the subjects were so different. At first, to be honest with you, when we tried to sequence it in a normal fashion – like an uptempo song, then a ballad, paced like you traditionally try to do, but it didn't make any sense. You didn't know why we went from this terrible thing to this light thing. It needed a faucet and a sink. It just didn't work. So Kathleen said, 'Oh yeah – slow ones, rockers, spoken. In a general way. If you're a ballad, you go over there. Door Number Three.' And it worked."

They refined their initial list of 25 tracks, Tom sharing with the Observer magazine that they found it made "for easier listening if I put them in categories. It's a combination platter, rare and new. Some of it is only a few months old, and some of it is like the dough you have left over so you can make another pie." He told to the Plain Dealer that as the pair sorted through their archives, they dealt with the inevitable song ideas that never fully materialised into finished tracks.

"I guess my feeling is, if you have songs left over from a record, I usually cut 'em up and use 'em for bait, to catch other songs. A good butcher uses every part of the cow, as they say. I guess it did have some kind of momentum. You think, 'What else would go well with this?' Y'know, like making supper."

To freshen up their recipe, as the pair started brainstorming they soon found new song ideas. Tom shared this birthing process in an Epitaph label promo interview, claiming that in some ways, it became a matter of artistic necessity, such that "gathering all this material together was like rounding up chickens at the beach. It's not like you go into a vault and check out what you need. Most of it was lost or buried under the house... You fall into the vat. We started to write just to climb out of the vat. Then you start listening and sorting and start writing in response to what you hear. And more recording. And then you get bit by a spider, go down the gopher hole and make a whole different record."

This new writing was, in truth, part of a broader pattern of continual writing that reflected Waits' prolific nature as a songwriter throughout his 35-year career. He explained to journalist Mick Brown that, following the release of 'Real Gone', he and Kathleen "just carried on and wrote a whole bunch of new songs. You say, you'd better keep going. We'd better get a holding tank. And then they say, 'Hey, the project's over.' But it doesn't really end until someone takes it from you and says, 'We need this – we have to master it.' So a lot of those we just kept writing."

Pulling back the curtain on how he and Brennan's 25-year collaborative musical relationship had matured, Tom quipped in his same dialogue with Mick Brown that, as with the broader nature of any long-term marriage itself, "it's an ongoing battle. Wait for the bell and come out fighting. The only trouble is when the gloves come off. We're always arm-wrestling over various things, and when you get into lines in a song, a line that you love... 'You know what? The weakest part about this song is that third line, scratch it...' 'Are you kidding me? I'm going to move it up front. It's the most important line in the song!'"

Waits confirmed in a conversation with the Chicago Tribune that "sometimes we put on the boxing gloves and come out fighting. My wife is a really great musician and composer. She's much more adventurous than I am. She's always trying to disrupt the whole thing and take it apart and put it back together with its tail in the wrong place. She's much more questioning and critical. I'm like, 'Okay, I'm done, done, done.' It's something you learn how to do after a while. It's like a sack race. Once you raise kids together writing songs with your wife is pretty easy."

Their parenting relationship fed into their creative one as song ideas began flowing. Waits painted a portrait for Mojo wherein "it would look like two birds in some weird mating ritual probably, kicking up dust, then flying away, coming back. I don't know, once you've had kids everything else is pretty easy collaboration-wise. It's kind of an extension of everything anyway – what you like, what I like, what we like, what I can enlighten you about, what I can hold you down and make you drink."

Tom added to Pitchfork that, in every respect, he felt Brennan was "a remarkable collaborator; we have a real rapport, and that's really what anybody who is working with anybody else is looking for. It clicks. Sometimes we go in the car, just take the tape recorder and go on a long trip. Sometimes we just sit around the piano – if we have a deadline, it tightens up the perimeters of the whole thing. We work independently and we work together. Hopefully we're coming at it from different angles."

Detailing how their writing styles differed even as they created together, Tom shared with NPR World Café that "I'm one of those people who likes to write in the car on the way to the studio. And she'll do that too. She's a good sport. You know, she's quick on her feet. And a 'remarkable collaborator'…if two people know all the same stuff, one of you is unnecessary. You know, we come at it from two different angles. She's got the rhumbas and the bossa novas and the Gregorian chants and…She had one of those record collections, at one point I said: 'Baby, I don't know if I'm marrying because I love you or just because you got such a great record collection.' It was a little bit of both I think. All my records were like, you know, out of their sleeves…in pizza boxes. But we had a lot of fun writing together. It's a hoot."

Waits was clearly appreciative of the partnership, offering the touching assessment to the Plain Dealer that "I'm a lucky man… She's outta this world, I don't know what to say. How does it work? I dunno. Trade secret, man. If I told you how it works, you wouldn't understand. What's the recipe for anything? It's more than the recipe. It's more than the sum of its parts. She has a remarkable imagination. And that's the nation where I live. She's bold, inventive and fearless. That's who you wanna go in the woods with, right? Somebody who finishes your sentences for you… We're a mom and pop corner store. It works. Keep it in the family."

As the musical foundations for what would become Waits' next studio LP emerged, he offered that "my wife is much more adventurous than I am," confessing in the same conversation with the Houston Chronicle that "my wife is much more adventurous than I am. She has a wilder mind than mine."

The material's varying tempos and musical paces began to reveal themselves, Tom quipping that "she wanted to call the 'Bawlers' disc 'Shut Up And Eat Your Ballads' – you know, for people who don't get enough slow songs in their diet. Any one of my songs probably could've fit into any of the three categories. Songs are either slower than your heart rate, at around the same tempo as the beating of your heart or faster, and you act accordingly."

Tom suggested to Mojo that, in the course of shaping the album's new material, "I think everybody's looking for something they've never seen before. You work on your songs, but your songs also work on you. So you absorb and you excrete and in some way you retain, and slowly you start to become some place that songs are passing through. I'd like to think that they enjoy blowing through you. There's something electric about you, maybe, some kind of a force left behind by music that passes through you. Like everybody likes to be around someone who does something well and loves doing it, so songs would be no different, right? Like 'Let's blow down there and see that guy.'"

As his muse began paying him visits, Waits confessed candidly to the Vancouver Province that "it's mystifying to a certain degree where the characters and ideas come from, but also very ordinary." He added in conversation with Mojo that, as he disappeared into the magic and mystery of his songwriting talent, "you kind of go into the world of a song. They're not necessarily autobiographical, sometimes you inhabit the lives of others. Or it's just a daydream. Songs write themselves sometimes. It's like you're walking out on the diving board and you keep walking until you fall in the water and every line keeps you in the air and if you come up with a bad line you fall into the water. I don't know how it works. If I did I'd probably stop doing it."

Waits next explained to Word magazine that once he'd discovered lines that intrigue his musical imagination, "You're always waiting for them to happen, the way cats wait for things to move around the house; you sit quietly and wait, you know. You never know when they're going to happen, and you want to be ready. I think that's what people look for in songs. I write down song titles usually, and usually something that you're going through emotionally will make a particular title leap out at you. This is what my wife says – there's something that you're already working on inside that this song will be the manifestation of. Now you have a container. The first thing that anybody ever created was a container… Once you're nourished in that most fundamental way, everything else will follow."

As he worked through nurturing any given song idea toward its broader compositional construction, Tom shared with journalist Bob Mehr that, even then, "you don't really know where your inspiration is going to come from. If you're drowning in the middle of the ocean, the sound of a helicopter would be rather pleasing. Other times, it's pretty annoying…The amazing thing about songwriting is that you don't really go to school to learn how to do it. You just learn by listening to other people's songs. You listen to Big Mama Thornton and Big Joe Turner and Big Irma Perkins. And Little Milton and Little Jimmy Dickens, Little Willie John, Little Stevie Wonder. All the littles – and all the bigs.

"And then everything you somehow absorb you will secrete in some way. Songs are not logical. There's nothing logical about a song, whether it's 'My Funny Valentine' or 'Ode To Billie Joe'. It doesn't make any sense how they come, you pull them out of the air really." Likening his song ideas at that point to "like capturing birds without killing them," Waits added in the same discussion with the Observer magazine that "sometimes you end up with nothing but a mouthful of feathers."

In an effort to avoid such moments of frustration, when he was working by himself, Tom revealed in a discussion with Spirit magazine that "I love nothing better than being in a room and the door locked, and the piano and the tape recorder going. It's a great job, making up tunes." Compared with the early days of his career when he would start with the piano, by the time three decades had passed Waits had reached the point where he shared with the Miami Herald that "I like to make melodies up without an instrument, like you're drawing in the air with your finger. More like the choreography of a bee."

Waits added to Pitchfork that, above a lot of other creative considerations, "I'm usually more concerned with how things sound than how they look on the page. Some people write for the page and that's a whole other thing. I'm going for what it sounds like right away, so it may not even look good on the page. But I'm still a word guy. I'm drawn to people who use a certain vernacular and communicate with words. Words are music, really. I mean, people ask me, 'Do you write music or do you write words?' But you don't really, it's all one thing at its best. Sometimes when you're making songs you just make sounds, and the sounds slowly mutate and evolve into actual words that have meaning."

From that foundation, Tom next explained in the same conversation that "slowly you develop your own voice. I like vocal word stuff. But I don't always write with an instrument, I usually write accapella. You're freer. You have no frets to constrict you, there are no frets on your voice, and that's a good feeling. So for composing melody, it's something you can do anywhere." When he was ready to begin defining those melody ideas in their lyrical context, the singer-songwriter explained to the Vancouver Province that "I write down titles for songs, I have a whole bunch of them. Sometimes, if you have a good one, the song has already begun to come into being."

Waits compared the process to music writer Ethan Dawes as "in some ways like bein' a character actor: you try to find the right voice for the song to make sure it fits, that's usually how it's worked, you try to expand it, most of what you absorb ultimately it's what your going to secrete, if you pay attention that is." As specific themes began to take shape, Tom revealed to the Miami Herald that often "the origins of them are very ordinary. And that's what's important to remember. You make these tunes, you have to put things in them that are kind of like a little voodoo doll: a little bone, a little hair. My theory is you've gotta put the names of towns, something to eat and some people in there. And above all, weather."

As he framed the lyrical story of a song against its musical soundscape, Waits – in a conversation with All Things Considered – explained that ultimately he thought of his songs as "kind of a movie for the ears. So if it's just underscoring and restating what you're already experiencing visually, I think you just kinda bat it away like a fly. Unless it has some kind of a nourishment from another dimension. So, that's what you try to do with a song."

Tom explained to the Plain Dealer that at the end of the day, "a great many songs are like riddles. You don't necessarily understand them. Those are the ones you keep singing in hopes of finding a new way in… Songs are sometimes cautionary tales. Or waltzes. Or rumbas. It's a common topic for a song. Have you heard the Bob Dylan radio show? Every week he picks a new theme. Songs about eyes, songs about marriage, songs about divorce, songs about prison, songs about coffee, songs about liquor, songs about the road, songs about home. All songs break down into one of those categories or another."

Waits added in conversation with the Orange County Register that songs are "in some kind of stream over your head. And then you're receptive and open and you're vibrating at the right place, you can just pull one right down, you know. Just grab it by the legs like a chicken, pull it right down." In the same conversation, Tom reasoned that ultimately "songs are hard, 'cause if they're too obvious they go right out the other ear. If they're not obvious enough they never go in. Nobody listens to a song like they're reading instructions. It's going in like someone who's telling you (his) dream. You're listening to it and connecting it up to your own dream and listening to the story in somewhat of a dream state yourself."

Waits described the original material that wound up completing 'Orphans' as "songs for all occasions. Some were written in turmoil and recorded at night in a moving car, others were written in hotel rooms and recorded in Hollywood during big conflamas. That's when conflict weds drama. At any rate these are the ones that survived the flood and were rescued from the branches of trees after the water's retreat.

"On 'Orphans', there is a mambo about a convict who breaks out of jail with a fishbone, a gospel train song about Charlie Whitman and John Wilkes Booth, a Delta blues about a disturbing neighbor, a spoken word piece about a woman who was struck by lightening, an 18th century Scottish madrigal about murderous sibling rivalry, an American backwoods acappella about a hanging. Even a song by Jack Kerouac and a spiritual with my own personal petition to the Lord with prayer. There's even a show tune about an old altar boy and a rockabilly song about a young man who's begging to be lied to. I think you will find more singing and dancing here than usual. But I hope fans of more growling, more warbling, more barking, more screeching won't be disappointed either."

Delving into the inspiration behind 'Road To Peace', Tom candidly shared with the Observer magazine that "I was pissed off. Started with a line I read in the paper one day: 'He studied so hard it was as if he had a future.' It was about this kid who got blown up in a suicide bomb on a bus in Israel. They say God doesn't give you anything he knows you can't handle. Well, I don't know if I believe that… I guess any time anyone from outside a situation voices an opinion, it's going to be, 'Who the fuck are you?' Don't matter what side you're on. But this song ain't about taking sides, it's an indictment of both sides. I tried to be as equitable as possible. I don't really know what a song like that can achieve, but I was compelled to write it. I don't know if any genuine meaningful change could ever result from a song. It's kind of like throwing peanuts at a gorilla."

Waits recalled to the Chicago Tribune that channeling that anger into song was a fairly effortless process. "It came right out of the New York Times and fell right out of the paper and onto the tape recorder. It's a hot topic and there were a lot of things in the article that moved me. All those lines (about the youthful suicide bomber) like, 'He studied so hard, it's as if he had a future, he told his mother he had a test that day.' Those were things I couldn't throw in the fireplace, so I thought maybe we can patch this into something without sounding too stiff. But then again that's probably the strength of it, that it reads like a news article."

Of 'Down There By The Train', Tom recalled to music writer Bob Mehr that he was first moved to record the song after "a friend who was playing guitar with (Johnny Cash) at the time, Smokey Hormel, said, 'Yeah, Johnny's going to be doing other people's tunes. Send us down something.' But the version (on 'Bawlers') isn't the original demo I sent."

Flattered by the initial invitation to write for the legendary Cash, Waits shared with journalist Mick Brown his memory that "when he was doing the first of those American Recordings with Rick Rubin…(and) somebody said, 'You got any songs for Johnny Cash?' I just about fell off my chair. I had a song and I hadn't recorded it. So I said, 'Hey – it's got all the stuff that Johnny likes – trains and death, John Wilkes Booth, the cross… Charles Whitman – he's the one that went up a tower in Texas and shot all those people. He was probably bipolar.

We got the famous last words of dying men here, all that sort of stuff. Oscar Wilde – 'Either that wallpaper goes or I do.' Isn't that beautiful? That at that final moment he could still be witty."

Turning to 'Long Way Home', which the singer-songwriter explained in a discussion with NPR World Café was first written for the Big Bad Love movie, he recalled "I didn't know what they wanted. So sometimes you have to create a riddle. I think those are the songs that last the longest. The ones that you don't necessarily understand. Not that that's one of those songs you don't understand. It's pretty clear. You know: 'It takes a long way home', you know? But sometimes there's a little nagging misunderstanding or it helps glue the song to the picture... because a song is really a complete item in itself. It's really a movie for the ears. So you don't wanna be redundant."

Waits was certainly not that with the composition of 'Army Ants', sharing in the same conversation with NPR that "most of that is from the Audubon Society field guides for insects. I think we both like the arcane measures of life, you know? And the little things that hold us all together. Those are 'fascinating facts'. And I guess I'm hooked on 'fascinating facts.' I thought those were interesting things about the insects, because they do live parallel lives with us I guess." he found a more personal muse for 'The Pontiac', telling the Plain Dealer that the song arose out of "a ride down to the corner store with my father-in-law, talking about endless catalogue of cars he's owned and the detail with which he remembers each one lovingly."

Of the tender 'First Kiss', he offered to journalist Mick Brown that "my theory is...if you're going to make a song it's like packing somebody a lunch. You've got to give me weather, a name of a town, you've got to give me something to do and something to eat. It helps with the atmosphere. If you want to invite somebody into a song of yours it's kind of like inviting them into your home, and you have to give them some place to sit down. Because there's too many songs that are already written that are well-furnished. 'With a new song you've got to use some old tricks.'"

Waits explained to the Plain Dealer that, when it came to selecting covers for the album, "It all belongs. It's all music. Most of us have some irreconcilable differences inside of us. Hey, look, Howlin' Wolf loved Gene Autry. There's no reason you can't do a Sinatra song, then talk about insects, all that stuff on the same record. You just try to hold the crowd.

"Hey, Memphis Minnie? They found a set list that she had. It had fallen inside of her guitar. She died in 1973. 'Warm My Wiener', all that stuff. She did a lot of blue material. But they found a set list in her guitar. And you know the very first song on the set list? It was the Woody Woodpecker song. She played dances where they had kids. She was a songstress. She would do a Broadway show tune, then do a blues, then do a dance-band hit or a children's song. All kinds of stuff together. It's just whether you can make it all make meaningful sense together. That's the real trick."

Singling out a few specific numbers in terms of why he and Brennan chose them for inclusion, Waits began with 'Young At Heart', sharing with Word magazine that "that song always moved me. My wife just thinks it's hilarious because she says, 'You sound so goddamned depressed singing it. When you say, And here's the best part/ You have a head start/ If you are among the very young at heart.' She says, 'I don't believe that bullshit for a minute."

Of the Daniel Johnston selection 'King Kong', Tom recalled in conversation with journalist Katherine Turman that he decided to try his own rendition after "Jim Jarmusch played me his version of 'King Kong' and I tried to stay as true to that as I could. If you hear the original, you'll see what I mean. I got all his records. I thought I'd really discovered this: it's real outsider art. The interesting thing about outsider art is that it's such big business.

"These outsider artists are creating false biographies for themselves, saying they're victims of mental illness and child abuse, and they grew up poor in the South and they're creating these false backgrounds. You aren't really qualified as an outsider unless you've had no formal art education, so you have to prove that you have no art education at all. It's an interesting turn of the tables."

A tribute to his hero Jack Kerouac rounded out this covers collection. Tom recalled to Now that "Kerouac's nephew had this song of Jack's, or at least some of his words he wanted me to record. I guess Jack was at a party somewhere and snuck off into a closet and started singing into a reel-to-reel tape deck, like, 'I left New York in 1949, drove across the country…' I wound up turning it into a song."

Not merely one song. Waits chose to craft two separate renditions of the tune, sharing with journalist Mick Brown that he ultimately wound up with "two versions of the same Jack Kerouac piece…one a ballad and one is blues… (the first) entitled 'Home I'll Never Be' and the other 'On The Road'. I made the song first with Primus, the rocker version, and then Hal Willner asked me to come down and play for an Allen Ginsberg memorial.

"There were a lot of people there talking about him. I didn't have a band. So I said, well, this is an actual song written by Jack Kerouac – an accappella song they found on one of the tapes. 'I left New York, 1949. To go across the country without a damn blame dime! Montana in the cold, cold fall! Found my father in a gambling hall…' Kerouac sang it alone on a microphone – it's on a collection of his work – and it's beautiful, very touching. So I tried to do my version like that. I ended up liking it. Somebody had the tape from that night, so we stuck it on there."

When all was said and done, Waits had assembled what Rolling Stone noted had "obviously began as an outtakes collection…(and) ended up…a definitive album." Its 54 tracks included an astonishing 30 newly composed songs. Billboard magazine described disc one, 'Brawlers', as "Waits' rock and blues record, evoking everyone from T Rex and Johnny Burnette to Sonny Curtis and Howlin' Wolf. It's a grand thing, since he hasn't released one like this before… 'Brawlers' digs deep into the American roots music that has obsessed Waits since the beginning of his long labyrinthine haul…"

The legendary music publication added that "'Bawlers' is the set's bridge, and it's easy to see why: it's the most accessible disc in the box…a collection of ballads, raw love songs, weepy wine tunes, wistful yet tentative hope – in the form of floppy prayers – and an under-the-table and wishing, bewildered, yet dead-on topical tome on the world's political situation. Disc three, entitled 'Bastards', is even edgier; it's Waits hanging out there with his music and muse on the lunatic fringe of experimentation... The eerie, strange, cabaret-in-a-carnival music... enlists banjos, accordion, tuba and big bass drum as simply the means to let these twisted words out of the box... This disc is the true mixed bag in the set: unruly, uneven, and full of feints and free-for-alls."

The Guardian began by reporting that, as with his last studio LP, "'Orphans' is once again co-produced with Kathleen Brennan, his wife and collaborator. Two of his children, Casey and Sullivan, also contribute, respectively, drums and guitar." Elaborating on the broader personnel that contributed to the production of the original material, Waits recalled in an Epitaph promo interview that "we met Karl Derfler, a wizard engineer who works at Bay View Studios in Richmond, California, in the science-fiction part of town. A battlefield medic, he...recorded all the new material." The band recorded this at a studio by San Quentin, and personnel included Charlie Musselwhite, the Club Foot Orchestra, Carla Kihlstedt and Marc Ribot.

Of working once again with his son Casey, Tom quipped in a conversation with journalist Bob Mehr that "I got him cheap 'cause he's still living at home. He's been playing the drums since he was about eight. I don't know any kid who's 21 and really wants to be hanging out with his dad and all of his old friends. But he gets a kick out of it."

Explaining what he felt set his son apart from any number of world-class session drummers who would have lined up for the chance to play with the legendary Waits, the singer-songwriter proudly offered to Pitchfork that "he's a big strong guy, taller than me. He's a giant of a man. He has a lot of interest in music, he does beatboxing and listens to music and it stays with him. He was playing with old-timers...but he was excellent, it was terrific playing together, as you'd imagine it would be."

Tom explained to Katherine Turman that "digitally you can recreate everything that was once done in analogue. As soon as vinyl left, someone put pops and cracks over a song. I guess, culturally, we're always burying something and digging it up, burying it in order to dig it up. They do the same thing with hairdos and shoes and furniture. It's what we do. As far as the sound goes, most of the people I know are always looking for some very obscure apparatus that will give them some unusual sound source that they can use in the studio. Then someone says, 'There's this thing called Amp Farm.' It's a farm, and you hit the thing and 700,000 sounds come up, and you can pick from there. There's no reason to have 700,000 amplifiers anymore."

In the same conversation Waits likened himself to the equivalent of "a director when I go into the studio," reasoning to Mojo magazine that visually it's required because "some of these songs are like aquariums and you can see things behind other things, everything's moving. You're really trying to capture something that's living. And the songs are living."

Sometimes he would keep a song's instrumental structure stripped down rather than. layered. "I think sometimes if a song is very well-constructed it doesn't need a lot of gewgaws, it doesn't need a lot of jewellery, and sometimes what you're adding to the song is a hairnet and a wristwatch and yellow socks. Some songs are created under very difficult circumstances and sung in luxury, and others you'll write in luxury and perform them under very difficult circumstances."

Billboard singled out his vocal tracks as "the epicentre of 'Orphans'... It's many expressions, nuances, bellows, barks, hollers, open wails, roughshod croons, and midnight whispers carry these songs and monologues to the listener with authority as an open invitation into his sound world, his view of tradition and his manner of shaping that world as something not ephemeral, but as an extension of musical time itself. As a vocalist, Waits, like Bob Dylan, embodies the entire genealogical line of the blues, jazz, local barroom bards, and travelling minstrels in the very grain of his songs... It is that voice that links all three of these discs together and makes them partners."

Word magazine agreed, concluding that "as much as this collection is demonstration of Waits' extraordinary range as a composer and musician, it is also testament to his singular talents as a singer. Nobody sounds like Tom Waits – but here, nobody sounds like Tom Waits in quite as many different ways and guises." Delving into the specifics of creating those varying layers of vocal personalities, Waits agreed that "at the centre of this record is my voice. I try my best to chug, stomp, weep, whisper, moan, wheeze, scat, blurt, rage, whine and seduce. With my voice, I can sound like a girl, the boogieman, a Theremin, a cherry bomb, a clown, a doctor, a murderer. I can be tribal. ironic or disturbed. My voice is really my instrument." More merely than just the starring player in his songs, Waits revealed to the Chicago Tribune that, in fact, "there's a backstage to your vocal activities, and then there's an onstage."

As he created the individual characters his voice brought to life on the album, the singer explained to Mojo that he became "the actor in the songs. Like, what's the voice for this song? What should this guy be wearing in this picture? You do that all the time when you're making songs, because you want it to be everything it can be." To fully flesh out that potential, Tom added to All Things Considered that, as he recorded, "I try to make different kinds of characters out of my voice. You know, I have a falsetto, and I try to sound like a cherry bomb, a clown and an old-fashioned crooner."

Waits felt he covered new ground in the course of creating the album's vocal personalities, confessing to music writer Ethan Dawes that, while he liked "all the spoken-word stuff, I'm still trying to hammer out my own unique hybrid of incorporating all the vocals and backing tracks. I've been doing the spoken word stuff for a long time and I'm tryin' to just sort of invent my own niche." 'Spidey's Wild Ride' was one of his personal highlights from the latter experiment, and Tom recalled to Now that "I had fun doing that song – just some singing and some beatboxing. It's very rudimentary yet, at the same time, very complete.

"What's interesting to me about hip-hop is that it doesn't have any conventional wisdom – the form is still being defined...(but) it's still largely a lawless territory.

If you want, you could record a mariachi calypso foxtrot with a Samoan singer in a bull ring. The production can also be very cheap – all you need is three fingers, a drum machine and a sampler and you can record a hit song in your closet. I've done some recording in the closet myself and the washroom, in the garage and in the car too, whatever."

Upon release on 16 November 2006, the conclusion was foregone among reviewers like the Guardian that 'Orphans' was "an outstanding musical creation… that nods to almost every known genre of American music, and some that have yet to be named, though to say so is pretty much a platitude at this stage in Waits' history," while the New York Times concluded for its part that the collection stood "alongside Mr Waits' best albums". The BBC felt it demonstrated "how he uses just about every native musical form of expression to achieve this high standing", adding that there was "something for every type of Tom Waits fan" among a collection that in the legendary broadcasting network's opinion was "easily up there with his best work".

Some critics – like American Songwriter – seemed as appreciative as fans themselves that Waits had succeeded in "rescuing some exceptional songs from being lost…forever". adding in a more modern context that "as much of Waits' brilliance has been found in his ability to create albums that are perfectly sequenced to showcase his eclecticism and range as an artist, having these songs separated into three stylistically themed albums… 'Orphans' succeeds in being the sketchbook of a master craftsman."

American Songwriter ranked the release Number 12 in its list of the 25 Best Albums of the Decade, an opinion Bloomberg TV shared, including the record among their list of the Best Records of the Decade, noting specifically that with 'Orphans', Waits had "provided a songwriting master class." Even with its pre-released material, Billboard – which ranked the album Number 6 on the Top 10 Albums of 2006 – would argue that "one cannot dismiss that, even though some of these songs have appeared elsewhere, 'Orphans' is a major work that goes beyond the origins of the material and drags everything past and present with sound and texture into a present to be presented as something utterly new, beyond anything he has previously issued."

Waits seemed satisfied with his latest accomplishment, explaining in an Epitaph promo interview that "Kathleen and I wanted the record to be like emptying our pockets on the table after an evening of gambling, burglary and cow tipping. We enjoy strange couplings, that's how we got together. We wanted 'Orphans' to be like a shortwave radio show where the past is sequenced with the future, consisting of things you find on the ground, in this world and no world, or maybe the next world. Whatever you imagine that to be."

Tom added to the Houston Chronicle that, at the end of any album cycle, "you try to make it a thoroughly balanced and meaningful listening experience for these strangers out there." While he knew how to please his audience, that magic formula came without any fixed ingredients, rather as an ongoing experiment that suited his preference for being "more of an innovator".

Waits shared his broader creative ambitions with the Chicago Tribune, observing that, "next year, I'll be on to something else," quipping that "my mind's like a grasshopper." The singer-songwriter added that between he and wife/collaborator Kathleen, "we're always making new tunes up – that doesn't ever stop. I love doing it. I love nothing better than being in a room with the door locked and the piano and the tape recorder going. It's a great job: making up tunes." Feeling that "the best stuff…is always the fresh material," Tom added in a closing thought to Pitchfork that – as an artist – he was ultimately driven by "what's up ahead. I don't really have one of those 'Oh, that was my big moment' things."

"I worry about a lot of things, but I don't worry about achievement." – TOM WAITS, 2009

"A legendary songwriter and performer…he is, without a doubt, one of the most original musical performers making records today."
– DAVID LETTERMAN

"Waits has now firmly sealed his place as one of the USA's major storytellers." – BBC

CONCLUSION: Looking Past The Confines Of Legacy...

By 2010, the four decades of balls and genius Tom Waits had invested into the record business – outlasting generations of contemporaries on his own artistic terms – had earned him a coveted and long overdue induction into the Rock and Roll Hall of Fame. Waits confessed to Rolling Stone magazine in the aftermath of the announcement that it had initially shocked him, quipping that "I am still recovering. I never really cared about the Rock and Roll Hall of Fame… but now I am surprised to discover how much I *do* care. I'm wondering if I did something wrong?"

One audience Waits had consistently thrilled throughout his career were his critics. He comically acknowledged to the LA Times in 2011 of that 40-year love affair that "I've never gotten any real strong verbal insubordination from any reviewers."

The BBC concluded by the end of the Millennium's first decade that "Waits has now firmly sealed his place as one of the USA's major storytellers," while even conservative-leaning media like the Wall Street Journal admiringly observed that "Mr Waits has composed a body of work that's…comparable to any songwriter's in pop today. A keen, sensitive and sympathetic chronicler of the adrift and downtrodden, Mr Waits creates three-dimensional characters who, even in their confusion and despair, are capable of insight and startling points of view. Their stories are accompanied by music that's unlike any other in pop history."

Setting Waits apart from his songwriting contemporaries, Interview magazine took note of the fact that "since his first appearance 20 years ago on the floors of little-known late-night clubs in the backstreets of LA, Tom Waits has been creating a universe all his own, an American dystopia sung in ballads, blues, laments and elegies. His vision and character are as American as Bruce Springsteen's. But where Springsteen sings of the American Dream Waits is stuck somewhere in the lost latitudes of an American nightmare."

It has been Waits' extraordinary voice, alongside his songwriting itself, that led listeners fearlessly through those darker musical territories. Spin magazine concluded it could "guide ships through dense fog. He sings songs that are poetic, hilarious, scary, touching, hallucinatory, and fine. Maybe he's like John Lee Hooker, Mose Allison, Neville Brand, François Villon, Soren Kierkegaard, Lenny Bruce and Wallace Beery rolled into one. Sometimes his band sounds like a Salvation Army combo covering a Stones tune. But nothing really sounds like Waits."

Picking up on that praise, the Chicago Tribune added that "with his gravel voice, a bunch of beatnik-influenced songs and a persona composed of equal parts Bohemian intellectual, streetwise hipster and garden variety gutter rat, Tom Waits has worn and continues to wear a variety of hats, literally and figuratively." In the opinion of the San Francisco Chronicle, Waits had proved himself "to be not only one of the most original voices in American music but also one of the most enduring talents of his generation." That influence is measurable in part by the Austin Chronicle's observation that "his songs have been covered by everyone from the Eagles and Rod Stewart to Austin's Jon Dee Graham."

The Rock and Roll Hall of Fame went further, citing "Screamin' Jay Hawkins, Solomon Burke, Marianne Faithfull, the Neville Brothers, Robert Plant and Alison Krauss and the Blind Boys of Alabama. He has recorded with the Rolling Stones, Bonnie Raitt, the Replacements and Roy Orbison. A tribute to his great influence is how many of his songs have been recorded by artists who usually write their own – including Bruce Springsteen ('Jersey Girl'), Tim Buckley ('Martha'), Johnny Cash ('Down There By The Train'), Bob Seger ('16 Shells From A Thirty-Ought Six'), T-Bone Burnett ('Time'), the Eagles ('Ol' 55'), Tori Amos ('Time'), Steve Earle ('Way Down In The Hole'), Elvis Costello ('Innocent When You Dream') and Rod Stewart ('Downtown Train')" among others."

While this trend had seemed to bother Waits in his earlier years – most notably in the case of the Eagles' early-Seventies cover of 'Ol' 55' – by 2010 Tom seemed to have gained a more favourable perspective on the whole affair. "I came around to thinking that it's a good thing. They're saying that there's something in there that's beyond its own personal revelation to you, something that is somewhat universal, the truths or the feelings are broad enough that they can be incorporated into somebody's else's experience, and that's good. You're always anxious to hear your songs done by someone you admire or respect, because that's what it's all about."

The moment of musical tribute that truly seemed to have been responsible for bowling over Waits' previous opinion on covers had come in the mid Nineties when he'd received word that the legendary Johnny Cash wanted to cover 'Down There By The Train'. Once he'd heard that, "I said, 'okay, that's it, I'll be leaving.' I was already thoroughly satisfied."

Speaking more generally, Waits recently told Now magazine that "over the years a number of different people have done versions of my songs that I've enjoyed. I thought what Jeffrey Lee Pierce did with 'Pasties And A G-String' was pretty cool... I saw Solomon Burke open for the Rolling Stones in Los Angeles not too long ago. He came out with his cape and sceptre and sat on this big throne and did my song 'Diamond In Your Mind' – that was pretty exciting. When you write songs you do it with the idea that other people might want to sing them. That's the part of the Tin Pan Alley tradition. What I do comes out of my fascination with that whole thing. You know, you sit at a piano with the window open and something blows in that goes through you and turns into a song."

Tom added his feeling that "anytime somebody does your tune, it's a good deal. That's really why you wrote it. Otherwise it'd be so deeply emotional and personal, nobody else would be able to understand or relate. When you write a song, the idea is to build a road that someone else is going to drive on someday. I think as I've gotten older, I understand that better. Plus, I've butchered a lot of other people's songs myself, so it's only fair." Ultimately, Waits seemed to view the multi-generational catalogue covers as a way of keeping his own broader collection of songs active in the popular musical conscious, reasoning to journalist Sean O'Hagan that "when someone else sings your song that means it's got a life."

Tom was careful to explain to journalist Nigel Williamson that while "being seen as part of a crowd bothered me, those are all great people." He drew the significant distinction that in the same time "I didn't identify with them, so I set out to find my own path," reasoning on a deeper level that "it's much easier to give in to certain patterns and currents that shape us all. It's much harder to swim the other way."

The singer-songwriter added to the New York Times that, throughout his career, he had instinctively felt it was important to "try to walk my own path. You have to believe in yourself and you have to ride out the seasons. Everybody wants it to be summer all the time, in relationships and with their career. And when the weather starts to turn, they think they better get out. So it takes a certain amount of persistence." Tom added to Musician magazine his feeling that while "music is social, but I'm not making music to be accepted. I think everyone has to go out on their own journey."

GQ magazine would conclude that, thanks to his commitment to creative independence, "Waits has had a musical career in this country unlike anybody else's. His was not a meteoric rise to fame. He just appeared – a rough, tender, melancholic, thoroughly experimental, lounge-singing, piano-playing, reclusive hobo in a $7 suit and an old man's hat – and that is what he has remained. For 30 years, as bigger and more conventional rock stars have shimmered and melted away in hot spotlights all around him, Tom Waits has stayed on his dimly lit side stage, sitting at his piano (or guitar or sousaphone or cowbell or 50-gallon oil drum) creating extraordinary sounds for a loyal audience."

Assessing his broader legacy in the context of that fan base, NPR recently added their assessment that "its difficult to overstate Tom Waits' importance and impact: With a career that spans more than 20 albums, he blends countless musical and theatrical styles, from classic jazz, blues and polka to rock and folk. Held together with his gravelly rasp, his music is instantly recognisable and endlessly compelling. Waits' visionary songwriting (with a major assist from wife Kathleen Brennan) and experimental nature have kept fans enthralled for decades."

Of those artists still alive that helped define a specific era of popular music, in the opinion of Time Out, "probably only Bob Dylan, Randy Newman, Elvis Costello and Nick Cave come close to Waits in stature or gift and none is ageing quite so gloriously or with such savage mystery and sheer aplomb." Dylan had acknowledged Waits as one of his contemporaries, and Tom was delighted. "Bob

Dylan is definitely a planet to be explored," he told Irish radio host Dave Fanning. "He changed music permanently. And so he's one of the giants, and when a giant acknowledges you, yeah of course it effects you." He added to the LA Times the note that personally, Dylan had had a huge influence on his own legacy as a songwriter, such that he regarded the fellow legend as a "planet to be explored by everyone... He's had a real profound effect on me as a songwriter, and everybody I know who writes songs. That almost goes without saying."

Analysing his own place in that small club of living legends, Tom recently confessed to radio DJ Fran Kelly that "I don't know where I fit into the whole thing, but obviously I fit in somewhere. They found a category for me at the record stores." Yet, as he declared to Now magazine, "if somebody doesn't like what I do I really don't care. I'm not chained to public opinion, nor am I swayed by the waves of popular trends. I just keep on doing my own investigations."

Waits speculated to Sean O'Hagan that "some day I'm gonna be gone and people will be listening to my songs and conjuring me up. In order for that to happen, you gotta put something of yourself in it. Kinda like a time capsule. Or making a voodoo doll. You gotta wrap it with thread, put a rock inside the head, then use two sticks and something from a spider web. You gotta put it all in there to make a song survive."

Reflecting on the success he'd achieved by taking extreme chances, Waits revealed in a conversation with fellow folk icon Beck that "my theory is that the innovators are the ones that open the door to things, and then behind them there's a huge crowd and they are trampled by the crowd behind them." The singer-songwriter acknowledged in a conversation with Daily Show host Jon Stewart that, "I've been lucky, you know? I take my own path and I turn around and I look behind me and there are people that are following me. And I think that I get a kick out of that." Commenting more directly on how that creative chance-taking had inspired newer generations of musicians, Tom offered to the Onion that "its nice to feel that you're having some effect, but I don't want to put too much stock on it or put too much weight on my contribution."

Tom observed to journalist Mickel Jollet that the image that people have of him "kind of goes with the subject matter I write about. Somehow people expect me to be someone who lives in the same kind of stories I write about. And you know, for the most part, I guess that's probably somewhat true. My records are kind of like dispatches of my own and people kick through that and find some truths for themselves. I'm just glad to be in the soup. I'm being influenced by everything around me and I'm influencing others and that's definitely where I wanted to be. I'm glad to be doing it. I'm one of the lucky ones, I get to have my musings. I throw it out there, and people give me money for it. My job isn't to predict what they'll like, but to try and inspire myself and hopefully as a by-product to inspire others."

Part of the secret to Waits' longevity has always been his belief that an artist is only as original or relevant as their next musical evolution. "The important thing is to continue to challenge yourself, 'cause I think that I would rather be a failure on my own terms than a success on somebody else's. This industry has a tendency to chew you up and spit you out – today's heroes are tomorrow's service-station attendants." Acknowledging that on some level sales did continue to matter, he told journalist Bob Mehr that "I guess you always hope that the demand is going to be greater than the supply. That's the American way. Otherwise, you're forced to give copies away with something else – like tyres."

The New York Times concluded in 2010 that, through that philosophy, Waits "has created and maintained his own peculiar zone – more like a back room or a bunker full of debris – in American music." The San Francisco Chronicle paid perhaps a greater compliment by acknowledging him as "the rare recording artist whose recent work is as fresh and challenging as anything he's done before."

Billboard magazine recently added that "at this stage of the game, any new Tom Waits record is an event. Listening through the music of his entire career is daunting, to say the least, but it's a journey no one else, with the possible exception of Bob Dylan, has taken before…The twists and turns of a songwriter wrestling and bellowing at and with his muse, but of a journeyman artist barely able to hold on to the lid of his creativity."

In that spirit, speaking to the LA Times late in the last decade of new music he was in the process of creating, Tom explained his eye was focused on the moment of his music-making, reasoning that "you're never sure how long it will take. You write two songs and you put them in a room together and they have offspring." Waits remained as experimental as ever, sharing that his laboratory consisted of "an old schoolhouse where we work. High ceilings, wood floors, just a room.

"Whether you're recording on a little hand-held tape recorder or with a $1,000 microphone, it's all the same drama. Oh my God, we're going to do something here. You have this device for capturing something that doesn't necessarily want to be captured. Songs are really just emotional containers of abstract things. Nobody really knows what they are. It's like diamond-cutting or hunting for bear or dropping out of a tree. Sometimes, it's like ping-pong. Other times it's like operating on a flamingo. Every song's different. Some are like empty swimming pools, and you've got to be the water."

Waits recently quipped in an interview with Australian television host Don Lane that, these days, he was concerned "primarily about whether there are nightclubs in heaven." But his closing thought – for the moment – was made to Sounds magazine that "we're all just writing our own obituaries; I mean, in 50 years from now it won't matter much, but I'm trying to do something for posterity I guess. I think it's important to consider that there might be young people listening to me and I might just inspire at least one of them…"

AUTHOR BIO

Nashville-based music biographer Jake Brown has published thirty books, including AC/DC: in the Studio, Iron Maiden: in the Studio, Heart: In the Studio (authorised and co-written with Ann and Nancy Wilson), Prince: In the Studio, Motörhead: In the Studio (co-written with Lemmy Kilmister), Rick Rubin: In the Studio, Dr. Dre: In the Studio, Suge Knight: The Rise, Fall and Rise of Death Row Records, 50 Cent: No Holds Barred, Biggie Smalls: Ready to Die, Tupac: In the Studio (authorised by the estate), as well as titles on Kanye West, R. Kelly, Jay-Z, the Black Eyed Peas, and other titles including Red Hot Chili Peppers: In the Studio, Motley Crue: In the Studio, Alice in Chains: In the Studio, Meat Puppets: In the Studio (co-written with Curt and Cris Kirkwood), Tori Amos: in the Studio, and Third Eye Blind: in the Studio (authorised).
Brown is also the co-author of founding Guns N'Roses guitarist Tracii Guns' authorised memoir, and a featured author in late funk pioneer Rick James' autobiography, Memoirs of Rick James: Confessions of a Super Freak, and is the co-author of What the Hell Was I Thinking?! by retired adult film star Jasmin St Claire. In February 2008, Brown appeared as the official biographer of record on Fuse TV's Live Through This: Nikki Sixx TV special and in November, 2010, appeared as biographer of record on Bloomberg TV's 'Game Changers' Jay Z special. Brown has received additional press in national publications including USA TODAY, MTV.com, The New York Post, Vibe, NPR, Billboard, Revolver, and Publishers Weekly among many others. Brown was recently nominated alongside Lemmy Kilmister for the 2010 Association for Recorded Sound Collections Awards in the category of Excellence in Historical Recorded Sound Research. Brown is also owner of the hard rock label Versailles Records, distributed nationally by Big Daddy Music/MVD Distribution and celebrating a decade in business this year.

ALSO AVAILABLE FROM
CHERRY RED BOOKS:

JOHNNY THUNDERS - IN COLD BLOOD
NINA ANTONIA

THE SECRET LIFE OF A TEENAGE PUNK ROCKER: THE ANDY BLADE CHRONICLES
ANDY BLADE

HELLS BENT ON ROCKIN: A HISTORY OF PSYCHOBILLY
CRAIG BRACKENBRIDGE

BEST SEAT IN THE HOUSE - A COCK SPARRER STORY
STEVE BRUCE

HEART OF DARKNESS - BRUCE SPRINGSTEEN'S 'NEBRASKA'
DAVID BURKE

ALL THE YOUNG DUDES: MOTT THE HOOPLE & IAN HUNTER
CAMPBELL DEVINE

BITTERSWEET: THE CLIFFORD T WARD STORY
DAVID CARTWRIGHT

KISS ME NECK - A LEE 'SCRATCH' PERRY DISCOGRAPHY
JEREMY COLLINGWOOD

CELEBRATION DAY - A LED ZEPPELIN ENCYCLOPEDIA
MALCOLM DOME AND JERRY EWING

OUR MUSIC IS RED - WITH PURPLE FLASHES: THE STORY OF THE CREATION
SEAN EGAN

THE DOC'S DEVILS: MANCHESTER UNITED 1972–77
SEAN EGAN

THE ROLLING STONES: COMPLETE RECORDING SESSIONS 1962–2002
MARTIN ELLIOTT

THE DAY THE COUNTRY DIED: A HISTORY OF ANARCHO PUNK 1980 TO 1984
IAN GLASPER

BURNING BRITAIN - A HISTORY OF UK PUNK 1980 TO 1984
IAN GLASPER

TRAPPED IN A SCENE - UK HARDCORE 1985–89
IAN GLASPER

THOSE WERE THE DAYS - THE BEATLES' APPLE ORGANIZATION
STEFAN GRENADOS

PWL: FROM THE FACTORY FLOOR
PHIL HARDING

IRISH FOLK, TRAD AND BLUES: A SECRET HISTORY
COLIN HARPER AND TREVOR HODGETT

A PLUGGED IN STATE OF MIND: THE HISTORY OF ELECTRONIC MUSIC
DAVE HENDERSON

EMBRYO - A PINK FLOYD CHRONOLOGY 1966–1971
NICK HODGES AND IAN PRISTON

GOODNIGHT JIM BOB - ON THE ROAD WITH CARTER USM
JIM BOB

INDIE HITS 1980–1989
BARRY LAZELL

FUCKED BY ROCK (REVISED AND EXPANDED)
MARK MANNING (AKA ZODIAC MINDWARP)

MUSIC TO DIE FOR - THE INTERNATIONAL GUIDE TO GOTH, GOTH METAL, HORROR PUNK, PSYCHOBILLY ETC
MICK MERCER

INDEPENDENCE DAYS - THE STORY OF UK INDEPENDENT RECORD LABELS
ALEX OGG

NO MORE HEROES: A COMPLETE HISTORY OF UK PUNK 1976 TO 1980
ALEX OGG

RANDOM PRECISION - RECORDING THE MUSIC OF SYD BARRETT 1965–1974
DAVID PARKER

PROHETS AND SAGES: THE 101 GREATEST PROGRESSIVE ROCK ALBUMS
MARK POWELL

GOOD TIMES BAD TIMES - THE ROLLING STONES 1960–69
TERRY RAWLINGS AND KEITH BADMAN

QUITE NATURALLY - THE SMALL FACES
TERRY RAWLINGS AND KEITH BADMAN

THE LEGENDARY JOE MEEK - THE TELSTAR MAN
JOHN REPSCH

DEATH TO TRAD ROCK - THE POST-PUNK FANZINE SCENE 1982–87
JOHN ROBB

ROCKDETECTOR: A TO ZS OF '80S ROCK / BLACK METAL / DEATH METAL / DOOM, GOTHIC & STONER METAL / POWER METAL AND THRASH METAL
GARRY SHARPE-YOUNG

ROCKDETECTOR: BLACK SABBATH - NEVER SAY DIE
GARRY SHARPE-YOUNG

ROCKDETECTOR: OZZY OSBOURNE
GARRY SHARPE-YOUNG

THE MOTORHEAD COLLECTOR'S GUIDE
MICK STEVENSON

TRUTH... ROD STEWARD, RON WOOD AND THE JEFF BECK GROUP
DAVE THOMPSON

NUMBER ONE SONGS IN HEAVEN - THE SPARKS STORY
DAVE THOMPSON

BLOCK BUSTER! - THE TRUE STORY OF THE SWEET
DAVE THOMPSON

CHILDREN OF THE REVOLUTION: THE GLAM ROCK STORY 1970–75
DAVE THOMPSON

YOU'RE WONDERING NOW - THE SPECIALS FROM CONCEPTION TO REUNION
PAUL WILLIAMS

DEATHROW: THE CHRONICLES OF PSYCHOBILLY
ALAN WILSON

TAMLA MOTOWN - THE STORIES BEHIND THE SINGLES
TERRY WILSON

CHERRY RED BOOKS

For contact, submissions and further
information, please visit
www.cherryredbooks.co.uk or email:
books@cherryred.co.uk